P9-DVZ-806

Tax Credits and
Intergovernmental Fiscal Relations

Tax Credits and Intergovernmental Fiscal Relations

By James A. Maxwell

THE BROOKINGS INSTITUTION
Washington, D.C.

© 1962 BY

THE BROOKINGS INSTITUTION

Published August 1962

Library of Congress Catalogue Card Number 62-18306

336.29
M465t

143102

To Ellen Mary

Mills College Library
Withdrawn

MILLS COLLEGE
LIBRARY

THE BROOKINGS INSTITUTION is an independent organization devoted to nonpartisan research, education, and publication in economics, government, foreign policy, and the social sciences generally. Its principal purposes are to aid in the development of sound public policies and to promote public understanding of issues of national importance.

The Institution was founded December 8, 1927, to merge the activities of the Institute for Government Research, founded in 1916, the Institute of Economics, founded in 1922, and the Robert Brookings Graduate School of Economics and Government, founded in 1924.

The general administration of the Institution is the responsibility of a self-perpetuating Board of Trustees. The Trustees are also charged with maintaining the independence of the staff and fostering the most favorable conditions for creative research and education. The immediate direction of the policies, program, and staff of the Institution is vested in the President, assisted by the division directors and an advisory council, chosen from the professional staff of the Institution.

In publishing a study, the Institution presents it as a competent treatment of a subject worthy of public consideration. The interpretations and conclusions in such publications are those of the author or authors and do not necessarily reflect the views of other members of the Brookings staff or of the administrative officers of the Institution.

BOARD OF TRUSTEES

Morehead Patterson, *Chairman*
Robert Brookings Smith, *Vice Chairman*
William R. Biggs, *Chairman, Executive Committee*

Arthur Stanton Adams	David M. Kennedy
Dillon Anderson	John E. Lockwood
Elliott V. Bell	H. Chapman Rose
Louis W. Cabot	Sydney Stein, Jr.
Robert D. Calkins	Donald B. Woodward
Leonard Carmichael	
Thomas H. Carroll	*Honorary Trustees*
Edward W. Carter	
Colgate W. Darden, Jr.	Daniel W. Bell
Marion B. Folsom	Mrs. Robert S. Brookings
Gordon Gray	Huntington Gilchrist
Huntington Harris	John Lee Pratt

Foreword

DEMANDS FOR additional federal financial assistance to state-local governments reflect a widespread belief that needed expenditures for education and other services cannot be financed out of state and local revenues. Many proposals for new or enlarged grants-in-aid for particular activities have been advanced. An influential body of opinion, while acknowledging the urgency of state-local needs, holds that adoption of these proposals may stimulate centralization and distort budget decisions at both the federal and state-local levels. Consequently, increasing attention has been given to the possibility of extending general purpose assistance to the states, leaving to them the decisions on the use of the resources.

Credits against the federal income tax have been suggested as one means of providing assistance to the states without stimulating federal control. Taxpayers would be allowed to offset against their federal income tax liability part of their payments of certain state taxes. This would make it possible for the states to raise additional revenue without increasing the total amount of taxes paid by their residents. Interest in such tax credits has also been prompted by dissatisfaction with state tax systems and concern over interstate tax competition.

This study examines these proposals for new tax credits and reviews the experience with credits against the federal estate tax and the payroll taxes under the unemployment compensation system. Tax credits are compared with general purpose grants-in-aid and revenue sharing. Special attention is given to estimates of the distribution of the benefits from tax credits among states and groups of taxpayers. The objective is to provide background for informed discussion and to make possible a better choice among alternatives rather than to support or oppose particular proposals.

James A. Maxwell is professor of economics at Clark University. His previous work in the field of intergovernmental fiscal relations includes *The Fiscal Impact of Federalism in the United States* (1946), *Federal Subsidies to the Provincial Governments in Canada* (1937)—both published by the Harvard University Press—and two studies for the National Bureau of Economic Research, *Federal Grants and the Business Cycle* (1952) and *Recent Developments in Dominion-Provincial Fiscal Relations in Canada* (1948), as well as many journal articles.

This study is one of a series that the Brookings Institution is undertaking in government finance. It was carried out under the general direction of Richard Goode. An advisory committee consisting of Richard Goode, Jesse Burkhead, L. L. Ecker-Racz, Harold M. Groves, and Lewis H. Kimmel made helpful suggestions to the author.

The Institution is grateful to Professor Maxwell, to Clark University for granting him leave of absence for this investigation, and to members of the Advisory Committee and others who contributed to this study.

The research was financed by a grant from the Carnegie Corporation of New York. The Institution is grateful for this support.

The opinions and interpretations are those of the author and do not necessarily reflect the views of staff members, officers, or trustees of the Brookings Institution or of the Carnegie Corporation of New York.

ROBERT D. CALKINS
President

May 1962

Author's Acknowledgments

WHATEVER I HAVE ACCOMPLISHED in analysis owes much to the guidance and criticism provided by Richard Goode, L. L. Ecker-Racz, and Joseph A. Pechman. The last-named is also largely responsible for the techniques of estimating the state-by-state income tax credits explained in Appendix B. My advisory committee made many useful suggestions, both general and specific, for improvement of my manuscript. Raymond E. Manning of the Legislative Reference Service detected a number of errors through his careful reading of my pages. Helpful advice concerning Chapter 3 was given me by Philip Booth, Ely M. Artenberg, and Leo Orwicz of the Department of Labor, Selma Mushkin of the Department of Health, Education, and Welfare, and Stanley Rector. Allen D. Manvel of the staff of the Advisory Commission on Intergovernmental Relations drew upon his extensive knowledge of state and local finance to suggest methods of estimating property tax deductions, and G. P. St.Clair of the Bureau of Public Roads performed the same service with respect to gasoline tax deductions. Woo Sik Kee served as my assistant during the period of my research. The Appendix section was mostly his responsibility, and it testifies to the care with which he carried out laborious calculations. It was my good fortune that the task of editing my manuscript fell upon Kathleen Sproul. She performed the task with diligent care and imaginative perception, smoothing over many rough spots in my exposition.

Finally, I owe a debt of gratitude to three institutions. The Carnegie Corporation of New York initiated the research and provided a grant to the Brookings Institution which made the research possible. Brookings requested me to undertake the research and provided me with stimulating associates and excellent working facilities. Clark University granted me leave of absence for a semester from my teaching and administrative responsibilities.

JAMES A. MAXWELL

Contents

Introduction

IN RECENT YEARS the opinion has been expressed in many quarters that, in the years ahead, state and local governments will experience serious difficulties in financing their functions. In the postwar years their expenditures have grown rapidly, and yet prospective demands seem likely to swell rather than abate.

Expenditure and Revenue Problems

James Bryant Conant recently estimated the "educational deficit" —that is, the difference between what was spent for the public schools (as of 1957-58) and what should have been spent—at $7 billion to $8 billion a year.[1] Still other demands upon state-local governments arise out of rapid growth of population and the continued shift to the suburbs. The rate of increase has been greatest among the young and the old, both heavy consumers of state-local services. For example, over the twenty years 1960-80 the total population of the United States is projected to increase by 44 per cent, while the school-age segment (5 to 17 years) rises by 51 per cent and

[1] See Conant, *The Child, The Parent, and the State* (Harvard University Press, 1959), pp. 55, 182-184.

1

the segment 65 years and over by 55 per cent.[2] The shift of population to the suburbs is generating needs for new schools, roads, parks, water systems and sewer systems; it is creating problems of urban renewal and of metropolitan transportation.

The rise of standards of living in the private sector of the economy can also be expected to be accompanied to an increasing extent by demands for improved standards of public services. In the American system most of the collective and civilian wants associated with increasing real income fall in the sphere traditionally assigned to state and local governments. Better public education, improved care for the mentally ill and the aged, expanded recreational facilities, more effective water-pollution control and sanitation—all of these are matters of some urgency. And American opinion seems to be moving toward acceptance of more generous governmental support for cultural activities and for programs to beautify the cities and countryside. In short, new programs are likely to emerge which will place additional expenditures upon state and local governments.

Are state and local revenues systems geared to finance new and growing demands? Revenues from present taxes will increase as national income rises but probably by less than demands for services traditionally provided by state and local governments. State-local revenues depend heavily on sales taxes and property taxes. The yields of these taxes are much less responsive to economic growth than income tax yields, which are dominant in the federal revenue system. Sales taxes and property taxes are regressive in incidence. Efforts to obtain more revenue and to lessen tax regressivity have been stalled in many states by archaic constitutional provisions, political conflict, and the fear of driving out business. Discontent with high federal taxes may sometimes be reflected in voters' opposition to state-local tax increases. Interstate tax competition in some cases takes the form of special exemptions or other conces-

[2] See U.S. Bureau of the Census, *Current Population Reports* (Series P-25, No. 187, Nov. 10, 1958), *Illustrative Projections of the Population of the U.S., by Age and Sex: 1960 to 1980,* prepared by Meyer Zitter and Jacob S. Siegel, pp. 16-17. This projection assumes continuation of 1955-57 fertility rates.

sions designed to attract business. Small differences in state taxes, which often seem to serve no important public purpose, impose additional costs and inconvenience on taxpayers whose activities extend across state lines.

Possible Remedies

Among the remedies for fiscal conflict, separation of federal-state sources of revenue and functions has the longest history. Separation of sources of revenue, short of war, existed in fact into the twentieth century because federal tax revenues came from customs and excises, while state and local revenues came from a miscellany of levies, none of which was tapped by the federal government. The federal government did, on occasion, make outright donations of federal land to the states, and at one time, in 1836, it made what amounted to an outright grant of money. Its revenues were then embarrassingly in excess of its current and prospective expenditures, and the federal debt was zero. Many of the states, on the other hand, were in financial need. A "deposit" of the surplus federal revenues—$37.5 million—with the states, according to their representation in Congress, was enacted, to be distributed in four installments. The deposit was, in fact, an unconditional grant, and this at a time when constitutional purism was at its height.[3]

Functions of government were always much less neatly separated than sources of revenue. Some intermingling can be found down the decades from the beginning, although the effort was made to draw and maintain broad lines of separation. Witness in the early years the lengthy and subtle debate over internal improvements, with President Madison averring the necessity in 1817 of "adequate landmarks" to guard the boundaries between the powers of "the General and the State Governments," and President Jackson in

[3] See James A. Maxwell, *The Fiscal Impact of Federalism in the United States* (Harvard University Press, 1946), pp. 14-15. Three installments were distributed; the fourth was postponed because of depression, and finally withheld. Some states, notably Virginia, attempted for years to secure the withheld quarter.

1834 fearful of "the entering wedge" which might "rive the bands of the Union asunder."[4] The theory of separation gradually was adulterated by practical exceptions and, in any case, lost its popular appeal. But it would have remained intact if, somehow, a flexible reallocation of governmental functions could have been arranged. Nothing of the sort happened, and it is unlikely ever to be managed well, even in a unitary system.

As a result, separation of sources and reallocation of functions stand as absolutes, outside the realm of practice. In practice, functions are often blended unsmoothly, revenues overlap, intergovernmental transfers are extensive and sometimes run in opposite directions so that state governments provide revenues for, and receive revenues from, local governments. And yet overlapping taxes mean, at best, duplication of administrative effort and duplication of compliance effort by taxpayers. Since the best is not achieved, they bring, as additional costs, tax conflict, discrimination, and complexity. These are tolerated because no scheme of separation offers different levels of government equal opportunity to meet their revenue needs. Yet one need not be driven by a passion for uniformity to believe that intergovernmental relations would be improved, taxpayer morale lifted, and growth of the national income encouraged by some reasonable rearrangement of the present techniques of tax collection.

Attention should, therefore, be given to devices for intergovernmental financial coordination in an effort to ease the strains. Might federal tax credits serve this purpose? Or tax supplements? Or tax sharing? Or grants-in-aid? And is the problem of state-local financial need a general one, common to all states, or is it selective and confined to the low-income states? Is there need of federal aid for specific functions? If the need is selective, would the different devices be equally effective in meeting it?

And what of the need of the federal government? In the next decade will the requirements of defense be overriding, so that the civilian functions of government at all levels must be somewhat neglected? While no firm answer to the last question (and to some other questions) can be provided, this study attempts to clarify the

[4] *Ibid.*, pp. 16-17.

issues. It seeks by analysis and by presentation of quantitative material to make possible a better choice among alternative public uses of resources.

Chapter 1 surveys government finances, present and future, in an endeavor to compare the financial situation of state and local governments with that of the federal government. Chapters 2 and 3 examine the two instances—death tax and unemployment insurance —in which the device of the tax credit has been employed, extracting the conclusions suggested by experience. Chapter 4 explores the individual income tax credit, a topic of some intricacy concerning which the opinions of students of public finance are not wholly in accord. Brief attention will be paid also to a sales tax credit. Chapter 5 appraises deductibility of state and local non-business taxes against the federal individual income tax, estimating their amount by principal types and by states, and comparing deductibility with crediting. Chapter 6 offers a brief analysis and comparison of other financial devices related to crediting—grants (conditional and unconditional), tax sharing, and tax supplements —and surveys the application of the variety of devices to specific taxes. In Chapter 7 an effort is made to draw conclusions.

EVEN WHEN CONCLUSIONS concerning particular devices of federal-state-local financial coordination are clear-cut, they may not add up to a clear-cut public policy. Tax credits have merits and demerits; so have tax deductions; grants-in-aid are not all of one piece, since the techniques that are appropriate to their use when the national objective is narrow in scope and for the short run will not be appropriate when it is broad and for the long run. "Our dual form of government," as Justice Joseph McKenna once remarked, "has its perplexities. . . ."[5]

[5] *Hoke* v. *United States*, 227 U.S. 322 (1913).

1

Government Finances, Present and Future

These States are the amplest poem,
Here is not merely a nation but a teeming Nation of nations . . .

Walt Whitman
"By Blue Ontario's Shore"

DURING THE FIRST THREE DECADES of this century, federal finances on the one hand and state and local finances on the other
showed an inverse alternation. In World War I, federal expenditures surged up and new revenues were tapped; the expenditures
and revenues of state and local governments, however, were on a
standby or maintenance basis. In the succeeding period of peace, the
federal Treasury passed abruptly from large deficits to unwieldy sur-
pluses because wartime expenditures declined more rapidly than did
tax collections; state and local government expenditures expanded
as the federal contracted, and not infrequently the expansion led to
financial difficulties.

The difficulties of state and local governments became general with the arrival of depression in the 1930's. As a result, the federal government intervened and assumed a large share in performance of welfare functions by relief spending, by additional grants-in-aid, and by establishment of cooperative programs, such as unemployment insurance and old age insurance.

During World War II, state and local finances once again were on a maintenance basis. With the peace, most economists expected that the behavior of federal and state-local finance would be similar to that of the 1920's, and for a very few years it was. But after 1948 the cold war became more and more manifest, and defense spending rose to levels hitherto unknown in our peacetime history.

Division of Spending

What, succinctly, is the current division of governmental spending—federal, state, and local—and what may be the projections for the years ahead? When the figures are assigned according to the final level concerned, "direct general" expenditure in fiscal 1960 was as follows:[1]

Federal	$ 76.7 billion	$426 per capita
State and Local	51.9	288
State $18.0 billion		
Local $33.9		
Total	$128.6 billion	$714 per capita

Federal direct expenditure may be split into two parts, defense and civilian, including in the former the expenditure not only for the national military establishment, but also for international relations and interest on the public debt.[2] The civilian portion was about one quarter of the total, as the following figures show.[3]

[1] Direct general expenditure excludes that for liquor stores, insurance funds, and a few other items. See U.S. Bureau of the Census, *Governmental Finances in 1960* (September 1961), p. 17.

[2] While some small part of the federal debt was incurred for non-defense purposes, a very large portion grew out of past wars.

[3] See *Governmental Finances in 1960*, p. 18.

Defense, International Relations,		
and Interest on Debt	$55.1 billion	72%
Civilian	21.6	28
	$76.7 billion	100%

State and local expenditure is almost wholly for civilian purposes—in 1960 a total of $51.9 billion, and thus more than double the federal spending for civilian purposes.

If defense is "the first duty" of government (in Adam Smith's phrase), it must take precedence over all other duties. The unusual characteristic of the military portion of expenditure for defense is that, to be efficacious, it must be *relative* to that of other major nations. A smaller amount will do just as much if there is multilateral disarmament; a larger sum will do no more if major nations all keep pace. If, therefore, military spending could safely be reduced, or even if this spending as a percentage of national product could be reduced, the civilian functions of government could and would be claimants for a larger expenditure. Since such functions are mainly performed at the state and local level, state and local expenditures would expand. A variety of needs—for expansion of educational facilities, because of the bulge in school-age population and because quality improvement is urgent; for urban renewal, to check the blight on our cities; for greater welfare expenditure, because of the bulge in the population 65 years and over; for rectifying public works deficiencies due to war and depression—all await state and local action.

The Decade Ahead

Assumptions concerning the level of defense spending in the decade ahead, imperative though they may be for projections of state-local expenditure, are notably precarious. The pessimistic assumption—that the future will necessitate a defense effort much larger than the present one—limits the expansion of state-local financing; the optimistic assumption—that defense spending will shrink, or even that its growth rate will simply equal that of the Gross National Product—permits relative growth of state-local spending. Most projections of state-local finance reckon that aggregate state-local spending by 1970 will be double (approximately) that of 1960. Since the income-elasticity of state-local taxes is low (1.0 to 1.2), compared to federal (1.5), the fiscal problems of state and local governments may be severe.[4] Nine tenths of state-local tax revenue comes from property, sales, and licenses, and only one tenth from income and death taxes; nearly nine tenths of federal tax revenue is from income and death taxes. The few states which rely on income-elastic taxes may expect buoyant revenues, but most should expect a lag. While tax rates and bases can, indeed, be raised, here also the leeway available to state-local governments, compared to the federal government, is modest.[5]

[4] Income-elasticity means the percentage change in revenue divided by the percentage change in GNP.

[5] I have examined with care the projections of Otto Eckstein (*Trends in Public Expenditures in the Next Decade,* Committee for Economic Development, April 1959), Gerhard Colm and Manuel Helzner ("Financial Needs and Resources Over the Next Decade: At All Levels of Government," *Public Finances: Needs, Sources, and Utilization,* Conference of the Universities-National Bureau Committee for Economic Research, Princeton University Press, 1961, pp. 3-21), Dick Netzer ("Financial Needs and Resources Over the Next Decade: State and Local Governments," *ibid.,* pp. 23-65), the Rockefeller Brothers Fund (*The Challenge to America: Its Economic and Social Aspects,* Special Studies Project Report IV, Doubleday, 1958), and Robert J. Lampman ("How Much Government Spending in the 1960's?" *Quarterly Review of Economics and Business,* Vol. 1, February 1961, pp. 7-17). The obsolescence rate of such studies is remarkably high. Moreover, an attempt to bring together the different sets of figures uncovers so many differences in assumptions that the value of a tabular comparison is questionable. Instead, a brief comment concerning some of the projections will be attempted.

Colm assumes that, in the next decade, defense spending as a per cent of GNP will decline slightly; Eckstein that it will be constant. The trend in state-local budgets will be less favorable than that in federal because of rising costs and income-inelastic revenues. Netzer contemplates "a defense effort far larger than the present one" (Netzer, *op. cit.,* p. 25). In his projections state-local financing will not be very troublesome. Several commentators (Allen D. Manvel —and Colm as instanced by Manvel—I. M. Labovitz, and Selma J. Mushkin, *Public Finances: Needs, Sources, and Utilization,* pp. 65-67) declared that the Netzer estimates of state-local expenditure were over-conservative and that, in any case, aggregates concealed area weaknesses. State-local governments in poorer areas would be unable to meet financial problems which richer areas might surmount. The estimates of the Rockefeller Brothers Fund differ from those just mentioned in that they were of *needs,* rather than, according to Eckstein (*op. cit.,* p. 14), of "what the political process is likely to produce." Robert J. Lampman, making an assumption about defense spending similar to Colm,

The estimates or projections, then, point to the likelihood that, in the decade ahead, the financial situation of the state-local governments will be less favorable than that of the federal government, even though maintenance of a precarious peace makes necessary a strong posture of defense. Some reallocation of fiscal resources to state-local governments may be appropriate. The situation that actually develops may, of course, be better or worse. If it is worse, state and local spending will have to be held to a maintenance level. If it is better—if peace breaks out—the historical financial problem of American federalism will emerge: How best to release resources from the federal level to the state-local level, and to the private sector of the economy? Here also use of devices for intergovernmental coordination will be relevant. In place of simple and direct reduction of federal taxation, it may be advantageous to couple reduction with credits, or supplements, or sharing; in place of tax reduction, it may be advantageous to provide grants-in-aid.

All of these devices will be examined in the subsequent chapters, with special attention to tax credits. For the purposes of this study, a federal tax credit is a device that allows federal taxpayers to offset (credit) an amount paid as a specified state (or local) tax against their liability for a specified federal tax, the ceiling of the creditable amount being stated in terms of the federal liability.[6] Interest in tax credits has recently been strong, partly because some people who recognize state-local financial needs doubt that the needs should or could be met by federal grants, and partly because new types of credits have been proposed which seem favorable to the needy states.

As a prelude to the main lines of analysis, two background subjects merit brief emphasis. First, the financial needs of state-local governments are not all of one piece; the levels of governmental

---

estimates that, in the decade ahead, state-local revenues will rise "by 50 to 70 per cent without changes in nominal tax rates," while expenditures will rise "on the order of 60 to 80 per cent" (Lampman, op. cit., p. 17).

[6] Credits against federal individual income tax are now provided for partially tax-exempt interest on federal bonds, for certain foreign taxes, for dividends from domestic corporations, and for retirement income.

provision and effort differ from state to state. Diversity of this sort is inevitable, not only because resources are unequal, but also because, in a federalism, safeguards for state (and local) autonomy receive special consideration. Some display of the heterogeneity of aggregate financing, state by state, seems essential to the discussion here, even though the measures of governmental provision and effort which will be used are inadequate, and even though the outlines will be depicted by broad strokes.

Second, federal financial action helpful to state governments may appear to overlook the urgent needs of local governments. Has the federal government a direct responsibility to aid local governments? The question is raised in this chapter to alert readers, rather than to provide an answer; in subsequent chapters, however, the issue will again be examined.

Governmental Expenditure and Effort

The detailed figures of state and local government expenditure and revenue provided in the *1957 Census of Governments* will be used here to indicate the diversity of levels that prevails from state to state.[7] Figures for a single year are, of course, less reliable than figures for several years. Moreover, the amount of state and local expenditure in a state is not, by itself, an ideal measure of governmental achievement, since quality of service may vary when the amount of expenditure is the same. Other factors—population densities, costs of services, and both physical and demographic features—affect the amount of governmental expenditure in a state.

General Expenditure and Revenue

With the above limitations in mind, however, per capita figures of state and local government expenditure may be regarded as rough shorthand measures of what state and local governments

[7] U.S. Bureau of the Census, *1957 Census of Governments*, Vol. 3, No. 5, *Compendium of Government Finances* (1959). Specific reference to pages consulted will be found in Appendix A, Tables 1 and 2; see footnotes below concerning that Appendix.

provide in each state. The *average* of state and local government expenditures per capita for the Nation is a sort of norm or standard of services to which, in 1957, citizens might aspire, and the per capita figures for each state may be expressed as "relatives" of this average (i.e. each figure is divided by the average). Thus, in 1957 the national average of state and local general expenditure per capita was $237.09; that of Nevada—the highest state—was $367.07, and its expenditure relative was therefore 155; that for Arkansas—the lowest state—was $148.03, and its expenditure relative was therefore 62.[8]

Expenditure of state and local governments in a state should be related to governmental "effort." General revenues raised by state and local governments *from their own sources,* when expressed per $1,000 of personal income for each state, may be taken as a rough measure of "effort." The average for the United States in 1957 was $99.40, North Dakota standing at the top with $158.57, and Delaware at the bottom with $67.96. Here again the state-by-state figures can be expressed as relatives of the average to secure "effort relatives"—for example, 160 for North Dakota and 68 for Delaware.[9]

The expenditure relatives and the effort relatives can be compared most readily by calculating "adjusted" effort relatives, i.e. relatives which show effort necessary in each state to achieve average expenditure per capita. (These relatives are simply the effort relatives divided by the expenditure relatives times 100). While concealing both actual effort and expenditure, the adjusted relatives serve the limited purpose of facilitating comparison of states in terms of effort needed to secure average expenditure per capita.[10]

For the purposes of this study, attention is concentrated on the few states which, in 1957, were in a very inferior situation. There were fifteen states which could have reached average expenditure for general government per capita only by an effort 20 per cent or more above average (see Table 1-1, column 1).

[8] See Appendix A, Table 1, columns 1 and 2.

[9] See *ibid.,* columns 3 and 4.

[10] See *ibid.,* column 5. The dominant determinant of the adjusted effort relatives is per capita income. If per capita state general expenditure and revenue were equal for each state, then the adjusted effort relative for each state would be U.S. per capita income divided by state per capita income times 100.

TABLE 1-1. *States with Highest Adjusted Effort Relatives for General Government and Local Schools, 1957*[a]

State	General Government (1)	Local Schools (2)	State	General Government (1)	Local Schools (2)
Mississippi	216	263	West Virginia	129	160
Arkansas	174	210	Virginia	126	131[b]
South Carolina	169	215	South Dakota	126	143
North Carolina	151	189	Louisiana	122	140[b]
Tennessee	149	170	Idaho	121	149
North Dakota	147	150	Maine	120	128[b]
Kentucky	146	156	Utah	116[c]	152
Georgia	138	172	New Mexico	114[c]	140
Alabama	132	187	Oklahoma	112[c]	147

[a] Source: Appendix A, Table 1, column 5, and Table 2, column 5.
[b] Outside the fifteen states with the highest relatives for local schools.
[c] Outside the fifteen states with the highest relatives for general government.

Local School Expenditure

The use of average figures as norms for *all* state and local government expenditure may be criticized, since the states are not homogeneous in their need for and appraisal of governmental functions. An exercise similar to that above may be more revealing if confined to state and local expenditure on *local* schools. The composition of this expenditure should be quite homogeneous among the states, and need per pupil should be fairly standard.

In 1957 average state and local general expenditure per pupil enrolled in public schools was $372.50, the top state being New York with $558.80, and therefore an expenditure relative of 150, while the lowest one was Mississippi with $170.90 and an expenditure relative of 46.[11] Governmental "effort" exerted for this function may be expressed as state-local expenditure for local schools, less federal grants, per $1,000 of personal income.[12] For 1957 the average for the

[11] See Appendix A, Table 2, columns 1 and 2.
[12] "Effort" for *all* functions was expressed by relating state and local *revenue* from their own sources to personal income. For a particular function, specifically

nation was $33.93, the highest state being South Carolina with $47.64 and an effort relative of 140, and the lowest, Delaware with $27.25 and an effort relative of 80.[13]

As in the exercise above, the two sets of relatives can be compared most readily by calculating "adjusted" effort relatives which indicate the effort needed by each state to achieve average expenditure for local schools per pupil enrolled. When the fifteen states with the highest relatives are listed in Table 1-1, it turns out that twelve of them appear also among the fifteen states with the highest adjusted effort relatives for general government. Three states—Virginia, Louisiana, Maine—in the bottom fifteen with respect to general government fall just outside the bottom fifteen with respect to local schools; and similarly three states—Utah, Oklahoma, New Mexico—in the bottom fifteen with respect to local schools fall a little outside the bottom fifteen with respect to general government.

The pattern that emerges from the two exercises is broadly similar when attention is focused on the states from which a great effort would have been necessary in 1957 to secure average expenditure for general government or for local schools. The states listed in Table 1-1 are submarginal in performance of state-local functions, and the fiscal effort necessary to alter this situation—if it is to be altered—is beyond their strength. It should also be observed that the adjusted effort relatives for local schools are regularly higher than those for general government. While the reason for this cannot be explored in detail, it seems that expenditure for local schools of the "rich" states is relatively higher than their expenditure for other functions. As a result the national average is pulled up—the distribution of state-by-state expenditure per pupil enrolled in public schools has a large positive skewness—so that both the number of

local schools, revenue figures are neither available nor necessary. Expenditure (after deduction of federal grants) in relation to income, may be taken to indicate "effort." The grants deducted were those for "school construction and surveys" and for "maintenance and operation of schools." These totaled $159.9 million in the fiscal year 1957, which was 1.3 per cent of total general expenditure for local schools.

For the grant figures see *Annual Report of the Secretary of the Treasury on the State of the Finances: Fiscal Year 1957*, pp. 580-581; for local school expenditure see *1957 Census of Governments*, Vol. 3, No. 5, p. 41.

[13] See Appendix A, Table 2, columns 3 and 4.

states falling below average and the deviation of their per pupil expenditure from average is large.

State-Local Financial Relations

In the recent past, both state and local expenditures have grown at a remarkable rate, despite the continued high level of federal expenditure. If the state portion is separated from the local, and if expenditure is credited to the level of government which is the source of the funds, state expenditure appears to have risen only slightly less fast than local (see Table 1-2).

In a federalism the states as political units have special significance. Indeed, a strict theory of federalism would require that the

TABLE 1-2. *State and Local General Expenditures, 1948 and 1960, Less Intergovernmental Payments*[a]

Function	Expenditure		Relatives for 1960 (1948 = 100)
	1948	1960	
	STATE		
Education	$2.2 billion	$ 8.1 billion	368
Highways	1.7	4.4	259
Public Welfare	0.9	1.6	178
All Other	2.9	6.8	234
Total	$7.7 billion	$20.9 billion	271
	LOCAL		
Education	$2.7 billion	$ 9.3 billion	344
Highways	1.0	2.1	210
Public Welfare	0.5	0.7	140
All Other	4.0	12.1	102
Total	$8.2 billion	$24.2 billion	295

[a] Source: U.S. Bureau of the Census, *Governmental Finances in 1960* (September 1961) pp. 18, 33; U.S. Bureau of the Census, *Historical Statistics of the United States, Colonial Times to 1957* (1960), pp. 725–730.

Federal intergovernmental payments have been subtracted from state and local general expenditures; state intergovernmental payments have been subtracted from local general expenditures.

federal government should operate through state governments, and not through local governments, because the latter are the creatures of the state governments. Moreover, on administrative grounds it would seem appropriate that the federal government deal with fifty states rather than with thousands of local governments. But the practicalities of actual situations have undercut this theory. Every large metropolitan area constitutes an *imperium in imperio;* its problems may transcend the boundaries of a state, and, even if they do not, it may object to controls exercised by a state legislature. In many states, there is a perennial urban-rural conflict. If the issues that arise were merely the result of differences in citizen preferences, each voter counting as one, the democratic process should appease the contending areas.

A basic difficulty is, however, that this process within states has been impaired by a gross maldistribution of representation in state legislatures so that a vote in some districts is worth 75 to 100 times a vote in others. State legislatures have failed to heed constitutional or statutory provisions which specify periodic reapportionment, and state courts have often denied judicial relief. Legislatures in which rural voters are overrepresented, relative to urban voters, make discriminatory decisions concerning state expenditure, taxes, and grants-in-aid. For example, in Colorado "the legislature allows Denver only $2.3 million a year in school aid for 90,000 children, but gives adjacent Jefferson County—a semi-rural area— $2.4 million for 18,000."[14] Is there some point at which denial of equal representation requires federal intervention and even remedy?

At present many urban communities in many states are dissatisfied with the financial treatment they receive from their state legislatures. They would be less than content with federal action which stopped with release of financial resources to state legislatures.[15]

[14] From brief for the United States as *amicus curiae* in the U.S. Supreme Court, October term 1960. This concerned the Tennessee reapportionment case *Baker v. Carr,* which the Court put over. In March 1962 the Court held by a 6 to 2 decision that the distribution of seats in state legislatures was subject to constitutional scrutiny by the federal courts.

[15] Many statements to this effect can be found in *Federal-State-Local Relations: State and Local Officials,* Hearings Before the Intergovernmental Relations Subcommittee of the House Committee on Government Operations, 85th

Some of this dissatisfaction is ill-founded. The attractiveness of the federal Congress and of the federal bureaucracy over that of the state legislature and the state bureaucracy is often the reaction of inexperience.

Nonetheless, local governments have cause to suspect that federal resources released by credits, or sharing, or grants to the state governments might not trickle down to them, despite their genuine needs. And yet no formula is available for federal use to assure a fair distribution. For the long pull, the federal government should endeavor to secure political adjustments, such as improvement of state constitutions, an equitable system of reapportionment, greater legislative flexibility, and stronger powers for the state executive, which will make state governments more responsive to citizen-needs and make citizens more able to express these needs by the democratic process.[16] This is the way to build a cooperative federalism.

IN THE CHAPTERS WHICH FOLLOW, the reality of state and local financial needs will be assumed. In what measure these needs will be met depends, to a very large degree, on one imponderable—the defense requirements of the nation. In the event that defense does not absorb a larger slice of GNP, or that its slice declines, the financial needs of state and local governments will grow in relative urgency. Therefore, an appraisal of the techniques by which the federal government may provide state-local governments with assistance is in order.

Inadequate performance of state and local functions may not, in

---

Congress, 1st and 2d sessions (1957-58). Thus Mayor Daly of Chicago declared, "I think a city of the size of Chicago should be able to go directly to its Federal Government with its programs, because we find in many instances the greater responsiveness, greater understanding, and all it would lead to. In my opinion, by sending a large city to the State and then to the Federal Government, there are long periods of delays, conferring with people in many instances who do not understand our problems, have no comprehension of our problems." See Part 2 of Hearings (Chicago, Ill., and Kansas City, Mo.), Oct. 16, 1957, p. 391.

[16] The Commission on Intergovernmental Relations in its *Report to the President* (June 1955), Part I, Chap. 2, "The Role of the States," argues for these and other changes.

the short run, threaten our national survival. But it does hinder the growth and efficiency of private economic functions, it deprives citizens of governmental services, and, in the long run, it saps our strength. Defects in the quality and quantity of our educational system are obviously harmful to the growth of our economy; so are inadequate highways. Welfare services for those not in the labor force—the very old and the young—represent public consumption, and they may have no direct effect on production and growth. But provision of a level appropriate to an affluent society is a humane duty.

2

The Death Tax Credit

> The [tax credit] act is a law of the United States made in pursuance of the Constitution and, therefore, the supreme law of the land, the constitution or laws of the states to the contrary notwithstanding. Whenever the constitutional powers of the federal government and those of the state come into conflict, the latter must yield.
>
> The contention that the federal tax is not uniform because other states impose inheritance taxes while Florida does not, is without merit. Congress cannot accommodate its legislation to the conflicting or dissimilar laws of the several states, nor control the diverse conditions to be found in the various states which necessarily work unlike results from the enforcement of the same tax.
>
> Justice George Sutherland
> *Florida* v. *Mellon*

THE CREDIT AGAINST the federal estate tax for state death tax payments is the most venerable instance of use of this device for federal-state taxes in the United States. State governments, by virtue of prior occupancy, long regarded death taxation as their preserve; they had therefore been irritated when, in 1916, a federal estate tax was enacted.[1] In the years after World War I, their officials campaigned vigorously for complete federal withdrawal.

[1] 39 Stat. 777.

Origin and Development

Both the federal administration and the Congress favored this
step. In 1924, as a preliminary to withdrawal, a 25 per cent credit
was enacted—that is, an estate subject to federal tax could subtract
amounts paid as state death taxes up to 25 per cent of the federal
tax.[2]

A few voices had expressed doubt that the states could successfully
utilize a system of death taxes, and they could illustrate their opinions by pointing out the small amount of state collections, the diversity of rates, exemptions, and definitions, and the unhealthy
growth of discriminatory practices, particularly in taxation of non-
resident decedents. The National Tax Association in 1924 spon-
sored a conference of state and local representatives to consider reform of death taxation, and this conference, meeting in Washington
in February 1925, appointed a nine-man committee of investigation,
headed by Frederic A. Delano, which was to report to a second
conference in November 1925. The deliberations of the Delano
Committee coincided with those of the House Ways and Means
Committee, and Representative William R. Green of Iowa, chairman of Ways and Means, invited the Delano group to consult with
the congressional group, prior to the November conference. In its
report to the conference the Delano Committee planned to recommend repeal of the federal estate tax within a period of six years,
and so stated during the Ways and Means hearings. No promises
concerning repeal were made by the congressional committee, but
it evidenced a strong feeling that when, within the interim of
years, the states should have rooted out discriminatory taxation and

[2] In 1918 taxpayers were allowed to offset against federal income tax and the
war-profits and the excess-profits tax the amounts of similar taxes paid to a
foreign country. The objective was to reduce international double taxation.
According to Andrew M. Tully, "there was apparently no direct connection"
between this offset and the death tax offset of 1924. See *The Tax Credit*, Special
Report of the New York State Tax Commission, No. 15 (1948), p. 1. Tully's
chapters on the death tax and unemployment insurance tax credits contain an
extensive bibliography of prior writings on these subjects.

For the legislation on the 1924 credit, see 43 Stat. 303.

made an approach to uniformity in definitions, exemptions, and rates, repeal could be considered again.[3]

At this very time, 1924-25, tax officials in many states were frightened by a threat to their system of death taxes—a threat which had arisen within their own ranks. Florida in 1924, by constitutional amendment, forbade enactment of death taxes by its legislature. By supplementing the attractions of its climate with the attractions of a tax-haven, Florida hoped that rich people would domicile themselves within its borders. Nevada took the same step, with the same hope, in 1925.

Against this background the credit device took on a new significance. Could it be used to eliminate the anarchistic moves by Florida and Nevada, to encourage all the states to reform their taxes, and to add to state and reduce federal revenues? In 1926 the 25 per cent credit was enlarged by Congress to 80 per cent, and the tax advantages sought by Florida and Nevada were thus largely canceled out, since the estate of a decedent in those states would pay the full federal tax.[4]

This was the turning point of the movement for repeal of the federal tax. Many state officials were, on the one hand, pacified by the 80 per cent credit, and, on the other hand, timid about the prospect of federal withdrawal. For a few years progress toward reform was made through state action, notably adoption of reciprocity, and through decisions of the Supreme Court, especially concerning situs of intangibles.[5] In 1931 credits for state taxes offset, on the average, 75.6 per cent of federal tax liabilities; the number of states using estate tax only had risen from two in 1925 to seven in 1932, and the number using estate and inheritance taxes jointly

[3] See James A. Maxwell, *The Fiscal Impact of Federalism in the United States* (Harvard University Press, 1946), p. 338.

[4] See 44 Stat. 126. Chairman Green was prepared to use the credit as a lever to expedite reform. See *Revenue Revision,* Hearings Before the House Committee on Ways and Means, 69th Congress, 1st session (1925), pp. 812-814.

[5] The Supreme Court held that intangibles should have a situs only in the state in which the decedent was domiciled. See Maxwell, *op. cit.,* pp. 340-341. The Court also denied the contention of Florida that the credit was unconstitutional; see *Florida* v. *Mellon,* 273 U.S. 12 (1927). The Justice Sutherland quotation heading this chapter is from p. 17 of the decision.

had risen from three to twenty-seven.[6] But in 1931-32 all such progress stopped because of the depression. Congress underlined the block when, in 1932, it enacted a supplementary estate tax (with an exemption of $50,000) to increase federal revenues. The 80 per cent credit against the 1926 tax was retained, but the idea of repeal was no longer contemplated. On several later occasions Congress increased the federal rates and altered the exemptions in order to increase federal collections, while excluding the states from participation.[7]

TABLE 2-1. *Federal Estate Tax Liability Before State Death Tax Credit, and State Death Tax Credit, Selected Years 1929-59*[a]

Year	Federal Estate Tax Liability Before State Death Tax Credit	State Death Tax Credit	
		Amount	Per Cent of Federal Tax Liability Before Credit
1929	$165.4 million	$122.1 million	73.8%
1939	330.2	53.1	16.1
1949	634.9	65.8	10.4
1959	1,346.3	131.5	9.8

[a] Source: Advisory Commission on Intergovernmental Relations, *Coordination of State and Federal Inheritance, Estate, and Gift Taxes* (January 1961), p. 41.

As a result, the state death tax credit in relation to federal estate tax liability declined, reaching 9.8 per cent in 1959, as Table 2-1 indicates. The federal objective of 1929—providing the states with a larger slice of death tax revenue—had been effectively sidetracked, and so also had been the original objective of federal withdrawal.

[6] See E. E. Oakes, "The Federal Offset and the American Death Tax System," *Quarterly Journal of Economics*, Vol. 54 (August 1940), p. 576. Also see Advisory Commission on Intergovernmental Relations, *Coordination of State and Federal Inheritance, Estate, and Gift Taxes* (January 1961), p. 39. The Advisory Commission report has been of great value in helping me to prepare these pages.

[7] The specific exemption, which was $100,000 under the 1926 act, was reduced to $50,000 in 1932 and to $40,000 in 1935. Further changes were made in 1942 and 1948.

Tax Coordination

What of the objective of tax coordination? Here one accomplishment must be conceded: the threat of disintegration of state death taxation through interstate competition was averted and, as of 1961, of the fifty states only Nevada had no death tax. The unruly behavior in 1924-25 of two states (Florida and Nevada), with 1 per cent of the population of the nation, had been stifled by the 80 per cent credit which did put a floor under state death tax liability. The credit, which gave a federal tax-reduction to estates of decedents for state death taxes, did discriminate against estates of decendents in Florida and Nevada in order to halt the spread of interstate competition in impairment of a tax.

Other aspects of tax coordination were not achieved through the credit. In 1926 some people were aware of the advantages of an integrated system of death taxes. Equity to the individual, administrative economy, easing of problems of compliance, all point to the conclusion that death taxation should be under federal authority. But in 1926 federal withdrawal in favor of the states was argued on the grounds of prior state occupancy and the legal theory that the states have, and the federal government has not, the right to regulate the descent and distribution of property at death. The weight of these arguments has diminished over the decades. After forty-odd years of unbroken federal occupancy, the historical plea of state occupancy seems unconvincing, and, while property does pass at death under state law, the constitutional right of the federal government to tax receipt of property at death is beyond dispute.

The argument that the fiscal need of the states exceeded that of the federal government was persuasive in the 1920's, and it has weight today. Here the question is whether or not death taxation is a logical or promising source of state revenue. Death tax revenue from its very nature is unstable for the nation as a whole, and this instability increases when the unit is a state because, in such case, the yearly number of returns is small and the composition of taxable estates is highly variable from state to state. Table 2-2 shows that in 1959 some states had a much smaller fraction of taxable estates over $200,000 than others: extremes were South Dakota and

TABLE 2-2. *Percentage Distribution of the Number of Taxable Federal Estate Tax Returns Filed During 1959 by "Net Estate Before Specific Exemption" Size Classes, for Fourteen States*[a]

State	Net Estate Before Specific Exemption							Totals
	Under $100,000	$100,000– 200,000	$200,000– 300,000	$300,000– 400,000	$400,000– 500,000	$500,000– 1,000,000	Over $1,000,000	
STATES WITH NO NET ESTATES OVER $1,000,000								
Alaska	28.6%	71.4%	0.0%	0.0%	0.0%	0.0%	0.0%	100%
New Hampshire	47.4	36.8	9.8	1.8	1.4	2.8	0.0	100
Nevada	47.4	36.8	7.0	3.5	3.5	1.8	0.0	100
South Carolina	53.0	31.6	8.6	3.0	1.2	2.6	0.0	100
Idaho	55.6	33.9	5.9	3.3	0.6	0.7	0.0	100
North Dakota	67.0	27.0	3.0	3.0	0.0	0.0	0.0	100
South Dakota	71.8	23.7	2.6	0.6	1.3	0.0	0.0	100
STATES WITH THE LARGEST RELATIVE NUMBER OF NET ESTATES OVER $1,000,000								
Rhode Island	37.9%	35.9%	10.3%	2.3%	2.9%	6.5%	4.2%	100%
Massachusetts	41.1	36.0	8.4	3.9	2.9	4.9	2.8	100
Delaware	40.8	40.9	8.3	1.7	1.6	4.2	2.5	100
New York	46.3	30.1	9.2	4.4	2.4	4.3	3.3	100
Connecticut	46.3	28.3	10.0	4.1	2.1	5.9	3.3	100
West Virginia	48.7	32.0	9.7	2.5	2.5	2.1	2.5	100
Wyoming	52.8	34.7	4.2	2.7	0.0	2.8	2.8	100

[a] Source: Derived from Advisory Commission on Intergovernmental Relations, *Coordination of State and Federal Inheritance, Estate, and Gift Taxes* (January 1961), p. 125, Table O.

North Dakota with 4.5 per cent and 6 per cent, Rhode Island and Connecticut with 26.2 per cent and 25.4 per cent.

In important respects the action of Congress in 1926 was misdirected because of a conflict of objectives. Tax coordination through an 80 per cent credit was hindered by the increase in the federal specific exemption from $50,000 to $100,000. This meant that numerous small estates, from which state revenue was (and is) derived, were excluded from the credit. Moreover, the credit was a *uniform* percentage of federal tax liability from a scale of progressive rates (running from 1 per cent on the first $50,000 of the net estate to a top rate of 20 per cent on the excess above $10,000,000). This meant that larger aggregate credits resulted for larger than for smaller estates, and for richer than for poorer states.

> One $25 million estate, for example, produces a larger tax credit for State taxes than nearly 3,000 separate $200,000 estates. Indeed, the tax credit on one $25 million estate exceeds the sum of all tax credits claimed on Federal estate tax returns filed in 1959 from 17 low wealth States.[8]

The modest contribution of the credit toward tax coordination stopped in the 1930's. Since then increasing complexity, structural disorder, and conflicting jurisdiction have become characteristics of state death taxation; it is hard to avoid the conclusion that these have retarded growth of the national income. State governments, under no pressure to move toward uniformity in type of tax, definitions, rates, exemptions, deductions, exclusions, and administrative practices, but under considerable pressure to secure additional revenue, have erected a complicated congeries. At the outset, in 1926, the states were left free to adjust to the credit as they wished; the credit was unconditional. Legislatures and state administrators were not motivated to undertake the difficult job of altering existing law in the direction of coordination, and the freeze of the credit which came with the depression of the 1930's encouraged slovenly legislation. E. E. Oakes has suggested that the credit was "at least a partial explanation" of state lethargy, "since any shortcomings reducing the yield of this tax would in the important cases be offset by the increased revenues from the supplementary levy on estates."[9]

[8] Advisory Commission on Intergovernmental Relations, *op. cit.*, p. 43.
[9] Oakes, *op. cit.*, p. 589.

TABLE 2-3. *State Death Taxes on Selected Size Estates, Left One Half to the Wife and One Fourth to Each of Two Adult Children*[a]

	Net Estate After Deductions, but Before Specific Exemptions								
$50,000		$100,000		$600,000		$1,000,000		$5,000,000	
Amount of State Tax	No. of States	Amount of State Tax	No. of States	Amount of State Tax	No. of States	Amount of State Tax	No. of States	Amount of State Tax	No. of States
$ 0– 99	1	$ 0– 399	2	$ 3,500– 8,499	11	$10,000–18,499	13	$100,000–139,999	15
100–199	4	400– 799	6	8,500–13,499	7	18,500–26,999	5	140,000–179,999	4
200–299	5	800–1,199	12	13,500–18,499	10	27,000–35,499	8	180,000–219,999	5
300–399	13	1,200–1,599	9	18,500–23,499	8	35,500–43,999	9	220,000–259,999	2
400–499	5	1,600–1,999	6	23,500–28,499	5	44,000–52,499	5	260,000–299,999	2
500–599	4	2,000–2,399	4	28,500–33,499	5	52,500–60,999	5	300,000–339,999	7
600–699	1	2,400–2,799	2	33,500–38,499	1	61,000–69,499	1	340,000–379,999	5
700–799	3	2,800–3,199	0	38,500–43,499	1	69,500–77,999	2	380,000–419,999	3
800–899	2	3,200–3,599	0	43,500–48,499	0	78,000–86,499	0	420,000–459,999	2
900–999	1	3,600–3,999	1	48,500–53,499	1	86,500–94,999	1	460,000–499,999	4
	39		42		49		49		49

[a] Source: Derived from Advisory Commission on Intergovernmental Relations, *Coordination of State and Federal Inheritance, Estate, and Gift Taxes* (January 1961), pp. 116–117, Table J.

Types of State Taxes

The Advisory Commissions' report described six types of state death taxes found in 1960 for forty-nine states and the District of Columbia, as follows (the twelve states marked with asterisks also had gift taxes):[10]

"Pick-up" tax only, in five states: Alabama, Arizona, Arkansas, Florida, and Georgia.

Estate tax only, in two states: North Dakota and Utah.

Estate tax and "pick-up" tax, in three states: Mississippi, New York, and Oklahoma.*

Inheritance tax only, in three states: Oregon,* South Dakota, and West Virginia.

Inheritance tax and "pick-up" tax, in thirty-five states and D.C.: Alaska, California,* Colorado,* Connecticut, Delaware, District of Columbia, Hawaii, Idaho, Illinois, Indiana, Iowa, Kansas, Kentucky, Louisiana,* Maine, Maryland, Massachusetts, Michigan, Minnesota,* Missouri, Montana, Nebraska, New Hampshire, New Jersey, New Mexico, North Carolina,* Ohio, Pennsylvania, South Carolina, Tennessee,* Texas, Vermont, Virginia,* Washington,* Wisconsin,* Wyoming.

Inheritance, estate, and "pick-up" tax, in one state: Rhode Island.*

No tax, in one state: Nevada.

The pure "pick-up" taxes—in five states—are modeled on the federal statute and aim "to impose a tax liability equal to the maximum credit . . . allowed under Federal law."[11] But several states have modified this pick-up pattern in order to raise more revenue. Thirty-nine states use inheritance taxes, and thirty-five of these use pick-up taxes as supplements in order to secure "unused" federal credits. No shorthand way exists to display the full variation in state death taxes, but Table 2-3 may serve to indicate the wide range of amounts of tax imposed by the states on net estates of varying amounts left one half to the widow and one fourth to each of two adult children. The wide differences in tax due from both large and small estates are startling. On net estates of $50,000 and

[10] See Advisory Commission, *op. cit.*, p. 35.
[11] *Ibid.*, p. 34.

CHART 2-1. *Proposed Estate Tax Credits as Per Cents of Personal Income in Relation to Per Capita Personal Income by States, 1959*[a]

Credits as Per Cents of Personal Income

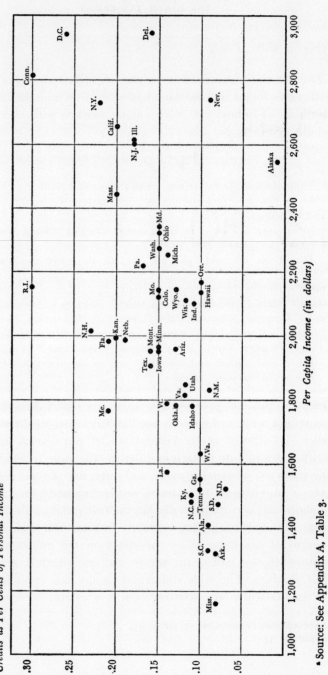

Per Capita Income (in dollars)

^a Source: See Appendix A, Table 3.

$100,000 the tax of the top states is nineteen times that of the low ones; on larger estates the tax is four to six times higher.

Revision Recommended by the Advisory Commission

On September 24, 1959, creation of a permanent Advisory Commission on Intergovernmental Relations was authorized (Public Law 86-380); on December 8, President Eisenhower announced its membership. The twenty-six members were drawn from Congress (three senators, three representatives), the Executive branch (three Cabinet officers), governors (four), state legislators (three), mayors (four), elected county officers (three), and the public (three). The Commission chose revision of the death tax credit as its first major effort at tax coordination in order to "revitalize an intergovernmental arrangement to which the States attach symbolic significance far and above its dollar and cent value."[12]

Alternative Credit Schemes

The recommendation was made that Congress increase the federal credit in order to spur the states toward coordination and to provide a modest increase in state revenues. Four alternatives were considered: (1) a straight increase in the credit, (2) supplements to the present credit, (3) credits based on the present tax liability (instead of that of 1926), (4) graduated or two-step credits, higher on low and medium estates than on large ones.[13]

The first three alternatives were discarded: the first because it, like the 80 per cent credit, would give no credit on estates below $100,000 and the credits given would increase progressively with the size of the estate; the second because it would not only retain the faults of the present credit but also add to its complexity; the third

[12] *Ibid.*, p. iv.

[13] The Commission offered two variants of the graduated credit: one equal to 80 per cent of tax up to $250,000 taxable estate, 20 per cent over $250,000; the second (Alternative No. 5) equal to 80 per cent of tax up to $150,000 taxable estate, 20 per cent over $150,000. See *ibid.*, p. 66.

because it would preserve the existing, and illogical, relationship of the credit to federal tax liabilities. The Commission favored the fourth alternative: specifically, replacement of the present system with a two-bracket graduated credit which would make available a relatively large share of federal tax liabilities in the lower tax brackets and a smaller share in the higher brackets. While the Commission made no recommendation about the size of the credit, regarding this as a policy decision for the President and the Congress, it illustrated the effects of a credit equal to 80 per cent of gross federal tax liability on the first $250,000 of taxable estates, and 20 per cent on the balance.[14] This would increase the aggregate credit (based on 1959 figures) from $131.5 million to $639.4 million, i.e., by 386 per cent.

The Commission pointed out that such a two-step credit, in comparison with one which provided a uniform percentage, would be more favorable to the smaller, non-industrialized states than the existing type of credit.[15] Table 2-4 shows, for five "rich" and five "poor" states, actual credits and estimated credits for 1959 under the fourth alternative. The increase for the former group is threefold, for the latter group, ninefold. This effect would, however, be somewhat erratic, as Chart 2-1 shows, and a positive correlation would remain between state per capita income and the amount of the proposed new credit.[16]

The two-step graduated credit, according to the Commission, would also "contribute significantly to the stability of the States' revenues because small and medium size estates are the hard core of their tax bases." Death taxes are, at best, an unstable source of revenue, and this instability is aggravated when the taxing jurisdiction is small. Yet the states, "because their facilities for deficit financing of operating costs (as distinguished from capital outlays)

---

[14] *Ibid.* Other illustrative credits are also given.

[15] *Ibid.*, pp. 70-73. The percentage increase going to the different states would, however, range quite widely from under 200 per cent to over 2,500 per cent.

[16] The value of Spearman's coefficient of rank correlation between state per capita income and the new credits as per cents of state personal income, 1959, is +.561; between state per capita income and the old credits as per cents of state personal income, 1959, is +.576. For the figures by states, see Appendix A, Table 3.

TABLE 2-4. *Credits in 1959 Compared to Alternative No. 4 Credits, for Five "Rich" and Five "Poor" States*[a]

State	1959 Credit (1)	Alternative No. 4 Credit[b] (2)	Per Cent Increase Over Present (1959) Credit (3)
	FIVE "RICH" STATES		
Delaware	$ 442 thousand	$ 2,144 thousand	385%
Connecticut	7,002	20,977	200
New York	25,833	99,762	286
California	16,015	79,576	397
Illinois	8,709	46,362	432
	$58,001 thousand	$248,821 thousand	329%
	FIVE "POOR" STATES		
South Dakota	$ 45 thousand	$ 856 thousand	1,802%
Alabama	461	3,946	756
South Carolina	255	2,819	1,005
Arkansas	196	1,965	903
Mississippi	215	2,093	873
	$1,172 thousand	$11,679 thousand	897%

[a] Source: Derived from Advisory Commission on International Relations, *Coordination of State and Federal Inheritance, Estate, and Gift Taxes* (January 1961), p. 68, Table 13.

[b] 80 per cent of gross federal tax liability on the first $250,000 of taxable estates, and 20 per cent on the balance.

are limited," need stable revenues.[17] The Commission recommended that two conditions be attached to the new credit: (1) revenue-maintenance, and (2) a shift to estate taxes.

Revenue-Maintenance

On the average, state death tax collections over the last decade have been about 2.8 times the old credit. This meant that many estates had paid state death taxes in excess of the amount that could be credited against the federal tax. If the federal credit were increased these estates could claim larger credits. For this reason "the

[17] Advisory Commission, *op. cit.*, pp. 15, 64.

immediate effect of an increase in the Federal credit, especially in the lower brackets, would be Federal tax reduction, not increased State collections."[18] Unless a state felt an urgent need for additional revenue, it might be loath to take action depriving its residents of the federal reduction. The Commission felt strongly that it was no part of its duty to recommend tax decrease (or increase); with respect to this it should be neutral. Accordingly, it declared that the new credit should be "conditional upon certification by the Governor to the Secretary of the Treasury that the estimated annual revenue level of his State's death taxes has been raised in an amount corresponding to the estimated aggregate increase in the tax credits on Federal estate returns filed from his State. This Commission further recommends that the States be required to maintain these higher tax rate levels for a period of five years."[19]

Estate Taxes

While the new credit, coupled with revenue-maintenance, would provide the states with additional revenue, it would, in itself, do nothing to alleviate the complexity of death taxation, a complexity "due largely to the prevalence of inheritance type taxes among the States." Tax simplification was an important objective, and therefore the Commission recommended "that the higher Federal estate tax credit . . . be limited to estate type State taxes, as distinguished from inheritance taxes."[20]

Statutory Format of Credit

The credits of 1924 and 1926 were expressed as a percentage of federal tax liability. This meant that any change in federal rates or exemptions would automatically affect state revenues. When in

[18] *Ibid.*, p. 76.

[19] *Ibid.*, p. 18. Revenue-maintenance had been recommended by the Joint Federal-State Action Committee as a condition for federal relinquishment of part of the tax on local telephone service. See *Final Report of the Joint Federal-State Action Committee to the President of the United States and to the Chairman of the Governors' Conference* (February 1960), pp. 68-70.

[20] Advisory Commission, *op. cit.*, p. 20.

1932, and subsequently, Congress did change the federal provisions, it avoided affecting state revenues by enacting a second and different scale of federal rates and exemptions, leaving the 80 per cent credit tied to the 1926 act and inapplicable to the new provisions. In 1954 this format was dropped in favor of a bracket schedule for computation of the credit. The Commission believes that this latter method is better both for the federal government and the states.

Division of the Tax

During its deliberations the Advisory Commission had, of course, considered whether death taxes should be *exclusively* a federal source or a state source of revenue. On economic grounds, the case for sole federal jurisdiction was strong. But on other grounds such a step was not feasible, and the Commission, therefore, considered another possibility. Was it possible to split death taxation according to the size of estates, giving the federal government exclusive jurisdiction over large estates, and the states over small ones? Would a 100 per cent credit for state taxes on small estates provide such a split? Some state administrators were fearful of this plan, feeling that the Internal Revenue Service would have no interest in "credit only" returns, and would, therefore, be slack in administering this part of the tax.

The Commission also explored division of the death tax field through a high federal exemption. Again, some state administrators were reluctant because they valued federal administrative help in property valuation, credits, and the like.[21] Elaborate administrative arrangements were not justifiable for the modest amounts of revenue derived from death taxation.

The Future

The plan of the Advisory Commission represents a serious attempt to move toward coordination of death taxation. The bait of a larger credit, combined with a requirement of revenue-maintenance, is to persuade the states to substitute estate for inheritance

[21] *Ibid.*, p. 87.

taxes. The Commission recommends a two-step graduated credit in an effort to make available relatively larger new revenues to the poorer states. The results to be obtained here must be slight because state death taxes, under any circumstances, will be unequally productive. The desideratum, toward which the new credit may be a step, is complete federal jurisdiction.

The Commission was conscious of this prospect. If the new plan were accepted by the Congress, if the states dutifully shifted to estate taxes, and if many of them conformed their taxes to the federal model, might not some "prefer to forgo their independent death taxes with their duplicate compliance and administration in exchange for a corresponding share of Federal collections"? The Commission wished to facilitate this development "when and if a consensus develops among the States in favor of central collection and State sharing."[22]

When the recommendations of the Advisory Commission come before the House Ways and Means Committee, a proposal which would accelerate unification may be made: that the federal exemption be lowered from the present $60,000 to, say, $25,000.[23] The recommendations, which are tied to the present federal rates and exemption, would continue in existence and tend to freeze the present tax differentials among the states arising because some states levy significant amounts of tax over and above the federal credit. The differentials are most important for estates $60,000 to $150,000. Dropping the federal exemption would reduce these differentials because state taxes would very likely conform more closely to the federal credits. The proposal would, to be sure, redistribute the interstate burden of state death taxes. A state which at present has the 1926 federal exemption would, by the above proposal, secure many new taxpayers compared with a state which already has a low exemption.

The effect of the proposal, even more than the recommendations

[22] *Ibid.*, pp. 21, 22.

[23] Information obtained by correspondence (December 1961) with Charles F. Conlon, Executive Secretary of the Federation of Tax Administrators.

of the Commission, would be to increase the dominance of the federal tax by extending coverage over a wider range of estates and tying the state taxes firmly into a national pattern.

SOME LESSONS CAN, perhaps, be drawn from experience with the death tax credit. (1) State governments will respond to the inducements of a credit; (2) state governments appreciate the assistance of federal administrative techniques; (3) a credit has inherent inflexibilities both at the federal and at the state level; (4) over time these inflexibilities, unless remedied, would impair tax coordination and engender state discontent.

MILLS COLLEGE
LIBRARY

3

The Unemployment Insurance Tax Credit

The plan of unemployment security we suggest is frankly experimental. We anticipate that it may require numerous changes with experience and, we believe, is so set up that these changes can be made through subsequent legislation as deemed necessary.

The Committee on Economic Security, 1935
Report to the President

WHEN, AFTER 1933, the Great Depression and the New Deal had weakened resistance to federal social legislation in the United States, some people advocated a federal scheme of unemployment insurance. But most interested persons favored some method of federal-state cooperation, and opinion crystallized around two plans: the tax-offset plan, and a grant plan. In both of them the federal government was to impose a uniform flat tax on employer payrolls, thereby removing the fear of interstate competition, and in both the states were required to pass unemployment insurance laws. The differences between the two plans stemmed chiefly from the degree of centralization thought to be desirable, with supporters of grants desirous of more federal controls and supporters of tax-offsets desirous of fewer.

Under the grant plan the proceeds of the uniform payroll tax were to be collected federally and then returned to each state, if and when a state passed a law which met prescribed federal standards concerning waiting period, rate and duration of benefits, and so on. Proponents argued that this plan would not easily be susceptible to constitutional attack, and, looking to the future, that it would offer opportunity for liberalization of unemployment compensation, since the payroll tax was to be wholly a federal tax, as well as an opportunity for the federal government to require new conditions in the state laws.[1]

The tax-offset plan had two tactical advantages. For one thing it was utilized in the Wagner-Lewis bill which was before Congress in 1934 and which had gained wide endorsement. For another, it seemed to hold a better promise of survival if federal legislation on unemployment compensation were struck down by the Supreme Court, a possibility very much in men's minds at the time. Unconstitutionality of a plan financed by federal grants would deprive the states of support for their laws, since the payroll tax was to be a federal tax; a similar fate for a plan financed by state payroll taxes, credited against a federal tax, would leave the taxes in operation even if the federal tax disappeared, and it might be hoped that the operation of unemployment insurance could be salvaged. Beyond these tactical advantages, the tax-offset plan appealed to those who wanted a minimum of federal controls at the outset.

[1] Arguments in favor of the grant plan are summarized in Eveline M. Burns, *Toward Social Security* (McGraw-Hill, 1936), pp. 209-213. "The grant-in-aid method of returning the money collected by the federal government to the states is much more effective than the tax offset method as a means of raising the standards of the state plans. Apart from the fact that the federal government could probably lay down more conditions under the grant-in-aid plan without running foul of the Supreme Court, it could also secure more effectively the fulfillment of those conditions. It could more easily refuse to make any grant to a state whose plan does not meet the federal requirements" (p. 211).

They desired experimentation with legislation and programs, differing in detail from state to state, so that the worth of several variants might be tested.[2]

Original Framework

The Committee on Economic Security, which had been created by President Franklin D. Roosevelt in 1934 to work out a general plan for social security, endorsed the tax-offset approach with one major modification.[3] Instead of an offset of 100 per cent, the committee recommended an offset of 90 per cent, with payment of the remaining 10 per cent of the federal tax into the federal Treasury. This revenue was to be the source of federal grants to the states to cover the cost of administration of their laws, and this new feature reflected the realization that some additional federal controls over the states would be desirable.[4] If the federal government gave grants—100 per cent grants—for administration of unemployment insurance, not only might state favor for the bill be generated, but reasonable uniformity of state administration might be secured.

Federal Conditions for Tax Credit

The desire of the Committee on Economic Security to establish a federal-state system that would impose a minimum of federal standards had met a ready response among members of Congress, who, as it turned out, were even more tender of states' rights than was the committee.[5] By Title IX of the Social Security Act (49 Stat.

[2] Controversy concerning the type of reserve was vigorous, with Wisconsin, Utah, and New Hampshire desirous of plant reserves.

[3] For the Committee's Report, see *Message of the President Recommending Legislation on Economic Security*, House Document No. 81, 74th Congress, 1st session (1935), pp. 1-41. The quotation heading this chapter is from p. 19 of the Report.

[4] The grants for administration were in Title III of the bill, while provision for the tax was in Title IX. The separation was supposed to improve the constitutionality of the measure.

[5] The House Ways and Means Committee report on the bill (H.R. 7260) declared: "The bill permits the States wide discretion with respect to the unem-

639) a federal unemployment tax, beginning at 1 per cent in 1936, rising to 2 per cent in 1937 and to 3 per cent for subsequent years, was imposed on payrolls of employers of eight or more workers, with specific exemption of agricultural workers, domestic servants, employees of nonprofit institutions, and governmental employees. If a state enacted a satisfactory unemployment insurance law, its employers were to receive credit for their payments under the state law up to 90 per cent of the federal tax. The federal rate of 3 per cent would therefore be reduced to 0.3 per cent by a state rate of 2.7 per cent. This 2.7 per cent was to be the standard rate of state tax because estimates of cost made for the Committee on Economic Security had indicated that such a rate would impose a reasonable burden and would finance the proposed benefits. The credit served the purpose of limiting the net federal rate to 0.3 per cent.

State unemployment insurance laws had to be approved by the Social Security Board before employers were entitled to receive credit against the federal tax. To secure approval, the laws had to meet six conditions; five of these were still relevant in 1961:

1. Payments of unemployment benefits were to be through public employment offices, or such other public agencies as the Social Security Board might approve.

2. All payments to the state unemployment funds were to be transferred immediately to the Secretary of the Treasury, who would credit them to each state.

3. Money withdrawn by the states from their unemployment trust funds was to be used only for payment of benefits.

4. Benefits were not to be denied to an unemployed eligible worker who refused new work (a) which arose because of a labor dispute, (b) which had hours, wages, or other conditions substantially below those prevailing for similar work in the community, (c) which required the worker to sign a "yellow-dog" contract or to join a company union. This was the so-called "labor standards" condition.

5. All rights conferred by the state law were to exist subject to the

---

ployment compensation laws they may wish to enact. The standards prescribed in this bill . . . are designed merely to insure that employers will receive credit against the Federal pay-roll tax only for payments made under genuine unemployment compensation laws." (*The Social Security Bill*, House Report No. 615, 74th Congress, 1st session, 1935, pp. 8-9.)

power of the legislature to alter the law at any time. In short, no vested interest could be claimed.[6]

The first three of the conditions listed above were, in essence, housekeeping regulations; their aim was to safeguard state funds and secure orderly payments to beneficiaries. The fourth was designed to hold the states to a pattern with respect to labor standards.

The federal act contained another set of conditions connected with the tax credit. The states were not required to impose a 2.7 per cent rate on all covered employers; those with favorable employment experience or adequate reserves could have their payments reduced below 2.7 per cent under the state law, and would still receive the maximum credit of 2.7 per cent against the federal tax. This system was called "merit" or "experience" rating, and the federal law stated certain conditions, relating particularly to reserves, which had to be met in order to warrant "additional credit."[7]

This summary statement of the tax-credit conditions imposed by Congress will, perhaps, be better appreciated by recollecting that the areas of unemployment insurance left by Congress for state decision included amount and duration of benefits, the length of the waiting period, eligibility requirements, and disqualification provisions. With respect to *coverage*, although the federal law did specify what types of employers would be subject to the federal tax, it did not limit state coverage to those so specified. State laws, for instance, could (and did) cover employers with less than eight employees. With respect to *contributions*, although the federal law did

---

[6] See 49 Stat. 640. The other condition of the original six, not now relevant, stipulated that no benefits were to be paid for unemployment occurring within two years after the beginning of contributions, thus ensuring solvency of the state funds by enabling reserves to be built up.

[7] See 49 Stat. 644. If contributions were to a pooled fund, a lower rate had to be based on three years of experience; if to a guaranteed-employment account, the balance had to be not less than 7.5 per cent of total wages payable by an employer; if to a separate reserve account, the balance had to be not less than five times the largest amount paid as compensation from it in any one of three preceding years and not less than 7.5 per cent of total wages payable by an employer in the preceding calendar year. Virtually all states have operated with pooled funds from the beginning. The "reserve-ratio" type of experience rating has been most popular, and as of 1961 was being used by thirty-three states.

indicate a standard rate of state tax—a rate expected to be widely used—it also provided that states could allow a lower rate than 2.7 per cent with no diminution of credit. As things have turned out, this latter provision has allowed the states substantial freedom in determination of employer contributions.

Administrative Grants and Federal Conditions

The grants to the states for administration of unemployment insurance were also subject to federal conditions.[8] The 2.7 per cent credit against a 3 per cent federal tax left a remainder—0.3 per cent (or 10 per cent of the gross tax)—for federal collection. This went into the general fund of the Treasury, but it was regarded as the source of the grants for administration. The grants were unusual in being 100 per cent grants. If a state was to secure them, its compensation laws had to meet a set of conditions similar to— indeed, sometimes identical with—those specified for the tax credit. The Social Security Board had to approve the state laws, and, furthermore, to certify to the Secretary of the Treasury that they met the federal conditions for receipt of grants.

The Board had considerable freedom in deciding the appropriate amount of a state grant. Its determination could be based on population, number of persons covered by the state law, "the cost of proper and efficient administration," and such other factors as it found relevant. It could also suspend a grant, after giving reasonable notice and an opportunity for fair hearing to the state agency, if proper administration was not observed. Clearly the strings attached here were more extensive and expansible than those attached to the tax credit. In deciding upon the appropriate amount of grant to each state, the Social Security Board (since 1949 the Secretary of Labor) was not bound by the amount collected in a state through the federal tax. In practice, a considerable number of states (twenty-five and the District of Columbia in fiscal 1960) have received administrative grants exceeding collections, and in some of these (fifteen in fiscal 1960) the grants have been substantially in excess.

[8] See 49 Stat. 626.

FROM THIS SKETCH, the unusual features of the federal tax become apparent. Its amount was reduced 90 per cent (from 3 per cent to 0.3 per cent) by enactment of state taxes, even though actual collections under the state taxes were much less than what would be produced by a 2.7 per cent rate. The proceeds of the net federal tax of 0.3 per cent were mostly committed to provide grants to the states for administration. When it turned out that something was left over, the states asserted claims against this remainder. In short, this federal tax was a device, not to raise federal revenue, but to secure other federal objectives.

The Social Security Act was signed into law on August 14, 1935. In the next two years the federal-state system of unemployment insurance went into operation more rapidly and smoothly than most people had dared to hope; the tax credit proved to be a powerful short-run device. At the urgent request of many states, the Social Security Board prepared a number of draft bills which met the minimum requirements of federal law, and these were widely copied. As a result, substantial uniformity was secured on matters about which no federal standards had been specified. Little objection to federal conditions was raised. The state acts were submitted for approval to the Board, and approval was duly given (approval had to be given within 30 days if a state law met the requirements of the federal act). By the middle of 1937 all states were in, and the efficacy of the 90 per cent credit as a stimulus was beyond dispute.

The Issue of Constitutionality

The hurdle of constitutionality was surmounted on May 24, 1937, by the narrow margin of a 5-4 decision of the Supreme Court. Justice Benjamin N. Cardozo spoke for the majority. Unemployment was a national problem, and the action taken by the federal government through the law in question was designed, not to coerce the states, but to give them a larger freedom in joining together to avert a common evil. The conditions imposed were not arbitrary.

. . . a wide range of judgment is given to the several states as to the particular type of statute to be spread upon their books. . . . In determining essentials Congress must have the benefit of a fair margin of discretion. One cannot say with reason that this margin has been exceeded or that the basic standards have been determined in any arbitrary fashion.[9]

Justice James C. McReynolds, on the other hand, believed that the majority decision opened the way for the "practical annihilation" of state freedom. And Justices George Sutherland and Willis Van Devanter felt that, by the provisions of the act,

> . . . the federal agencies are authorized to supervise and hamper the administrative powers of the state to a degree which not only does not comport with the dignity of a quasi-sovereign state—a matter with which we are not judicially concerned—but which denies to it that supremacy and freedom from external interference in respect of its affairs which the Constitution contemplates—a matter of very definite judicial concern.[10]

No one can say, now or ever, what the Court would have decided had a more centralized plan of unemployment insurance been submitted. But it does seem that the range and extent of federal conditions weighed heavily with the Court and that, for this reason, the caution of the framers of the plan was wise. A federal-state scheme was put into operation, and it was not struck down by judicial veto.

Legislative History, 1935-61

Despite numerous congressional investigations and repeated presidential recommendations, the federal legislative structure of unemployment insurance was changed very little during the years between 1935 and 1957.

Coverage

Minor changes aside, the only important enlargement in federal coverage came in 1954 when it was extended to employers of four or more persons (the original figure in the bill when introduced

[9] *Steward Machine Co.* v. *Davis*, 301 U.S. 593-594.
[10] *Ibid.*, pp. 613-614.

into Congress in 1935).[11] As of 1960, some 13 million workers were
still excluded. Most states have gone beyond the federal coverage,
especially for small firms, and in 1960 twenty-four states were covering firms with fewer than four employees, and twenty were covering
some with one or more.

Wage Base

In the original act the payroll tax was imposed on all covered
wages. In 1939 the base became the first $3,000 of annual wages in
order to make this base coincide with the payroll base of the Old
Age and Survivors Insurance system, and here it has remained
(even though the base of the OASDI tax has been lifted by stages
to $4,800).[12] In 1939 taxable wages (with a $3,000 ceiling) represented 98 per cent of total covered payrolls, while at present they
represent less than two thirds. The narrow base limits collections,
"accentuates cyclical variation in the employers' tax burdens . . .
and forces higher tax rates on certain industries."[13]

Resistance to increase in the base has been strong, especially in the
low-wage states. In 1958 an increase to $3,600 would have made 80
to 90 per cent of wages taxable in nine low-income states (North
Dakota, New Hampshire, Vermont, Hawaii, Maine, Mississippi,
North Carolina, Arkansas, South Carolina), and only 60 to 70 per
cent in seven high-income states (Delaware, Michigan, New York,
Illinois, Wisconsin, Ohio, New Jersey).[14] By 1961, however, nine
states had enacted a base for their own taxes which exceeded the
federal base: Alaska, $7,200; California, $3,800; Delaware, Hawaii,
Massachusetts, Nevada, Oregon, Rhode Island, and West Virginia
—each $3,600.[15]

[11] 68 Stat. 1130.
[12] 53 Stat. 1393.
[13] Richard A. Lester, "Financing of Unemployment Compensation," *Industrial and Labor Relations Review*, Vol. 14 (October 1960), pp. 62-63.
[14] See Minutes of the Committee on Benefit Financing, Interstate Conference of Employment Security Agencies, Jan. 5-7, 1960, Appendix II, Table 2. Opponents of a higher base argued also that "new" and seasonal employers would be affected more severely than "rated" employers.
[15] Bases effective Jan. 1, 1954, in Nevada; Jan. 1, 1955, in Delaware; Jan. 1,

Title XII

In 1944, Congress, worried that the states might not be able to finance unemployment benefits during reconversion of industry from war to peace, established a federal unemployment account from which states could secure advances if their own unemployment trust funds became dangerously low.[16] The federal account secured its money from the excess of federal collections, through its 0.3 per cent tax on payrolls, over administrative expenditures for employment security programs. At this time collections had exceeded expenditures by about $645 million. As it turned out, the states were in no need of advances; the provision expired on March 31, 1952.

Meanwhile, the states had become convinced that the proceeds from the federal tax should be used only for the employment security program, and that payment of excess collections into the general fund of the Treasury was wrong. This agitation, carried on with vigor by the Interstate Conference of Employment Security Agencies led, in 1954, to passage of the Reed Act, which established Title XII on a permanent basis.[17] The excess of collections from the federal tax over expenditures for administration was to be segregated and earmarked for use to build a loan fund upward of $200 million; it was estimated that this amount would be achieved in three to four years. From this fund, states with depleted reserve accounts could obtain non-interest bearing repayable advances. The advances could be repaid at any time, but if they had not been repaid after four years the credit against the federal tax received by employers in the borrowing state was to be reduced from 90 per cent to 85 per cent, with a cutback of 5 points in each subsequent year until the advance was paid. (Or, to put the matter differently, the rate of the federal tax would go up from 0.30 per cent to 0.45 per cent to 0.60 per cent, etc.)

1960, in Rhode Island, Alaska, Oregon; Jan. 1, 1962, in California, Hawaii, Massachusetts, and West Virginia. Oregon's base becomes $3,800 when fund is below 6 per cent.

[16] 58 Stat. 789.

[17] 68 Stat. 668.

Looking still further ahead, the law provided that, after a loan fund of at least $200 million had been accumulated, any excess of federal collections was to be transferred to the accounts of the states in the proportion that the taxable payroll of each was to aggregate taxable payrolls of all states. As will appear later, the assumption of a continued excess of collections was soon to prove unfounded.

Temporary Unemployment Compensation Act, 1958

During the recession of 1957-58 concern over the large number of workers who had exhausted the benefits to which they were entitled under state laws led to further federal legislation.[18] If states agreed to participate, additional benefits would be paid to "exhaustees" (workers who had exhausted their benefits after June 30, 1957). The amounts paid in benefits, while originally to be provided from the federal Treasury, were to be repaid by November 1963. If repayment had not been made, the offset-credits against the federal tax were to be reduced—that is, the federal tax on employers in the participating states was to increase by 0.15 per cent in 1963, and by an additional 0.15 per cent in each year thereafter, until the advance had been covered. Sixteen states and the District of Columbia participated in the full program, receiving advances of $445.7 million.[19]

Increase in the Federal Tax, 1960

The rate of the federal tax was raised (effective January 1, 1961) from 3 per cent to 3.1 per cent by Congress in 1960, the credit being left at 2.7 per cent.[20] The *net* tax was therefore raised from 0.3 per cent to 0.4 per cent for two purposes: to meet higher administrative expenses and to provide a larger loan fund.

Under the operations of the Reed Act in the three fiscal years 1954-56, excess collections of $198.7 million were credited to the

[18] 73 Stat. 14; 47.
[19] See *Unemployment Compensation*, Hearings Before the Senate Committee on Finance, 87th Congress, 1st session (1961), p. 34.
[20] 74 Stat. 980.

loan fund, and in the three fiscal years 1956-58, $138.1 million was credited to the state accounts. For fiscal 1959, however, federal tax collections fell short of administrative expenditures by $422,000 and a recurrence of this situation was certain. The 1960 act provided that the proceeds of the 0.4 per cent federal tax would go to a trust fund account from which Congress could appropriate annually a sum not to exceed $350 million for administrative grants to the states. Any remainder, after federal administrative costs of the program (Labor and Treasury Departments) were financed, was to go to build up the loan fund to a level of the greater of $550 million or 0.4 per cent of aggregate state taxable wages. Conditions on which an advance could be made were tightened and provisions for repayment were accelerated. An advance for a month would be made only if reserves on hand plus expected collections seemed inadequate to meet expected benefit payments during the month. Repayment of advances had to begin after two years at a rate double that under the prior statute.

Temporary Extended Compensation Act, 1961

During the recession of 1960-61 the problem of a growing number of exhaustees reappeared, and Congress responded by providing temporary benefits to unemployed workers who had exhausted their rights under state law.[21] The measure differed from that of 1958 in its method of finance. Whereas the 1958 act provided that repayment of federal advances would be made through reduced offset-credits against the federal tax on employers in a participating state, the 1961 act severed collections in a state from benefits in that state. Collections, through a temporary increase of four tenths of 1 per cent for two calendar years (1962-63) in the federal tax rate, were to be pooled. As a precedent, Secretary of Labor Arthur J. Goldberg cited the procedure concerning grants for administration. Federal tax collections to provide them were pooled, with allocation of grants to states according to need as reckoned by the De-

[21] 75 Stat. 8.

partment of Labor. He argued that this approach was logical and equitable because "in abnormal, prolonged unemployment there is a Federal responsibility."[22]

Was this the opening wedge for imposition of federal standards? The report of the Senate Finance Committee declared:

> Information received by the committee indicates that, in effect, employers in about 40 States would be paying part of the cost of temporary extended unemployment compensation in the other 10 States. The committee is concerned that even though the tax to provide for payment of the benefits provided by the bill would be imposed uniformly on employers in all of the United States, the benefits provided by the bill would vary widely from State to State, depending upon the scope of each State law and the conditions of unemployment prevailing in each of the several States, and such payments would be paid out of such pooled funds. This constitutes a departure from the concept of unemployment insurance which has been in effect since the inception of the Federal-State unemployment compensation program in 1935.[23]

The Senate Finance Committee amended the bill as passed by the House (H. R. 4806) to provide that the cost of temporary extended unemployment compensation paid in each state would be borne by taxes on employer payrolls in each state. If collections from the two-year increase in the federal tax were inadequate to cover benefit payments, the deficiency was to be made up, beginning in 1964, by reduction of the credit against the federal tax, i.e., increase of the federal tax on employers in the state. If, on the other hand, an excess of revenue was received from any state, this was to be credited to that state's account in the trust fund.

By a narrow vote (44-42), the Senate rejected this feature of the committee's report.

[22] *Unemployment Compensation*, Senate Finance Committee Hearings (1961), p. 133.
[23] *Temporary Extended Unemployment Compensation Act of 1961*, Senate Report No. 69, 87th Congress, 1st session (1961), p. 6.

Questions of Conformity

As has been indicated, the efficacy of the credit device in stimulating the enactment of state legislation according to a desired pattern could hardly be improved. Every state law by mid-1937 was certified to the Secretary of the Treasury as approved for the tax credit. Thereafter changes in state laws, or in administration and interpretation of them, had to be watched because each year, on December 31, the Social Security Board (since 1949 the Secretary of Labor) must certify to the Secretary of the Treasury that each state law is in conformity. He shall not certify if, "after reasonable notice and opportunity for hearing to the State agency," he finds a law not in conformity.[24] It is the job of the Labor Department's Bureau of Employment Security to observe and check upon developments by consultation with and reports from state and regional officials.

An Interstate Conference of Employment Security Agencies was set up in 1937 to provide a channel of communication between the states collectively and the federal government, and among the states themselves, in discussion of common problems. It established a number of technical committees—Benefit Financing, Legislative, Fraud Prevention and Detection, Interstate Benefits Payment, and ten others—which make reports and recommendations to the whole Conference.

The staff of the Bureau of Employment Security, in doing its job, does not make rulings; it raises issues of conformity and attempts to work out with state officials how, within the limits of conformity, state objectives can be accomplished. Frank T. de Vyver, who was a member of the Federal Advisory Council of the Bureau of Employment Security from 1948 to 1954, has summed up the position as follows:

Although there has never been a year-end refusal by the Bureau to certify the conformity of a state law with federal standards, there have

[24] *Internal Revenue Code* (1954), Sec. 3304(c).

been several close calls and a number of interesting arguments both over matters of general principle and over specific questions of tax reductions provided in the state's experience rating procedures. At least two times the Bureau's stand has led to amendments of federal legislation and in other instances a state governor has vetoed the proposed state legislation because the Bureau indicated that a conformity issue might be raised. Usually, however, although the arguments may get heated, issues have been settled to the mutual satisfaction of the state and the Bureau.[25]

Voluntary Contributions

Some of the more interesting issues of conformity concern experience rating. In 1947, Minnesota amended its unemployment insurance act to permit employers to make voluntary contributions to the state fund in order to secure a more favorable experience rating. Such a contribution has the same effect as a required tax contribution under a reserve-ratio system or under a benefit-ratio system of experience rating in bringing about a lower tax rate for an employer, and this may readily be managed when an employer is close to the bottom of a rate bracket. The Commissioner for Social Security ruled the amendment out of conformity with the experience-rating sections of the federal law because of the timing allowed to the contributions. But Congress in July 1947 amended the federal law to make statutory provision for voluntary contributions, as well as for specific timing (see 61 Stat. 416, applying to *Internal Revenue Code,* 1954, Sec. 3303-d); therefore in December 1947 the Minnesota law could be certified. As of January 1, 1960, employers in twenty-six states could obtain reduced rates by voluntary contributions.[26]

Non-Charging

At present practically all state laws have "non-charging" provisions because they recognize that certain benefit costs should not be

[25] De Vyver, "Federal Standards in Unemployment Insurance," *Vanderbilt Law Review,* Vol. 8 (February 1955), p. 416.

[26] See U.S. Bureau of Employment Security, *Comparison of State Unemployment Insurance Laws* (BES No. V-141, Jan. 31, 1960), p. 41.

charged to individual employers in measuring employment experience. An example would be where, after benefits had been paid to a worker, the case is appealed and the original determination (that benefits were due) is reversed.[27] In 1940 an Oregon law authorized non-charging "where the unemployment of the individuals is due to an act of God, a catastrophe not attributable to the employer, or by operation of law." The Social Security Board held that this provision would prevent a true measure of the unemployment experience of employers, and the provision was repealed. In 1953 the Secretary of Labor, after a hearing, held an Alabama amendment not in conformity with Section 3303 (a) (1) of the Internal Revenue Code because it permitted non-charging when the operations of a business were impaired because of severe damage to its plant.[28]

In numerous similar cases the Secretary of Labor has held to the principle that only benefits which do not reflect *workers'* risk of unemployment may be non-charged. In 1956, as an aftermath of the fall hurricane, Connecticut and Pennsylvania passed amendments to their laws which provided for non-charging of benefits and waiving of the waiting period in disaster situations. The state legislatures had, however, taken the precaution of providing that the amendments were contingent upon approval by the Secretary, and no conformity issue was, therefore, raised. The Secretary ruled against the amendments. In his opinion, to omit charges when the unemployment compensated was not within the control of an employer would mean that few charges could be required, "since, in the last analysis, most unemployment is beyond the control of any individual employer."[29] The "unemployment risk" referred to in the federal law is that of insured individual *workers,* and all risks of unemployment of workers must be charged.

[27] *Ibid.,* p. 37.
[28] See Edwin R. Teple and Charles G. Nowacek, "Experience Rating: Its Objectives, Problems, and Economic Implications," *Vanderbilt Law Review,* Vol. 8 (February 1955), p. 396.
[29] U.S. Bureau of Employment Security," Unemployment Insurance Program Letter," No. 419 (May 2, 1956). The Connecticut amendment was defective also in that omission of charges was provided for *all* employers during a specified ten-week period, whether or not they had been affected by the floods.

The California Conformity Issue

The most notable dispute concerning conformity arose in 1949 over application of the so-called "labor standards" section of the California act—a section required by federal law.[30] California had not amended its law, but the Secretary of Labor held that the law had been changed by the state *interpretation* of the law. The Secretary's position was that unemployed seamen, "some of whom were even receiving unemployment benefits," had been denied benefits when they refused to take "new work" open by reason of a labor dispute. The California position was that the claimants had been denied benefits *because* they were involved in a labor dispute. When the maritime strike occurred, were the claimants who were out of work, although members of the union, in a technical employer-employee relationship? The Department of Labor believed they were not; the California agency held that they were, and its position was upheld by the state appeals tribunal.

The Department of Labor agreed, however, that sanctions should not be applied. Instead, California was to take up other similar cases, making decisions which took into account the department's decision; this was done, and benefits were allowed by the state.

The Knowland Amendment

The quarrel had aroused state administrators, who saw in it a federal attempt to force them to administer and apply state law through federal pressure—an interference with the normal process by which state administrative action can be appealed and determined under state law. California sought remedy from Congress.

In June 1950, a Social Security bill dealing only with the Old Age and Survivors Insurance system was before Congress. During final debate in the Senate, an amendment concerned with the

[30] The state of Washington, involved at the same time in a similar dispute, agreed to reverse its decisions and to accept the position of the Secretary of Labor.

labor standards provisions of the unemployment insurance system was introduced from the floor by Senator William F. Knowland of California. (No hearings were held on the proposal.) A flood of telegrams poured in, alleging arbitrary action by the Secretary of Labor. The Department of Labor, in defense, alleged that the Knowland amendment would nullify the powers of the Secretary to enforce federal labor standards, because it would deny him the power to hold a state law out of conformity so long as it *contained the words* required by federal law. Nonetheless, despite strong opposition from a good many members of both House and Senate, the amendment was passed.[31] The portion of the federal law which declared that a state must not have "changed its law" was altered to declare that the state must not have "amended its law" with respect to the labor standards provision.[32] Moreover, the power of the Secretary to decide on noncompliance arising out of an administrative interpretation of the state law must not be exercised, if the issue had been taken to the courts, until the highest state court had made its decision.

The Knowland amendment had a direct bearing on the resolution of the issue between California and the Department of Labor, since it declared that claimants must exhaust their remedies under state law before the Secretary had jurisdiction. This process was not completed until 1955. By then the California Appeals Board had reversed the allowance of benefits, the lower California courts had sustained this denial, and the Supreme Court of California had refused to review. Only at this point could the Department of Labor act once more.

In June 1955, California was informed that a question was being raised concerning conformity of its law, and a hearing was scheduled for August. The outcome was a recommendation by the examiner that California not be held out of "substantial compliance."

Tactically the Secretary of Labor was now in an awkward posi-

---

[31] See 64 Stat. 560. For a record of the dispute, see *Congressional Record*, Vol. 96, Pt. 7 (June 19, 1950), pp. 8781-8786, and Pt. 9 (August 16, 1950), pp. 12652-12671.

[32] *Internal Revenue Code* (1954), Sec. 3304(c).

tion, since the interpretation of the law by California had been bolstered by full administrative and judicial review. The first reaction of Secretary James P. Mitchell was to announce to the Conference of Employment Security Agencies that, in principle, he favored judicial review of his decisions; then, somewhat later, he appointed a three-member advisory panel to review the controversy and offer him advice.[33] The panel upheld the position of California, and the Secretary himself accepted this finding. The long controversy, therefore, represented a setback for the Bureau of Employment Security.

Judicial Review

The California controversy awakened a strong sentiment among the states, operating through the Interstate Conference, to secure judicial review of the decisions of the Secretary of Labor. Under the law the decisions of the Secretary are final; a state has no appeal. The penalty for nonconformity would be withdrawal of the credit against the federal tax; the state payroll tax would apply and also the federal tax. The penalty has never been applied because the severity of this sanction has always brought conformity, whether by compromise or capitulation. It cannot be doubted that any Secretary of Labor would hesitate to withhold federal tax credits from employers in a state, and that state officials would be chary of incurring the penalty.

Which of the two parties, in such a tug and pull, has been the more timid? While the state administrators seem to believe their bargaining position to be weaker, evidence of weakness is not palpable. Backed by an effective body in the form of the Interstate Conference, with easy access to Congress, the states appear to have strengthened their position since 1935. Nonetheless, the threat of holding a state law in nonconformity has been used enough to make many of the states want judicial review.

[33] The panel membership was: Dean G. N. Stevens of the University of Washington Law School, Chief Judge N. Cayton of the Court of Appeals of the District of Columbia, Dean John Ritchie III of the University of Wisconsin Law School.

Even though Secretary Mitchell had declared his intention to propose legislation providing for judicial review of the decisions of the Secretary, it did not prove easy for representatives of the states to agree with the Labor Department upon suitable legislation. When the states, through the Interstate Conference, attempted to get direct congressional action, they made no progress.[34] At last in 1960 it seemed that the Interstate Conference and the Labor Department were going to agree on a judicial review bill, but new technical difficulties arose because the department wanted the bill to clarify the meaning of the Knowland amendment.

The difficulty concerned Section 3304 (c) of the *Internal Revenue Code,* which declared that a state law should not be held in noncompliance because of an interpretation "of State law with respect to which further administrative or judicial review is provided under the laws of the State." The department wished to amend the section to make it clear that the Secretary, in raising questions of conformity concerning the "labor standards" provision, did not have to wait on a decision by a state Supreme Court. The "labor standards" provision was to be applied uniformly in all jurisdictions, and to be applied also without undue delay. The members of the Interstate Conference felt that the suggested amendment would be an extension of the present powers of the Secretary, and this they would not concede.[35]

Perhaps the position of the Interstate Conference here is legalistic. Operation of a federal-state system, comprising some fifty ju-

[34] Some other federal departments were fearful of judicial review. Several grant programs of the Department of Health, Education, and Welfare gave its Secretary power to make decisions concerning state performance. Judicial review for unemployment insurance might be a precedent for a similar move concerning grant programs.

[35] Some states may decide to push their advantage. In April 1960 the Regional Director of the Bureau of Employment Security questioned a decision by an Indiana Review Board which seemed in conflict with the federal standards provision, since the claimant employee was offered work vacant because of a strike and work completely different from his prior work. The Director of the Indiana Employment Security Division questioned the jurisdiction of the Labor Department, citing the words of Section 3304(c) quoted above. While admitting that the Indiana decision to deny benefits might well be questioned, he believed that the department had no legal right to intervene in the case because the review processes of the state had not been exhausted by the claimant.

risdictions, cannot but be cumbersome and slow in the best of circumstances. To add judicial review would be to add delay. The danger of abuse of his power by the Secretary of Labor is remote; if it should develop, Congress will be responsive to state complaints. The tax sections of the federal unemployment insurance act do require close supervision of state legislation and administration by the Bureau of Employment Security in an effort to see that federal conditions have been met. This has not prevented development of a marked heterogeneity of state programs—greater than was anticipated in 1935. This heterogeneity narrows the features of unemployment insurance acceptable to all the states even when it unites them in opposition to federal action. As a result, the national interest has, in several respects, been pushed into the background.

On the other hand, it may be that the operations of the Department of Labor are excessively *sub rosa* and that, for this reason, the state administrators are unduly fearful of the federal bureaucracy. The Bureau of Employment Security has developed techniques to persuade the states; it has "a well-developed lexicon of phrases running from mildly implied suggestion that a state mend its ways to expression of grave doubt that a state is in conformity if it continues its practices."[36] Doubtless maneuver and pressuring are of the essence in our legislative and administrative process. But they should be accompanied by release of information so that a public opinion can evolve.

Financial Difficulties

The most unexpected developments in the program of unemployment insurance of the past quarter-century have grown out of experience rating. No one in 1935 foresaw, even dimly, the consequences of experience rating, because no one foresaw the favorable employment record that was to follow the 1930's. Gradually it became clear that the standard rate of 2.7 per cent was too high; had Congress then permitted a flat reduction of the standard rate, development of the program would have been different. But this

[36] *The Advisor* (Unemployment Benefits Advisors, Inc.), Feb. 10, 1956, p. 5.

was not permitted and soon many states found their reserves to be excessive. Experience rating, whatever its other merits or demerits, did offer a way by which states could reduce the average level of rates, and gradually the states turned to it.

The early financial practices of the states reflected strongly the impact of the great depression. In 1938 state tax rates averaged 2.75 per cent of taxable wages, and in forty-eight states the maximum weekly benefit was $15. This conservatism endured into the years of World War II when twelve states levied about $200 million in additional war-risk contributions on firms with greatly expanded payrolls, in the expectation that such firms would, postwar, be a drain on the system. Congress manifested a similar concern in 1944 by establishing a federal unemployment account from which, in the event of postwar need, advances might be made to the states. In this year (1944) "trust fund interest was more than sufficient to finance the year's benefit payments in all but three states."[37] From the beginning of the program to September 30, 1945, state contributions and interest totaled $9.3 billion, while benefit payments were only $2.3 billion. At this time 67.2 per cent of eligible workers could have been paid benefits of maximum duration from the funds then available.[38] The states were, in this respect, not in a uniform situation, but even the state with the lowest figure (Illinois) was in a strong financial situation. When, therefore, unemployment during reconversion was handled with ease, and when, thereafter, employment continued high, the states turned to a more intensive use of experience rating as a way to lower their tax rates. Chart 3-1, which relates annual benefit cost rates to annual contributions, 1946-52, shows that average contributions exceeded average benefits in most of the states, as indicated by the concentration of dots above the diagonal line.[39]

[37] *Issues in Social Security,* a Report to the House Committee on Ways and Means, by the Committee's Social Security Technical Staff, 79th Congress, 1st session (1946), p. 445.

[38] *Ibid.,* pp. 446, 599. It is ironic to find that Alaska could at that time have paid benefits for a maximum duration to 292.5 per cent of its covered labor force; at present its trust fund is insolvent.

[39] Both costs and benefits are expressed as percentages of *total* wages in covered employment because benefits are generally based on a worker's total wages and not on taxable wages.

CHART 3-1. *Average Annual State Contributions and Benefits as Per Cents of Total Wages, 1946-52*[a]

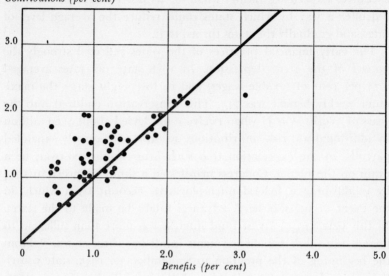

Contributions (per cent)

Benefits (per cent)

CHART 3-2. *Average Annual State Contributions and Benefits as Per Cents of Total Wages, 1953-59*[a]

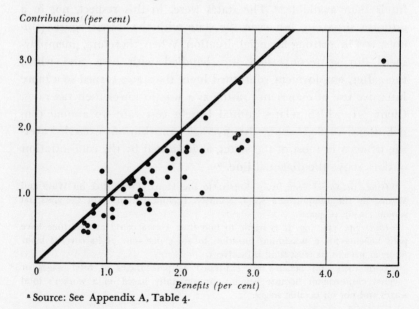

Contributions (per cent)

Benefits (per cent)

[a] Source: See Appendix A, Table 4.

This favorable financial experience was, however, soon to be reversed; costs came to outstrip contributions, and the protective devices against weak financing contained in many state laws often failed to work either because their "triggers" were geared to statistics which were out of date or because the triggers were spiked by legislative or executive intervention. Chart 3-2 shows that in 1953-59 benefits exceeded contributions in most of the states, as indicated by the concentration of dots below the diagonal.

TABLE 3-1. *Average Cost (benefit) Rates and Tax Rates, 1954-58 and 1960, as Per Cents of Taxable Wages, for Selected States*[a]

State	Average 1954–58		Average 1960	
	Benefit Rates	Tax Rates	Benefit Rates	Tax Rates
United States	1.9%	1.3%	2.3%	1.9%
Alaska	4.4	2.7	3.3	2.9
Delaware	1.2	0.6	1.6	2.5
Michigan	3.1	1.6	2.6	2.9
Oregon	2.5	1.6	2.1	2.7
Pennsylvania	2.9	1.7	3.1	3.1
West Virginia	2.3	1.1	2.5	2.7
Illinois	1.5	0.8	1.7	2.1
Maryland	1.7	0.9	2.7	2.8
Ohio	1.7	0.7	2.8	1.5
Rhode Island	2.9	2.7	2.3	2.7
Tennessee	2.4	1.7	1.9	1.7

[a] Source: *Report of the Committee on Benefit Financing*, Interstate Conference of Employment Security Agencies (September 1959), pp. 3, 15; U. S. Bureau of Employment Security, *The Labor Market and Employment Security* (May 1961), p. 14.

In a 1959 report the Committee on Benefit Financing of the Interstate Conference singled out six jurisdictions as especially out of line—Alaska, Delaware, Michigan, Oregon, Pennsylvania, and West Virginia (see Table 3-1), and mentioned five others as possibly in need of loans. Except for Alaska and Rhode Island, tax rates in these states were not high. The table shows also the sharp increase in tax rates by 1960.[40]

[40] This inattentiveness to sound financing was not general among the states. Thirty-four had provided for suspension of rates below the standard rate when

Other financial features of the system needed attention. As has been noted, during the recession of 1957-58 the number of persons exhausting benefits grew at an alarming rate, and Congress enacted the Temporary Unemployment Compensation Act of 1958. At this very time, moreover, loan funds provided under the Reed Act of 1954 were running short, and administrative expenditures exceeded collections from the federal tax of 0.3 per cent. Alaska had already borrowed $8.3 million and Michigan $113 million from the fund; Pennsylvania had requested an advance of $112 million, and Delaware, West Virginia, and Oregon were eligible, since their reserves were less than the amounts paid out in benefits in the preceding twelve months. The fear expressed in 1955 by two members of the Kestnbaum Commission—New Jersey Governor Alfred E. Driscoll and Colorado Governor Dan Thornton—that the loan fund might invite "irresponsible action by the States" seemed to be justified.[41]

The Reed Act had, indeed, an *ex post* sanction of some severity: if a loan had not been repaid by the fourth January after it had been made, the rate of the federal tax, applicable to employers in the state, was to go up. And the same type of sanction was to be used to secure repayment of federal advances under the Temporary Unemployment Compensation Act of 1958. Was this also an invitation to irresponsible finance? Was it not necessary that steps be taken, *ex ante,* to ensure adequate benefit financing? Should the federal government impose minimum reserve requirements on the states? Should it provide that states could borrow only when their systems met specified financial standards?[42] And what if the increases in the federal tax in order to pay back advances were badly timed in terms of the business cycle? Any automatic formula, dependent on the calendar, runs this risk.[43]

---

reserves fell below a certain level; twenty-six had provided for an automatic increase in their wage base if Congress increased the base of the federal tax beyond $3,000; and six had actually provided a higher base for the state tax.

[41] Commission on Intergovernmental Relations, *Report* (June 1955), pp. 201-202, footnote 4.

[42] The Federal Advisory Council made such recommendations in March 1960. See Minutes of the Committee on Benefit Financing, January 1960, p. 26.

[43] The Committee on Benefit Financing had before it in February 1961 a resolution which would allow postponement of repayment of advances under

Conclusion

After two decades the federal-state system of unemployment insurance fell into serious financial trouble. The tax credit device, in this its most ambitious use, proved inflexible in adapting to a changing environment. Original overestimates of costs and underestimates of revenues built norms into the system which were unrealistic: a standard state tax rate of 2.7 per cent; a taxable wage base of $3,000; additional credits against the federal tax which pushed tax rates down too far and opened differentials among the states. By the mid-1950's some states thought they had gone too far in lowering rates and liberalizing benefits. But a shift in methods of finance was not easy; many states procrastinated, fearful that change would be an acknowledgement of weakness.

The changes in methods of finance since 1935 fly in the face of certain original concepts, of which the most important was limitation of interstate competition.[44] In 1938 tax collections were 3.1 per cent of total wages in covered payrolls; in 1960 they were approximately 1.3 per cent. (See Table 3-2 and Chart 3-3.) Taxable wages were 97 per cent of total wages in 1938; they were only 62 per cent in 1960. The appropriate comparison is, therefore, of collections as a per cent of total wages. Employers paid on the average less than half the original standard rate, and received credit against the federal tax for sums more than twice as large as they actually paid. But national figures conceal the fact that, with respect to collections, there is no national system. The rate differences among states are great. In 1960 the estimated average rate in terms of taxable wages was, on the one hand, 0.5 per cent in Colo-

---

the 1958 act if a state maintained a tax rate of at least 2.7 per cent for a two-year period preceding the due date. See Minutes, February 1961, p. 10.

[44] "The failure of the States to enact unemployment insurance laws is due largely to the fact that to do so would handicap their industries in competition with the industries of other states. . . . A uniform Nation-wide tax upon industry, thus removing this principal obstacle in the way of unemployment insurance, is necessary before the States can go ahead." See House Report No. 615, 74th Congress, 1st session (1935), p. 8.

TABLE 3-2. *State Unemployment Insurance Collections as Per Cent of Total Wages in Covered Payrolls, 1938-60*[a]

Collections as Per Cent of Total Wages		Collections as Per Cent of Total Wages	
1938	3.1%	1950	1.2%
1939	2.8	1951	1.3
1940	2.6	1952	1.1
1941	2.4	1953	1.0
1942	2.1	1954	.8
1943	2.0	1955	.8
1944	1.9	1956	.9
1945	1.7	1957	.9
1946	1.2	1958	.9
1947	1.3	1959	1.0
1948	1.0	1960	1.3[b]
1949	1.0		

[a] Source: Minutes of the Committee on Benefit Financing, Interstate Conference of Employment Security Agencies, February 1961, Exhibit A.
[b] Based on data for twelve months ending October 1960.

rado and Iowa, 0.8 per cent in Virginia; on the other hand, it was 3.1 per cent in Pennsylvania, 2.9 per cent in Michigan, 2.8 per cent in Maryland, 2.7 per cent in Oregon, Rhode Island, Washington, and West Virginia.[45]

In short, the uniform tax rate, which in 1935 was thought to be an important technique to avoid and prevent interstate competition in the financing of unemployment insurance, has disappeared. A multiplicity of rates now prevails, and the average level differs significantly from state to state. The technique used to bring this about was experience rating. But with or without it, the overriding fact is that the cost of unemployment insurance differs widely from state to state. The chief reason is the different incidence of unemployment, although the state differentials have been widened also

[45] See *Unemployment Compensation,* Senate Finance Committee Hearings (1961), p. 28.
    Richard A. Lester has described the spread in rates as follows: "Most states have 8 or more different tax rates below the standard rate of 2.7 per cent. In half the states, the regular tax schedule has a top rate 9 to 30 times as high as the bottom rate, and some 14 other states have a minimum rate that can be zero—no state tax." ("Financing of Unemployment Compensation," p. 63.)

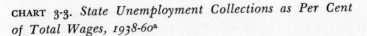

CHART 3-3. *State Unemployment Collections as Per Cent of Total Wages, 1938-60*[a]

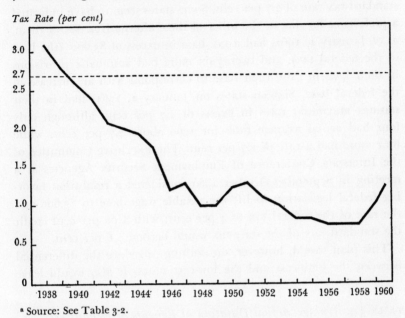

Tax Rate (per cent)

[a] Source: See Table 3-2.

by state action designed "to minimize the tax on the employer both from the contribution side and the benefit side."[46]

[46] Teple and Nowacek, *op. cit.*, p. 404. The authors go on to say: "Such devices include lower minimum and maximum rates, crediting of trust fund interest to employers' accounts, non-charging of benefits, different systems of experience rating, and stricter disqualification and entitlement conditions for benefits. . . . The competitive advantage traceable to these factors is probably small, however, compared to the advantages the employer enjoys by virtue of having his establishment located in a state with a low rate of unemployment."

For the week ending January 28, 1961, insured unemployment as a per cent of average covered employment during the twelve months ending March 1960 varied among the states as follows:

Hawaii	3.6%	West Virginia	13.4%
Texas	4.7	Montana	14.1
Virginia	5.1	Alaska	20.1

See *Temporary Unemployment Compensation and Aid to Dependent Children of Unemployed Parents,* Hearings Before the House Committee on Ways and Means, 87th Congress, 1st Session (1961), pp. 21-22.

This, then, is the major problem, and it cannot be solved by a uniform increase in the taxable wage base, or an increase in the standard tax rate of 2.7 per cent. Some states seem to have indicated a preference for one or the other of these alternatives. Six of them, as of January 1, 1961, had a tax base in excess of $3,000 (the base of the federal tax), and twenty-six more had automatic provisions in their laws to raise their base to correspond with an increase in the federal base. Sixteen states on January 1, 1961, had in their statutes *maximum* rates in excess of 2.7 per cent, although only four had actual average rates for 1960 above 2.7 per cent, while four more had a rate of 2.7 per cent. The Executive Committee of the Interstate Conference of Employment Security Agencies at a meeting in September-October 1960 considered a resolution favoring federal legislation to lift the taxable wage base to $3,600 and the rate of the federal tax to 4 per cent; with a 90 per cent credit the standard rate of the state tax would become 3.6 per cent.

This plan would, however, do nothing to reduce the differential between the high-cost and the low-cost states. It also would leave

TABLE 3-3. *Average Actual Duration of Benefits of Exhaustees, Fiscal Year 1960*

Average Weeks of Benefit	Number of States[a]
13.0-14.9	5
15.0-16.9	3
17.0-18.9	10
19.0-20.9	13
21.0-22.9	7
23.0-24.9	5
25.0-26.9	6
27.0-28.9	0
29.0-31.0	1
	—
	50

[a] Figures are derived from *Unemployment Compensation,* Hearings Before the Senate Committee on Finance, 87th Congress, 1st session (1961), p.22, Table 11. The "number of states" includes the District of Columbia; it does not include Wisconsin, for which comparable data were not available. The highest figure was that of Pennsylvania, with 30 weeks.

untouched the problem of the duration of benefits. In 1958 and again in 1961 the federal government passed temporary legislation which provided extension of benefit payments to "exhaustees." Congress appeared to acknowledge a federal responsibility to finance prolonged unemployment, and this did persuade many states to move. By January 1, 1961, forty-one states had provided a maximum duration of twenty-six weeks, fourteen went beyond, and only nine fell short of this duration.[47] Average actual duration, however, seldom reached twenty-six weeks even in a year of fairly high unemployment, as Table 3-3 indicates.

The Social Security Board, at least as late as 1948, desired and hoped to achieve a federal system of unemployment insurance. Although unsympathetic to this approach, Congress has been unreceptive also to numerous other approaches put before it.[48] The sanguine expectation of 1935 was that a federal-state program would produce valuable experiments and adaptation to variation in actual situations. Something of the sort has happened, but the impact of the experiments has been erratic, and some of the heterogeneity which has emerged impairs the efficient operation of unemployment insurance. In not a few respects the states have exaggerated the importance of details; they have been jealous of each other and of the federal government. Some of them have lost sight of the national interest in unemployment insurance.

A defect of our legislative process, exaggerated by federalism, is that marginal adjustments in an established program are sluggish. Tax credits operate to enhance this defect because they are inflexible. As a device to stimulate prompt action, their power is massive; as a device in operation, they oppose mutation. Special countervailing efforts to assure adjustments in the initial program are, therefore, indicated.

---

[47] The nine states and their maximum weeks payable were as follows: Alabama, 20; Montana, 22; North Dakota, 24; South Carolina, 22; South Dakota, 24; Tennessee, 22; Texas, 24; Virginia, 20; West Virginia, 24. See *Unemployment Compensation*, Senate Finance Committee Hearings (1961), p. 18.

[48] These are summarized by Wilbur J. Cohen, "Some Major Policy Issues in Unemployment Insurance and General Assistance" in *Studies in Unemployment*, prepared for the Special Senate Committee on Unemployment Problems, 86th Congress, 2d session (1960), pp. 317-320.

4

Individual Income Tax Credit

> The basic difficulty at present in certain states is that the
> legislatures, for one reason or another, have refused to pass
> the necessary tax bills to restore the state finances to a
> healthy condition. . . . Therefore, a thorough exploration
> of the use in one way or another of the power of Congress
> to cajole or coerce the states into putting their own finan-
> cial houses in order seems to me well worth the effort.
>
> James Bryant Conant
> *The Child, the Parent, and the State*

PROPOSALS HAVE RECENTLY been advanced that a credit be allowed against federal individual income tax for state income tax
payments. The proposals have come from Orville L. Freeman, Walter
W. Heller, George Meany, Robert R. Nathan, Harvey E. Brazer,
Stanley H. Ruttenberg, Morton Grodzins, and John W. Gardner.
Barry Goldwater has suggested that property tax payments for
schools be credited against federal individual income tax payment,
and Robert Heller has made a similar proposal, except that in his

plan only increases in property tax payments over a base year would be creditable.

The objectives sought to be achieved by this mixed group of proponents are themselves diverse.[1] The objective most frequently stated is that of opening up new avenues of revenue, and therefore of expenditure, for state (and local) governments. The expenditure most to be encouraged is that for education, and, on this account, the tax credit is favored since it would put the federal taxing power at the service of the states "with little danger of control" (Gardner). Another objective is stimulation of over-all progression, thus raising more revenue more equitably, "rather than enacting regressive sales and excise taxes" (Meany). A credit would "strongly induce if not force 17 states, with over one-third of the Nation's population," to adopt individual income taxes (W. W. Heller). Another and related objective is "interstate equalization"; Orville Freeman and Walter W. Heller believed that a graduated credit (to be described later) would "automatically help redress the balance between richer and poorer states." Still another objective is tax

---

[1] See Orville L. Freeman (then Governor of Minnesota), "Strengthening the States' Tax Base," Statement presented at the 51st Annual Meeting, Governors' Conference, August 1959; Walter W. Heller (then Professor of Economics, University of Minnesota), "Deductions and Credits for State Income Taxes," in *Tax Revision Compendium*, Submitted to the House Ways and Means Committee, 86th Congress, 1st session (1959), Vol. 1, pp. 419-433; George Meany, President of the AFL-CIO, Statement in *Goals for Americans*, Report of the President's Commission on National Goals (Prentice-Hall, 1960, for the American Assembly), p. 29; Robert R. Nathan, of Robert R. Nathan Associates, and Edward D. Hollander, "The Role of Individual Income Taxes in Federal-State-Local Fiscal Relations," *Tax Revision Compendium*, Vol. 1, pp. 224-225; Harvey E. Brazer, Professor of Economics, University of Michigan, "The Deductibility of State and Local Taxes under the Individual Income Tax," *ibid.* p. 417; Stanley H. Ruttenberg, Director, Department of Research, AFL-CIO, *Money and Credit*, Report of the Commission on Money and Credit (Prentice-Hall, 1961), p. 125; Morton Grodzins, Professor of Political Science, University of Chicago, "The Federal System," *Goals for Americans*, p. 278; John W. Gardner, President of Carnegie Corporation, "National Goals in Education," *ibid.*, p. 99; Barry Goldwater, U.S. Senator for Arizona, *Washington Post*, January 29, 1961; Robert Heller, of Robert Heller and Associates, "A Proposal for Financing Tax-Supported Education," *Harvard Educational Review*, Summer 1958, pp. 214-231.

Earlier proposals for credits are discussed by Andrew M. Tully, *The Tax Credit*, Special Report of the New York State Tax Commission, No. 15 (1948), Chap. 7.

coordination and financial reform, through reduction of tax conflict and of compliance and tax administration costs.[2] None of the proponents was explicit concerning this last objective, although there was mention of minimizing interstate competition—overcoming "the paralyzing fear that taxes will discourage the location and expansion of industry in the taxing state" (Freeman).

Not one of the proponents regarded a tax credit primarily as a technique to secure reduction of federal taxation. This is especially to be noted because the original use of the credit device—the 25 per cent credit of 1924 and the 80 per cent credit of 1926 against the federal estate tax (see Chapter 2)—was mainly for this purpose, and also because important issues of theory are resolved when tax reduction is eschewed as an objective.

Types of Credit

An income tax credit is an offset allowed to individuals against a federal individual tax liability for payment of specific state (and local) taxes. The ceiling or maximum allowable credit is stated as a percentage or portion of the federal tax, allowable if the state (or local) tax is at least equal to the credit. The federal government may designate conditions for the credit, of which the simplest is that only a specified type of tax be eligible. In actual practice and in discussion, federal credits usually have been linked to a similar state tax. But a credit could, conceivably, be allowed against income tax for dissimilar state and local taxes, and indeed the creditable state death taxes, while of the same genus, are of several species.

A Flat Percentage Credit

Most earlier discussions of an income tax credit assumed that the credit should, in form, be a flat percentage of the federal tax. If, for example, the federal liability of an individual was $100, a

[2] Brazer favors a tax credit as a substitute for deductibility of state and local personal taxes against federal individual income tax. This position will be analyzed in Chapter 5.

credit of 7 per cent would entitle him to reduce his federal liability by $7, assuming his state tax was at least this amount.

Graduated Credit

Recently, schemes for graduated credits have been advanced. Walter W. Heller proposed to the House Ways and Means Committee in 1959 a credit against federal income tax up to 20 per cent of the first $200 of tax liability, 10 per cent of the next $300, and 1 per cent of the remainder—as ceiling amounts which would apply when state income tax payments were equal to or larger than the credit.[3] Thus an individual with a federal tax liability of $600 and a state tax payment in the prior year of $71 could subtract this entire $71 from his federal liability. A flat percentage credit of 7 per cent would allow him to subtract $42. Should the allowable credit vary according to the type of return? While Heller made no differentiation, it seems reasonable to assume that his scale should apply to joint returns and that the scale for returns of other persons should be 20 per cent of the first $100 of federal tax liability, 10 per cent of the next $150, and 1 per cent of the remainder.[4]

How appraise the two types of credit? With a flat percentage, Congress would have to determine the appropriate rate, and this decision might hinge upon how large or how small a reduction of federal tax it wished to provide. A regressively graduated credit would, in addition, force Congress to determine the scale, since very many scales would bring the same aggregate deduction in federal tax, and the choice of graduation would be difficult. The Heller scale, given above, appears at first sight to serve an "equalization" purpose by confining almost all of the reduction in federal tax to recipients of low incomes.

[3] See *Tax Revision Compendium*, Vol. 1, pp. 419-433. Governor Freeman proposed the same scheme in his Statement to the Governors' Conference in 1959.

[4] This differentiation is made in the calculation of the allowable credits by states for 1958, presented in Appendix B. Further differentiation of the "other" group would, of course, be defensible, but refinement of this sort would complicate the calculation without bringing much change in the aggregate or in the state-by-state results.

Credit of a Flat Sum

A third type of credit might be a flat sum—for example, $32.50 for a single person and $65 for a married couple. Such a credit is, of course, simply a variant of the Heller type, serving to confine federal tax reduction through the credit even more rigorously to the lower end of the income scale. Geographically, this and the Heller scheme would provide a relatively larger reduction in states where low federal tax payments were numerous.

The particular figures mentioned here— (1) 7 per cent of federal tax liabilities; (2) 20 per cent of the first $200 of federal liability, 10 per cent of the next $300, and 1 per cent of the remainder for joint returns, with a modified scale for "other" returns; (3) $65 for a married couple and $32.50 for a single person—all would yield (approximately) the same aggregate amount of credits, and subsequent statistical analysis in this chapter will rest on them.[5] The main purpose of this analysis is to measure, state by state, what would be made available by each credit.

Federal Tax Reduction

The first result of a federal credit, regardless of type, would be federal tax reduction. The federal government would collect less in federal income tax from residents in all states which collected an income tax. As noted in Chapter 2, federal tax reduction was a prime motive behind the death tax credits of 1924 and 1926; the credits were to be a prelude to federal abandonment of this tax field. At that time forty-five states (as well as Alaska and Hawaii) had some form of death tax, while three states—Florida, Nevada, and Alabama—did not. Florida and Nevada had just emphasized their status by passing constitutional amendments forbidding death taxes, a step which greatly alarmed the other states. The 80 per cent credit of 1926 seemed, therefore, to be a way to stifle unruly

[5] The aggregate amount used in the analysis is not meant to suggest the appropriate size of a federal credit. As is explained in Appendix B, the particular aggregate chosen—approximately $2.4 billion for 1958—was simply the amount calculated for a Heller-type credit.

behavior by two states, containing about 1 per cent of the nation's population. In such circumstances a federal tax reduction discriminating against these two states and Alabama seemed justifiable.

What is the relevance of this precedent for an income tax credit? As of 1961, thirty-two states (and the District of Columbia) were levying individual income taxes, which yielded 20.4 per cent of their tax revenue. Except for the addition of Alaska (then a territory) in 1949 and West Virginia in 1961, the roll of income tax states has been constant since 1937. For the fifty states as a whole, in 1961 the individual income tax produced 12.4 per cent of tax revenue. In states which now have income taxes, the immediate effect of a federal credit would be tax reduction, the amount and distribution depending upon the coincidence of state and federal payments by individuals. Immediately, individuals in the eighteen states who pay federal, but not state, income tax would secure no tax reduction because they would have nothing to credit. In short, the immediate impact of a credit would be discriminatory; individuals similarly circumstanced would secure different tax reductions depending upon the state in which they resided.

The federal government, in providing a credit, would of course have objectives other than tax reduction. No doubt can exist that an important aim of some advocates of an income tax credit is to push state governments into income taxation. The credit would, as the Groves-Gulick-Newcomer report declared in 1943, "underwrite a minimum of direct taxation and progression in the State tax systems."[6] Universal adoption by the states of individual income taxation would improve the progressivity and built-in flexibility of their revenue systems.

Other financial reforms might also be achieved if the federal government not only required adoption of income tax, but also specified other conditions. (Presumably only taxes applying to total income of individuals, reasonably defined, would be eligible; the New Hampshire and Tennessee taxes, for instance, which apply only to income from intangibles, would not count.) The more limited and precise the form of the credit, the more could it be used to mold the structure of the state taxes. As will be seen later, any

[6] *Federal, State, and Local Government Fiscal Relations,* Report of the U. S. Treasury Committee on Intergovernmental Fiscal Relations, Senate Document No. 69, 78th Congress, 1st session (1943), p. 448.

credit related directly to federal tax liability would have effects on the amount of the state personal exemption and scale of rates. Another relevant federal condition might be a uniform definition of tax jurisdiction in order to minimize double taxation. Many reasonable variants exist, and in framing such a definition it should be recognized that a uniform definition for the states might differ from the federal definition. While a tax credit would do nothing in itself to eliminate dual administration of income taxes, conditions requiring uniformity would tend to make dual administration superfluous. Marked reduction in conflicting taxation, in costs of administration and compliance—these are appealing goals, even at the cost of a marked reduction of state tax autonomy.

Impact on States With and Without Income Tax

The immediate impact of a federal credit on a state would vary depending on whether it had or had not an income tax, and, if it had, whether the tax yielded more or less in the aggregate than the maximum amount of the available credit. To be concrete, assume that the federal government offered a credit with a ceiling equal to 7 per cent of federal tax liability. For 1958, total federal tax liability was $34,304 million, and 7 per cent of this would be $2,400 million.[7] This is the maximum amount which individuals could claim as credits.

States Without Income Tax

Residents of the then nineteen states without income taxes had, in 1958, a federal tax liability of $16,090 million, and 7 per cent of this is $1,126 million (see Table 4-1). If these states levied income

[7] Tax liability for 1958 is used here because 1958 was the most recent year for which reports from *Statistics of Income* (Internal Revenue Service, 1960) were available at the time the computations shown in Appendix B, Table 1, were made. The 7 per cent figure is chosen because it gives approximately the same aggregate credit value as two other types of credit which are to be examined here in some detail.

TABLE 4-1. *Hypothetical 7 Per Cent Federal Tax Credit, 1958, for Nineteen States Without State Individual Income Tax*[a]

State	Federal Income Tax	7 Per Cent Credit
Connecticut	$ 719.8 million	$ 50.4 million
Florida	718.7	50.3
Illinois	2,622.1	183.5
Indiana	826.0	57.8
Maine	128.3	9.0
Michigan	1,607.5	112.5
Nebraska	223.9	15.7
Nevada	76.3	5.3
New Hampshire[b]	101.8	7.1
New Jersey	1,539.4	107.8
Ohio	2,040.7	142.8
Pennsylvania	2,368.0	165.8
Rhode Island	171.7	12.0
South Dakota	80.2	5.6
Tennessee[b]	405.4	28.4
Texas	1,540.5	107.8
Washington	622.9	43.6
West Virginia[c]	237.4	16.6
Wyoming	59.9	4.2
Total	$16,090.5 million	$1,126.2 million

[a] Source: Column 1, U. S. Internal Revenue Service, *Statistics of Income, 1958: Individual Income Tax Returns* (1960), p. 66.
[b] New Hampshire and Tennessee tax income from intangibles.
[c] West Virginia adopted an income tax in 1961.

taxes with the same base and the same exemptions as the federal tax, and with a scale of rates which for every adjusted gross income class was 7 per cent of the federal scale, they would secure a revenue of $1,126 million. Governors and legislatures in some states, harassed for money to meet urgent public needs, might hail the credit as a bonanza, costless in the aggregate to their taxpayers, since the amount of the new state tax would be exactly matched by the reduced amount of federal tax liabilities. Other governors and legislatures might inveigh against federal coercion, confident that this stand would bring political profit. In some states opposition to income taxation is strongly fortified by constitutional provision. But one may guess that, in time, the opposition would capitulate. In Michigan, the bait of $112.5 million; in New Jersey, $107.8 million; in Illinois, $183.5 million—all at the expense of the federal treasury —might be potent.

States With Income Tax

The immediate gain in 1958 for the twenty-nine states with individual income taxes would be quite diverse in the short run and assuming their taxes are not altered.[8] As is shown by Table 4-2, eleven of these states in fiscal 1959 collected sums *less* than 7 per cent of federal tax liabilities of their residents in 1958. For all eleven the shortage was $168.2 million—that is, collections would have to increase by 55 per cent to absorb the credit. The aggregate figures do not, of course, show the shortage with accuracy. Personal exemptions for state individual income taxes are usually higher than those for the federal tax (the Louisiana exemption in fiscal 1959 for a single person was $2,500, and for a married couple $5,000), and state rates are not geared to pick up a 7 per cent credit. In a state with high exemptions and low rates, residents with low incomes who pay no state tax would not gain from the credit, and even those with larger incomes might not secure the full amount of the allowable credit.

It is, however, reasonable to assume that these states would alter their exemptions and rates so as to maximize the credits which their residents could take against federal income tax liabilities. Even if this were done, many taxpayers would still secure a tax reduction because of the credit. In Louisiana, for example, if state collections were raised to $28.9 million (the maximum creditable amount), federal liabilities would become $383.4 million ($412.3 million less $28.9 million), and this amount, added to the new state collections, would give an aggregate of $412.3 million instead

[8] Hawaii and Alaska, not then states, and the District of Columbia also had income taxes.

TABLE 4-2. *Eleven States with Revenue from Individual Income Tax, Fiscal 1959, Less Than 7 Per Cent of Federal Tax Liability, Calendar 1958*[a]

State	Federal Tax Liability, 1958 (1)	7 Per Cent of (1) (2)	State Income Tax, Fiscal 1959[b] (3)
Arizona	$ 194.2 million	$ 13.6 million	$ 9.0 million
Arkansas	143.4	10.0	8.4
California	3,816.2	267.1	160.7
Georgia	437.0	30.6	29.4
Kansas	362.5	25.4	22.1
Louisiana	412.3	28.9	11.7
Mississippi	127.7	8.9	6.4
Missouri	782.0	54.7	34.0
New Mexico	130.1	9.1	6.8
North Dakota	73.4	5.1	4.5
Oklahoma	325.0	22.8	15.0
Total	$6,803.8 million	$476.2 million	$308.0 million

[a] Source: Column 1, U. S. Internal Revenue Service, *Statistics of Income, 1958: Individual Income Tax Returns* (1960), p. 66; column 3, U. S. Bureau of the Census, *Summary of State Government Finances in 1959* (1960), p. 11.

[b] The fiscal year of forty-four states ended June 30; the other four states had endings as follows: Alabama, September 30; New York, March 31; Pennsylvania, May 31; Texas, August 31.

of the pre-credit aggregate of $424 million ($412.3 million plus $11.7 million). In short, the credit would allow an over-all reduction in taxes equal to the amount of state income tax collections pre-credit.

Questions for future consideration are these: Should the federal government, through a credit, provide such a tax reduction? Or should it, as a condition for the credit, require (for example) that Louisiana income tax collections reach $40.6 million ($11.7 million plus $28.9 million), so that total collections, federal and state, do not diminish? Only by such a requirement would the credit be divorced from a reduction of taxes.

As Table 4-3 shows, eighteen states in fiscal 1959 had individual income taxes the yields of which exceeded 7 per cent of federal tax liabilities of their residents in 1958. For Oregon, at one extreme, the

TABLE 4-3. *Eighteen States with Revenue from Individual Income Tax, Fiscal 1959, in Excess of 7 Per Cent of Federal Tax Liability, Calendar 1958*[a]

State	Federal Tax Liability, 1958 (1)	7 Per Cent of (1) (2)	State Income Tax, Fiscal 1959[b] (3)
Alabama	$ 341.9 million	$ 23.9 million	$ 24.6 million
Colorado	329.3	23.1	34.7
Delaware	153.5	10.7	27.1
Idaho	93.7	6.6	13.7
Iowa	435.9	30.6	36.0
Kentucky	351.2	24.6	45.9
Maryland	685.1	48.0	81.5
Massachusetts	1,124.5	78.7	155.0
Minnesota	565.0	39.6	76.5
Montana	100.3	7.0	9.4
New York	4,494.1	314.5	565.8
North Carolina	405.3	28.4	60.7
Oregon	343.7	24.1	77.1
South Carolina	182.0	12.7	18.4
Utah	127.7	8.9	12.3
Vermont	47.3	3.3	9.6
Virginia	558.8	39.2	71.8
Wisconsin	700.5	49.0	121.2
Total	$11,039.8 million	$772.9 million	$1,441.3 million

[a] Source: See Table 4-2.
[b] See Table 4-2.

state yield was 3.2 times the 7 per cent credit; for Alabama, at the other extreme, the state yield barely exceeded the credit. Once again it should be noted that such a comparison of totals is imprecise, since segments of the income tax scale of these eighteen states might produce collections less than the allowable 7 per cent credit.[9] It is

[9] Figures given by Walter W. Heller (*Tax Revision Compendium*, Vol. 1, p. 421) for Minnesota show that the 1956 Minnesota tax liabilities for the gross income group $1,000 to $1,999 were less than a 5 per cent credit, even though total Minnesota liabilities exceeded the total credit by 160 per cent.

possible that, in response to a credit, when collections in some brackets exceeded the maximum credit values, states might lower rates for these brackets, while raising them for other brackets. But for most taxpayers in these eighteen states the state tax would overtop a 7 per cent credit and no significant alteration of the state tax would be needed to maximize the value of the credit.

The figures below illustrate the case of a married taxpayer in New York with an adjusted gross income of $10,000.

	Before Credit	After Credit
Federal tax	$2,200	$2,046 ($2,200 less 7%)
State tax	308	308
Total	$2,508	$2,354

His state tax of $308 exceeds a 7 per cent credit ($154). Inauguration of the credit would reduce his federal tax and his aggregate tax by $154. If the state government is to pick up this sum and other similar sums, it must raise its rate structure.[10]

Since the rate structure in some of the eighteen states in Table 4-3 is relatively high in comparison with their sister states, this may cause political hesitation. Yet the questions may be asked: Why should the Congress give a 7 per cent tax reduction to residents of these states? Why should not *revenue-maintenance* be a condition of the credit, following the precedent of the recommendation concerning a new death tax credit by the Advisory Commission on Intergovernmental Relations?[11] The condition should not be expressed as an absolute amount of dollars. If a federal credit made possible a potential tax reduction of $2.1 million in a year to residents of a state, revenue-maintenance should not mean that, in the future, the state government would raise $2.1 million additional

[10] The personal exemption for New York is the same as the federal exemption ($600), but in nineteen states (and the District of Columbia) of the thirty-two in 1961 (twenty-nine in 1958) with individual income taxes, the personal exemption was larger than the federal.

[11] Revenue-maintenance was also recommended by the Joint Federal-State Action Committee in 1957 as a condition of a tax credit against the federal local telephone tax. This will be discussed in Chapter 6.

by income tax. The value of a federal credit would increase in later years as federal tax liabilities grew. The requirement should be that a state income tax *structure* be enacted, estimated to increase state collections at the time and in the future by an amount which will match the decrease in federal collections caused by the credit; or that the aggregate of post-credit collections—federal plus state—at least equals pre-credit collections as a percentage of taxable income. Only by such a requirement would taxpayers be left no better or no worse off with respect to their income taxes; only by it would the federal government avoid discriminatory tax reduction.[12]

One important objection to revenue-maintenance should, however, be recognized. If the Congress rated highly the objective of tax coordination and regarded individual income taxes as a superior means of raising state revenue, then it might forgo revenue-maintenance, using the credit merely as a lever to reduce tax conflict and to push states into income taxation. States without income tax would have to enact income taxes in order to secure the credit—taxes which provided a uniform definition of tax jurisdiction. These states would, in effect, provide for revenue-maintenance even though this was not a federal requirement. States with income tax would be pushed toward a uniform definition of tax jurisdiction, but they would be free to allow use of the credit by their taxpayers to secure a tax reduction.

A generation ago this plan seemed more plausible than it now does. Recently, concern over the fiscal adequacy of state-local tax systems has been acute, and therefore the objective of revenue-maintenance has been given top priority. Revenue-maintenance could, moreover, be coupled with conditions to assure tax coordination. An income tax credit could be utilized both to provide state-local governments with additional financial resources and also to reduce tax conflict.

---

[12] How compliance with a requirement of revenue-maintenance would be ascertained and enforced, I shall not explore. The Advisory Commission on Intergovernmental Relations proposed that, with respect to its new death tax credit, the governor of a state certify to the Secretary of the Treasury that the requirement had been met. It would seem also that, in all cases, the Secretary of the Treasury should make a certification to the President and the Congress.

Revenue-Maintenance and Structural Inflexibility

One consequence of a revenue-maintenance requirement would be inflexibility of state income tax structure. Rates and exemptions would, to some extent, be frozen at the level indicated by the requirement. This inflexibility would, of course, take time to become manifest. The first consequence of a credit, coupled with revenue-maintenance, would be a substantial increase of revenue for the state governments. But expenditures would soon grow and, in time, states might wish to make stronger use of income tax than is indicated by the credit. Nothing in the credit scheme would prohibit states from raising their income tax rates (and most states have collected death taxes in excess of the creditable amounts). Moreover, even if a credit scheme were simply maintained and not liberalized by the Congress, its income-elasticity would produce a growing annual sum. Nonetheless, a credit would put some curb on the willingness of state legislatures to change the rate structure (and other features) of their income taxes.

Would it also limit the freedom of action of the Congress? Again, the answer is affirmative. If a credit were provided, Congress, in making future changes in the federal income tax, would have to consider the effects on state revenues. This problem was encountered in 1932 when Congress wished to increase its death tax revenues and yet to exclude the states from participation. Congress, therefore, enacted a separate statute with a new rate structure and new exemptions to yield additional federal revenues, while leaving intact the 1926 federal death tax structure, including the 80 per cent tax credit. In 1954, however, a new technique was devised whereby the death tax credit was expressed, not as 80 per cent of federal tax liability under the 1926 act, but as amounts relevant to taxable estates falling in various brackets. For example, under the old formulation the credit on a taxable estate of $50,000 was 80 per cent of the tax liability of $7,000—or $5,600; under the new formulation the credit was stated in relation to the size of the taxable estate.[13]

[13] *Internal Revenue Code*, Sec. 2011(b).

Similarly, tax credits for income tax could be expressed as amounts in relation to adjusted gross income brackets. And this formulation would, in effect, assure the states that Congress, in changing the federal tax, would not automatically affect the credits; it would also allow Congress to change the rates of the federal tax without affecting the credit. Technically, this formulation is an improvement. Nonetheless, a credit does limit the freedom of Congress to change a tax against which a credit has been given; the limitation is modest if the credit is modest, and large if the credit is large.

Another inflexibility of a credit plus revenue-maintenance would be that existing income tax differentials, state by state, would be continued and reinforced. Oregon, with its relatively stiff state income tax, would have to raise its income tax revenue by the amount of the credit, just as would Washington, with no present income tax.

Revenue-maintenance might seem also to raise an administrative and compliance problem. A credit would require a state in the position of Oregon to add enough to its rate structure to absorb the credit. The *total* amounts paid to the state by individuals would be considerably in excess of the amounts necessary to absorb the credit, and only part of their payments would be creditable against their federal tax. This should, however, cause no serious difficulty. If the state enacted a pick-up tax to fulfill the revenue-maintenance requirement, the individual payments of it would be wholly creditable. If, as another alternative, the state revised its entire income tax structure in such a way as to meet the *aggregate* requirement, payments of individual taxpayers might not rise by amounts which coincided precisely with payments under a pick-up tax. But, again, this would not be objectionable. The requirement should be interpreted with some latitude, and certainly it should not mean that additional tax payments at every level of taxable income must match the maximum allowable credit.

The argument may be illustrated as follows. If a taxpayer in an income tax state paid, pre-credit, $150 in federal tax and $50 in state tax—a total of $200—a 10 per cent credit with a revenue-maintenance requirement might be met by a pick-up tax which raised his state payment by $15 to $65. A narrow interpretation of the requirement would specify that, if his state tax were only raised to $60, the allowable credit would be $10, and such an interpretation would create an administrative and compliance problem. The requirement should, however, be in *aggregate* terms, and additional payments of state income tax by individuals at various levels of taxable income might not equal payments of a pick-up tax. Some might be smaller, and some larger, so long as the aggregate collections from the state tax equaled the aggregate federal credits.

Effects on Progression

A Flat Percentage Credit

A credit in the form of a flat percentage—7 per cent—would, it appears, induce states *without* income tax to adopt taxes which, in structure, would maximize credit values for their residents. Such state pick-up taxes would ideally copy the federal tax with respect to exemptions and definition of income, while the rates would be set so as to collect 7 per cent of the federal tax liability in every bracket. These rates would be 7 per cent of the federal marginal or bracket rates, and therefore progressive, but the progression of federal and state rates together would be the same after as before adoption of the credit. Moreover, the total amount taken by individual income taxes from residents of every state would be unchanged, the federal "take" being down in each case by an amount equal to the take of a state government.

The effects of a 7 per cent credit on states *with* income tax would be similar, assuming revenue-maintenance to be required. Such states might, if permitted, add a pick-up tax to their system, leaving the prior tax unchanged. Administratively and in terms of cost of compliance, this would be an inferior choice. A better alternative would be to enact a new state tax which aimed to collect from each taxpayer an amount equal to the old tax which he would have paid, plus an amount equal to 7 per cent of his federal liability. Here again over-all progression, and the total take from residents of each state, would be unchanged. There would be no interstate equalization. As will be shown later, a 7 per cent credit scheme would be advantageous to the state governments of the richer states simply because tax liabilities of individuals for federal income tax are relatively greater there.

The Heller-Type Credit

A credit graduated regressively—for example, the Heller scale of 20 per cent of the first $200 of federal tax, 10 per cent of the next $300, and 1 per cent of tax in excess of $500—would confine most of the initial reduction of federal tax in income tax states to persons with modest incomes. A married person with a federal tax liability of $500 would secure a credit of $70, i.e., a reduction of his federal tax to $430 (down 14 per cent), whereas the credit for a married person with a federal tax of $10,000 would be $165, i.e., a reduction to $9,835 (down 1.7 per cent). But if, as has been argued above, revenue-maintenance is required, what low-income persons gained through reduction of federal tax would be taken from them by an increase of state tax. In the present eighteen non-income tax states, a pick-up tax geared to the Heller credit would collect $40 from the married person with a federal tax liability of $200, $70 from one with $500, $75 from one with $1,000. The relevant adjusted gross incomes to be linked with these taxes for a married couple and for a single person (taking the standard deduction) are shown in Table 4-4. It will be noticed that the effective rates of the pick-up tax would be regressive except at low levels of income. The table shows also the effective rates of a state tax enacted in response to a revenue-maintenance requirement for a flat credit of $65 (married couples) and $32.50 (single persons).

The precise effect of the Heller-scale credit, coupled with strict revenue-maintenance, on progression in states with income taxes would, of course, depend on the prior scale. All that can be stated is that progression of the state income tax would be diminished. Possibly such a change should, in the circumstances, be regarded as irrelevant or unimportant because a regressive credit increases the progression of the federal tax and leaves total progression unchanged. Congress may be thought to determine the progression of the federal tax after consideration of individual incomes net of all state and local taxes. To be sure, selection of an ideal set of rates

TABLE 4-4. *State Pick-up Taxes and Their Effective Rates When Geared to Maximum (1) Heller-Scale Credits and (2) Flat Credits on Federal Tax Liability for Various Adjusted Gross Incomes*

AGI	Federal Tax	State Pick-up Tax Geared to		Effective Rate of State Pick-up Tax	
		(1) Heller Credit	(2) Flat Credit[a]	(1) Heller Credit	(2) Flat Credit
MARRIED COUPLES, FILING JOINTLY AND TAKING STANDARD DEDUCTION					
$ 1,875	$ 100	$20	$65	1.1%	3.5%
2,450	200	40	65	1.6	2.7
4,100	500	70	65	1.7	1.6
6,790	1,000	75	65	1.1	1.0
10,000	1,636	81	65	0.8	0.7
20,000	4,532	110	65	0.6	0.3
SINGLE PERSONS, TAKING STANDARD DEDUCTION					
$1,225	$100	$20	$32.50	1.6%	2.7%
1,775	200	40	32.50	2.3	1.8
3,400	500	70	32.50	2.1	1.0
4,900	800	73	32.50	1.5	0.7

[a] For married couples, $65; for single persons, $32.50.

for the nation is now imperfectly performed because of the diverse impact on individual incomes of state and local taxes. An ideal federal scale for residents of New York, where state taxes are progressive, is not ideal for residents of Washington or New Jersey, where state taxes are regressive. Greater uniformity of state and local taxation would simplify this congressional decision.

Interstate Equalization

It has sometimes been thought that a federal credit, either as a flat percentage or with the Heller scale, would be equalizing.[14] Equalization—that is, a redistribution of income from richer to

[14] Heller has stated: "Either substitution of a Federal credit for deductibility, whether as a flat percentage of the Federal tax or on a sliding-scale basis, or

poorer states—now takes place through federal income tax, since more revenue is collected, relative to income or population, in richer states than in poorer.[15] If the realistic assumption is made that the federal credit brings *no change in the amount of interstate distribution of federal expenditure,* then no redistribution is effected through a credit scheme which is coupled with a strict revenue-maintenance requirement.

The reason is that individuals everywhere, pre-credit and post-credit, would pay the same total amount of income tax. The level and distribution of state expenditure would, presumably, change upward with the amount of state income tax collections, but no interstate equalization would result because collections and expenditures would offset. The credit may be regarded as an alternative to outright federal tax reduction, and just as it is realistic to assume no alteration in the amount or distribution of federal expenditure because of the reduction, it is realistic to make the same assumption with respect to a federal credit. The difference between an outright federal tax reduction and a credit with revenue-maintenance is that in the latter case the states are required to pick up the reduction, while in the former they are not. When they do pick it up, the alterations in federal collections, state by state, are offset, so that no change in equalization results. With outright federal tax reduction, however, changes in equalization are bound

---

supplementation of deductibility by a sliding-scale credit would serve to reduce somewhat the existing interstate inequalities of income." (*Tax Revision Compendium,* Vol. 1, p. 425.) Equalization is declared to be a goal which "we customarily seek." (*Ibid.,* p. 422.) Nathan and Hollander appear to hold these same beliefs.

Fifteen years ago I thought a regressively graduated income tax credit would be of greater advantage to "poor" states, and more effective in redistribution of tax burdens, interstate, than now appears to be the case. See Maxwell, *The Fiscal Impact of Federalism in the United States* (Harvard University Press, 1946), p. 269.

[15] The revenue is, of course, used to provide federal expenditure, and it is likely that the benefits accruing from federal expenditure reinforce the equalization arising from revenue-collection. However, interstate allocation of benefits from federal expenditure which is collective, e.g., that for national defense, must be arbitrary and is perhaps inherently illogical, since collective benefits cannot really be allocated.

to occur (even when federal expenditure stays the same) because the interstate incidence of the reduction would be uneven.[16]

Even though a tax credit coupled with revenue-maintenance brings no equalization, the contention may be made that poor states gain more because their needs, relative to their fiscal capacity, exceed those of rich states. A tax credit may extricate poor states from financial difficulties which are more acute than those of rich states.

Suppose that revenue-maintenance is *not* required as a condition for the credit. A great variety of responses, state by state, would occur. Possibly the response of states without income taxes would be about the same whether or not revenue-maintenance were required; they would tend to enact pick-up taxes. The response of states with income taxes is less certain. Some states, if not pressed for revenue, might allow their taxpayers to retain the full amount of the reduction of federal taxes resulting from the credit. In such case, under the Heller scale the accruals to income would be greater for small than for large incomes. The federal income tax would become more progressive in these states and, therefore, some redistribution of income would result. Some poor states have as residents a greater relative number of low-income federal income taxpayers. If a poor state and a rich state—Alabama and Delaware, for example—both regarded a Heller-type credit simply as a tax reduction to be permitted to accrue to their taxpayers, some interstate equalization would occur, if the reduction were relatively greater for Alabama.[17]

[16] If the assumption is made that the federal credit does reduce federal expenditure, then the distribution of the expenditure interstate is bound to be altered; the gain a state secures from a credit may be more than offset, wholly offset, or partly offset by the loss of federal expenditure. Changes in interstate equalization may occur. Another assumption might be that the loss of federal revenue from a tax credit is made up by increase in other federal taxes (federal expenditure remaining unchanged). Here also states might gain or lose in net receipt of federal benefits, depending on the incidence of the new federal taxes in comparison with the incidence of the credits. Finally, if a revenue-maintenance requirement is loosely interpreted, so that payments of individual taxpayers did not rise by sums which coincided with those which accomplished a complete pick-up, some modest equalization might occur.

[17] The distribution of the number of returns of federal individual income tax, 1958, taxable and nontaxable, by adjusted gross income classes for Alabama

The record seems to show that most advocates of graduated credits wish to open new avenues of revenue to state governments, rather than to give taxpayers a reduction of federal income tax. They expect state governments to move in as the federal government withdraws. Thus Freeman speaks of the credit as an "instrument which will give the states full access to the best tax of all, the income tax." Nathan and Hollander write that "ways must be found to open new avenues to State and local revenues which will enable the States to find reliable, responsive, and economic sources of revenue."[18] Of the other proponents, Gardner, Meany, and Grodzins are explicit in endorsement of the credit as a device to increase state and local taxing power.

Quantitative Impact of Credits by States

Inevitably a flat percentage credit provides larger relative sums for rich than for poor states. The Heller-type credit was designed, among other purposes, to remedy this result by setting an inelastic ceiling on credits so that, as federal tax liability grew, the credit values above $70 would grow very modestly. In Appendix B, Table

and Delaware is given below. Of the returns, 29 per cent for Alabama and 43 per cent for Delaware had an adjusted gross income of $5,000 or more.

AGI	Percentage Distribution	
	Alabama	Delaware
Under $1,000	14%	8%
$1,000 under $ 2,000	15	12
2,000 under 3,000	17	14
3,000 under 4,000	14	11
4,000 under 5,000	11	12
5,000 under 6,000	11	12
6,000 under 7,000	6	8
7,000 under 8,000	4	5
8,000 under 9,000	3	7
9,000 under 10,000	2	2
10,000 or more	3	9
	100%	100%

[18] Freeman, Statement at Governors' Conference (1959); Nathan and Hollander, *Tax Revision Compendium*, Vol. 1, p. 223.

Heller's calculations (*ibid.*, pp. 422, 424, and 426) assume absorption of a federal credit by the states.

CHART 4-1. *Three Types of Credits as Per Cents of Personal Income in Relation to Per Capita Income, by States, 1958*[a]

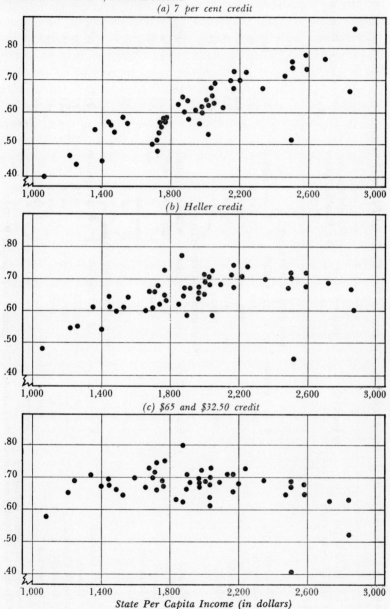

Credits as Per Cents of Personal Income
(a) 7 per cent credit

(b) Heller credit

(c) $65 and $32.50 credit

State Per Capita Income (in dollars)

[a] Source: See Appendix B, Table 1.

TABLE 4-5. *Estimates of Three Maximum Credits as Per Cents of Personal Income, 1958, for Fifteen States*[a]

Rank in Per Capita Income, 1958[b]	7 Per Cent (1)	Heller Scale (2)	$65 and $32.50 Per Taxable Return (3)	As Per Cent of Personal Income		
				(1)	(2)	(3)
FIVE HIGH-INCOME STATES						
1. Delaware	$ 10.7 million	$ 7.5 million	$ 6.7 million	.86%	.60%	.54%
2. Connecticut	50.4	45.1	41.7	.77	.69	.64
3. New York	314.6	286.9	276.4	.75	.68	.66
4. Nevada	5.3	4.9	4.7	.78	.72	.68
5. Illinois	183.5	172.3	162.6	.76	.71	.67
FIVE MIDDLE-INCOME STATES						
23. Kansas	$ 25.4 million	$ 27.9 million	$ 28.9 million	.60%	.66%	.69%
24. Nebraska	15.7	17.7	18.8	.57	.64	.68
25. Hawaii	7.1	7.9	8.1	.62	.68	.70
26. Minnesota	39.6	43.7	44.7	.61	.67	.69
27. Iowa	30.5	35.4	37.2	.58	.67	.71
FIVE LOW-INCOME STATES						
46. North Carolina	$ 28.4 million	$ 35.1 million	$ 42.8 million	.45%	.55%	.68%
47. Alabama	23.9	27.1	30.3	.55	.62	.69
48. South Carolina	12.7	16.9	20.2	.44	.58	.69
49. Arkansas	10.0	11.8	14.3	.47	.55	.66
50. Mississippi	8.9	11.1	13.7	.39	.48	.60

[a] Source: Appendix B, Table 1.
[b] District of Columbia not ranked here, although it is ranked in Appendix B, Table 1.

1, a report is given of the state-by-state impact for 1958 of these
two credits, as well as of the third type by which an absolute ceiling
per taxable return is set. Each of the three types yielded approximately the same aggregate credit for the fifty states (Alaska and
Hawaii are included) and the District of Columbia. (Appendix B
also gives a report of the techniques by which the measurements
were made.)

The general tenor of the results may be seen from examination of
Table 4-5, which shows figures for fifteen states—the five richest,
the five middle income, and the five poorest in terms of per capita
income in 1958. The Heller-type credit, in comparison with a flat
7 per cent credit, would reduce the sums made available to the
richer states, and increase those made available to the poorer states.
(See Chart 4-1.) But both increases and decreases are, perhaps, less
than might have been expected.[19] If supplementation of the revenue
sources of poor states compared with rich states is an objective, the
power of tax credits is modest even when their form is deliberately
and strongly shaped to this end.

Nonspecific Revenue-Maintenance

In the preceding pages the assumptions were made that (1) the
credits could be secured by residents of a state only for state income
tax payments, and (2) a revenue-maintenance requirement would
induce state income tax rates, or additions to rates, which would
pick up the tax reductions of the federal credit. These assumptions
are convenient, but not essential.

If, for crediting, states had to have an income tax, then those
without the tax would enact one (with pick-up rates). But states
with an income tax which is adequate, without change, to enable
residents to absorb the credits, might choose to meet a revenue-
maintenance requirement in other ways. If the credit were provided

[19] The values of the Spearman rank correlation between state per capita
income and (a) 7 per cent credits, (b) Heller credits, and (c) $65 and $32.50
credits per taxable return, each as per cents of state personal income, are
respectively +.865, +.586, and —.192.

through the Heller scale, a state might conceivably leave the tax reduction in the hands of low-income persons, and raise the taxes on middle and upper incomes. Indeed, the spirit of the Heller scale might indicate this action to be appropriate. On the other hand, the tax relief given to low-income people by the federal credit might be regarded by the states as justification for imposing additional taxes on them.

Another possibility should be noticed. The federal government might allow crediting against income tax for payments of some state (local) tax other than on income, and it might regard the requirement of revenue-maintenance as met if states raised the appropriate amounts of revenue from *any* tax.

Credit for State Sales Tax

In 1960 state governments raised nearly twice as much from taxation of general sales as from taxation of individual income; fourteen states had general sales taxes only, twelve had income taxes only, nineteen had both types of tax. In terms of existing usage, therefore, the retail sales tax might be considered as appropriate for crediting.[20] How might a credit against federal income tax for state retail sales taxes be handled? An individual would be allowed the amount of his annual sales tax payment as a credit, not to exceed 7 per cent of his federal liability, or the appropriate amount under the Heller scale. In states with both an income tax and a sales tax, the federal government might allow taxpayers to take a credit *either* for income tax *or* for sales tax on the ground that this procedure would not favor taxpayers in the nineteen states and the District of Columbia which had both taxes. Such a policy would, however, discriminate against residents of the three states (Nebraska, New Hampshire, and New Jersey) which had neither.[21]

[20] If a credit is regarded as a possible substitute for deductibility of state (and local) taxes, then a sales tax credit might be regarded as a substitute for deductibility of sales taxes.

[21] Texas, long without either tax, has adopted a sales tax, which became effective January 1, 1961.

In 1961 the Internal Revenue Service issued a series of state-by-state sheets of figures showing, by adjusted income classes, 1960 average sales tax payments of residents in each of the thirty-four states and the District of Columbia.[22] These figures are used here to illustrate how a credit for sales tax would work. The allowable credit under a percentage scheme (7 per cent) would regularly exceed the sales tax payment for high-income persons; under the Heller scale, however, this would not be the case, since the allowable credit is geared to favor persons with a federal tax liability of $500 and less.

Consider, first, the effect of enactment of an alternative credit scheme, with the Heller scale, on a state with neither sales tax nor income tax. Presumably the state would be pushed toward use of one or the other without much delay. If a sales tax were chosen, it would be framed so as to collect approximately $40 from a husband and wife with a federal liability (before sales tax credit) of $200, $70 from a couple with a liability of $500, etc.; for a single person the figures of collections and liabilities would be half those just given. In short, the scale of the sales tax induced by the credit would be such as to maximize credit values. In comparison with an income tax, a sales tax aimed to pick up maximum credits would be imprecise. Whereas a pick-up income tax would collect from individuals exactly what they gained from a credit, a sales tax would not; the reason is that the base of a state income tax could be made identical with that of the federal income tax, while that of a state sales tax (resting on consumption) could not.

At the lower end of the scale, a sales tax, even when food and medicine are exempt, reaches persons who pay no federal income tax, and therefore credits there would be unused (see columns 2 and 3 in Table 4-6). For a married couple with an adjusted gross income of $1,250 the federal tax would be zero, while a sales tax at the rate of 3 per cent, exempting food and medicine, would col-

[22] U.S. Internal Revenue Service, Documents No. 5306-No. 5339 (1961). Family size classification is also shown, for all except eight states and the District of Columbia. The sheet for Hawaii states only that "two per cent of . . . [adjusted gross income] up to $15,000 is a reasonable estimate of the sales tax paid by the average taxpayer in Hawaii."

lect $22. This could be remedied only if the state sales tax provided a refund, or enlarged the exemption of commodities consumed by low-income persons. For adjusted gross incomes above $5,750, sales tax payments again exceed the credits. This divergence could be modified and reduced by some alteration of the credit scale and of the base of the tax. Even so, the conclusion is obvious that a pick-up sales tax would be much less precise in maximizing credit values than a pick-up income tax.

Consider next the effect of an alternative credit scheme on a state with a sales tax already in operation. The tendency would be to adjust collections so as to maximize the credits, especially by reducing unused credits. As mentioned above, something might be accomplished to relieve low-income persons by exemption of "necessities" or by a refund. Changes of this sort, induced by the credits, would give state tax reductions to some and increases to others, even supposing the total of state revenue were maintained. It is conceivable that a state with high sales tax collections might be induced by the credit to lessen its collections if revenue-maintenance were not required.

As in the case of income tax credits, a revenue-maintenance requirement for a state without sales tax would be, in effect, a requirement that credits and the loss of federal revenue be maximized.[23] But states with a sales tax could, of course, maximize credits without maintaining revenue, and thereby allow their residents to secure a reduction of federal income tax. A revenue-maintenance requirement for such states would mean that the states must raise additional revenue equal to the credit.

In states with an income tax and not a sales tax, and similarly in states with a sales tax and not an income tax, might the alternative credit tempt states to add the missing tax? Suppose that, at the time a credit was allowed, a state had a sales (income) tax which was more than adequate to maximize the credits for its residents. Might there be a temptation to reduce its sales (income) tax to the credit-induced scale, and to meet the revenue-maintenance requirement

---

[23] The requirement could, literally, be this for income tax. As has been indicated, it could not be for sales tax.

TABLE 4-6. *Illustrative State Sales Tax Payments and Heller Credits in Relation to Federal Income Tax Liabilities of Married Couples with Various Adjusted Gross Incomes*

AGI	Married Couple		
	Federal Income Tax[a] (1)	State Sales Tax[b] (2)	Heller Credit, Maximum (3)
Under $1,000	$ —	$ 15	$ —
$ 1,250	—	22	—
1,750	75	27	15.00
2,250	165	33	33.00
2,750	255	38	45.50
3,250	345	44	54.50
3,750	435	50	63.50
4,250	525	56	70.25
4,750	615	61	71.15
5,250	705	68	72.05
5,750	795	73	72.95
6,250	894	79	73.94
6,750	993	86	74.93
7,250	1,091	92	75.91
8,250	1,290	103	77.90
9,250	1,488	114	79.88
10,500	1,758	129	82.58
19,500	4,362	214	108.62

[a] Standard deduction assumed.
[b] The figures are taken from U. S. Internal Revenue Service, Document No. 5332, "Residents' Average State General Sales Tax Payments: Rhode Island" (1961). Rate of tax is 3 per cent, and food and medicine are exempt.

by enacting the missing tax? Should the requirement of revenue-maintenance permit such a move, or should it specify use of the same tax for crediting and for revenue-maintenance?

In states with both sales and income taxes, might not an alternative credit induce a shift in degree of reliance by the state? Probably revenue-maintenance would tend to be met by collecting additional revenue through the tax used less intensively at the time.

Conclusion

If, in the future, Congress reduces federal individual income tax, it could promote national objectives by executing the reduction via tax credits. Any crediting device should contain some conditions in order to justify its use; indeed, the merit of a credit in comparison with outright and overt tax reduction inheres in imposition of conditions. One condition might be revenue-maintenance, which would require the states to utilize the revenue sources relinquished by the federal government. The broad justification would be that, since state (and local) governments in the foreseeable future have important functions to perform which will strain their means of finance, federal help in raising the needed revenue is warranted. The chief defect of the condition of revenue-maintenance is its inflexibility. If the state tax creditable against the federal income tax had to be similar—if only a state individual income tax were acceptable —existing income tax differentials would be frozen into state tax structures. Moreover, enactment and acceptance of a credit puts some block on the ability and willingness of states to alter their creditable tax.

Another set of conditions might aim at fiscal reforms, and here the list could be long and specific. A federalism, with its extra layer of governments in the form of states, has exceptional ability to generate tax conflict and complexity, and multiple compliance and administrative costs in tax collection. Much of the time the conflicts, complexities, and multiple costs are sheer waste; they express an anarchy of autonomy; they impede efficient government and hinder economic development. Relief from them would be clear gain. Against the risk that the force and vigor of state governments *might* be impaired can be set the certainty of a reduction of interstate competition, of federal help in assessing, collecting, and administering important state taxes, and of larger state revenues. The over-all efficiency of government in the United States would be improved.

The two objectives of financial assistance and fiscal reform—with their indicated conditions or techniques—are not mutually exclusive; they might well be implemented together.[24] To forgo fiscal reform and require merely revenue-maintenance would be to disregard the national interest in tax coordination. To forgo revenue-maintenance and require simply some measure of tax coordination would discriminate in favor of taxpayers in states which, at the time of introduction of the credit, had income taxes, and it would overlook the federal interest in improving the precarious financial position of very many state and local governments.

[24] James Bryant Conant may well have had this in mind in the passage quoted at the beginning of this chapter—from *The Child, the Parent, and the State* (Harvard University Press, 1959), p. 57. An exploration of ways whereby Congress might use its power "to cajole or coerce the states into putting their own financial houses in order" might discover ways to achieve financial assistance and fiscal reform. The "national 'educational deficit' "—Conant's phrase (*ibid.* p. 55)—of our public schools would be reduced or eliminated.

5

Deductibility of State and Local Taxes

> In our earliest income tax acts, the idea that net income after taxes is the true measure of taxpaying ability seems to have been implicit.
>
> C. Harry Kahn
> *Personal Deductions in the Federal Income Tax*

THE DEDUCTIBILITY OF state and local taxes is examined here because some economists believe that income tax credits would be a superior substitute for deductibility, and that, if credits could be provided, deductibility should be abolished. To appraise this proposition certain questions need to be answered. What purposes, if any, does deductibility now serve? Are these the same purposes that would be served by crediting, or are the two, in this respect, dissimilar? How do the two devices compare in the amount of reduction of federal income tax that they provide in the aggregate, by states, and by individual income classes?

Rationale of Deductibility

The right of individuals to deduct their nonbusiness state and local tax payments from income in computing the taxable base for federal income tax has long been established. At present almost all state and local taxes paid by individuals qualify—taxes on property, sales, gasoline, individual income, and motor vehicles, as well as some few excise taxes.[1]

What is the rationale or justification of deductibility of these taxes? In logic, two broad grounds may be advanced.

1. Deductibility may be regarded as a *refinement* of gross income in order to reach taxable income. Congress may be thought to allow deductions and exemptions in order to secure the best base on which to levy a progressive federal income tax. The economic status of a person for purposes of levy of the federal income tax is to be measured after deduction of state and local taxes. These taxes are unavoidable personal expenses for the individual; they are levied to provide citizens over the nation with governmental services of a vital and intimate sort. In equity the base for the federal tax should exclude these costs, and Congress should determine the marginal rates of the federal tax in relation to this base. Acceptance of this

[1] Prior to 1942 federal practice was that only sales taxes "paid" by, and imposed directly on, the consumer were deductible. Yet states wished to impose such taxes on retailers, or wholesalers, or distributors because collection from them was relatively efficient and because this technique avoided giving exemptions to certain purchases. Congress recognized the problem, and in 1942 provided that state and local retail sales taxes should be deductible by the consumer, even when imposed on the retailer, so long as the amount of the tax was separately stated to the consumer. (Revenue Act of 1942, section 122; 56 Stat. 820.)

In 1951 the deduction was similarly extended to state gasoline taxes imposed on the wholesaler or retailer but separately stated to the consumer. (65 Stat. 40.) State cigarette taxes are deductible if the consumer is liable for the tax. A number of states which collect the cigarette tax by means of stamp taxes have amended their laws to provide expressly that the impact of the tax is on the purchaser, even though payable in advance by the distributor. The Commerce Clearing House *Federal Tax Reports 1961* indicated that the cigarette tax was deductible by the consumer in approximately twenty-four of the forty-seven states (and the District of Columbia) which impose cigarette taxes.

justification, be it noted, leads to dismissal of any argument concerning the unequal value of deductibility to the recipients, since this unequal value is a result of the decision of Congress to impose graduated rates. The refinement of gross income does complicate the tax return and increase problems of administration and compliance.

2. Deductibility may be regarded as a means of assisting "in the financing of activities in the public interest."[2] It is an indirect way of subsidizing state and local governments in raising revenue for governmental purposes. In a federalism, the national government must exercise restraint in its use of the power to tax. Most of the principal taxes are strongly utilized by it, but in using them it should recollect that citizens pay state and local taxes, and that state and local governments collect taxes in order to perform their functions. Such a rationale would indicate that all or most general taxes should be deductible if, thereby, an effective subsidy is provided for state and local governments. Is this subsidy effective? Has it been utilized by state and local governments, or is it an outdated survival with no present justification? Answers to some of these questions may be sought by examining deductibility of the main types of state and local taxes.[3]

Excises

Most economists, while critical of deductibility as such, have been more critical of deductibility of taxes on property and on consumption than of taxes on individual income. Some taxes on consumption, notably those on motor fuel and on motor vehicles, are levied on a benefit basis. The benefits should be regarded as individual consumption and the taxes as payments for specific services rendered by state and local governments.[4]

[2] C. Harry Kahn, *Personal Deductions in the Federal Income Tax* (Princeton University Press, 1960) , p. 88. The quotation heading this chapter is from p. 101.

[3] Some of the readers of my manuscript did not find persuasive the arguments presented in this chapter. They did not believe, as I do, that our federal tax system justifies deductibility of state-local taxes in order to refine gross income; they felt, moreover—as I do not—that deductibility is an inefficient subsidy.

[4] William Vickrey, *Agenda for Progressive Taxation* (Ronald Press, 1947), pp. 94-95.

Deductibility of excises on "luxuries"—cigarettes, liquors, and the like—is criticized on other grounds. If such excises have a sumptuary justification, deductibility reduces some of their efficacy in restraining consumption. Moreover, nonsmokers gain nothing from deductibility and are, therefore, subjected to discrimination. The awkwardness of the legal distinction between excises imposed directly on the consumer, and those not so imposed, persists for these taxes and, as a result, cigarette taxes are not deductible in some states. These criticisms, be it noted, do not apply to deductibility of general sales taxes. Still another flaw is that most taxpayers lack adequate records on which to base claims for deduction of excises and even of sales taxes. The Internal Revenue Service cannot easily verify the accuracy of claims, and the probable result is petty cheating by many taxpayers.

Property Taxes

Deductibility of property taxes is criticized as discriminatory in favor of the owner-occupant of residential property and against the tenant. As Harvey E. Brazer puts it: "Both undoubtedly bear the property tax as part of their housing costs. But the tenant is not permitted to deduct any part of his rent while the owner-occupier may deduct the property tax in full."[5]

A partial retort might be that Congress has deliberately chosen to subsidize home ownership, and that at present more than 60 per cent of residences are owner-occupied. Property taxation is a general tax by which local governments across the nation raise 87 per cent of their tax revenue. If deductibility of property tax were abolished, the base of the federal tax would be larger, and, as a *quid pro quo*, the federal government could lower its income tax rates. Should the effort be to equate, for each person, the enlargement of his tax base with the lower rate, so that the amount of his federal tax is unchanged? The advantage of such a change in form is not easy to detect. Or should the opportunity be taken to provide a different distribution of federal tax? The usual argument

[5] Brazer, "The Deductibility of State and Local Taxes Under the Individual Income Tax," *Tax Revision Compendium*, Submitted to the House Ways and Means Committee, 86th Congress, 1st session (1959), Vol. 1, p. 414.

is that the income tax of homeowners should be increased relative to that of renters. In either case, what would the effects be on the finances of local governments, bound as they are to reliance on property tax? Would voters be more resistant than at present to increases in property tax, if deductibility were abolished? It seems very likely that they would.

The argument of Brazer that the property tax is "a general user charge, and as such should no more be deductible for individual income tax purposes than are other expenses incurred as part of the taxpayer's ordinary cost of living"[6] is not persuasive. Occasionally, user charges are added to the property tax, and no justification for deductibility of such charges can be offered. But most property taxes are not assessed as measures of user benefits, else the childless owner-resident of a valuable house would pay less than what, in fact, is levied.

This summary argument indicates that the rationale for deductibility of property tax is much superior to that for deductibility of those excises which are levied on a benefit basis, as well as those which have a sumptuary purpose. The general property tax, minor exceptions aside, is not levied on a benefit basis. Its coverage is wide, and it will continue to be the main—almost the sole—tax resource of local governments. Whatever is the subsidy provided through deductibility of personal taxes, local governments share in that subsidy mainly through property tax deductibility.

Income Taxes

What is the case for deductibility of individual income taxes? As pointed out in Chapter 4, income taxation is presently (1961) employed by only thirty-two states (and the District of Columbia). If deductibility were limited to income taxes, state governments would be under pressure to adopt income taxation, whereas the present inclusion of all important taxes removes any such pressure.

Deductibility of a *progressive* state income tax—the only kind worth considering here—brings the surprising result that "after a certain point in the income scale, the cost of a state income tax as

* *Ibid.*

an addition to federal income tax, measured as a per cent of income, declines rather than rises."[7] If, for example, the marginal federal rate on taxable income of $1,000 is 20 per cent, and the state rate is 2 per cent, the combined rate is not 22 per cent, but 21.6 per cent; if the marginal federal rate on taxable income of $100,000 is 72 per cent and the state rate is 7 per cent, the combined rate is not 79 percent, but 74 per cent. The increase in the marginal rate because of the state tax is 1.6 per cent, rather than 2 per cent, in the first case; 2 per cent rather than 7 per cent in the second case.[8]

The same example may be utilized to argue that this deductibility decreases the progression of the federal tax. The marginal federal rate on taxable income of $1,000 is lowered from 20 per cent to 19.6 per cent by deductibility of the state tax; that on taxable income of $100,000 is lowered from 72 per cent to 67 per cent. The relative difference between the original pair of rates (20 per cent and 72 per cent) is greater than that between the derived pair (19.6 per cent and 67 per cent). The steeper the state progression, the more does deductibility lessen the steepness of the federal scale. The value of a fixed deduction from federal income tax to a taxpayer depends on (1) the marginal rate of his federal tax and (2) his taxable income (his tax base). *Any* deduction from adjusted gross income lessens the tax base; when the amounts of the deduction rise as incomes rise, as in the case with payments under a progressive state income tax, the erosion of the base of the federal income tax is larger in the upper brackets than in the lower. This erosion is compounded by the progression of the federal rates, since even a fixed deduction is worth more to a taxpayer if he has a 30 per cent marginal federal rate than if he has one of 20 per cent.

How serious is this objection? If one argues that income *after* deduction of state (and local) income taxes is the appropriate base on which federal income tax should be levied, the weakening of progression seems irrelevant.[9] Congress should set the marginal

---

[7] Kahn, *op. cit.*, p. 106.

[8] The formula for the increase in the marginal rate due to the state tax, when S = state marginal rate and F = federal marginal rate, is $S(1 - F)$.

[9] This position is taken by Melvin I. White, "Deductions for Nonbusiness Expenses and an Economic Concept of Net Income," in *Federal Tax Policy for Economic Growth and Stability*, Papers Submitted by Panelists, to the Joint

TABLE 5-1. *Effects of State Income Tax (New York) and State Sales Tax (Michigan) on Federal Income Tax Liabilities, and on Combined Liabilities, of a Married Taxpayer with Two Dependents, 1960*

AGI	Taxable Income[a]	Federal Tax Without Deductibility (1)	State Income Tax (2)	State Sales Tax[b] (3)	Federal Tax After Deductibility of[c] Income Tax (4)	Federal Tax After Deductibility of[c] Sales Tax (5)	Combined Taxes (2)+(4) (6)	Combined Taxes (3)+(5) (7)
$ 2,000	$ 0	$ —	$ —	$ 54	$ —	$ —	$ —	$ 54
4,000	1,600	320	—	95	320	301	320	396
6,000	3,600	720	34	135	713	693	747	828
10,000	7,600	1,592	200	206	1,548	1,547	1,748	1,753
30,000	27,600	8,348	1,965	308	7,503	8,216	9,468	8,524

[a] Before deduction of state tax or other allowed deductions.
[b] Column 3 is from U.S. Internal Revenue Service, Document No. 5322, "Residents' Average State General Sales Tax Payments: Michigan" (1961).
[c] Columns 4 and 5 are computed as follows: (4) $3,600 less $34 equals $3,566; tax at 20% equals $713. (5) $3,600 less $135 equals $3,465; tax at 20% equals $693.

rates of the federal tax by considering income after deductions for
state income taxes. The progression of the income tax should be
viewed on the basis of the combined liability of a taxpayer for two
income taxes, since both are paid out of the same income.

This position, while plausible, is over narrow. As has already
been argued, other nonbenefit and general state and local taxes take
away income from individuals as clearly as does income taxation.
If Congress, in setting federal income taxes, looked at levels of individual incomes after state (and local) income taxes, and those alone,
it would, in effect, be taxing individuals more heavily in states
without income taxes than individuals in states with such taxes. A
more logical position is that Congress should set federal rates, etc.,
in relation to individual incomes after deduction of *all* general and
nonbenefit taxes.

Another, and related, argument in favor of deductibility of state
income taxes is that, thereby, states are given an opportunity to
enact progressive income taxes without fear of impairing their
competitive position vis-à-vis states without income tax. Deductibility, it is declared, means that part of the cost to taxpayers in a
state is borne by the federal Treasury. The Treasury collects less
from a taxpayer in an income tax state than it does from a taxpayer with an identical taxable income in a state with no income
tax.

The comparison often runs as follows. If a taxpayer has a taxable
income of $3,600 in State A, which has no income tax, his federal
tax will be $720. A similar taxpayer in State B, which collects $34
in income tax from him, finds his federal tax reduced to $713, and
he, therefore, really pays only $27 more as a result of the state in-
come tax. Similarly, a taxpayer with a taxable income of $27,600
would pay a federal tax of $8,348 in State A. In State B an income
tax of $1,965 would reduce his federal tax to $7,503, so that his
combined payment would be only $1,120 more than the single pay-
ment in State A. (See columns 1, 4, and 6 in Table 5-1.) In the face
of this situation, why have states been reluctant to use progressive
income taxes? The explanation offered is that they have failed to

Committee on the Economic Report, 84th Congress, 1st session (1955), p. 361.
He writes: "Consequently, a person's economic status before levying the Federal
income tax is properly measured after a State or local income tax."

appreciate the effects of deductibility, or perhaps that many persons think of, and are sensitive to, marginal rates.[10]

The above comparison between a state with an income tax and a state without one is defective. A state without income tax must raise revenue by alternative taxes; therefore, a comparison should be made between sales tax payments, for example, in one state and income tax payments in another, both taxes producing approximately the same total revenue. The figures given in Table 5-1, columns 2 and 3, represent the state tax liabilities of a married person with two dependents in New York and Michigan in 1960.[11] These amounts are deductible in computing federal tax liabilities, and these liabilities, after such deductions, are shown in columns 4 and 5. For adjusted gross incomes of $10,000 and under, deduction of the state sales tax reduces the federal tax more than does deduction of the state income tax; for AGI's above $10,000 the opposite result is obtained.

If, next, the figures of combined tax liability are compared—columns 6 and 7—it appears that, at lower levels of AGI, the tax differential is unfavorable to the sales tax state, while at higher levels it is favorable. The illustrative differentials of Table 5-1, arising out of use (a) of a state income tax and (b) of a state sales tax, in relation to the situation of a state with neither, are summarized thus:

	Net Cost to Taxpayer of	
	State Income Tax	*State Sales Tax*
AGI	(col. 6 minus col. 1)	(col. 7 minus col. 1)
$ 2,000	$ —	$ 54
4,000	—	76
6,000	27	108
10,000	156	161
30,000	1,120	176

Again it appears that the combination of federal income tax and state income tax (which is deductible) will produce a combined tax

[10] Kahn, *op. cit.*, p. 106, offers these reasons.

[11] In 1960 the per capita yield of the state income tax in New York was $45.07; that of the general sales tax in Michigan was $46.43.

on high-income persons appreciably greater than the combination of federal income tax and state sales tax (deductible). Deductibility reduces the federal tax in both situations, but for high incomes deductibility of a progressive state income tax does not compensate for the much larger amounts taken by such a tax. The result is, then, that an interstate differential does exist between income tax states and sales tax states, in favor of the latter, with respect to those persons who are believed most likely to migrate for tax reasons.

Deductibility of state income taxes is declared to have the merit that combined federal and state income tax rates, which would be confiscatory *without* deductibility, cannot be confiscatory.[12] So long as the states and Congress are legally free to impose taxes without reference to action by the other level of government, the danger of confiscation is present. Deductibility greatly reduces this danger. Brazer declares, however, that "this argument has only very limited application" because few states have high marginal rates, and that a better protection against confiscation would be reduction of the highest federal rates.[13] But states with income tax are unlikely to regard lower federal rates as an equivalent for abolition of deductibility, because deductibility is a long-established privilege, whereas reduction of the highest federal rates would be a mutable congressional decision.

IN SUMMARY, THEN, the case for deductibility of state and local gasoline taxes and excises is weak. That for deductibility of the major taxes—property, income, sales—is stronger. These are *general* taxes. Property tax deductibility gives, indirectly, a federal subsidy to local governments. Deductibility of income and sales taxes is, in some measure, a coordinating device which reduces interstate tax-differentials and protects against combined rates which would be confiscatory. Except as a means of encouraging use

[12] Twenty states as of 1961 allowed the federal income tax to be deducted from the income subject to their taxes. The effect of this is to reinforce the deductibility of states taxes from the federal tax. Deductibility of federal taxes against the federal income tax is no longer allowed by federal law.

[13] See *Tax Revision Compendium*, Vol. 1, p. 416.

of income taxes by the states, limitation of the privilege of deductibility to income taxes seems to offer no clear advantages. Both state income taxes and general sales taxes reduce the incomes of taxpayers—who are no more free to avoid the one than the other.

Other questions, however, merit analysis. What is the amount of taxes eligible for deduction by types and by states? Do "deductions for taxes constitute an increasing proportion of income as income rises"?[14] What is the cost of deductibility to the federal Treasury? Should deductibility be dropped in favor of a credit against federal income tax? Quantitatively, what would be the effects, state by state?

Taxes Eligible for Deduction

Information concerning the amounts of particular types of state and local taxes actually deducted is not available, since *Statistics of Income* shows only national aggregates of total taxes deducted on itemized returns. The amount of taxes itemized has grown rapidly since the end of World War II because of the rapid rise of home ownership (and therefore of mortgage interest), of installment debt, of personal incomes, and of state and local taxes.

Figures of tax deductions on itemized returns are deficient, however, since such returns in 1958, for example, were only 35 per cent of all returns and accounted for only 52 per cent of adjusted gross income reported. Those who filed the remaining returns claimed the standard deduction and received no separate deduction for state and local taxes. What amount of state and local taxes would be deducted if there were no standard deduction? Or, to put the question differently, what amount of potential deductions of state and local taxes is concealed by the standard deduction? And what are the amounts of the principal types of state and local taxes eligible for deduction?

In Appendix C, Table 1, a reckoning is provided of taxes eligible for deduction by types of tax and by states for 1957. (The year 1957 was selected because the *1957 Census of Governments* provides details not available for any other year.) The reckoning starts with

[14] Brazer states that they do; see *ibid.*, p. 413.

TABLE 5-2. *Estimated Nonbusiness State and Local Tax Payments Eligible for Deduction, 1957*[a]

Tax Payment	Amount	Per Cent
Property	$ 3,449 million	29.4%
Individual Income	1,754	15.0
Motor Vehicle and Operators Licenses	847	7.2
Gasoline	1,645	14.0
General Sales	4,029	34.4
Total	$11,724 million	100.0%

[a] Source: See Appendix C, Table 1.

figures of state and local tax collections, 1957. But collections of property tax and gasoline tax, in particular, are much in excess of the amounts eligible as personal or nonbusiness deductions from AGI. The problem, therefore, was to refine the figures of collections *in the aggregate and by states.* This reckoning, especially that by states, required many assumptions and estimates concerning which differences of opinion could arise. The figures should, therefore, be regarded as rough approximations which, it is hoped, may soon be made obsolete by a more direct and sophisticated calculation from tax returns of individual income. This would be a relatively simple operation. It is a minor scandal that the federal government should provide to individuals, through deductibility, a large annual tax reduction without knowledge of its incidence by income size or by states.

Table 5-2 shows that in 1957 taxes eligible for deduction totaled $11,724 million, with general sales and property taxes the dominant components.[15] Figures of tax deductions itemized on tax returns are not available for 1957, but for 1958 the total was $7,480 million. If the 1957 total of $11,724 million of taxes eligible for deduction is increased by 5 per cent to provide a rough estimate for 1958, a

[15] Kahn, *op. cit.,* pp. 231-233, presents similar figures for 1946 and 1956. If the methods of calculating deductible property taxes and gasoline taxes used by me are correct, Kahn's figures for them are too high. The principal component of the property tax figure offered for 1956 by Kahn was taken from U.S. Office of Business Economics, *Survey of Current Business,* July 1957, p. 23, Table 39, Line 6, "Taxes on owner-occupied farm and nonfarm dwellings." I believe that these annual figures are much too high.

Deductible Taxes Per Capita (in dollars)

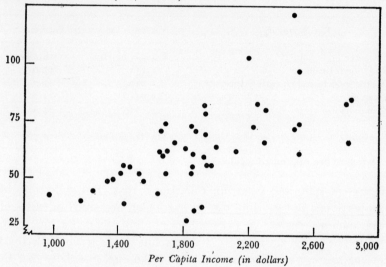

Per Capita Income (in dollars)

CHART 5-2. *Deductible Taxes as Per Cents of Income in Relation to Per Capita Incomes, by States, 1957*[a]

Deductible Taxes as Per Cents of Income

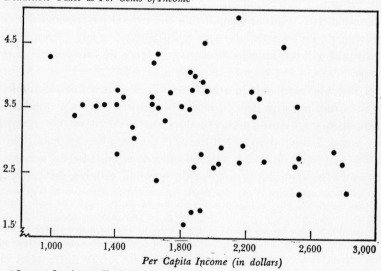

Per Capita Income (in dollars)

[a] Source: See Appendix C, Table 1.

TABLE 5-3. *Estimated Nonbusiness Deductible Taxes, Per Capita and as Per Cents of Personal Income, 1957, for Fifteen States*[a]

Income Rank	State	Deductible Taxes	
		Per Capita	Per Cent of Income
	FIVE HIGH-INCOME STATES		
1.	Connecticut	$85	3.0%
2.	Delaware	62	2.2
3.	New York	95	3.7
4.	California	118	4.7
5.	New Jersey	57	2.3
	FIVE MIDDLE-INCOME STATES		
23.	New Hampshire	$54	2.9%
24.	Minnesota	60	3.2
25.	Florida	54	3.0
26.	Nebraska	32	1.7
27	Iowa	75	4.1
	FIVE LOW-INCOME STATES		
45.	Alabama	$49	3.5%
46.	North Carolina	49	3.7
47.	South Carolina	44	3.7
48.	Arkansas	40	3.4
49.	Mississippi	42	4.3

[a] Source: See Appendix C, Table 1.

figure of $12,310 million is secured. (However, the roughness of the estimate should be underscored.) The difference between this figure and the total of itemized taxes—$7,480 million—is $4,830 million.

Deductible Taxes by States

The aggregate amounts, and the per capita amounts, of deductible taxes by states are shown in Appendix C, Table 1. Also shown are deductible taxes as per cents of personal income by states. What relationship is there between per capita aggregate deductible taxes and per capita incomes by states? Calculations of the Spearman measure produces a value of + .658, indicating a loose correlation (see Chart 5-1). The figures of deductible taxes per capita, and of such taxes as per cents of income, are shown in Table 5-3 for fifteen states—five high-income, five middle-income, and five low-income. The looseness of the correlation is evident, since two of the high-income states, Delaware and New Jersey, have lower per capita deductible taxes than Iowa, one of the middle-income states. When deductible taxes as per cents of personal income are compared with personal income by states, the correlation becomes negative and insignificant (the value of the Spearman measure is $-.263$; see also Chart 5-2). In short, the reduction of federal income tax through deductibility is only moderately advantageous to the rich states.

Deductible Taxes Compared with Taxes Deducted

If, in 1958, the amount of state and local taxes eligible for deduction was approximately $12,310 million, and the total of such taxes actually itemized was $7,480 million, how is the difference of $4,830 million to be accounted for? A small part of it arises because some persons pay state and local taxes who do not file federal tax returns. Joseph A. Pechman has estimated that AGI reported on federal returns is 9 to 10 per cent less than actual AGI.[16] The recipients of this AGI must be supposed to pay some state and local non-business taxes, and a rough estimate of this amount (see tabulation below) is $830 million.[17]

	AGI	Tax-Deductibility
Reported on Tax Returns	$281.2 billion	
Not Reported	28.1	
Total	$309.3	$12,310 million
Reported on Itemized Returns	145.4	7,480
Remainder	$163.9	$ 4,830
Reported on Standard Deduction Returns	135.8	4,000
Not Reported	$ 28.1	$ 830

[16] Pechman, "What Would a Comprehensive Individual Income Tax Yield?" in *Tax Revision Compendium*, Vol. 1, pp. 255; 256, Table 3.

[17] Since AGI reported on tax returns for 1958 was $281.2 billion, some 10 per cent additional—$28.1 billion—was received, but not shown on the returns, making a total of $309.3 billion to absorb a potential tax-deductibility of

The remainder of the difference—$4,000 million—is accounted for and concealed by the standard deduction. In 1958, on 38.3 million returns (out of a total of 59.1 million) the standard deduction was used; on only 20.8 million were deductions itemized.[18] Itemization rises rapidly as adjusted gross income increases, the most notable jumps coming for the AGI classes above $10,000 because the standard deduction has a ceiling of $1,000. Persons with AGI of $10,000 or less, and a diminishing few with higher incomes, may be presumed to choose to itemize chiefly because this is a tax-saving choice.

Tax deductions on returns with itemized deductions, 1958, as per cents of AGI, taxable and nontaxable, are shown in Table 5-4. It will be noticed that the regression of the per cents is much steeper for nontaxable returns than for taxable returns (although both show regression). At the low end of nontaxable returns are persons who pay no federal income tax, but who do pay appreciable sums in state and local taxes.[19] The itemized nontaxable group drains returns from the adjacent group of itemized taxable returns, while both groups attract persons who, by itemizing, reduce their tax base beyond what it would be reduced by using the standard deduction. This attraction may be assumed to operate for every AGI class, so that the percentages which tax deductions are of AGI on returns with itemized deductions (see Table 5-4) are larger than on all returns because, in every class, persons choose to itemize as a tax-saving device. But the *pattern* displayed on itemized returns, taxable and nontaxable together, may be assumed to hold as a pattern of *potential* tax deductions on returns which used the standard deduction.[20]

$12,310 million. AGI on itemized returns was $145.4 billion and it accounted for $7,480 million of tax deductions. The remainder, $4,830 million, has been split proportionally between AGI reported on standard deduction returns and AGI not reported, i.e., $4,000 million to the former and $830 million to the latter.

[18] It is sometimes forgotten that the standard deduction provides the benefits of deductibility. Thus Brazer states: "The impact of the optional standard deduction operates to deny the [tax] deduction to more than 70 per cent of all taxpayers." (*Tax Revision Compendium*, Vol. 1, p. 417.)

[19] *Tax* deductions are only 20 per cent of total deductions on nontaxable returns which itemized in 1958, and *total* deductions for this group comprised 41 per cent of its total AGI.

[20] Kahn, *op. cit.*, p. 179, has noticed "that tax payments of those who itemize and those who use the standard deduction are closer in amounts than some other [deductible] expenditures are."

TABLE 5-4. *Tax Deductions as Percentages of AGI, Taxable and Nontaxable Returns with Itemized Deductions, 1958*[a]

AGI Class			Nontaxable Returns	Taxable Returns	All Returns
Under $600			41.0%	—%	41.0%
$ 600 under $	1,000		13.2	4.9	10.3
1,000 "	1,500		11.6	6.0	8.8
1,500 "	2,000		10.1	5.7	7.3
2,000 "	2,500		8.4	5.6	6.4
2,500 "	3,000		7.8	5.1	5.7
3,000 "	3,500		7.8	5.2	5.6
3,500 "	4,000		6.6	5.2	5.4
4,000 "	4,500		6.9	5.1	5.2
4,500 "	5,000		6.9	5.2	5.3
5,000 "	6,000		7.9[b]	5.2	5.3
6,000 "	7,000		—	5.2	5.2
7,000 "	8,000		—	5.2	5.2
8,000 "	9,000		—	5.1	5.1
9,000 "	10,000		—	5.0	5.0
10,000 "	15,000		—	5.1	5.1
15,000 "	20,000		—	5.0	5.0
20,000 "	25,000		—	4.9	4.9
25,000 "	50,000		—	4.7	4.7
50,000 "	100,000		—	4.5	4.5
100,000 "	150,000		—	4.3	4.3
150,000 "	200,000		—	4.5	4.5
200,000 "	500,000		—	4.3	4.3
500,000 "	1,000,000		—	4.0	4.0
1,000,000 or more			—	3.5	3.5

[a] Source: Derived from U. S. Internal Revenue Service, *Statistics of Income, 1958: Individual Income Tax Returns* (1960), pp. 42-43.
[b] For nontaxable returns, the class is "$5,000 or more."

This hypothesis seems to be credible because the pattern of tax deductions displays a broad similarity to the pattern of the incidence of state and local taxes. Two sets of incidence figures are shown in Table 5-5: (1) R. A. Musgrave's calculation of certain state and local taxes as percentages of adjusted money income classes, 1954, and (2) George A. Bishop's calculation of the same taxes as percentages of net national product for 1958. In both cases

TABLE 5-5. *Estimated Incidence of Certain State and Local Taxes, 1954 and 1958*[a]

Adjusted Money Income Class	Estimated Incidence of Certain State and Local Taxes, 1954[b]
Under $2,000	10.5%
$ 2,000 under $ 3,000	9.5
3,000 " 4,000	8.9
4,000 " 5,000	8.7
5,000 " 7,500	8.4
7,500 " 10,000	7.9
10,000 or more	6.4
	8.1%

Net National Product	Estimated Incidence of Certain State and Local Taxes, 1958[b]
Under $2,000	11.2%
$ 2,000 under $ 4,000	9.3
4,000 " 6,000	8.4
6,000 " 8,000	7.5
8,000 " 10,000	7.1
10,000 " 15,000	6.3
15,000 or more	4.9
	7.3%

[a] Source: For the 1954 figures see R. A. Musgrave, "The Incidence of the Tax Structure and Its Effects on Consumption," *Federal Tax Policy for Economic Growth and Stability*, Papers Submitted by Panelists to the Joint Committee on the Economic Report, 84th Congress, 1st session (1955), p. 98, Table 2. For the 1958 figures see George A. Bishop, "The Tax Burden by Income Class, 1958," *National Tax Journal*, Vol. 14 (March 1961), p. 54, Table 6.

[b] Includes individual income taxes, excises, sales taxes, and property taxes. I have excluded inheritance and gift taxes, and taxes on corporate profits.

inheritance and gift taxes and taxes on corporate profits are excluded. Now it must be avowed that tax deductions are not the same as actual taxes paid or as incidence of taxes; that the concept of AGI is not the same as that of adjusted money income used by Musgrave or of net national product used by Bishop; and that, for these reasons, comparability must not be stressed.[21] For my pur-

[21] Kahn, *ibid.*, pp. 97-100, argues that the incidence of taxes should not be reckoned from figures of tax deductions because (1) deductions are inaccurate

TABLE 5-6. *Estimate of Potential Tax Deductions on Standard Deduction Returns, 1958*[a]

AGI Class	AGI on Returns with Standard Deduction (1)	Tax Deductions as Per Cent of AGI Itemized Returns (2)	(1)×(2) (3)	Estimate of Potential Tax Deductions[b] (4)
Under $600	$ 1,266 million	41.0%	$519 million	$259 million
$ 600 under $ 1,000	2,272	10.3	234	117
1,000 " 1,500	4,553	8.8	401	200
1,500 " 2,000	5,160	7.3	377	188
2,000 " 2,500	6,403	6.4	410	205
2,500 " 3,000	7,575	5.7	432	216
3,000 " 3,500	8,492	5.6	476	238
3,500 " 4,000	9,097	5.4	491	245
4,000 " 4,500	9,734	5.2	506	253
4,500 " 5,000	9,803	5.3	520	260
5,000 " 6,000	17,140	5.3	908	453
6,000 " 7,000	13,341	5.2	694	346
7,000 " 8,000	10,657	5.2	554	276
8,000 " 9,000	8,015	5.1	409	204
9,000 " 10,000	6,220	5.0	311	155
			$7,242	$3,616
10,000 or more			384	384
Total			$7,626 million	$4,000 million

[a] Source: Column 1, U. S. Internal Revenue Service, *Statistics of Income, 1958: Individual Income Tax Returns* (1960), p. 55; column 2, see Table 5-4.
[b] Column 4 is 49.9 per cent of column 3. For explanation, see text.

pose the sole point to be made is that, in view of the regressivity of aggregate state and local taxes, it is not surprising to find a similar regressivity displayed by personal tax deductions.

If, then, tax deductions as percentages of AGI on itemized returns are assumed to provide the pattern of tax deductibility which would be displayed in default of the standard deduction, the next step is to find a correction for the overestimate which is present in the aggregate and in every AGI class. It will be recalled that a rough estimate of the aggregate of state and local deductible taxes concealed in standard deduction returns in 1958 was $4,000 million (see tabulation on page 110).

How should this amount be allocated by AGI classes? For AGI's above $10,000 the standard deduction has a ceiling of $1,000 per return. As a result, its aggregate value for returns with AGI larger than $10,000 is simply the number of returns times $1,000, which for 1958 is $1,254 million. How much of this may be attributed to *tax* deductions? On itemized returns with AGI above $10,000, tax deductions were 30.6 per cent of total deductions. This percentage may be assumed to represent the tax deduction portion of $1,254 million, i.e., $384 million. Accordingly, the $384 million representing the potential tax deductions of standard deduction returns above $10,000 is subtracted from the $4,000 million representing potential tax deductions in all standard deduction returns, leaving $3,616 million to be allocated to AGI classes below $10,000.

The argument was offered earlier that the actual pattern of tax deductions by AGI classes on itemized returns indicated the pattern of potential tax deductions on returns which used the standard deduction, although every one of the percentages in the pattern would be too large. The latter expectation is amply fulfilled when the percentages of Table 5-4 are applied to AGI's reported on returns using the standard deduction, 1958. As Table 5-6 shows, the aggregate—$7,242 million—is double the ceiling aggregate of $3,616 million already derived. Accordingly, each of the figures of column

reports of taxes paid in the preceding year, (2) the composition of deductions is not known, (3) taxes legally deductible are not a good basis to study economic incidence. As may be guessed, I regard these points as overmeticulous for my purpose.

3 is multiplied by 3,616 ÷ 7,242 (49.9 per cent), to arrive in column 4 at estimates of potential tax deductions on standard deduction returns by AGI classes, 1958.

The final result of this computation of state and local taxes eligible for deduction in 1958 is as follows:

Reported on itemized tax returns	$ 7,480 million
Estimated for standard deduction returns	4,000
Estimated as unreported in tax returns	830
Total	$12,310 million

Regressivity of Tax Deductions

While some of the calculations made above are hypothetical and uncertain, the regressivity of deductions of state and local taxes in the aggregate is certain, and this regressivity is large toward the lower end of the income scale. Tax deductions constitute a decreasing proportion of income as income rises and, therefore, serve to increase the progressivity of the federal tax. Abolition of deductibility would, in this sense, strike harder at small- and middle-income taxpayers than at those with large incomes. Reduction of the standard deduction would logically be a part of abolition of deductibility, and this step also would strike more severely at taxpayers with AGI below $10,000.

These generalizations need qualification in two particulars. First, aggregate figures of tax deductions conceal interstate differences. In such states as Oregon and New York, where progressive state taxation of individual incomes is important, state taxes in the aggregate are progressive. But even in Oregon collections from individual income tax are only one fourth, and in New York only 13 per cent, of total state and local tax receipts. Second, Congress should not be assumed to set the scale of progression without assumptions concerning the effects of deductibility; it could couple abolition of deductibility with a reduction of rates which would favor small- and middle-income taxpayers.

Cost to the Federal Treasury

The indubitable advantages of deductibility to state and local governments are purchased at a cost to the federal Treasury. A calculation for 1958, using the method devised by Kahn, produced an estimate of $2,020 million for taxable returns which itemize (Table 5-7).[22] The right to deduct certain state and local taxes brings a reduction of federal tax, and since any deduction which does not diminish with increasing income brings a larger tax cut per dollar of deduction to high-income persons, deduction of state and local taxes is valuable to high-bracket incomes. If taxes itemized on 1958 returns were not deductible, the federal Treasury would have assessed $14.5 million additional in tax (85 per cent of the $17 million of taxes deducted) on the bracket with AGI of $1 million or more; it would have assessed $181.2 million additional on the bracket $5,000 and under $6,000 (20 per cent of $905.8 million). The $14.5 million is 6.2 per cent of the actual liability of the high bracket; the $181.2 is 12.5 per cent of tax liability of the low bracket.[23]

It is obvious that the modest regressivity of tax deductions (which becomes almost proportionality for incomes above $10,000) is swamped by the steep progression of the federal rates. State and local taxes do increase with increases in income, even though they do not increase proportionally, and the right of deduction from the federal tax base mounts in relative value, bracket by bracket.

[22] See Kahn, op. cit., p. 230, Appendix G, from which the following is briefly excerpted: "Average marginal rates of tax were computed by dividing the change in average tax liability between two income groups by the change in average taxable income between the same two income groups. . . .

"Deductions in given income groups were then multiplied by the marginal rate of tax. . . ."

[23] If the federal bracket-rates are set in the light of deductions and exemptions, the calculations of cost given above are irrelevant.

TABLE 5-7. *Estimated Cost to the Federal Government of Tax Deductions on Taxable Itemized Returns, 1958*[a]

AGI Class	Average Marginal Rate of Federal Tax, 1958 (1)	Tax Deductions, 1958 (2)	Cost to Federal Government (3)
$ 600 under $ 1,000	0.20	$ 2.9 million	$ 0.6 million
1,000 " 1,500	.20	17.5	3.5
1,500 " 2,000	.20	39.3	7.9
2,000 " 2,500	.20	74.0	14.8
2,500 " 3,000	.20	105.3	21.1
3,000 " 3,500	.20	160.0	32.0
3,500 " 4,000	.20	223.9	44.8
4,000 " 4,500	.20	287.5	57.5
4,500 " 5,000	.20	368.7	73.7
5,000 " 6,000	.20	905.8	181.2
6,000 " 7,000	.21	861.7	181.0
7,000 " 8,000	.22	688.3	151.4
8,000 " 9,000	.22	528.4	116.3
9,000 " 10,000	.23	376.7	86.6
10,000 " 15,000	.27	895.7	241.8
15,000 " 20,000	.32	364.0	116.5
20,000 " 25,000	.40	231.5	92.6
25,000 " 50,000	.54	510.0	275.4
50,000 " 100,000	.67	262.6	176.0
100,000 " 150,000	.74	69.3	51.2
150,000 " 200,000	.84	29.3	24.6
200,000 " 500,000	.89	47.9	42.7
500,000 " 1,000,000	.85	14.0	11.9
1,000,000 or more	.85	17.0	14.5
Total		$7,081.2 million	$2,019.6 million

[a] Source: Column 1 calculated by the method described in C. Harry Kahn, *Personal Deductions in the Federal Income Tax* (Princeton University Press, 1960), p. 104 and p. 230, Appendix G; column 2 from U. S. Internal Revenue Service, *Statistics of Income, 1958: Individual Income Tax Returns* (1960), p. 42.

Comparative Advantages to Individuals and States of Deductibility and of the Heller Credit

Individual Taxpayers

In Table 5-7 the estimated cost to the federal Treasury from tax deductibility on taxable itemized returns, 1958, was reckoned at $2,020 million. This leaves out of account the cost arising out of potential tax deductibility in returns with the standard deduction. This potential, on taxable and nontaxable returns, was reckoned in Table 5-6 at $4,000 million. The calculation is, however, too hypothetical to justify a further calculation by AGI classes of the tax-cost to the federal Treasury from this deductibility. In the aggregate the tax-cost almost surely exceeds what would be the cost of the Heller credit ($2,427 million for 1958; see Chapter 4, footnote 5, and Appendix B, Table 1). The relevant figures are brought together in Appendix A, Table 5, so that investigating or inquiring readers may make a calculation for themselves. But some indication may be offered here of how individual taxpayers would fare if the Heller credit were provided as a substitute for tax deductibility in 1958.

1. At the very bottom of the AGI scale (below $2,000) the substitution would bring net disadvantages. The reason is that the credit assumes and rests upon the existence of a federal tax liability, while deductibility here wipes out any liability.

2. For AGI $2,000-$10,000 the credit as a substitute for deductibility would have brought a federal tax reduction.

3. For AGI of $10,000 or more substitution of the credit for deductibility would have brought an increase of federal tax because the absolute value of the credit, after reaching $70 (when tax liability for a joint return is $500), rises only by $1 per $100 of federal tax liability.

States

Earlier in this chapter, it was shown that, for 1957, the positive correlation between deductible taxes and personal income by states is modest, that is, rich states gain little in relative advantage through tax deductibility. (See Table 5-3, Charts 5-1 and 5-2, and page 110.) In Chapter 4, it was shown that a moderate positive correlation exists for 1958 between per capita income and Heller credits as per

TABLE 5-8. *Ten States Losing Most and Ten Gaining Most in Rank by Substitution of Heller Credits, 1958, for Deductibility of State and Local Personal Taxes, 1957*[a]

Rank in Per Capita Income, 1957[b]	Rank with Respect to		Rank	
	Deductible Taxes as Per Cent of Income, 1957	Heller Credits as Per Cent of Income, 1958	Loss	Gain
(1)	(2)	(3)		
TEN STATES LOSING MOST				
49. Mississippi	5	49	44	
42. Georgia	10	41	31	
32. New Mexico	4	34	30	
47. South Carolina	17.5	47	29.5	
46. North Carolina	19.5	48.5	29	
41. North Dakota	12	40	28	
48. Arkansas	24	48.5	24.5	
30. Arizona	8	31	23	
33. Vermont	6	27	21	
45. Alabama	19.5	37.5	18	
TEN STATES GAINING MOST				
23. New Hampshire	42	1		41
6. New Jersey	45.5	6		39.5
18. Rhode Island	40	4		36
14. Pennsylvania	37	5		32
8. Nevada	38	7		31
15. Wyoming	43	16		27
10. Ohio	39	12		27
11. Maryland	28	3		25
36. Idaho	44	19		25
7. Illinois	35	11		24

[a] Source: Column 1, U. S. Bureau of the Census, *1957 Census of Governments*, Vol. 3, No. 5, *Governmental Finances*, p. 62; column 2, derived from Appendix C, Table 1, column 8; column 3 derived from Appendix B, Table 1, column 7 (which includes Alaska and Hawaii, as column 3, here, does not).
[b] The ranks are for the forty-eight states and the District of Columbia.

cents of personal income by states. (See pages 86 to 89.) These results raise doubts concerning the likelihood that poor states would gain relatively by substitution of the Heller credit for tax deductibility.

The doubts are strengthened by a related comparison by which states are ranked according to (1) deductible taxes as per cents of personal income, 1957, and (2) Heller credits as per cents of personal income, 1958. Examination of the gain or loss in rank from substitution of the Heller credit for deductibility is then made. Table 5-8 shows the ten states gaining, and the ten losing, most in rank from the switch. While the outcome is somewhat inconclusive, poor states are dominant in the losing group, and rich states in the gaining one.

Credits as a Substitute for, or Supplement to, Deductibility

Both tax deductions and tax credits can be regarded as an indirect federal subsidy to state and local governments. Recent discussion has mentioned a credit against federal income tax as a substitute for deductibility, sometimes of *all* state and local taxes now deductible, and sometimes of state and local income taxes. But a credit has also been suggested as a supplement to deductibility.[24]

That a credit against federal income tax for state income tax payments should be a supplement to deductibility would mean that some individuals could use state income tax payments twice to reduce their federal tax. They could continue their present practice of using their state income tax payments as deductions from federal

[24] Heller advocates a credit either as a substitute for, or supplement to, deductibility. He writes: "Either substitution of a Federal credit for deductibility, whether as a flat percentage of the Federal tax or on a sliding-scale basis, or supplementation of deductibility by a sliding-scale credit would serve to reduce somewhat the existing interstate inequalities of income." His discussion runs wholly in terms of deductibility and crediting of state *income* taxes. See *Tax Revision Compendium*, Vol. 1, p. 425.

Brazer discusses, and is critical of, deductibility of all state and local taxes. But in suggesting crediting he does not make clear whether he wants it in lieu of all tax deductions, or merely of deduction of state income tax payments. See *ibid.*, p. 417.

taxable income, and they could use them also to secure a credit against federal tax. Such a provision would appear to hold out special inducements for states *without* income taxes to enact such taxes, because this would allow residents who paid state income tax to secure a double (partial) recoupment. Individuals in states *with* income taxes would secure partial recoupment through the credit, but they would not make any new gain through deductibility. If, as has been suggested, the credit carried a requirement of revenue-maintenance, individuals in these states would gain through deduction of their additional income tax payments. But the amounts payable under the existing income tax would not count as credits.

To enact a credit as a supplement might seem somewhat prodigal of federal revenue, but this would not be a fatal difficulty so long as Congress, in reckoning the credit, was aware of the double recoupment and took account of it.

Would it be feasible for Congress to provide an income tax credit and, at the same time, abolish the right of deductibility of state income tax payments? The credit would be a substitute for deductibility of these tax payments, but deductibility of other state and local personal taxes would be retained. In this case, individuals in states *with* income tax would, if the credit were equal in value to the right of deductibility, be no better and no worse off. Individuals in states *without* income tax, when these states were induced by the credit to enact an income tax, would gain a new tax advantage without any compensating loss. In short, a credit for income tax as a substitute for the right to deduct income tax payments would appear to discriminate against states presently with income taxes.

Another possibility—and the most plausible one—is that an income tax credit would be a substitute for deductibility of all state and local personal taxes. As has been noticed earlier, such a credit would compel states without income taxes to enact them in order to enable their residents to secure credits.[25]

---

[25] Of the thirty-two jurisdictions (1960—including the District of Columbia and not including West Virginia) taxing individual income, in only ten was this tax the major source of revenue (Alaska, Delaware, Maryland, Massachusetts, Minnesota, New York, Oregon, Vermont, Virginia, Wisconsin); in thirty-

Similarities and Differences in the Devices

Many of the supposed differences between the two techniques stem merely from the fact that deductibility is a long-established right, covering all the chief state and local personal taxes, while crediting is a proposal. The federal government at present can do little to enlarge deductibility; it also can do little to reduce deductibility, except by a *quid pro quo*, because established concessions are hard to withdraw or modify. But the same political and administrative generalizations are applicable to old credits; they also are inflexible. New credits—credits in the planning process—*are* flexible; they can be shaped by Congress by means of conditions. But if deductibility were new, or if a new start could be made with it, similar conditions and limits could be framed. It would, for instance, if the slate were clear, be easy to specify that only state (and local) income tax payments be deductible; that these payments be deductible according to a graduated scale so that, for example, 100 per cent of the first $200 of state tax liability be deductible, and 50 per cent of the additional liability.

But, while the abstract similarity between the two techniques should be indicated, the practical fact is that tax deductibility has been used up, and crediting has not. If, therefore, a crediting scheme could be substituted for existing deductibility, Congress would regain freedom of action to move toward certain fiscal objectives—such as tax coordination—as well as toward elimination of certain undesirable features of deductibility. And perhaps some strategy could be devised to keep crediting flexible for the future.

Certain differences between the techniques of deductibility and crediting against income tax should not, however, be overlooked. Even assuming *tabula rasa*, crediting is inherently less open-end and more "political" than deductibility. It is less open-end because,

---

one states a general sales tax or gross receipts tax was the chief source. A married resident of New York (no sales tax) with two dependents and an AGI of $12,400 would now pay approximately $200 in state income tax, and this reduces his federal tax (if he itemizes) by approximately $44; a resident of Rhode Island (no state income tax) in a similar situation would pay a general sales tax of $182, and secure the same reduction in his federal tax.

while a credit is framed in terms of liability for federal income tax, a tax deduction is framed in terms of state and local tax payments. Both federal and state-local tax liabilities may be expected to grow over time, but the shape of the former will depend somewhat on specific congressional decisions, while that of the latter will depend upon uncoordinated decisions by thousands of governments.

Moreover, with respect to type of tax which can be deducted or credited, deductibility has more flexibility. Any personal tax can be deducted from the income tax base without difficulty; it is less easy to frame a scheme for crediting other state and local taxes against the federal income tax, because crediting seems to imply the assessment by state and local governments of a similar tax. How, for example, could a scheme for crediting property tax payments be managed? Or sales tax payments? To be sure, something could be worked out, but more care with details would be necessary than for deductibility, if only because a credit is against tax liability, whereas a deduction is against the tax base. Deductibility, as it now operates, gives the states flexibility with respect to the form and type of their taxes. A crediting device would be more restrictive; indeed, it would probably be designed to encourage some measure of uniformity. Furthermore, a credit against federal income tax, expressed as a percentage, reduces the liabilities of persons at the bottom level, whereas deductions wipe out their liabilities. If the credit against federal income tax for taxes other than state income tax could not be managed—if the credit were limited to state income taxes—then states without income tax would have to enact income taxes in order to participate in the credit.

Another important practical difference between deductibility and crediting is that the former may be presumed to give some subsidy to local governments, whereas crediting would operate directly to aid state governments. This difference is associated with the question of revenue-maintenance. Even *tabula rasa* the federal government could not, if it chose to give the right of deductibility of property taxes, require revenue-maintenance, because it could not test and enforce compliance. This right has, of course, long been provided, and local governments have received thereby some indirect federal subsidy unassociated with any federal requirement.

Similarly a credit against federal income tax for property tax payments, if it could be devised, would not be coupled with a revenue-maintenance requirement. It would simply be an outright reduction of federal tax liability.[26]

The conclusion follows that a proposal to substitute a credit for deductibility must consider the effect on local governments. The financial benefits stemming from a credit, coupled with revenue-maintenance, would accrue directly to state governments; whatever loss resulted from abolition of deductibility would accrue to local governments, and it is not clear how this could be offset. Should the Congress, in providing a credit, specify that some share of the revenue-benefits be passed on to local governments? A meaningful provision of this sort would be difficult to frame and hard to administer.

Finally, a substitution would not improve the relative financial position of the "poor" states, or that of individuals at the bottom of the AGI scale.

[26] As noted in Chapter 4, Robert Heller has proposed a credit against federal income tax, both personal and corporate, for future *increases* in state and local taxes used for education (*Harvard Educational Review*, Summer 1958, pp. 214-231). The plan seems to require administrative steps of considerable complexity, which, even if feasible, would be annoying and costly. It would, moreover, favor school districts which are financially strong.

6

The Variety of Devices: A Comparison

> If the commerce and industry and population move-
> ments of this country have taken on a complex Nation-
> wide character, the safeguarding and promotion of this
> development becomes a national responsibility. If the eco-
> nomic system is beset by multiple tax burdens, compliance
> and administrative costs, and by upsetting differentials, it
> is the duty of the Federal Government to remove these ob-
> stacles to economic activity and progress. It is not an im-
> pairment of State rights to create conditions under which
> the States will find it advantageous to cooperate and to
> enact and enforce desirable measures, which in the absence
> of such conditions do not appeal to the self-interest of the
> individual States. This is not to deny, however, that insofar
> as practicable local responsibility should be preserved.
>
> Treasury Committee, 1943
> *Federal, State, and Local Government Fiscal Relations*

AMONG THE VARIETY of financial devices by which the federal
government may provide financial assistance to state and local
governments are tax sharing, tax supplements, tax deductibility, tax
credits, unconditional grants, and conditional grants. Of this galaxy
only the last—conditional grants—provides federal control over the

uses to which the financial assistance is put. All the others make revenue available to state and local governments through federal cooperation and some measure of federal control.

The degree of federal control is slight for TAX SUPPLEMENTS, because a state has the right to decide on the rate or rates of the supplement to the federal tax. If the base of the tax is specific—a package of cigarettes, a gallon of gasoline—then the taxing decisions of both the collecting government and the other government can be quite independent. But if the base of the supplement is the tax liability of taxpayers to the collecting government, as when a state government assesses its citizens a percentage of their federal liability for individual income tax, a federal taxing decision has a direct effect on state collections, willy-nilly. A recipient state government can, however, avoid such effects by expressing its levy in terms of the federal liability arising from the federal law at a point of time.

The device of DEDUCTIBILITY of state and local taxes also brings little or no federal control. Yet it has become institutionalized and widespread as a "right"—without examination by Congress of its rationale. As was indicated in Chapter 5, it should be tidied up and structured on some logical basis.

The operation of TAX SHARING requires centralized control. As a federal-state device, the rationale behind its use is that certain taxes can be collected and administered more economically at the federal, i.e., the national level, than at the state level. Less resources are required by government to levy and collect a given aggregate revenue; less are required by taxpayers to comply with the tax law. The advantage is greater for some taxes than for others; it is large for income tax, both individual and corporate, small for gasoline tax, probably nonexistent for property tax. Even though quantification of costs of collection and compliance is not possible, little doubt can exist that, for income taxation, the savings to be secured by centralization would be substantial.

Tax sharing requires that one jurisdiction should control both levy and administration of the tax, and the other jurisdictions be entitled merely to a share of collections. They are, however, entitled to a share according to some agreed and uniform basis; they are not dependent on the arbitrary and variable decision of the collecting government. When they sacrifice their own right to collect a tax, they gain the right to a predetermined slice of revenue which can be used by them as they please. If the collecting government does give direction to expenditure, the shared tax is no longer pure; it has acquired something of the characteristic of a grant. Since sharing is according to some formula,[1] the actual receipts of numerous recipient governments can be equally appropriate only if the formula measures their needs for the revenue, which will seldom happen. Some of the recipient governments may, therefore, oppose loss of the right to collect the tax, because their take, even if inefficiently secured, can be made to match their needs.

The device of TAX CREDITS, as actually employed in the United States, may tie the hands of the state governments, as in the case of the unemployment insurance credit, or it may leave them much discretion, as in the case of the death tax credit. In all cases, however, initiative lies with the federal government, and justification of the use of a credit must usually be that some federal objectives, wholly beyond the objective of federal tax reduction, are served. Within the area of tax administration, a credit can be utilized to bring some order out of the disorder which has arisen through joint and uncoordinated use of a tax source. Joint occupancy is to be allowed to continue, but subject to federal specifications. Compared to a tax supplement, which permits a state government merely to tie on to a federal levy, a credit permits continuance of a state levy, and yet shapes the form and amount of the levy by the bait of reduction of federal collections. The size of the bait and the amount of conformity specified are elastic. This is the virtue and the danger of the credit device.

In actual practice, this elasticity has been apparent at the time of introduction of a federal credit—and it has been lost thereafter. The credits for the death tax and for unemployment insurance both illustrate this generalization. The conformity required by the former was modest, by the latter extensive. But what was done at the outset has not been changed, despite emergence of situations unforeseen

[1] For example, a percentage of federal collections, distributed to the states according to population, or consumption, or domicile of taxpayers. Some specific proposals will be noticed later.

in 1926 and 1935. In short, the potential for flexibility of the device has been unutilized and latent. While activation of this potential will seem to some to bring impairment of states' rights, a more persuasive view is that it should be regarded as removal of "obstacles to economic activity and progress."[2]

Grants, Conditional and Unconditional

The chief difference between conditional and unconditional grants is indicated by their titles: the former have conditions, specifications, controls, while the latter have not. If the federal government is interested in stimulating state-local performance of a function, and in guiding the nature of the performance, a conditional grant is indicated; if it is interested merely in providing state-local governments with financial help, leaving to them how this shall be used, an unconditional grant is indicated. Between these two limits, infinite variation is possible.

Conditional Grants

Federal use of these grants, over the decades, has been extensive; indeed, their use has been so extensive and disheveled as to suggest the lack of an over-all plan. Congress, detecting a national interest in a specific governmental function which, constitutionally and by precedent, was handled at the state and local levels, has made shift with conditional grants.

The variety of grant formulas cannot be examined here. But there is one feature of many recent formulas that, because of its significance for unconditional grants, needs mention: the considerable interstate redistribution of income which has occurred (1) because the revenue allocated to the states in grants is raised by a progressive federal tax system which drains more from the rich

[2] *Federal, State, and Local Government Fiscal Relations*, Report of the U.S. Treasury Committee on Intergovernmental Fiscal Relations, Senate Document No. 69, 78th Congress, 1st session (1943), p. 449. The Committee quotation heading this chapter is also from p. 449.

than the poor states,[3] and (2) because the allocation formulas, state by state, are based on need.

This may be illustrated by a summary look at the grant formula in the public school assistance bill of 1961 (S. 1021, H.R. 4970) as submitted to the Congress. Nine "rich" states, and the District of Columbia, were to be allotted for fiscal 1962 the minimum grant of $15 per public school pupil in average daily attendance. All other states would have an additional allotment depending upon the ratio of their personal income per public school pupil to the personal income per pupil for the United States. As a result, the allotment for Mississippi, the poorest state, would be $29.67. Mississippi would thus secure almost twice as much per public school pupil as the nine "rich" states. The incidence of federal taxes levied to raise the grants is, however, probably less than one fourth as much per pupil in Mississippi as in the nine "rich" states.[4] Similarly the redistributive effect of the progressive tax system is greater than that of the allocation formulas of other conditional grants.[5] Moreover, the equalization that occurs through these grants is a by-product, an accidental result.

The Kestnbaum Commission did not believe that equalization "of the general fiscal capacities of the States is by itself a proper objective of National policy." It did hold, however, that an equalizing formula in a grant was reasonable in order to attain the objective of a grant program in low-income states.[6]

It would seem that this generalization logically requires the support of two related concepts: (1) a standard fiscal effort on the part of the states, (2) a national minimum level, or foundation program,

---

[3] The grants for employment security administration and for highway construction are exceptions. The former come from payroll taxes; the latter from taxation of motor fuel and certain automotive excises.

[4] No very recent figures of incidence by states are available. But see Commission on Intergovernmental Relations, *Report to the President* (June 1955), Appendix E, Table 9; Howard G. Schaller, "Federal Grants-In-Aid and Differences in State Per Capita Incomes, 1929, 1939, and 1949," *National Tax Journal*, Vol. 8 (September 1955), pp. 287-299.

[5] Selma Mushkin has pointed out that federal expenditure brings a redistribution of income in favor of the poorer states. See "Federal Grants and Federal Expenditures," *National Tax Journal*, Vol. 10 (September 1957), pp. 193-213.

[6] Commission on Intergovernmental Relations, *op. cit.* (1955), p. 135.

which should be provided even in the poorest state.[7] If poor states, after making a standard effort to support some function in which there is a definable federal interest—for example, primary and secondary public education—are unable to provide a level which, in the opinion of the Congress, is an acceptable minimum level, Congress should provide grants by an equalizing formula. Equalization of this sort is self-limiting; it stops when the national minimum has been achieved. Moreover, unless a federal grant program is intended to stimulate expenditure on a specific function in all states, its allocation should be limited to states which, through a standard effort, cannot achieve a national minimum level of performance. When the judgment of the federal government is that a function is being underperformed solely or chiefly because of lack of state resources, it is wasteful to offer grants to those states which, by an average effort, could provide a program at a level above the national minimum.[8]

Unconditional Grants

The federal government in the United States has never utilized unconditional grants, but in two other federal countries—Australia and Canada—they have a long history.[9]

Such grants are akin to the devices examined above (especially to credits), even if the kinship is not obvious at first sight. A purpose of the federal government in the use of any of the devices is to provide or release financial resources for state and local governments. Federal action by way of an unconditional grant shifts federal revenues *directly* to the other governments; federal tax reduction, or credits, or supplements, require action by the state governments if they are to benefit. In this respect the unconditional grant is similar to federal sharing, but it is different in that neither is the

[7] These concepts are elaborated in James A. Maxwell, *Federal Grants and the Business Cycle* (National Bureau of Economic Research, 1952), pp. 59-64.

[8] *Ibid.*, pp. 7-9.

[9] Although the 1836 distribution of excess federal funds to the states was essentially an unconditional grant, in its original form as authorized by Congress it was a "deposit"; see Introduction, section on Possible Remedies.

total amount dependent upon the receipts from a particular tax, nor is its allocation to each state dependent upon collections originating within the boundaries of the state. Decisions concerning total amount and state portions of a grant are, however, made according to some principles, even though the actual factors or variables embodied in an unconditional grant scheme are often numerous and complex.

An unconditional grant, unlinked to any specific federal source of revenue, can be made as "equalizing" as Congress desires, while credits against federal income tax, on the assumptions specified earlier, provide no equalization. Even for the Heller credit, maximum credits per state, expressed as per cents of state personal income, will be less for poor than for rich states. And since what a state government may pick up as new revenue is the same as what the federal government relinquishes, the Heller credit brings no interstate equalization. In short, the credit brings a substitution of state for federal taxation, the amount and type of substitution being limited and controlled. An unconditional grant *may* provide interstate equalization, since the amount provided for each state does not depend upon the amount taken from it in federal taxes. The money disbursed as grants is raised by a progressive system of federal taxes; the state-by-state allocation of the grants may be inversely progressive, that is, the share of a poor state may be larger than that of a rich one in terms of per capita income, population and so on.

Moreover, equalization is more expansible through an unconditional grant than through a conditional one, because the relevant minimum or foundation level to be achieved may embrace all state and local functions, and not simply those in which there is a definable federal interest. In providing an unconditional grant, the federal government does not manifest an interest in specific state-local functions; rather, does it provide revenue which state and local governments may use as they choose. But the logic of the grant is that the federal government has an interest in enabling standard state and local functions to be performed at an average level, assuming the revenue-effort of state and local governments to be acceptable.[10]

[10] Compare Chapter 1, section on Governmental Expenditure and Effort.

Unconditional Grants in Australia and Canada

As noted above, unconditional grants have had extensive and varied use in Australia and Canada. A brief examination of their history in these two federal countries may cast some light on their advantages and disadvantages.

Australia

Special unconditional grants have been paid to a limited number of Australian states for half a century. At first the grants were *ad hoc*, since the expectation and hope was that they would be temporary. But after 1933 the temporary matured into the semi-permanent because of the work of a three-member Commonwealth Grants Commission. The commission, itself appointed in the first place for a three-year term, formulated principles upon which a consistent policy has been built, and its grant recommendations from the outset have been accepted by the Commonwealth government.

The grants under discussion have been both unconditional and "special"; unconditional because no federal strings were attached; "special" because they went only to three states—Tasmania, Western Australia, and South Australia. These three were, to use the words of the commission, "marginal states"; they contained "a large area on the fringe of the rather exiguous portion of the continent which is cultivable."[11] In 1933 the three contained less than 20 per cent of the population of Australia, although they embraced over half of its area (not counting the territories). Chiefly producers and exporters of raw materials, they failed to prosper in the 1920's; with the depression of the 1930's they were in desperate shape and their governments were near bankruptcy.

The commission early affirmed the generalization that a state government was entitled to a special grant if its fiscal position was

[11] Commonwealth Grants Commission, *First Report* (Canberra, 1933), p. 55. At present only Tasmania and Western Australia are claimant.

so impaired that it could not function on a standard comparable to that of the other states. Fiscal need by itself was a basis for special grants. But need should be interpreted with "austerity," and a state government should make strong efforts to solve its own problems. Accordingly, the commission took as "normal" the standards of expenditure and taxation of the nonclaimant states; it related the finances of the claimants to these norms and recommended grants which fell somewhat short of filling the deficiency between their expenditure and the normal. Claimancy in itself, the commission believed, should bring some penalty in the levels of provision and effort. And while the grants were provided without strings, the recipient governments knew that their whole system of expenditure and revenue was under scrutiny and would be taken into account by the commission; loose financial practices would be exposed and reform would be expected.[12]

The Commonwealth Grants Commission has continued in operation to the present. While numerous modifications and improvements in method have been made, subtle refinements have never been attempted and at all times the staff has been very modest in size. The value of the commission's contribution is certain, and yet, to an outsider, the clue to this success is elusive. The commissioners have been established and respected men. Perhaps for this reason their broad judgments and imprecise measurements have been accepted without quibble, rather than picked apart and discarded. The commission has not hesitated to be critical publicly of state fiscal behavior. It has assessed penalties for mistakes and awarded bonuses for wisdom without arousing rancor or envy. Two other characteristics also help explain its success: (1) It has stood outside the direct stream of political pressures and rested its decisions, as far as possible, on objective economic criteria; (2) its clientele, the claimant states, comprised only a small fraction of the nation—less than one fifth in population—and the grants to them made modest demands on the Commonwealth budget—recently less than 3 per cent of its tax revenue. If a similar perform-

---

[12] For an appraisal of the work of the commission, see Eric J. Hanson, *Australian Commonwealth Grants Commission: A Quarter Century of Fiscal Judgement* (Canadian Tax Foundation, 1960).

ance elsewhere could be assumed, every federalism should establish a similar body and utilize similar techniques.

Canada

This country has a system of unconditional federal grants to the provinces stretching back to the time of confederation in 1867. Throughout the history of the grants up to World War II, the determinants were political rather than economic. Sentiment for a revision of dominion-provincial relations, and especially financial relations, was precipitated by the ruinous incidence of the depression of the 1930's upon provincial finances. In 1937 a Royal Commission (the Rowell-Sirois Commission) was appointed; and in 1940 it recommended certain major changes in governmental functions and finances.

The commission did not conclude its deliberations until Canada had entered the war. At a Dominion-Provincial Conference called late in 1940 to consider the recommendations of the commission, three of the (then) nine provinces contended that action in wartime would be unwise. It is not merely coincidence that these three—Ontario, Alberta, and British Columbia—would not have been recipients of a new set of unconditional federal grants, based upon provincial fiscal need, which the commission had recommended. The conference broke up, but not before the federal Minister of Finance had bluntly indicated the severity of the wartime financial measures he meant to use, and secured provincial promises of full cooperation.

In April 1941 the federal government obtained provincial relinquishment of the field of income taxation, individual and corporate, for the duration of the war and one year after. The provincial governments received as compensation roughly the equivalent of their collections in 1940.

In August 1945 the Dominion-Provincial Conference on Reconstruction assembled at Ottawa. After protracted negotiations it foundered, and in June 1946 the federal Minister of Finance offered, as substitutes for the wartime tax agreements, proposals which he would negotiate with individual provinces. The following financial arrangements emerged: seven of the nine provinces signed tax-rental agreements by which the federal government for five years was given sole occupancy of the fields of personal income tax, succession duties, and corporation taxes (other than a 5 per cent tax on corporate net income which was to be collected by the federal government and turned over to the provinces). When Newfoundland joined the Dominion in 1949 it signed a similar tax-rental agreement. But Ontario and Quebec stayed outside. The details of the compensation paid to the renting provinces are too complicated to be presented here. Broadly, three options were offered, each resting chiefly upon a per capita payment and designed to provide yearly sums which would be attractive to certain provinces.

When new agreements were negotiated in 1952 for a second five-year period only modest changes were made because the agreements were negotiated in the shadow of the Korean war. However, an option was worked out which persuaded Ontario to sign tax-rental agreements with respect to individual income tax and corporation taxes.

The third agreement, for 1957 to 1962, was more generous and sophisticated in formulation. The financial responsibilities of the federal government had eased somewhat, and, besides, some general ideas concerning the principles of compensation had evolved. As earlier, tax-rental of individual and corporation income tax and succession duties was provided, but compensation to the provincial governments now had three separate components.

1. A renting province was to receive payment equal to (1) 10 per cent of the yield in the province of the federal individual income tax, (2) 9 per cent of the similar yield of the federal corporation income tax, (3) 50 per cent of the similar yield of federal succession duties, averaged over a three-year period. Eight provinces signed rental agreements for all three taxes; Ontario rented the individual income tax, but levied its own corporation taxes and succession duties; Quebec chose to levy all three taxes. When a province did not rent a tax, the federal tax on taxpayers in the province was reduced or abated by the rates stated above—10 per cent, 9 per

cent, 50 per cent—designated as "standard" rates. By this scheme tax uniformity and simplified collection were achieved over the nation.

2. The federal government agreed to provide "tax-equalization" payments to the governments of those provinces where the tax-rental payments were below the average per capita yield of the standard rates in the two provinces with the highest per capita yield at the standard rates. The stabilization payments were not subject to agreement; they were paid whether or not a provincial government signed a tax-rental agreement. This explicit recognition of the principle of equalization was an important innovation. While the Rowell-Sirois Commission had recommended equalization subsidies, federal Ministers of Finance until 1956 had been fearful of them.

3. The federal government, by what were called "stabilization" arrangements, set a series of floors under its payments to the provinces. The annual payments to a province were not to fall below 95 per cent of average payments in the two previous years.[13] The aim was, of course, to protect provincial governments against a cyclical or a secular shrinkage in subsidy receipts.

Each financial arrangement had brought a liberalization in its terms, whether modest as in 1952, or large as in 1956. Yet the provincial governments were dissatisfied, and in 1957 a new federal government enlarged its payments in two respects. It raised the "standard" rate of the individual income tax from 10 per cent to 13 per cent; it provided special unconditional grants to the four Atlantic provinces (these were called the Atlantic Provinces Adjustment Grants), contending that this was a further application of the principle of equalization.[14]

During 1960-61 a number of conferences of dominion-provincial officials were held to work out a scheme to replace the agreements expiring on March 31, 1962. Each provincial premier wanted better financial terms, whether on the basis of need, or justice, or con-

[13] Other alternative floors were provided.
[14] Special financial provision was made for Newfoundland by the Terms of Union in 1949 and again in 1959.

stitutional right. For example, Premier Frost of Ontario believed "that constitutionally each province is entitled to one-half the productivity or yield of the fields of personal income and corporation taxes"; Premier Lesage of Quebec wanted complete federal withdrawal from the field of succession duties, equalization payments "calculated on the basis of the per capita yield of the personal and corporate income taxes in the province where such yield is highest" (instead of the average of the two highest provinces), and a lifting of the stabilization floor from 95 per cent to 100 per cent.[15] Other premiers made other requests. The effect was to strengthen the conviction of Prime Minister John G. Diefenbaker and Minister of Finance Donald M. Fleming that the rental agreements had to some extent, "transferred the interest of provincial Premiers and their treasurers from their own taxpayers to the federal treasury."[16]

The federal government, therefore, proposed a number of changes, and legislation was passed in 1961 to make them effective in the following year.[17] In an effort to strengthen the financial responsibility of the provincial governments, the tax-rental system was to be discontinued, and the provincial governments were to impose their own taxes in the three jointly occupied fields. However, in order to make room for the provincial taxes, the federal government proposed to alter its own taxes as follows:

1. To reduce the *corporation tax* rate by 9 percentage points, i.e., by the amount of the then "standard" rate, or the parallel amount of the abatement allowed to nonrenting provinces. Withdrawal in favor of the provinces beyond this level seemed unwise because corporation profits are usually national in scope and origin, and because they are quite variable over time.

2. To reduce the yield of the federal *personal income tax* by approximately 20 per cent over a five-year period. The "standard" rate of 13 per cent allowed the provinces in 1961 was, in effect, to be raised to 20 per cent by reduction of the federal take.

3. The federal government had, in 1958-59, shifted from *succession duties* to an estate tax. If a provincial government chose not to impose

[15] *Dominion-Provincial Conference, July 25-27, 1960* (Ottawa, 1960), p. 24 (Frost), pp. 130-131 (Lesage).

[16] *Ibid.*, p. 9. The words are those of the Prime Minister.

[17] The effective date for the change in the individual income tax and in the corporation income tax was January 1, 1962; for that in the estate tax, April 1, 1962. The new arrangements were for a five-year period.

succession duties of its own, the federal government would pay it half the yield from the federal estate tax in the province. If, however, a provincial government levied succession duties, the abatement of federal rates (50 per cent of the yield) then in existence would be continued.

The federal government was well aware of the accomplishments of the rental system in securing tax uniformity and simplified administration and compliance. In order to retain these advantages it offered "to undertake the collection of the personal income tax or the corporation income tax, or both, for any Provinces which so desire, on condition that the Province under its laws defines the tax base, i.e., taxable income, to be identical at all times with the Federal definition."[18] A single joint return would be employed and the federal government would make no charge to the provincial governments for collection.

The equalization feature of the financial arrangements was to be changed only in two details. First, the formula was to include not only the yields from the three major taxes, but also one half of "the three-year moving average of gross natural resource revenues as determined by the Dominion Bureau of Statistics."[19] The aim was to broaden the base from which equalization grants were to be measured. Second, instead of the average yield of the relevant revenues in the two highest-yielding provinces, the ceiling of the grants was to be the average national yield. The Prime Minister declared that this shift was "based on financial realism." Equalization to the revenue yield of the top province was, in his opinion, an impractical goal. As a further move toward equalization the Atlantic Provinces Adjustment Grants were increased, and the special grant to Newfoundland was continued for five years.

No significant changes were made in the floor or stabilization arrangements.

WHILE A SOLID APPRAISAL of the dominion-provincial financial arrangements cannot be ventured here, it would seem that achievement of approximate uniformity of rates and base of the three im-

[18] Statement by the Prime Minister to the Dominion-Provincial Conference, February 23, 1961.
[19] *Ibid.*

TABLE 6-1. *Per Capita Federal Individual Income Tax Liability, by States, 1958*[a]

State[b]		Per Capita Liability	State		Per Capita Liability	State		Per Capita Liability
1. Del.	(1)	$358.5	18. Wyo.	(16)	$186.1	35. N.Mex.	(34)	$143.9
2. D.C.	(2)	301.1	19. Mo.	(20)	184.4	36. Va.	(35)	143.2
3. Conn.	(3)	299.6	20. Alaska	(9)	182.2	37. Okla.	(36)	143.1
4. Nev.	(5)	286.9	21. Wis.	(23)	181.3	38. Me.	(38)	135.6
5. N.Y.	(4)	274.0	22. Ind.	(22)	179.8	39. La.	(43)	130.5
6. Ill.	(6)	266.7	23. N.H.	(30)	174.2	40. W.Va.	(42)	126.3
7. N.J.	(7)	266.7	24. Minn.	(27)	169.5	41. Vt.	(40)	124.4
8. Calif.	(8)	258.8	25. Kans.	(24)	169.3	42. S.D.	(41)	119.5
9. Md.	(11)	230.4	26. Hawaii	(26)	168.2	43. N.D.	(39)	118.3
10. Mass.	(10)	226.4	27. Texas	(32)	165.4	44. Ky.	(45)	117.4
11. Wash.	(13)	223.8	28. Ariz.	(29)	164.6	45. Tenn.	(46)	115.8
12. Ohio	(12)	215.6	29. Nebr.	(25)	161.8	46. Ga.	(44)	113.1
13. Penn.	(15)	214.1	30. Iowa	(28)	159.5	47. Ala.	(48)	106.1
14. Mich.	(14)	210.2	31. Fla.	(31)	157.2	48. N.C.	(47)	91.1
15. R.I.	(17)	199.6	32. Mont.	(19)	151.0	49. Ark.	(50)	80.9
16. Ore.	(21)	198.1	33. Utah	(33)	149.3	50. S.C.	(49)	77.6
17. Colo.	(18)	194.8	34. Idaho	(37)	145.3	51. Miss.	(51)	60.2
						U.S.		$197.0

[a] Source: U.S. Internal Revenue Service, *Statistics of Income, 1958: Individual Income Tax Returns*, p. 79; U.S. Office of Business Economics, *Survey of Current Business*, August 1960, p. 17; U.S. Bureau of the Census, *Statistical Abstract of the United States: 1961*, p. 10.
[b] Figures in parentheses are ranks in terms of per capita personal income.

portant direct taxes must have had beneficial results. And yet the provincial governments have been restive, complaining that they were deprived of flexibility of decision and that their rental payments, or abatements, or equalization grants were inadequate, despite an increase of 57 per cent from 1956-57 to 1960-61. An outsider gains the impression that, increasingly, the arrangements have again become "political." The long history of unconditional grants in Canada, 1867-1940, is replete with political maneuvering. It may be that this sterile background was not erased when a new start was attempted in 1941.

Application of Assistance Devices to Specific Taxes

This survey of the main characteristics of the spectrum of intergovernmental financial devices will next be supplemented by a survey of their application to particular taxes.

Application to Individual Income Tax

Sharing. Discontinuance of state income taxes in return for some slice of federal collections raises, in acute form, the question of the proper basis for sharing. The figures of federal collections, by states, provided by the Commissioner of Internal Revenue are not satisfactory in terms of origin of income. A taxpayer may file his federal return and make his payments at his residence or his place of business, and the federal government has no direct interest in determining the origin of the income of the taxpayer. But most states which tax income do have an interest, because they tax nonresidents on income originating within their borders. Is the share of a state to depend on the origin of income or on the domicile of taxpayers?

Assuming this decision to be made, sharing either on the basis of origin or of domicile would provide the richer states with the lion's share. This is the inevitable result of distribution resting on progressive taxation of individual incomes. (See Table 6-1.) Should sharing rest on some other basis? In such case the linkage between the source of the income and the receipt of the distribution is impaired or broken. If the basis of sharing is population, the break may seem not to be sharp; if the basis is some measure of need, the break will seem drastic. But economic objectivity will be impaired by all such bases. The proper course would be, instead of professing linkage, to place the proceeds of income tax in the federal Treasury and to distribute money to the states on some basis chosen on its own merits.

Accepting the premise that sharing on the basis of origin of income is necessary, what share of federal collections might the states request? Their present utilization of income taxation is quite diverse as has been noticed previously. L. L. Ecker-Racz and I. M. Labovitz have measured this diversity by expressing state collections as a percentage of federal collections in each state.[20] In 1958 the range ran from Oregon, which collected an amount equal to 28.7 per cent of federal collections, to Oklahoma, which collected 4.2 per cent.[21] Voluntary relinquishment by Oregon of the right to tax individual income would probably require receipt of an annual amount of about one fourth of federal collections in Oregon. Ecker-Racz draws a conclusion as follows:

> Since practical political considerations would probably prescribe uniform sharing with all the states, it would require (at current federal collection levels) an additional federal tax levy of the general magnitude of $10 billion to finance this coordination device. In other words, the federal government would have to distribute to the states, on the average, about $6 for every $1 of their own tax they abandoned.[22]

Even if distribution of some smaller slice were negotiated, *uniform* sharing would give some states—especially those with no income taxes—windfall and abundant revenues in comparison with others which do now utilize the tax.

[20] Ecker-Racz and Labovitz, "Practical Solutions to Financial Problems Created by the Multilevel Political Structure," *Public Finances: Needs, Sources, and Utilization*, Conference of the Universities—National Bureau Committee for Economic Research (Princeton University Press, 1961), pp. 146-147.

[21] Neglecting Tennessee and New Hampshire, which have a limited income tax.

[22] Ecker-Racz and Labovitz, *op. cit.*, p. 148.

Federal collections of individual income tax are unstable; they are sensitive to cyclical swings. Stability of shared revenues could probably be provided by averaging, although the state-by-state components of the total would be often more unstable than the total itself.

State Supplements. This device is somewhat less centralizing than outright sharing, since states could specify the rate or rates of the supplement.[23] One, and the simplest, form of supplement is to express the state tax as a percentage of the federal tax liability. Alaska uses this method. Utah used it from 1951 to 1955; New Mexico used it from 1953 to 1955 on an option basis for individuals with AGI of less than $10,000. Three difficulties have been disclosed: (1) the method may be an unconstitutional delegation of state legislative powers to the Congress; (2) when federal rates or base are changed, the state secures more or less revenue than it reckoned; (3) the option technique allows taxpayers a chance to choose the option which lessens their tax.

Another form of supplement is the adoption by a state of the federal tax base, applying its own scale of rates. In 1961 twelve states did this, with certain modifications.[24] Constitutionally the states cannot tax interest on federal obligations. They wish to tax the income from securities of sister states and their local governments, which the federal government excludes from its tax base. Other, and more unique, state idiosyncrasies cannot be listed here. The more numerous are the modifications of the federal base, the less is the gain from simplicity of compliance and administration.

The discussion above assumes state collection and administration of its own tax. But these could, as in Canada, be delegated to the federal Treasury. In this case one additional difficulty would arise, because the states would have to forego taxation of the income of nonresidents.

[23] *Ibid.*, pp. 149-150.
[24] Alaska, Hawaii, Idaho, Iowa, Kentucky, Minnesota, Montana, New Mexico, New York, North Dakota, Vermont, and West Virginia. See Advisory Commission on Intergovernmental Relations, *Tax Overlapping in the United States, 1961* (September 1961), p. 62.

The advantages of federal collection-state sharing of individual income tax are obvious. All questions of conflicting taxation would be eliminated. The different definitions of income, exemptions, deductions, etc., would vanish. Citizens with equal incomes and similar family circumstances would pay the same amount of income tax. Dual administration also would be eliminated, with a marked reduction in administrative costs. Compliance costs, similarly, would shrink because taxpayers would make a single return to a single taxing authority. While no quantitative measure of these advantages is feasible, it must be large. And yet, for reasons indicated above, achievement of the advantage is very unlikely, short of a national emergency or formulation of some scheme of federal-state financial coordination which goes beyond a single tax.

Application to Corporation Income Tax

Credits. The question of credits for state taxes on corporation income against the federal tax on corporation income has not been given serious attention. Thirty years ago Robert Murray Haig declared that "the technical problems" of such a credit had "received practically no consideration or discussion." By way of illustration, he posed a series of questions that needed answers:[25]

> What types of state corporation taxes shall be recognized as offsets against the federal tax? Must they be *net* income taxes? Shall a tax which stresses corporate excess as well as net income, like the Massachusetts tax, or a tax which provides for a flat minimum and a low capital stock tax alternative, like that in New York, be deemed acceptable? What would be the status of a state net income tax with an alternative tax on gross such as has been suggested in New York? What would be done with a state corporation tax purely on gross, and will any distinction be made between a tax on gross which is in lieu of property taxes on the corporation and one which is in addition thereto? Shall property taxes imposed on corporations be accepted for the credit, and if so, how shall property be defined? Shall it include real estate and, if not, how shall real estate be defined? Shall corporate excise taxes which include in their base certain interests or other items which the Federal

[25] "The Coordination of the Federal and State Tax Systems," *National Tax Association, Proceedings of the Twenty-Fifth Annual Conference on Taxation,* September 12-16, 1932, p. 230.

Government is without power to tax be accepted in partial settlement of the federal levy? How shall the problem of variation in practice regarding basic dates for valuation of assets be met? Shall there be a limitation upon the amount eligible for credit from each state and, if so, on what basis shall this allocation be made? What shall be done about the various special types of public utility taxes? How shall the state taxes on banks be treated? Of what significance would the credit be for the state insurance taxes, which are almost exclusively on gross, in view of the virtual collapse of the federal net income tax on such companies?

The Treasury Committee on Intergovernmental Fiscal Relations, reporting in 1943, refused to worry about such issues, declaring that, if a federal credit were to be provided, then a federal definition of acceptable taxes would be made and the states might be left to "adapt their laws to the Federal definition."[26] Implicitly, then, a strict definition would induce a great deal of tax coordination.

What advantages would a corporation income tax credit bring? It would, of course, push all states into taxation of corporation net income (thirty-six states and the District of Columbia now tax it), but this tax, unlike the tax on individual incomes, has no enthusiastic support from any group. Neither is it a tax for which the states, historically or otherwise, have a special claim, nor one they may hope to secure in the future. A credit would open revenues to state governments, but mainly to the richer and more industrialized states. Interstate differentials with respect to the net burden of state corporation taxes are not significant because of deductibility, the great weight of the federal tax compared with state taxes, and the fact that the federal tax is nearly proportional. The need for coordination among the states themselves, especially with respect to jurisdictional claims and allocation of income derived from interstate business, is important; federal resolution of these problems may be required. But a tax credit does not seem to be a necessary or desirable device to this end.

Sharing. Complete federal collection of corporation income tax with distribution of some share to the state governments has been

---

[26] *Federal, State, and Local Government Fiscal Relations* (1943), p. 450.

TABLE 6-2. *Collections of Federal Corporation Income Tax Per Capita, Fiscal Year 1959, by States*[a]

State[b]	Per Capita Collections	State	Per Capita Collections	State	Per Capita Collections
1. Del.	(1) $877.9	18. Md.	(10)[c] $63.5	35. Ore.	(15) $39.0
2. N.Y.	(4) 306.8	19. Wash.	(12) 62.4	36. Idaho	(37) 39.0
3. Ill.	(6) 164.3	20. Okla.	(36) 61.7	37. Tenn.	(43) 35.9
4. Ohio	(11) 136.0	21. Texas	(31) 57.7	38. Ala.	(47) 35.7
5. Mich.	(13) 133.7	22. Kans.	(24) 56.3	39. Mont.	(29) 34.8
6. Conn.	(2) 116.7	23. Nev.	(3) 54.3	40. Ariz.	(28) 32.4
7. Mo.	(18) 109.2	24. Iowa	(30) 53.4	41. W.Va.	(39) 28.3
8. Minn.	(27) 99.8	25. Va.	(34) 52.9	42. Vt.	(35) 27.9
9. Penn.	(14) 97.0	26. Nebr.	(25) 51.8	43. Wyo.	(17) 25.7
10. Mass.	(9) 93.6	27. Ky.	(44) 51.3	44. S.C.	(48) 23.8
11. Wis.	(21) 90.0	28. Ga.	(41) 50.2	45. N.Mex.	(33) 22.2
12. N.J.	(7) 84.9	29. Hawaii	(19) 49.6	46. S.D.	(46) 19.9
13. Calif.	(5) 76.7	30. Utah	(32) 48.7	47. Ark.	(49) 16.6
14. Colo.	(20) 69.2	31. La.	(4) 46.6	48. N.D.	(42) 16.4
15. Ind.	(22) 65.7	32. Fla.	(26) 43.7	49. Alaska	(8) 15.1
16. N.C.	(45) 65.3	33. N.H.	(23) 42.8	50. Miss.	(50) 12.0
17. R.I.	(16) 64.6	34. Me.	(38) 40.7	U.S.	$102.1

[a] Source: *Annual Report of the Secretary of the Treasury on the State of the Finances, Fiscal Year 1959*, p. 436; U.S. Office of Business Economics, *Survey of Current Business*, August 1960, p. 17; U.S. Bureau of the Census, *Statistical Abstract of the United States: 1961*, p. 10.
[b] Figures in parentheses are ranks in terms of per capita personal income for calendar 1959.
[c] Includes District of Columbia.

given only casual attention. The objections to such a move are important. What is to be the basis on which to determine the share for each state? Ecker-Racz and Labovitz have pointed out that federal collections by states reflect where the federal return was filed and the federal tax paid. Usually a single federal return is made at the principal place of business of the company.[27] Therefore the figures of federal collections by states give no accurate report of where income was earned; they overstate the income earned in the states where corporations have their headquarters (see Table 6-2). State governments attempt to tax all corporate income originating within their own borders, and the nonindustrial states, therefore, collect much of their revenue from corporations which make their federal income tax payments elsewhere.

As a result, if state-by-state collections of revenue from corporate income tax are expressed as percentages of federal collections as reported by the Commissioner of Internal Revenue, the per cents are usually high for the nonindustrial states. In Ecker-Racz's calculations, 1953-58, Mississippi has by far the highest per cent (43.8), with Arkansas in second place (with 25.8). On the basis of these figures, a negotiation which sought the substitution of federal collection-state sharing for the present situation would have to concede a generous share to states like Mississippi and Arkansas.[28] Any sharing based on origin of income is sure to favor the richer states; sharing based on other criteria—origin of sales, destination of sales, payrolls, etc.—might be more favorable to the poorer and less industrialized states. But so long as economic criteria of the origin of income are utilized, sharing will be advantageous to the rich states.

Application to Excises

Over the decades one argument for reduction or repeal of certain federal excises has been that state governments could and would pick up those that were relinquished. Recently, however, this expectation has dimmed, and interest has shifted to federal credits,

---

[27] See Ecker-Racz and Labovitz *op. cit.*, pp. 154-156.

[28] *Ibid.*, pp. 155-156.

coupled with a requirement of revenue-maintenance. A strong effort to accomplish this with respect to the tax on local telephone service was made recently by the Joint Federal-State Action Committee. Appointed in 1957 by President Eisenhower with the endorsement of the Governors' Conference, the committee had a membership of nine governors, seven top-ranking federal officials, and the chairman of the executive committee of the Governors' Conference. The failure of this imposing group to secure crediting for the telephone tax is instructive.

Local Telephone Tax. This federal tax is at the rate of 10 per cent. If the federal tax were withdrawn, could the state (and local) governments pick up the tax? Certain compliance problems of a change-over are apparent. The telephone companies would have to prepare records, on the basis of the origin of a phone call (records not necessary for purposes of federal tax), because interstate calls cannot be taxed by the states. And if the federal tax were dropped some states might, for a variety of reasons, be reluctant to enact an equivalent tax. All in all, it is very doubtful that the state and local governments, unassisted, could pick up the revenue lost by the federal government. Yet this is a tax which could be administered by state and local governments, which would yield appreciable revenue in every state, and which would not bring interstate movement.

In 1957 the Joint Federal-State Action Committee recommended that the federal tax on local telephone service "be changed so as to provide a 40 per cent tax credit to those states enacting a 4 per cent local telephone tax, not counting taxes already levied prior to the adoption of the credit device."[29] The credit was, therefore, a device to link federal tax reduction with state-local absorption, and revenue-maintenance was to be a condition of the credit. The federal government, by retaining a portion of the tax, would retain intact techniques of administration and definition to which the state-local governments could tie. The recommendations of the

[29] *Final Report of the Joint Federal-State Action Committee* (February 1960), p. 35. See also James A. Maxwell, "Recent Developments in Federal-State Financial Relations," *National Tax Journal*, Vol. 13 (December 1960), pp. 310-319.

committee fell on deaf ears; Congress gave them no attention. But they are important because of explicit recognition of conditions to be associated with the credit device.

Why was the Congress uninterested? Chiefly because the Action Committee coupled to the credit federal withdrawal of two small federal grant programs—vocational education and construction of waste treatment facilities. This coupling not only offended supporters of the grants, but also posed an insoluble problem of establishing an equivalence, state by state, between the gain from the credit and the loss from the grants. While the allocation of the grants by states was somewhat erratic, low-income states usually received more per capita than high-income states did. Telephone tax collections, on the other hand, varied directly with state per capita income. In fiscal 1958 the per capita collection was $0.95 in Mississippi—the lowest state—and $3.48 in New York—the highest. The credit, therefore, was 3.7 times as much per capita for New York as for Mississippi. The per capita grants for Mississippi were, however, three times greater than those for New York.

The Action Committee, in response to criticism, dropped the credit to 30 per cent, coupling this move with recommendation of a new grant to the states. The new grant, which in the aggregate amounted to 1 per cent of the collections from the telephone tax, was to go to the thirty-seven states not appropriately compensated through the credit for the loss of the two federal grants.[30] The proposed new grant had three features which were unique: (1) it was to be unconditional, i.e., no specification was made concerning use; (2) its basis and amount rested upon no logic except to bridge a gap between the value of a credit and of relinquished grants; (3) it was to be given only to thirty-seven of the forty-eight states.

[30] The formulation was not simple. Briefly, it meant that eleven states would secure only the 30 per cent credit, because it would exceed the loss of grants by more than 40 per cent. For six states and the District of Columbia the credit would provide a revenue in excess of the grants, but less than 40 per cent in excess. Accordingly, the amounts of their new grants were to be enough, when added to the credit, to bring their receipts to 140 per cent of the amount of the old grants which were to be relinquished. For thirty-one states the credit would provide a revenue less than the old grants. They were to receive new grants large enough to bring their receipts up to 140 per cent of the amount of the old grants.

Admissions Tax. While this tax seemed suitable for state-local administration, in case of repeal of the federal tax, in 1950 the American Municipal Association suggested crediting as an intermediate step.[31] But interest in the tax has fallen in recent years because of a sharp decline in revenue as a result of shrinking attendance and enlarged exemptions.

Tobacco Taxes. Federal tobacco excises produced $2 billion in fiscal 1961, with over 90 per cent coming from cigarettes. All but three states have cigarette taxes, and a few tax other tobacco products. (A few localities have tobacco taxes.) In 1961 the state governments secured $986 million from taxes on tobacco products, over 5 per cent of their tax revenue. For thirty years methods of tax coordination have been discussed, most attention being given to tax sharing. In 1943 the Treasury Committee on Intergovernmental Fiscal Relations recommended an increase of 2 cents per standard package in the federal tax, with distribution of the proceeds to the states according to population, urban population being weighted at 150 per cent, conditional upon state withdrawal from the tax.[32] Crediting received little attention because the administrative procedures of the federal Treasury differ markedly from those of the state (and local) governments.

The Treasury collects tobacco taxes from a small number of manufacturers, whereas the states must collect from wholesalers within their jurisdiction, and, in the case of retailers' out-of-state purchases, from retailers. Organized and unorganized evasion is combatted by costly techniques. Since 1949 the federal government, through the Department of Justice rather than the Treasury, has assisted effectively by penalizing sale of cigarettes, interstate, to other than licensed distributors. No doubt can exist that state (and local) collection remains costly and relatively inefficient.

Federal collection of cigarette tax for the states, or a federal credit, would require a uniform state-tax rate, and this would cause

---

[31] U. S. Treasury Department, *Federal-State-Local Tax Coordination* (1952), p. 76.

[32] *Federal, State, and Local Government Fiscal Relations* (1943), pp. 506-508.

difficulty. As the tabulation below of state cigarette excises (September 1, 1961) shows, differences in the rates are appreciable, indicating differences in willingness to utilize this source of revenue.[33]

Rate for Standard Package	Number of States
2 cents	2
2½ "	1
3 "	5
3½ "	1
4 "	7
5 "	9
6 "	12
7 "	6
8 "	5
	48

In 1961, Oregon, North Carolina, and Colorado had no state tax on tobacco products; at the other extreme were Alaska, Louisiana, Montana, New Mexico, and Texas with 8-cent rates. A federal collection and distribution at the level of 5 cents per package, which would bring a large increase in revenue to the three states without tax, would bring a decrease to the five states in the 8-cent group (assuming withdrawal were required). This same situation indicates also that mere reduction of the federal tax would not likely bring state pick-up.[34]

Liquor Taxes. When, after 1933, the federal government and the states made a fresh start at taxation of liquor, efforts to secure co-ordination through tax sharing fell to the ground. At the time it seemed that a golden opportunity, seldom offered in the field of taxation, had been missed; but in retrospect the outcome seems explicable, even inevitable. Taxation and regulation of this busi-

[33] See Advisory Commission, *Tax Overlapping in the United States, 1961*, p. 92. The District of Columbia is included.

[34] This has been pointed out by Ecker-Racz and Labovitz, *op. cit.*, p. 173.

To meet the difficulty, the suggestion has at various times been made that state taxes be collected from manufacturers, thereby enabling states to set their own level of rate.

ness appear inseparable, and passage of the Twenty-First Amendment envisaged state, rather than national, regulation. By the amendment, transportation and importation of liquor into any *state*, "in violation of the laws thereof," was prohibited. The hope of tax coordination was, therefore, an illusion in view of the immiscible attitudes of segments of the nation.

Yet the hodgepodge of taxation which emerged, if not surprising, is certainly confusing, and only the broad results will be presented here. Federal tax revenue has overtopped state and local nearly five to one. In fiscal 1960 federal taxes on alcoholic beverages yielded $3,106 million, compared to a state-local yield of $671 million ($649 million state; $22 million local). But sixteen states secured most of their revenue by the liquor monopoly system, of which the net yield in 1960 was $237 million. Federal tax rates, both on distilled liquor and on beer, are three or four times higher than state rates.[35] The diversity of the yield by states from taxes and licenses is great: in 1957 $1.84 and $2.53 per capita in Mississippi and Kansas; $6.20 and $6.07 per capita in Massachusetts and North Dakota. This diversity, together with the heterogeneity of attitude, make sharing appear to be an unpromising device. Crediting is equally so, since federal collection is at the producer level, while state is at the wholesale and retail levels. Cooperation among state administrators and with federal officials is well developed and has brought good results. Proposals for centralizing state collection of liquor taxes at the manufacturer level have been considered, but nothing has been worked out.

Motor Fuel. Until 1956 the gasoline tax seemed one of the most likely candidates for some scheme of sharing, crediting, or even federal withdrawal. The states administered the tax with fair success, and all of them used it—albeit at different rates. The Federal-Aid Highway Act of 1956 shelved such plans—at least for some years ahead—by reserving all federal collections of gasoline tax for a highway trust fund and by initiating an expanded program of highway construction.

[35] See *The Federal Revenue System: Facts and Problems, 1961*, Staff Report for the Joint Economic Committee, 87th Congress, 1st session (1961), pp. 133, 288.

Retail Excises. The federal government levies excises on luggage, jewelry, furs, and toilet preparations at the retail level, and a miscellany of excises at the manufacturers' level. The amounts of revenue of the retail excises are too small to warrant a crediting plan. The excise on jewelry is the most important in yield—$165.7 million in fiscal 1960; the collections per capita by states range widely, being five times greater in New York than in Mississippi.[36]

Conclusion

When a tax is levied by all, or almost all, the states, use of a federal credit or a supplement seems within reach.[37] Unless this is so, a credit or a supplement will appear as a device to coerce states into use of a tax. A supplement requires, in addition, that all taxing jurisdictions employ the same tax base; a credit does not, although the national benefits from it are reduced when many varieties of the same tax are accepted for crediting. If requirements for crediting are strict—in particular, if a uniform base is a condition —these questions arise: Why not centralize administration completely in federal hands? Why not convert the scheme to a shared tax? The logic of the tax supplement, however, does not point to this outcome because it would allow individual states to designate

[36] The federal government has never had a general sales tax, and therefore crediting of state sales taxes has not received attention. An ingenious plan, never published, for enactment of a federal general sales tax solely to provide state and local revenues, has been suggested by Joseph A. Pechman, although he is not an advocate of it. As a supplement and accompaniment of a 20 per cent credit against federal income tax, the federal government "would enact a 3 per cent retail sales tax, but waive it in all states that levy a [sales] tax of this size or larger." In effect the federal government would give a 100 per cent credit for new state sales taxes. No general revenue-maintenance requirement was to be assumed. The 20 per cent credit against income tax was to force all non-income tax states to enact such a tax to absorb the credit; the 3 per cent federal sales tax with a 100 per cent credit for new sales taxes, similarly, would force all non-sales tax states to enact such a tax. All states would have both taxes; the greatest increases in revenue would accrue to states with neither tax and the least to states with both.

[37] Also, if a tax is not used by *any* of the states, a credit may be more feasible than it would be if the tax were in partial use.

the rates to be charged their residents and, therefore, to determine the annual amounts to be collected for each of them.

None of these devices gives any direction to state (or local) expenditure, and in this they are like an unconditional grant and unlike a conditional one. A conditional grant does give direction to expenditure; it can be, and has been, used to achieve national objectives with respect to selected functions. The price is, of course, federal intervention, and this is indicated when the national interest in specifics is clear. But if, over the nation, opinion concerning the specifics of intervention is discrete, a conditional grant may be neither advisable nor feasible. It is this latter situation which, for decades, has defeated attempts to provide federal grants for primary and secondary education.

While unconditional grants, like credits and supplements and shared taxes, give no assurance of specific expenditure, they are more flexible than any of these with respect to aggregate amount and allocation by states. In Australia and Canada this flexibility is indicated by the fact that unconditional grants have been provided for a limited number of states. This is a feat not yet accomplished by a conditional grant, even when the purpose was primarily to provide financial assistance for well-established activities rather than stimulus for new activities. When grants for education were under consideration in Congress in 1948-49, the original Taft bill (S.472) limited the grants to half the states and adjusted the amounts inversely to *relative* poverty, so that states got more when their per capita income was low. In its progress through the Senate the bill was altered so that some grants were provided for every state, and thereby its inherent logic was impaired.

Why this happened is not obscure. With respect to a *specific* function, every state could show need—absolute need. This was true even of rich states which led all the rest in terms of actual provision of educational services. And yet when all states were cut into a conditional grant program for education, the effect was to hinder adoption of the measure—both because need, except when measured relatively, becomes large and because conditions for the grant become more necessary and more onerous.

An unconditional grant may surmount—or evade—these handicaps of a conditional grant. Measurement of need for all standard governmental functions, lumped together, will be relative.[38] In terms of provision of all such functions of state and local governments, no observer can deny that the accomplishment in poor states is relatively inferior, and this not because of waste or lack of financial effort. Unconditional grants to these states, based on relative financial need, could be modest in amount. And the logic of *relative* financial need might guard against extension of the grants to all states.

[38] See Chapter 1, section on Governmental Expenditure and Effort.

7

Conclusion

> Everyone seems to want a degree of centralization, in
> those activities which are objects of his special interest, far
> larger than a wise economy of centralizing devices could
> possibly grant.
>
> Henry C. Simons
> *Personal Income Taxation**

OVER THE DECADES the philosophy of most Americans has been
that public programs should be executed by state and local governments if possible, by the federal government if necessary. Recently
the disturbed state of the world, together with increasing citizen
awareness of pressing public needs, may have weakened the force
of this conviction. The merits of federalism have been downgraded;
those of centralized government have been elevated.

And yet the belief is reasonable that, short of war, growth in
the complexity and the scope of governmental duties should enhance the merits of federalism. Some governmental decisions must

* Simons, *Personal Income Taxation* (University of Chicago Press, 1938), p. 215.

156

be made at the federal level, but there are many governmental services affecting the diverse daily life of the people about which uniform regulation and administration from a central source would be mischievous as well as impracticable. Centralized decision would be irresponsive to the variety of state and local needs.

The case for federalism—for decentralized decision and administration—rests on more than an appeal to efficiency. This is a dynamic nation; the appropriate way to handle governmental functions does not stay put. In such circumstances, state and local governments provide limited laboratories for experimentation in administration. Even more important is the fact that the state and local governments are bulwarks of democracy. Only where the people of a nation have adequate powers of decision can they develop a public spirit, and the specific knowledge and techniques that give life to free institutions.

A strong belief in federalism should not, however, be regarded as synonymous with an extreme belief in "states' rights." States' rights can be defined so as to have genuine meaning, but this meaning should not be twisted to block adjustments in the relative responsibilities of federal government and state-local government. In the modern world changes must be made, and rigid resistance to change can be injurious to the success of federalism.

IN THE PRECEDING CHAPTERS some of the financial devices of cooperative federalism have been analyzed. Cooperative federalism discards separation of governmental functions and of sources of revenue as irrelevant in the modern United States. Morton Grodzins has argued that, even historically, separation never existed; it was always an irrelevant theory.

> The American federal system has never been a system of separated governmental activities. . . . It is a misjudgment of our history and our present situation to believe that a neat separation of governmental functions could take place without drastic alterations in our society and system of government.[1]

[1] Grodzins, "The Federal System," in *Goals for Americans:* Report of the President's Commission on National Goals (Prentice-Hall, 1960, for the American Assembly), pp. 268, 271.

Even if this historical deduction is disputed, the contention is convincing that now, and in the foreseeable future, cooperative federalism must be our trust. The federal government has, therefore, an essential role to play in helping to finance and coordinate state and local activities.

To accomplish its aims the federal government has available a variety of devices, and it has a modicum of experience with most of them. The device given most intensive analysis in these pages is the tax credit. Experience in its use is, perhaps, more instructive negatively than positively; mistakes to be avoided are more visible than are guide-lines to be followed.

Experience with Tax Credits

The first federal tax credit—that against the federal estate tax for state death tax payments—was aimed inexactly at several objectives, none of them sharply defined and some of them in conflict. The federal government wished to yield a larger slice of death tax revenue to the states, and also to secure some measure of tax coordination. An 80 per cent credit, provided in 1926, did decrease the federal revenues and enable the states to increase their revenues if they picked up the allowable credits. But a sharp rise from $50,000 to $100,000 in the specific exemption of the federal tax meant that many small estates or inheritances which paid a state tax were excluded from the credit. Moreover, Congress attached as a condition to the credit only that a state death tax be levied. The push toward uniformity was, therefore, merely the inducement to each state government to maximize the value of the credit for its taxpayers.

After 1932 the force of even this modest persuasion was impaired when Congress froze the 1926 credit and, at the same time, enacted a supplementary estate tax to increase federal revenues. The relative value of aggregate credits in relation to aggregate federal estate tax liabilities declined from 76 per cent in 1931 to 10 per cent in 1959. The states, under decreasing pressure to accomplish uniformity and under growing pressure to secure more revenue, en-

acted death taxes which varied in type, definitions, rates, and exemptions, so that complexity and structural disorder became serious
problems.

In 1961 the new Advisory Commission on Intergovernmental Relations proposed revision and increase of the credit in an effort to
achieve tax coordination and to provide state governments with
additional revenue. Two conditions would be attached to the
credit: (1) a shift to estate taxes and (2) revenue-maintenance, i.e.,
that each state raise the annual level of its death tax revenue by an
amount equal to the increase in the tax credits secured on federal
returns filed from the state.

The second tax credit for which there is experience is that
against the federal unemployment insurance tax, enacted in 1935.
While the death tax credit was devoid of conditions, this one
carried a substantial set of federal requirements. Beyond doubt the
credit with its conditions secured prompt creation of a system of
unemployment insurance over the nation, and this system, at the
outset, had considerable uniformity in its major provisions. But in
the years since 1935 unforeseen developments have impaired the
equity and efficiency of the system. Instead of a uniform rate of payroll tax, a variety of rates prevails, and the average rate differs
greatly from state to state. The danger of interstate competition,
which had held back state provision of unemployment insurance
before 1935, has reappeared. Other flaws in the present federal-
state scheme have led some to believe that it should be replaced by
a purely federal scheme. However this may be, the tax credit, in
this its most ambitious use, has proved inflexible. Possibly, even
probably, the credit was not the right technique to secure a good
system of national unemployment insurance for the long run.

THE EXPERIENCE SKETCHED ABOVE indicates that in the case of
the death tax the federal government failed to impose enough
conditions to secure national objectives, while in the case of the unemployment insurance tax it imposed conditions which erred in
the opposite direction. How achieve the right combination? The
essential characteristics of the conditions of a credit should be sim-

plicity and flexibility: simplicity in order to avoid detailed and extensive federal supervision; flexibility so that, as federal objectives alter over time, the conditions may be modified.

Proposals for Income Tax Credits

Proposals have recently been advanced that credits against federal individual income tax liability be allowed for state income tax payments. Such a scheme would discriminate against residents of the states without income tax, of which there are presently eighteen. While this discrimination would be removed if these states enacted income taxes, the enactment would stem from federal coercion. One proposal—that of Walter W. Heller—was examined in Chapter 4. A regressively graduated credit is suggested, so that a larger percentage credit would be received for a small than for a large tax liability. Beyond a doubt crediting of this sort has a potential which might promote two broad national objectives: (1) helping state governments to finance their functions, (2) securing tax coordination.

If emphasis is given by Congress to coordination, individuals would be allowed to credit certain state income tax payments against certain of their federal payments, provided the form of the state tax met federal conditions aimed at reducing conflict. States with a creditable tax already in operation could allow their residents to use the credit simply to reduce their federal taxes; these states would not, in this case, secure any additional revenue.

If, on the other hand, emphasis is given to use of the credit to provide all states with additional financial resources, individuals in a state would be allowed credits provided that state tax payments were increased *pari passu* as federal payments were lowered. In this way crediting is coupled with a condition of revenue-maintenance, so that total payments—federal plus state—by individuals in a state are unchanged. Unless revenue-maintenance is required, crediting is merely an indirect means of reducing federal revenue. Its justification, in comparison with overt federal tax reduction, would have to rest on the national advantage secured through tax coordination and use of the creditable tax—for example, the individual income tax—by a larger number of states.

Revenue Maintenance as a Condition

If revenue-maintenance is made a necessary condition of crediting, the question arises: How may the condition be met? Here the *form* of the credit is important. A regressively graduated credit will open relatively more sources of revenue to "poor" states than a credit expressed as a uniform percentage of federal tax-liability. And such a credit opens to state governments the opportunity to raise this new revenue predominantly from low and middle incomes by enacting a scale of regressive rates in order to maximize the value of the credits. The objection that, thereby, the tax systems of state governments are made less progressive than otherwise is unconvincing.

State tax systems have always been regressive, or only modestly progressive, for the simple reason that state governments cannot successfully apply much progression in taxing large incomes or estates. Large incomes (estates) are mobile and almost always national in origin. Only with difficulty can they be equitably segmented for purposes of state taxation. Moreover, taxation of low and middle incomes provides state governments with relatively stable revenues. That a credit—specifically an income tax credit—does not add to over-all progression or provide interstate equalization, as some proponents have supposed it would, seems a minor flaw.

A requirement of revenue-maintenance does not preclude other conditions aimed at tax coordination. The federal government might make specifications concerning the acceptable state tax, and here the Advisory Commission on Intergovernmental Relations has provided a precedent by its recommendation that only estate-type death taxes be eligible for a new and enlarged death tax credit. An individual income tax credit, for example, might specify that the states define income so as to exclude income of nonresidents. Conditions of this sort, once accepted and put into operation, might well lead to a further step in centralization, namely complete federal collection and administration of the tax in question, each of the states having the right to designate the rate-supplements which it wished to be collected from its residents. The nation, in this case, would have eliminated the tax conflict and waste of resources which now occur through multiple administration and compliance costs.

In Appendix B, Table 1, estimates are offered of the maximum income tax credits which would, under certain assumptions, have accrued to the individual states in 1958. While the estimates are rough, a significant improvement in accuracy could be secured only by a more elaborate compilation of *Statistics of Income, 1958: Individual Income Tax Returns,* state by state. The estimates show that even the Heller-type credit would not be effective in strengthening the relative revenue sources of the poor states.

The potential merits of crediting as a device of tax coordination and financial aid should not obscure recognition of the dangers disclosed by the two instances of actual use, especially the danger of inflexibility. The states were pushed by the credits into patterns subject to change only by desuetude. In the case of the death tax credit, Congress reneged within seven years on the objectives it espoused at the time the credit was provided; in the case of the unemployment insurance credit, Congress allowed its objectives to molder because of the difficulties of revision of the original scheme. Even if Congress has clear objectives when it provides a credit, these are bound to require redefinition over time, and provision for redefinition should be written into the original scheme. Indeed, an inherent and built-in defect of intergovernmental financial arrangements is their insusceptibility to easy modification. The reason is obvious—that they *are* intergovernmental.

Yet the defect can, perhaps, be abated, if not banished. Congress should indicate its objectives when it enacts a device, not by a vague preamble, but by a specific and precise declaration. Congress should assume the responsibility, through its committee structure, of securing annual reports on the operation of a device. Congress ought, probably, to set a time-span on a device, so that re-enactment or termination will be necessary. It may be also that representatives of state and local governments should, somehow, be tied into the annual reporting and review through a body such as the Advisory Commission on Intergovernmental Relations.[2]

Credits as a Substitute for Deductibility

Crediting of state income taxes against the federal tax has been suggested as a substitute for the long-established right of individuals to deduct payments of state and local personal taxes from adjusted gross income. The desire to abolish deductibility arises (1) because of its untidy rationale—indeed, the lack of any rationale for deductibility of benefit taxes; (2) because deductibility of certain other taxes, notably property taxes and excises, is discriminatory against classes of people, e.g. renters of residential property, and nonsmokers; and (3) because the higher the income of a taxpayer, the larger the reduction in federal tax through deductibility.

Some of these objections are unconvincing. Though the case is clear for abolition of deductibility of taxes which are, in effect, specific user charges, a similar step with respect to general taxes (on property, income, consumption) is not. The discrimination against renters of residential property, associated with deductibility of property taxes on owner-occupied dwellings, could be removed by taxing imputed rent as income; it is not an inherent fault of deductibility. The objection that deductibility is more valuable to people with high incomes than to those with low incomes assumes implicitly that the scale of progression of the federal tax is determined without reference to the deductions allowed from income by Congress. The opposite assumption is more plausible: that Congress determines the rates only after adjusted gross income has been refined by subtraction of deductible taxes. In a federalism the national government should exercise discretion in utilizing sources of revenue, bearing in mind that state and local governments provide essential services, financed by taxes which reduce individual in-

---

[2] My own view is that Congress is responsive to the opinions of state and local governments when these secure expression through recognized and responsible channels. When federal legislation has overlooked legitimate state and local interests, the reason has been congressional ignorance of what these interests are.

comes. Tax deductions stand for *governmental* outlays which, as much as federal expenditures, go for public purposes.

Some critics have exaggerated the advantages that deductibility brings to the rich states. They forget that aggregate state and local taxes are regressive. As a result, these taxes are advantageous as deductions to residents of states with regressive taxes. The critics forget also that deductibility now provides some indirect subsidy to local governments, while crediting, most probably, would subsidize only state governments. In Appendix C, Table 1, state-by-state estimates of the amounts of taxes eligible as deductions in 1957 are offered. The method used is to refine figures of state and local tax collections so as to secure figures of personal or nonbusiness taxes. Comparisons are made also of amounts of deductible taxes with taxes actually deducted. The quantitative results strengthen the belief that "poor" states would be losers from substitution even of the Heller-type credit for deductibility.

The case for the substitution of crediting for deductibility must rest on the proposition that crediting, as a new broom, would sweep away a few of the anachronistic advantages to the individual taxpayer which are now embedded in deductibility. More important, it would stimulate steps toward tax coordination and orderly intergovernmental finance and, if coupled with revenue-maintenance, provide all state governments with additional revenues. These advantages might, perhaps, be gained with less resistance, especially from states without income tax, if crediting against federal income tax were permitted for payments of state general sales tax, as well as for payments of state income tax.

Other Devices: Grants and Tax Sharing

Tax credits, coupled with revenue-maintenance, are not geographically equalizing; they bring no interstate transfer of resources. Geographical equalization has never been an explicit federal objective, although it has often been an incidental result. Indeed, both the federal tax system and the federal expenditure program are equalizing.

Conditional Grants

Of all federal-state financial devices, conditional grants display what appear, at first sight, to be equalizing objectives, since the formulas for allocation of federal money assign more to poor than to rich states. But here also equalization is an incidental result. The explicit and important congressional objective is to accelerate accomplishment of some specific program by the poor states. Moreover, even in these grant programs, the progressive federal tax system which collects the amounts to be distributed as grants accomplishes more equalization than the grant formulas do.

When a grant program is specific—when it is for a defined activity —Congress has always provided for receipt of grants by all states, rich and poor. One reason is that "need" for a specific service is measured by absolute standards, and therefore all states, in this sense, will show "need." New York, a rich state, will have educational needs, even though its actual provision per pupil enrolled will greatly exceed average provision. Of course, if the grant program is designed to stimulate expenditure in *all* states, grants for *all* states are indicated. But if the aim is simply to ensure provision of a foundation or minimum-level program in all states, then grants for all states are wasteful. Such grants should be limited to those states which cannot, by a reasonable effort, be expected to provide this level through their own finances.[3]

Specific or conditional grants by definition carry some federal requirements in order that federal objectives be promoted. The requirements can be, and have been, tight or loose, broad or limited in range. If there is a national consensus concerning the objectives of a grant, Congress is likely to frame conditions with little trouble; if, however, national opinion is diverse, agreement over conditions will be hard to secure. A conditional grant program affects state-local decisions concerning expenditures, and

[3] Stimulative programs may be economic and developmental in objective, or they may be welfare-oriented. In the latter case an equalization formula is indicated; in the former it is not. For example, in allocating federal grants to the states for construction of interstate highways, the relevant criteria should be economic.

federal "interference" will be charged if established patterns are disturbed.

A tax credit with broad requirements is less likely to raise objection so long as the states are prepared to utilize the creditable tax. A credit gives no federal direction concerning how the state revenues are to be used. Nonetheless, a credit may be a step toward centralization since, if the states conform a tax to federal specifications, complete federal administration will seem to be a natural sequence with the states entitled to decide simply on the rate or rates which they wish to be levied as supplements to the federal tax.

Unconditional Grants

When a grant program is unconditional, the logical rationale for it is limited equalization; the formula should rest on the twin concepts of a standard effort and a minimum level of provision of a representative group of governmental services. Such an equalization formula is self-limiting and the program associated with it will be modest in scope, since "need" is measured relatively—by comparison with the actual provision of the services in all the states. The federal objective is to enable the poor states to achieve this level by grants which bridge the gap between it and what they can provide by their own efforts. The most obvious objection to such a formula is that the self-limiting feature will be broken by "political" pressures. About this, the experience of two other federal countries is contradictory: in Australia the claimant ("poor") states, in receipt of equalizing grants, have not demanded or received "political" grants; in Canada the claimant provinces strive to be "equalized to the top," and the actual grant decisions have often been political.

Tax Sharing

Still another device is tax sharing, which would require complete federal administration of a tax with the states entitled to a share of collections on some uniform basis. The device is, therefore, centralizing in its connotations; besides, agreement on a formula for sharing would be very difficult to secure. If the formula allocated the proceeds of, for example, individual income tax according to origin of the income or the domicile of the taxpayer, the richer states would get the lion's share. On the other hand, any basis of allocation resting on state need would break the linkage between the source of the income and the receipt of the distribution. Moreover, any plan for sharing would face a problem arising out of unequal present use of income tax by the states. Oregon in 1958 collected an amount equal to 28.7 per cent of federal collections in the state. If this performance were to set the standard for a scheme —and uniform sharing would seem necessary—the federal government would find the scheme expensive. Similar problems would arise in federal collection-state sharing of any tax.

PHILOSOPHERS HAVE OBSERVED that life is richer than logic, and, by an obvious parallel, the armory of devices examined here defies simple and categorical appraisal. Intergovernmental financial cooperation can be advanced by many devices, and, so long as illogic is avoided in their construction, the devices should be appraised in the light of the objectives which the Congress has in mind. Tax credits, for instance, can be utilized to advance tax coordination and to provide financial resources for state governments, and only by misuse might they be framed so as to aggravate tax conflict or so as to be dissipated in tax reduction. But tax credits do not provide for equalization, and they tend to be inflexible. If equalization is to be emphasized, the appropriate device is the unconditional grant; if stimulus to specific governmental functions, the conditional grant. Since federal objectives in assisting state and local governments are manifold, there is no inconsistency in logical use of several devices.

Appendixes

Appendix A

Tables

TABLE A-1. *State-Local Expenditure Per Capita for General Government, and General Revenue from Own Sources per $1,000 of Personal Income, 1957*[a]

State	Per Capita General Expenditure (1)	Expendi- ture Relative (2)	General Revenue per $1,000 of Income[b] (3)	Effort Relative (4)	Adjusted Effort Relative (5)
1. Nevada	$367.07	155	$120.04	121	78
2. Wyoming	328.21	138	126.18	127	92
3. Connecticut	322.96	136	82.81	83	61
4. California	322.26	136	111.18	112	82
5. New York	298.42	126	105.56	106	84
6. Washington	292.70	123	110.99	112	91
7. Massachusetts	291.34	123	99.52	100	81
8. Montana	282.21	119	120.59	121	102
9. Colorado	280.50	118	115.27	116	98
10. New Mexico	278.64	118	133.51	134	114
11. Louisiana	275.94	116	141.05	142	122
12. Arizona	272.86	115	115.30	116	101

[a] Source: Column 1, U. S. Bureau of the Census, *1957 Census of Governments*, Vol. 3, No. 5, p. 46. Column 2, calculated from column 1 divided by average, times 100. Column 3, *1957 Census of Governments*, Vol. 3, No. 5, p. 61. Column 4, calculated from column 3 divided by average, times 100. Column 5, calculated from column 4 divided by column 2, times 100.

[b] Revenue in fiscal 1957, personal income in 1957.

State	Per Capita General Expenditure (1)	Expenditure Relative (2)	General Revenue per $1,000 of Income[b] (3)	Effort Relative (4)	Adjusted Effort Relative (5)
13. Oregon..........	$271.41	114	$122.96	124	109
14. Kansas..........	270.82	114	114.28	115	101
15. Michigan........	262.43	111	99.74	100	90
16. Minnesota.......	260.64	110	119.11	120	109
17. North Dakota....	257.82	109	158.57	160	147
18. Oklahoma........	247.90	105	117.67	118	112
19. Vermont.........	245.66	104	116.23	117	113
20. South Dakota....	244.41	103	129.37	130	126
21. Maryland........	243.43	103	88.28	89	86
22. Delaware........	242.02	102	67.96	68	67
23. Wisconsin........	239.18	101	110.34	111	110
24. New Hampshire..	238.68	101	95.65	96	95
25. New Jersey......	237.00	100	82.10	83	83
26. Florida..........	234.58	99	110.50	111	112
27. Iowa............	234.36	99	113.12	114	115
28. Idaho...........	232.77	98	118.59	119	121
29. Utah............	232.73	98	113.36	114	116
30. Illinois...........	225.60	95	83.08	84	88
31. Ohio............	222.29	94	81.97	82	87
32. Rhode Island.....	209.61	88	84.34	85	97
33. Indiana..........	206.22	87	84.64	85	98
34. Texas............	204.85	86	97.61	98	114
35. Maine...........	203.37	86	102.36	103	120
36. Nebraska........	202.13	85	93.27	94	111
37. Pennsylvania.....	196.57	83	87.07	88	106
38. Missouri.........	191.48	81	77.71	78	96
39. Georgia..........	187.18	79	107.92	109	138
40. Virginia..........	179.54	76	95.55	96	126
41. Alabama.........	177.75	75	98.18	99	132
42. North Carolina...	161.66	68	102.40	103	151
43. Tennessee........	160.71	68	100.89	101	149
44. West Virginia....	155.29	66	84.17	85	129
45. Kentucky........	153.37	65	94.00	95	146
46. South Carolina...	153.14	65	109.41	110	169
47. Mississippi.......	151.64	64	137.26	138	216
48. Arkansas........	148.03	62	107.08	108	174
United States[c]..	$237.09	100	$ 99.40	100	100

[c] Excludes Alaska, Hawaii, and other territories.

TABLE A-2. *State-Local General Expenditure for Local Schools per Pupil Enrolled, and General Expenditure for Local Schools, Less Federal Grants, per $1,000 of Personal Income, 1957*[a]

State	Per Pupil School Expenditure (1)	Expenditure Relative (2)	Net School Expenditure per $1,000 of Income[b] (3)	Effort Relative (4)	Adjusted Effort Relative (5)
1. New York........	$558.80	150	$32.98	97	65
2. Delaware.........	489.60	131	27.25	80	61
3. California.........	474.10	127	37.91	112	88
4. Connecticut.......	458.10	123	28.60	84	68
5. New Jersey.......	455.70	122	28.69	85	70
6. Minnesota........	439.10	118	43.43	128	108
7. Illinois...........	435.10	117	27.66	82	70
8. Wyoming.........	429.90	115	45.77	135	117
9. Washington.......	427.70	115	40.17	118	103
10. Oregon...........	427.20	115	42.86	126	110
11. Arizona...........	419.60	113	46.94	138	122
12. Michigan.........	414.20	111	36.33	107	96
13. Massachusetts.....	409.70	110	27.78	82	75
14. Montana.........	404.00	108	41.22	121	112
15. Wisconsin.........	401.30	108	33.22	98	91
16. Ohio.............	392.90	105	31.34	92	88
17. Nevada...........	378.60	102	29.27	86	84
18. Pennsylvania......	378.30	102	29.60	87	85
19. Colorado.........	377.20	101	36.58	108	107
20. Maryland.........	377.10	101	30.59	90	89
21. Kansas...........	373.50	100	39.21	116	116
22. Texas............	359.40	96	38.12	112	117

[a] Source: Column 1, U. S. Bureau of the Census, *1957 Census of Governments*, Vol. 3, No. 5, p. 41, for figures of general expenditure for local schools. From these, federal grants for "school construction and surveys" and for "maintenance and operation of schools" are deducted; see *Annual Report of the Secretary of the Treasury, 1957*, pp. 580–581. For enrollment figures, see *1957 Census of Governments*, Vol. 3, No. 5, p. 65. Column 2, calculated from column 1 divided by average, times 100. Column 3, *ibid.*, Vol. 3, No. 5, p. 61, for figures of school expenditure per $1,000 of personal income. Federal grants are deducted as follows: (a) calculate grants as per cents of school expenditure, (b) multiply school expenditure per $1,000 of personal income by these per cents, (c) subtract these figures from the figures of school expenditure per $1,000 of personal income. Column 4, calculated from column 3 divided by average, times 100. Column 5, calculated from column 4 divided by column 2, times 100.

[b] Expenditure in fiscal 1957, personal income in calendar 1957.

State	Per Pupil School Expenditure	Expenditure Relative	Net School Expenditure per $1,000 of Income[b]	Effort Relative	Adjusted Effort Relative
	(1)	(2)	(3)	(4)	(5)
23. Iowa.............	$358.20	96	$39.33	116	121
24. Missouri..........	352.40	95	29.77	88	93
25. Rhode Island......	349.80	94	24.03	71	76
26. New Hampshire...	349.60	94	29.94	88	94
27. New Mexico......	349.20	94	44.73	132	140
28. Indiana...........	348.70	94	32.59	96	102
29. Louisiana.........	337.00	90	42.65	126	140
30. Florida...........	332.50	89	32.15	95	107
31. Utah.............	328.50	88	45.36	134	152
32. Nebraska.........	326.00	88	32.56	96	109
33. Vermont..........	315.20	85	36.66	108	127
34. South Dakota.....	313.60	84	40.76	120	143
35. North Dakota.....	312.60	84	42.68	126	150
36. Oklahoma.........	295.40	79	39.31	116	147
37. Idaho............	294.60	79	40.20	118	149
38. Georgia...........	251.60	68	39.85	117	172
39. Maine............	249.80	67	29.15	86	128
40. South Carolina....	243.30	65	47.64	140	215
41. Virginia...........	242.40	65	28.88	85	131
42. Kentucky.........	239.00	64	33.79	100	156
43. North Carolina....	239.00	64	41.01	121	189
44. West Virginia.....	223.90	60	32.68	96	160
45. Tennessee.........	223.40	60	34.47	102	170
46. Alabama..........	196.10	53	33.52	99	187
47. Arkansas.........	178.90	48	34.10	101	210
48. Mississippi........	170.90	46	41.01	121	263
United States[c]...	$372.50	100	$33.93	100	100

[c] Excludes Alaska, Hawaii, and other territories.

TABLE A-3. *Present and Proposed Estate Tax Credits by States in Relation to Per Capita Personal Income, 1959*[a]

State	Per Capita Personal Income (dollars) (1)	Credit Under Present Law (millions) (2)	Credit Under Alternative No. 4[b] (millions) (3)	Personal Income (millions) (4)	Present Credit as Per Cent of Personal Income (5)	Alternative Credit as Per Cent of Personal Income (6)
1. Delaware........	$2,946	$ .4	$ 2.1	$ 1,314	.03%	.16%
2. Dist. of Col.	2,943	1.0	5.8	2,210	.05	.26
3. Connecticut.....	2,817	7.0	21.0	6,904	.10	.30
4. Nevada.........	2,745	c	.7	752	d	.09
5. New York......	2,736	25.8	99.8	45,103	.06	.22
6. California.......	2,661	16.0	79.6	40,783	.04	.20
7. Illinois.........	2,610	8.7	46.4	25,734	.03	.18
8. New Jersey.....	2,608	6.2	28.0	15,429	.04	.18
9. Alaska.........	2,550	c	c	556	d	.01
10. Massachusetts...	2,444	5.2	25.2	12,380	.04	.20
11. Maryland.......	2,343	1.8	10.5	7,108	.03	.15
12. Ohio..........	2,328	6.8	32.1	21,979	.03	.15
13. Washington.....	2,271	1.4	9.6	6,363	.02	.15
14. Michigan.......	2,253	9.4	23.8	17,493	.05	.14
15. Pennsylvania....	2,222	8.2	42.6	24,732	.03	.17
16. Oregon........	2,171	.4	3.8	3,842	.01	.10
17. Rhode Island....	2,156	1.5	5.4	1,837	.08	.30
18. Wyoming.......	2,149	.2	1.0	707	.02	.13
19. Missouri........	2,145	2.1	13.5	9,248	.02	.15
20. Hawaii.........	2,139	.2	1.2	1,290	.02	.10
21. Colorado........	2,123	1.1	5.8	3,737	.03	.15
22. Wisconsin.......	2,116	1.4	10.3	8,258	.02	.12
23. Indiana.........	2,102	1.5	10.4	9,712	.02	.11
24. New Hampshire.	2,010	.2	2.7	1,200	.02	.23

[a] Source: Columns 1 and 4, U. S. Office of Business Economics, *Survey of Current Business* (August 1960), p. 17. Columns 2 and 3, Advisory Commission on Intergovernmental Relations, *Coordination of State and Federal Inheritance, Estate, and Gift Taxes* (January 1961), p. 68. Column 5, calculated from column 2 divided by column 4. Column 6, calculated from column 3 divided by column 4.

[b] 80 per cent of the gross federal tax liability on the first $250,000 of taxable estates, and 20 per cent on the balance.

[c] Less than $50,000.

[d] Less than 0.005 per cent.

State	Per Capita Personal Income (dollars) (1)	Credit Under Present Law (millions) (2)	Credit Under Alternative No. 4[b] (millions) (3)	Personal Income (millions) (4)	Present Credit as Per Cent of Personal Income (5)	Alternative Credit as Per Cent of Personal Income (6)
25. Kansas.........	$1,994	$ 1.9	$ 8.5	$ 4,238	.04%	.20%
26. Nebraska.......	1,981	.6	5.4	2,797	.02	.19
27. Florida.........	1,980	3.5	19.9	9,273	.04	.21
28. Minnesota......	1,962	2.7	9.9	6,660	.04	.15
29. Arizona........	1,959	.4	3.1	2,388	.02	.13
30. Montana........	1,955	.3	2.1	1,318	.02	.16
31. Iowa...........	1,953	.7	8.2	5,398	.01	.15
32. Texas..........	1,908	5.4	29.6	18,041	.03	.16
33. Utah...........	1,848	.6	1.9	1,626	.03	.12
34. New Mexico....	1,833	.2	1.6	1,681	.01	.09
35. Virginia........	1,816	.8	8.2	7,058	.01	.12
36. Vermont........	1,789	.2	1.0	694	.03	.14
37. Oklahoma.......	1,786	.9	5.4	4,138	.02	.13
38. Idaho...........	1,782	.1	1.4	1,187	.01	.11
39. Maine..........	1,768	.5	3.5	1,713	.03	.21
40. West Virginia....	1,635	.5	3.1	3,053	.02	.10
41. Louisiana.......	1,575	.9	7.2	5,169	.02	.14
42. Georgia.........	1,553	.7	6.1	6,081	.01	.10
43. North Dakota...	1,526	c	.7	972	d	.07
44. Tennessee.......	1,521	.6	5.5	5,362	.01	.10
45. Kentucky.......	1,514	.7	5.2	4,548	.01	.11
46. North Carolina..	1,485	1.3	7.6	6,771	.02	.11
47. South Dakota...	1,476	c	.9	1,020	d	.08
48. Alabama........	1,409	.5	3.9	4,607	.01	.09
49. South Carolina..	1,332	.3	2.8	3,148	.01	.09
50. Arkansas........	1,322	.2	2.0	2,370	.01	.08
51. Mississippi......	1,162	.2	2.1	2,528	.01	.08

State	1946–52		1953–59	
	Contribution Rate	Benefit Cost Rate	Contribution Rate	Benefit Cost Rate
Alabama....................	1.32%	1.41%	1.24%	1.50%
Alaska.....................	1.96	1.90	3.06	4.77
Arizona....................	1.56	.74	1.33	.98
Arkansas...................	1.47	1.20	1.23	1.51
California..................	2.10	2.31	1.50	1.55
Colorado...................	1.14	.40	.56	.76
Connecticut................	1.30	1.26	1.30	1.84
Delaware...................	.64	.64	.75	1.19
Dist. of Col................	.61	.53	.65	.76
Florida....................	1.09	.85	.80	.81
Georgia....................	1.25	.81	1.26	1.32
Hawaii.....................	1.06	.95	.98	1.18
Idaho......................	1.95	.91	1.56	1.99
Illinois....................	.97	1.18	.92	1.42
Indiana....................	.79	.74	1.00	1.41
Iowa.......................	1.11	.51	.63	.77
Kansas.....................	1.17	.92	1.09	1.25
Kentucky...................	1.74	1.14	1.93	2.64
Louisiana..................	1.64	1.35	1.24	1.32
Maine......................	1.70	1.75	1.59	2.09
Maryland...................	1.08	1.32	1.04	1.69
Massachusetts..............	1.66	1.96	1.90	1.81
Michigan...................	1.55	1.31	1.71	2.65
Minnesota..................	1.03	.79	.92	1.53
Mississippi.................	1.79	1.23	1.41	1.88
Missouri...................	1.22	.98	.84	1.18
Montana...................	1.94	.89	1.28	2.05
Nebraska...................	.87	.52	.78	.99
Nevada....................	1.73	1.35	1.96	1.98
New Hampshire.............	1.61	1.82	1.69	1.81
New Jersey.................	1.96	1.89	1.97	2.67
New Mexico................	1.75	.48	1.21	1.03

[a] Source: Derived from Committee on Benefit Financing, Interstate Conference of Employment Security Agencies, *Your Financial Responsibility* (September 1960).

State	1946–52		1953–59	
	Contribu-tion Rate	Benefit Cost Rate	Contribu-tion Rate	Benefit Cost Rate
New York...................	2.12%	2.08%	1.76%	2.15%
North Carolina...............	1.51	.95	1.39	1.63
North Dakota................	1.56	.86	1.50	1.90
Ohio.......................	.98	.84	.86	1.55
Oklahoma..................	1.09	1.15	.94	1.26
Oregon.....................	1.56	1.72	1.63	2.31
Pennsylvania................	.98	1.27	1.72	2.67
Rhode Island................	2.33	3.07	2.70	2.71
South Carolina...............	1.33	.94	1.24	1.30
South Dakota................	1.06	.46	.88	.86
Tennessee...................	1.53	1.47	1.63	2.09
Texas......................	.78	.36	.54	.73
Utah.......................	1.46	1.27	1.20	1.30
Vermont....................	1.54	1.39	1.21	1.60
Virginia....................	.91	.70	.62	.85
Washington..................	2.24	2.19	2.17	2.32
West Virginia...............	1.27	1.16	1.18	2.28
Wisconsin...................	.79	.55	1.04	1.48
Wyoming...................	1.20	.56	1.06	1.48

TABLE A-5. *Tax Deductions on Itemized Returns, Taxable and Non-taxable, and Estimated Tax Deductibility on Standard Deductions Returns, 1958*[a]

(in millions)

AGI Class	Returns with Itemized Deductions			Returns with Standard Deductions	Total
	Taxable (1)	Non-taxable (2)	Total[b] (3)	(4)	
Under $600	$ —	$ 4	$ 4	$259	$ 263
$600 under $1,000	3	15	18	117	135
$1,000 under $1,500	17	33	51	200	251
$1,500 under $2,000	39	39	78	188	266
$2,000 under $2,500	74	48	122	205	327
$2,500 under $3,000	105	47	152	216	368
$3,000 under $3,500	160	45	205	238	443
$3,500 under $4,000	224	38	262	245	507
$4,000 under $4,500	288	33	321	253	574
$4,500 under $5,000	369	28	397	260	657
$5,000 under $6,000	906	36	942	453	1,395
$6,000 under $7,000	862	9	871	346	1,217
$7,000 under $8,000	688	7	695	276	971
$8,000 under $9,000	528	1	530	204	734
$9,000 under $10,000	377	1	378	155	533
$10,000 under $15,000	896	4	900	384[d]	1,284[d]
$15,000 under $20,000	364	2	366		366
$20,000 under $25,000	232	1	232		232
$25,000 under $50,000	510	2	512		512
$50,000 under $100,000	263	1	264		264
$100,000 under $150,000	69	c	70		70
$150,000 under $200,000	29	1	30		30
$200,000 under $500,000	48	2	50		50
$500,000 under $1,000,000	14	c	14		14
$1,000,000 or more	17	1	18		18

[a] Source: Columns 1, 2, and 3, U. S. Internal Revenue Service, *Statistics of Income, 1958: Individual Income Tax Returns.* Column 4, see Table 5-6, in Chapter 5.
[b] Due to rounding, detail will not necessarily add to these totals.
[c] Less than $50,000.
[d] Includes estimated tax deductibility on all standard deduction returns with AGI of $10,000 or more.

Appendix B

Method of Estimating the Heller-Type Credits for State Income Taxes[1]

QUANTITATIVE INVESTIGATION of credits by states is hindered and impaired by the paucity of state-by-state figures in Internal Revenue Service, *Statistics of Income: Individual Income Tax Returns*. In the issue for 1958 returns, one finds in Table 16 (pp. 67-70) state-by-state figures given for the number of returns (taxable plus nontaxable), adjusted gross income, and income tax after credits—all of these for only twenty AGI classes, rather than the twenty-five classes used to show national figures.

In 1959, Walter W. Heller calculated tax credits, using only information available in Table 16 of the *Statistics of Income, 1956*.[2] This simple calculation rested on AGI, with no account taken of taxable vs. nontaxable returns, of the different types of taxpayers (single, joint returns, etc.), or of the number of dependents.

On a national basis, refinements to take account of these factors can be made. The first step of the calculation is to treat the nation as one large state, using the twenty AGI classes of Table 16, *Sta-*

[1] The method described here was suggested by Joseph A. Pechman.
[2] See Heller, "Deductions and Credits for State Income Taxes," *Tax Revision Compendium*, Submitted to the House Committee on Ways and Means (1959), Vol. 1, p. 426.

tistics of Income, 1958. This will be called Step 1. An illustration of the method of calculating the Heller credit of 20 per cent against the first $200, 10 per cent against the next $300, and 1 per cent against federal tax liability in excess of $500 is given below for the AGI classes $4,000 and under $5,000.

STEP 1.[3]

AGI Classes	Average liability	20% of the first $200	10% of the next $300
	(1)	(2)	(3)
$4,000 under $5,000	$398.81	$40.00	$19.88

1% of the remainder	Average credit	Number of returns taxable and nontaxable	Credit value
(4)	(5) = (2)+(3)+(4)	(6)	(7) = (5)×(6)
$0	$59.88	7,385,219	$442,226,914

One refinement was to calculate the value of credit, if nontaxable returns are eliminated. This is called Step 2.

STEP 2.[4]

AGI Classes	Average liability	20% of the first $200	10% of the next $300
	(1)	(2)	(3)
$4,000 under $5,000	$423.54	$40.00	$22.35

1% of the remainder	Average credit	Number of taxable returns	Credit value
(4)	(5) = (2)+(3)+(4)	(6)	(7) = (5)×(6)
$0	$62.35	6,954,051	$433,585,080

Another refinement—Step 3—was to distinguish between joint and "other" returns. Instead of giving the same credit to each return, tax returns were split into two groups: (1) joint and (2) "other" returns, including here, single, separate returns of husbands and wives, heads of household, and surviving spouse. For the Heller

[3] See *Statistics of Income, 1958: Individual Income Tax Returns*, p. 27, Table 1. Average liability is obtained through division.

[4] *Ibid.*, p. 53, Table 10.

credit a modified formula (20 per cent against the first $100, 10 per cent against the next $150, and 1 per cent against the remainder of federal liability) was applied to tax returns other than joint returns. No change was made for joint returns.

STEP 3: JOINT RETURNS.[5]

AGI Classes	Average liability	20% of the first $200	10% of the next $300
	(1)	(2)	(3)
$4,000 under $5,000	$337.21	$40.00	$13.72

1% of the remainder	Average credit	Number of returns, joint taxable	Credit value
(4)	(5)=(2)+(3)+(4)	(6)	(7)=(5)×(6)
$0	$53.72	4,718,376	$253,471,159

STEP 3:"OTHER" RETURNS.

AGI Classes	Average liability	20% of the first $100	10% of the next $150
	(1)	(2)	(3)
$4,000 under $5,000	$605.73	$20.00	$15.00

1% of the remainder	Average credit	Number of returns, "other" taxable	Credit value
(4)	(5)=(2)+(3)+(4)	(6)	(7)=(5)×(6)
$3.56	$38.56	2,235,675	$86,207,628

In a further refinement—Step 4—AGI classes were split into the smaller groups as actually given in Table 10 of *Statistics of Income, 1958,* to see whether this move would bring more accurate credit values. The calculation of Step 4 disclosed that the broader income classes tend to underestimate credit values under the sliding-scale plan. The correction was so small, however, that it has been ignored, and no illustration of Step 4 is given here.

Finally, account was taken in Step 5 of marital status and number of exemptions. This calculation was made only for AGI classes

[5] See *ibid.*

up to $5,000 and is not illustrated because the results were insignificant.

In reckoning credits for each of the fifty states and the District of Columbia it seemed appropriate to use as a pattern national figures after elimination of nontaxable returns (Step 2), and to distinguish between joint and "other" returns within each of the merged (twenty) AGI classes (Step 3). This national pattern is applied as a refinement of the figures for each state provided in Table 16 of *Statistics of Income, 1958*.

Starting with the figures available in Table 16, Table 1, and Table 10, an illustration of the Alabama calculation for the Heller credit is given below for the AGI class $4,000 and under $5,000.[6]

AGI Class	*Number of returns, taxable plus nontaxable*	*Number of taxable returns as per cent of all returns*
(1)	(2)	(3)
$4,000 under $5,000	89,547	94.2%

Number of taxable returns	*Number of taxable joint returns as per cent of all returns*	*Number of taxable joint returns*
(4) = (2)×(3)	(5)	(6) = (2)×(5)
84,353	63.9%	57,221

Number of "other" taxable returns	*Income tax after credits*[7]	*Income tax for joint returns as per cent of taxes for all returns*
(7) = (4)−(6)	(8)	(9)
27,132	$29,504,000	54.0%

Income tax for joint returns	*Income tax for "other" returns*	*Average tax for joint returns*
(10) = (8)×(9)	(11) = (8)−(10)	(12) = (10)÷(6)
$15,932,000	$13,572,000	$278.40

[6] For columns 1, 2, and 8, see *Statistics of Income, 1958*, pp. 67-70, Table 16. For column 3, see *ibid.*, pp. 27 and 53, Tables 1 and 10; computed by dividing number of taxable returns by that of all returns within each of merged (20) AGI classes. For column 5, using the same tables as in column 3, the ratio for each income class was computed by dividing the number of joint taxable returns by all returns. For column 9, using Table 10, the ratio for each income class was computed by dividing income tax for joint returns by total tax liability.

[7] Since this millions figure is rounded in *Statistics of Income, 1958*, the others in this calculation have been rounded.

20% of the first $200	10% of the next $300	1% of the remainder
(13)	(14)	(15)
$40.00	$7.80	$0

Average credit per joint return	Credit value	Average tax for "other" taxable returns	20% of first $100
(16)=(13)+(14)+(15)	(17)=(16)×(6)	(18)=(11)÷(7)	(19)
$47.80	$2,735,000	$500.20	$20.00

10% of the next $150	1% of the remainder	Average credit per "other" return	Credit value
(20)	(21)	(22)=(19)+(20)+(21)	(23)=(22)×(7)
$15.00	$2.50	$37.50	$1,017,000

Applying the same national ratios to each appropriate AGI class, the same calculation was made for each of the fifty states and the District of Columbia. The values of state-by-state income tax credits were totaled to obtain national aggregate figures.

Besides the Heller credit two other credits were calculated: (1) a flat credit of $65 for a joint return and $32.50 for each "other" return, (2) a credit of 7% of federal tax liability. Why $65 and $32.50? Why 7%? The aim was simply to use figures which would produce approximately the same *aggregate* credit as did the Heller credit. The Heller scheme was put on the public record in 1959 (*Tax Compendium*, Vol. 1, pp. 419-434), and it had been espoused previously by (then) Governor Orville Freeman of Minnesota. Accordingly it was regarded as the anchor-credit. Since all three types of credit plans produced approximately the same total for 1958, it is possible to make a ready comparison of state-by-state incidence.

The methods of calculating the flat credit and the 7% credit are not illustrated, since these are simple. The former is secured through multiplication of the number of taxable returns in each AGI class by $65.00 or $32.50; the latter through reckoning 7% of the appropriate tax liability.

The total national credits obtained for 1958 were $2,429.5 million under the $65 and $32.50 flat credit, $2,426.8 million under the Heller credit (20%-10%-1%) and $2,401.1 million under the 7% credit. (See Table B-1.)

TABLE B-1. *Estimates of Maximum Credits (7%, Heller-Scale, $65 and $32.50 per Taxable Return), and Credits as Per Cents of Personal Income, by States, 1958*[a]

(dollar items in millions)

State[b]	Personal Income	Federal Income Tax Liability	Flat 7% Tax Credits	Tax Credits Under Heller Scale	$65 Credit for Joint and $32.50 for "Others"	Flat Per Cent Credits as % of Personal Income	Heller-Scale Credits as % of Personal Income	Flat Amount Credits as % of Personal Income
	(1)	(2)	(3)	(4)	(5)	(6) = (3) ÷ (1)	(7) = (4) ÷ (1)	(8) = (5) ÷ (1)
1. Delaware........	$ 1,248	$ 153	$ 10.7	$ 7.5	$ 6.7	0.86%	0.66%	0.54%
2. Dist. of Col....	2,126	231	16.2	14.4	13.7	.76	.68	.65
3. Connecticut....	6,506	720	50.4	45.1	41.7	.77	.69	.64
4. New York......	42,157	4,494	314.6	286.9	276.4	.75	.68	.66
5. Nevada........	685	76	5.3	4.9	4.7	.78	.72	.68
6. Illinois........	24,230	2,622	183.5	172.3	162.6	.76	.71	.67
7. New Jersey.....	14,442	1,539	107.8	104.1	98.7	.75	.72	.68
8. California......	37,131	3,816	267.1	253.0	240.6	.72	.68	.65
9. Alaska.........	527	39	2.7	2.4	2.2	.52	.46	.41
10. Massachusetts..	11,677	1,125	78.7	81.9	81.2	.67	.70	.70
11. Maryland......	6,661	685	48.0	49.2	48.6	.72	.74	.73
12. Ohio..........	20,527	2,041	142.8	145.6	141.4	.70	.71	.69
13. Washington....	5,977	623	43.6	44.6	42.8	.73	.75	.72
14. Michigan......	16,581	1,607	112.5	112.8	110.3	.68	.68	.67
15. Pennsylvania...	23,589	2,368	165.8	170.6	168.8	.70	.72	.72
16. Wyoming......	676	60	4.2	4.6	4.7	.62	.69	.69
17. Rhode Island...	1,726	172	12.0	12.6	12.7	.70	.73	.73
18. Colorado......	3,508	329	23.0	24.0	24.0	.66	.68	.69
19. Montana.......	1,342	100	7.0	8.0	8.5	.52	.59	.63
20. Missouri.......	8,644	782	54.7	56.6	56.8	.63	.65	.65
21. Oregon........	3,528	344	24.1	25.2	24.7	.68	.72	.70
22. Indiana........	9,122	826	57.8	63.1	63.2	.63	.69	.69
23. Wisconsin.....	7,648	701	49.0	54.6	55.2	.64	.71	.72
24. Kansas........	4,214	362	25.4	27.9	28.9	.60	.66	.69

25. Nebraska........	$ 2,759	$ 224	$ 15.7	$ 17.7	$ 18.8	.57%	64%	.68%
26. Hawaii..........	1,158	102	7.1	7.9	8.1	.62	.68	.70
27. Minnesota.......	6,486	565	39.6	43.6	44.7	.61	.67	.69
28. Iowa...........	5,256	436	30.5	35.4	37.2	.58	.67	.71
29. Arizona........	2,202	194	13.6	14.3	15.9	.62	.65	.68
30. New Hampshire.	1,105	102	7.1	8.6	8.9	.64	.78	.80
31. Florida........	8,367	719	50.3	50.6	54.6	.60%	.60%	.65%
32. Texas..........	17,129	1,541	107.8	106.8	110.5	.63	.62	.64
33. Utah..........	1,516	128	8.9	10.8	11.5	.59	.72	.76
34. New Mexico....	1,554	130	9.1	9.9	10.4	.59	.64	.67
35. Virginia.......	6,660	559	39.1	43.2	45.7	.59	.65	.69
36. Oklahoma......	3,954	325	22.8	25.0	26.6	.58	.63	.67
37. Idaho.........	1,127	94	6.6	7.7	8.2	.58	.68	.73
38. Maine.........	1,642	128	9.0	10.9	11.9	.55	.66	.72
39. North Dakota...	1,063	73	5.1	6.5	7.5	.48	.61	.70
40. Vermont.......	645	47	3.3	4.2	4.8	.51	.66	.74
41. South Dakota...	1,132	80	5.6	6.9	7.7	.50	.61	.68
42. West Virginia...	2,960	237	16.6	19.4	20.8	.56	.66	.70
43. Louisiana......	4,933	412	28.9	30.2	32.1	.59	.61	.65
44. Georgia........	5,672	437	30.6	34.4	38.0	.54	.61	.67
45. Kentucky......	4,336	351	24.6	28.1	30.2	.57	.65	.70
46. Tennessee......	5,028	405	28.4	30.8	35.0	.56	.61	.70
47. North Carolina.	6,318	405	28.4	35.1	42.8	.45	.55	.68
48. Alabama.......	4,379	342	23.9	27.1	30.3	.55	.62	.69
49. South Carolina.	2,924	182	12.7	16.9	20.2	.44	.58	.69
50. Arkansas.......	2,152	143	10.0	11.8	14.3	.47	.55	.66
51. Mississippi.....	2,298	128	8.9	11.1	13.7	.39	.48	.60
United States[c]....	$359,227	$34,304	$2,401.1	$2,426.8	$2,429.5	0.67%	0.68%	0.68%

[a] Source: Column 1, U. S. Office of Business Economics, *Survey of Current Business*, August 1960, p. 17. Column 2, U. S. Internal Revenue Service, *Statistics of Income, 1958: Individual Income Tax Returns*, pp. 67–70. Columns 3, 4, and 5, estimates.

[b] Ranked according to per capita income, 1958.

[c] Column 2 total excludes "other areas" as defined in *Statistics of Income, 1958*, p. 70, footnote 4.

The estimations made for each state are rough, since within each of the merged (twenty) AGI classes there are some quantitative variations regarding types of returns, types of taxpayers, and the amounts of federal tax liabilities that taxpayers have. A major improvement in the accuracy of the estimates could probably only be secured if the reports in *Statistics of Income: Individual Income Tax Returns* were compiled state by state in the same detail as they are for the nation.

Appendix C

Estimation of Certain Taxes Eligible as Personal Deductions by States

ONLY THE AMOUNTS of personal taxes deducted by AGI classes on itemized returns are shown in Internal Revenue Service, *Statistics of Income: Individual Income Tax Returns*. Information is not available concerning aggregate amounts and amounts by types of taxes eligible for deduction, either nationally or state by state. Attempts to remedy this deficiency in information were made for the year 1957 by methods described below, relating to property tax, gasoline tax, and motor vehicle and operator licenses.[1] Main sources of material were the U.S. Bureau of the Census, *1957 Census of Governments*, especially Vol. 3, No. 5, *Governmental Finances*, and Vol. 5, *Taxable Property Values in the United States*, and U. S. Public Roads Administration, *Highway Statistics, 1957*. Of the major taxes most difficulty was encountered in determining the personal or nonbusiness portion of property tax and gasoline tax collections.

[1] All the property values are for 1956. It seemed reasonable to assume that valuations in 1956 were relevant for tax revenue in 1957.

Property Taxes

Real Property

The methods described below were devised with the generous assistance of Allen D. Manvel of the staff of the Advisory Commission on Intergovernmental Relations. The bulk of property taxes eligible as personal deductions are on owner-occupied dwellings of which nonfarm are 97 per cent and farm 3 per cent. Since satisfactory figures for farm dwellings are unavailable, the core of the calculation deals with owner-occupied nonfarm dwellings. It is probable that most farmers regard property taxes on their farms as business costs and not as personal deductions.[2] The rationale of the calculation outlined below is refinement of state-by-state figures of assessed value of nonfarm dwellings. The fraction which this value is of all property subject to general property tax is assumed to be the same as the fraction of general property tax revenue eligible as a personal deduction.

For purposes of the calculation the states are divided into two groups, with the exception of Iowa: (A) those with small or no exemptions of real property tax, (B) those with relatively large exemptions (California, Florida, Georgia, Indiana, Louisiana, Mississippi, New York, Oklahoma).

GROUP A CALCULATION, ILLUSTRATED FOR ARIZONA: 1. What is the assessed value of nonfarm residential property subject to tax in 1956? The calculation (based on *1957 Census of Governments,* Vol. 5, *Taxable Property Values in the United States,* Table 3 and Table 2), is as follows:

Locally assessed value of nonfarm dwellings (1)	Tax-exempt real property (2)	Assessed value of nonfarm dwellings subject to general property tax (3) = (1) − (2)
$345 million	$49 million	$296 million

The assessed value of all property subject to general property tax

[2] Estimates of property tax payments eligible for personal deductions do not include figures for farm dwellings.

was $1,239 million (Vol. 5, Table 2), and the assessed value of taxable nonfarm dwellings is 23.9 per cent of this.

2. What fraction of nonfarm dwellings is owner-occupied? For Arizona the figure is 62.6 per cent.[3] But this ratio needs adjustment because owner-occupied units are more valuable on the average than rented units. In 1957 space rental value of owner-occupied dwellings for the United States was $21,890 million and that of tenant-occupied was $10,453 million.[4] Thus, the former as a ratio of the total was 67.7 per cent. The division of this ratio by the ratio of owner-occupied $\left(\dfrac{67.7}{60.7}\right)$ gives a weighting ratio of 1.115 for the nation. Applying this 1.115 to the ratio of owner-occupied, the adjusted ratio for Arizona becomes 62.6 × 1.115 = 69.8 per cent.

3. The total revenue from general property tax in Arizona was $77.2 million (Vol. 5, Table 1), and therefore the property tax on nonfarm residential dwellings becomes $77.2 million × 23.9 per cent = $18.5 million. Of this $18.5 million, owner-occupied may be assumed to provide 69.8 per cent, i.e., $12.9 million.

GROUP B CALCULATION, ILLUSTRATED FOR FLORIDA: The gross assessed value of nonfarm dwellings and farms was $4,293 million, of which $3,861 million—89.9 per cent—was nonfarm (Vol. 5, Table 3). Homestead exemptions totaled $2,388 million (Vol. 5, p. 6) and 89.9 per cent may be assumed to be for nonfarm dwellings, i.e., $2,147 million.

The adjusted ownership ratio for Florida was 73 per cent (same adjustment as for Group A), and therefore the assessed value of owner-occupied dwellings was $\dfrac{73}{100}$ of $3,861 = $2,819 million. Exemptions of $2,147 million reduce this to $672 million, which is the assessed value of owner-occupied dwellings subject to general property tax. Since the total assessed value of property subject to

[3] Interpolation was made between 1950 and 1960 by using data available in U. S. Census Bureau, *Census of Housing, 1950*, Vol. 1; *ibid.*, *National Housing Inventory, 1956*, Vol. 3; and *ibid.*, *Census of Housing, 1960* ("*Advance Reports*").
[4] U. S. Office of Business Economics, *Survey of Current Business*, July 1960, p. 16, Table 15.

tax was $4,530 million (Vol. 5, Table 2), owner-occupied dwellings were 14.8 per cent. *Revenue* from the general property tax was $229 million (Vol. 5, Table 1), and 14.8 per cent of it gives $33.9 million attributable to owner-occupied dwellings.[5]

Iowa requires a special computation. It provides a "homestead tax credit" against a portion of the assessed value of a homestead and the amount of the total state repayment in 1957 was $28.7 million.[6] The general property tax revenue was $235.5 million and the assessed property value subject to tax was $4,607 million (Vol. 5, Table 2). Therefore, if there were no state repayment the nominal property tax rate in Iowa would be $\frac{264.2}{4,607.0} = 5.74$ per cent. If this nominal rate were applied to the assessed value of the residential property subject to tax, the property tax would be $953 million $\times$ 5.74 per cent = $54.7 million. From this "would be" tax yield the residential portion of the credit payment should be deducted in order to get the property tax on nonfarm dwellings.[7]

After a calculation is made for each state the state totals are added to secure a national figure of $3,172 million for forty-eight states and the District of Columbia in 1957.

Personal Property

Household personal property is subject to local assessment for general property tax in thirty-five states: Alabama, Alaska, Arizona, Arkansas, California, Florida, Georgia, Illinois, Indiana, Iowa, Kansas, Kentucky, Maine, Maryland, Massachusetts, Michigan, Minnesota, Missouri, Montana, Nebraska, Nevada, New Hampshire, New Jersey, New Mexico, North Carolina, North Dakota, Oklahoma, Rhode Island, South Dakota, Tennessee, Texas, Ver-

[5] It should be noted that, out of eight states in Group B, five states have homestead exemptions. For the remaining three states (California, Indiana, and New York) without homestead exemptions the amounts of tax exemptions were deducted from the gross assessed values of nonfarm dwellings before the adjustments for owner-occupied were made.

[6] Oral information from Allen D. Manvel, staff of the Advisory Commission on Intergovernmental Relations.

[7] With exceptions described above, the remaining part of the calculation for Iowa is the same as Group B.

mont, Virginia, West Virginia, Wyoming.[8] The bulk of personal property taxes eligible for personal deduction consists of taxes paid on household goods. It seems appropriate to assume that the $277 million of personal property taxes estimated by the Department of Commerce as deductible for the nation should be distributed among these thirty-five states.[9]

Gross assessed value of nonfarm residential properties is provided in *1957 Census of Governments*, Vol. 5, Table 3; and Table 7 in the same volume gives the ratio of assessed value to sales price, state by state. Starting with these figures, the first step is to estimate the sales value of nonfarm residential properties and then to use this as an *indicator* to determine the appropriate amount of deductible personal property taxes for each of the thirty-five states. Illustrative figures for Arizona are given below. The assessed value of its nonfarm dwellings was $345 million, and the size-weighted average ratio of assessed to sales value was 20.1 per cent. Application of 20.1 per cent to $345 million gives $1,716 million of estimated sales value as an *indicator*. A similar calculation can be made for each of the thirty-five states, and the indicators can be totaled to secure a national figure of $226.1 billion.

How can one use the state indicators to reckon personal property taxes eligible for deduction by states? The ratio of a state indicator to the sum of all state indicators is assumed to be the same as the ratio of personal property taxes eligible for deduction to the sum of all deductible personal property taxes. For example, if we have the

Arizona indicator as estimated	$1,716 million
U.S. aggregate of indicators	$226.1 billion
U.S. aggregate of deductible personal taxes	$277 million
Arizona personal property taxes eligible for deduction are calculated as follows:	

$$\frac{1.7}{226.1} \times \$277 \text{ million} = \$2.2 \text{ million}$$

[8] Advisory Commission on Intergovernmental Relations, *State and Local Taxation of Privately Owned Property Located on Federal Areas*, Exhibit 3 (April 1961).

[9] *Survey of Current Business*, July 1960, p. 19, Table 21. This $277 million is, of course, much less than the total of property tax on personal property, including business property.

This $2.2 million of deductible personal property taxes should be added to the previous estimate of $12.9 million of deductible real property taxes to give $15.1 million of property taxes eligible for personal deduction in Arizona. After a similar addition of real and personal property taxes is made for each state, the state figures are totaled to secure a national figure of $3,450 million for forty-eight states and the District of Columbia in 1957, i.e., $3,172 million real property plus $277 million personal property.

Gasoline Taxes and Motor Vehicle and Operators' Licenses

Gasoline Taxes

The methods employed below were devised with the generous assistance of G. P. St.Clair of the staff of the U. S. Bureau of Public Roads. A special table, "Estimated passenger car motor fuel consumption and state gasoline tax rates, 1957" was prepared by the Bureau (through St.Clair).[10] The figures of this table were then refined by elimination of gasoline taxes paid for business purposes.

A FIRST STEP is to eliminate the amount of gasoline consumed by taxicabs, since passenger car gasoline consumption listed in the table includes gasoline consumption by all types of automobiles. Illustrative figures for Pennsylvania are given below. The gallon mileage of an average taxicab is estimated by applying the equation developed by the Bureau of Public Roads, $Gt = 0.063405 + 0.02033\ Ru$, in which Gt represents the gallons per mile of passenger cars, and Ru, the ratio of urban driving to total driving. Ru, however, can be reckoned as 1 in the case of taxicabs.[11] Thus the

---

[10] The table was prepared by going through the following steps: (1) tabulation of the 1957 vehicle miles of passenger cars separately; (2) using the average miles per gallon for passenger cars in 1957, as given in *Highway Statistics, 1957*, Table VM-1, calculation of the gallons consumed by the passenger cars; (3) the values of gallons consumed in each state were adjusted pro rata so that the totals conform with the totals given in *ibid.*, Table G23.

[11] Since $Ru = 1$, $Gt. = 0.083735$ and mileage per gallon is $\dfrac{1}{0.083735}$ or 11.94.

average vehicle mileage estimated for the taxicab was twelve miles per gallon.

For an average taxicab the estimated national average is 25,000 miles per year.[12] Due to the lack of data available for different states, the national average is used for all forty-eight states and the District of Columbia. Dividing this annual mileage by the estimated gallon mileage $\left(\dfrac{25,000}{12}\right)$ gives annual consumption of 2,083 gallons per taxicab.

Number of taxicabs in Penna.[13]	Annual gasoline consumption by an average taxicab	Gasoline consumption by taxicabs in Penna., 1957
(1)	(2)	(3) $(1) \times (2)$
4,246	2,083 gallons	8,844,000 gallons

The gasoline consumed by taxicabs of Pennsylvania in 1957, therefore, is estimated at 8,844,000 gallons.

A SECOND STEP is to eliminate the amount of gasoline consumed by publicly-owned automobiles. *Highway Statistics, 1957* gives state-by-state figures for the number of publicly-owned automobiles.[14] For Pennsylvania: federal, 635; state, county, and municipal, 11,151; thus a total of 11,786. Since the average vehicle mileage per gallon for publicly-owned automobiles is not significantly different from that of all passenger cars in the nation, 14.4 miles per gallon is derived by dividing the total passenger car vehicle mileage by the total gallons consumed by passenger cars in 1957 $\left(\dfrac{528,232 \text{ million}}{36,677 \text{ million}}\right)$.[15] By using a technique parallel to that described for eliminating gasoline consumption by taxicabs, as the

---

[12] Oral information, Bureau of Public Roads.

[13] Preliminary table, Bureau of Public Roads.

[14] P. 49, Table MV-7.

[15] Total passenger car vehicle miles traveled and total passenger car gasoline consumption were provided by a special table (May 9, 1961). Approximately 0.6 miles more per gallon were consumed on the average by publicly-owned automobiles (oral information, Bureau of Public Roads), but this difference was not taken into account in the estimation.

figures below show, 1957 gasoline consumption by publicly-owned automobiles in Pennsylvania is reckoned at 9,547,000 gallons.

Number of publicly-owned automobiles	*Vehicle- mileage per gallon*	*Average annual mileage per publicly-owned car*[16]
(1)	(2)	(3)
11,786	14.4 miles	11,670 miles

Annual gasoline consumption by an average publicly-owned car	*Gasoline consumption by publicly-owned automobiles in Penna., 1957*
(4)	(5)
(3) ÷ (2)	(1) × (4)
810 gallons	9,547,000 gallons

Subtracting the amount of gasoline consumed by the taxicabs and publicly-owned automobiles from the total passenger car gasoline consumption (2,131,509,000 gallons) gives the figure of private non-commercial passenger car consumption in Pennsylvania. This was 2,113,120,000 gallons for 1957.

A THIRD STEP is to eliminate from this remainder the portion of gasoline consumption which is business or nonpersonal. The Bureau of Public Roads has broken down passenger car mileage by purposes of trip, as follows:[17]

1. Earning a living:
   To and from work
   Related business

2. Family business:
   Medical and dental
   Shopping
   Other

3. Education, civic, and religious

4. Social and recreational:
   Vacations
   Pleasure rides
   Other

The only purpose which is nonpersonal is "related business" travel done chiefly by traveling salesmen and agents, farmers, professionals and semiprofessionals, craftsmen, personal-service workers, etc. Unfortunately figures are available for only twenty-two states. Figures for the remaining states have been assigned as follows.

The Pennsylvania ratio of 15.5 per cent for "related business"

[16] Estimated mileage (oral information, Bureau of Public Roads).
[17] U. S. Bureau of Public Roads, *Public Roads*, December 1954, Table 18.

travel was given to Connecticut, Delaware, District of Columbia, Illinois, Indiana, Maine, Maryland, Massachusetts, New Hampshire, New Jersey, New York, Ohio, Rhode Island, Vermont, Virginia, West Virginia. The average ratio of Louisiana, Mississippi, Tennessee, and Kentucky—19.4 per cent—was given to Alabama, Florida, Georgia, North Carolina, South Carolina. The average ratio of New Mexico, Oklahoma, and Louisiana—25.6 per cent—was given to Texas; the average ratio of New Mexico and California—22.2 per cent—to Arizona; the average ratio of Kansas and South Dakota—24.1 per cent—to Nebraska; the Wisconsin ratio of 19.5 per cent to Michigan and Minnesota; the Wyoming ratio of 15.0 per cent to Nevada; and the Colorado ratio of 15.5 per cent to Utah.

The refinement of the Pennsylvania figure is shown below:

Gasoline consumption by passenger cars (excluding taxicabs and publicly-owned cars) (1)	*Related business travel mileage as per cent of all travel by passenger cars* (2)
2,113,120,000 gallons	15.5 per cent
Estimated gasoline consumption for related business (3) (1)×(2)	*Gasoline consumption by passenger cars for personal use* (4) (1)−(3)
327,534,000 gallons	1,785,586,000 gallons

A FOURTH AND FINAL STEP is to calculate the state tax. If the rate did not change in 1957, this is simple. But if, as in Pennsylvania, a change occurred, the appropriate rate has to be applied to the appropriate gallonage. In Pennsylvania the rate changed from six cents to five cents on June 1. Gasoline consumption for the period of January through May in Pennsylvania was 744 million gallons, and therefore this aggregate tax was (744,000,000 × 6 cents) $44,640,000. Consumption for June through December was 1,041,600,000 gallons and therefore this aggregate tax was (1,041,600,000 × 5 cents) $52,080,000. The total for 1957 was $96,720,000 and this is the amount which is eligible as a personal deduction.

A similar calculation was made for every state, and the amounts of eligible gasoline taxes estimated for forty-eight states and the

TABLE C-1. *Estimates of Nonbusiness Deductible Tax Payments by States, 1957, Totals, Per Capita, and as Per Cents of Personal Income.*[a]

(deductible taxes in millions; per capita amount in dollars)

State	Individual Income Tax (1)	General Sales Tax (2)	Gasoline Tax (3)	Motor Vehicle and Operators' Licenses (4)	Property Tax (5)	Total Deductible Taxes (6)	Deductible Taxes, Per Capita (7)	Deductible Taxes as Per Cent of Personal Income (8)
Alabama..........	$ 30.2	$ 77.4	$ 27.9	$ 3.9	$ 15.4	$ 154.8	$49	3.5%
Alaska...........	7.1	—	n.a.	n.a.	n.a.	n.a.	n.a.	n.a.
Arizona..........	15.1	38.3	10.4	2.0	15.1	80.9	75	4.1
Arkansas.........	5.4	35.8	13.9	7.0	8.3	70.4	40	3.4
California........	143.3	756.7	185.9	143.5	411.6	1,641.0	118	4.7
Colorado.........	23.2	47.7	18.5	4.4	37.4	131.2	79	3.9
Connecticut......	—	79.2	27.8	10.7	74.7	192.4	85	3.0
Delaware.........	14.5	—	4.3	1.6	6.4	26.8	62	2.2
Dist. of Col......	26.2	20.4	7.0	4.4	9.4	67.4	83	3.3
Florida..........	—	100.9	52.9	29.1	45.8	228.7	54	3.0
Georgia..........	26.0	124.3	36.1	9.7	12.3	208.4	55	3.9
Hawaii...........	15.3	38.1	n.a.	n.a.	n.a.	n.a.	n.a.	n.a.
Idaho............	10.1	—	6.9	3.3	5.4	25.7	40	2.4
Illinois..........	—	342.2	86.0	45.0	237.9	711.1	73	3.0
Indiana..........	—	123.8	54.9	18.5	83.4	280.6	62	3.1
Iowa.............	28.7	86.7	26.7	26.2	39.9	208.2	75	4.1
Kansas...........	13.3	51.3	20.4	9.7	32.7	127.4	61	3.3
Kentucky.........	56.3	—	31.6	4.4	27.6	119.9	39	2.9
Louisiana........	29.3	95.1	28.8	4.4	4.9	162.5	53	3.3
Maine...........	17.1	17.1	11.5	4.8	22.7	56.1	60	3.6
Maryland.........	51.4	45.8	27.9	9.8	81.2	216.1	75	3.5
Massachusetts.....	111.2	—	44.1	16.7	206.8	378.8	78	3.3
Michigan.........	—	328.8	83.1	36.0	226.2	674.1	87	4.0
Minnesota........	64.4	—	29.0	26.0	79.6	199.0	60	3.2

	Column 1	Column 2	Column 3	Column 4	Column 5	Column 6	Column 7	Column 8
Mississippi	$6.0	$59.3	$17.4	$6.3	$1.6	$90.6	$42	4.3%
Missouri	47.3	100.6	22.8	19.8	64.8	255.3	60	3.1
Montana	7.6	—	.8	3.3	9.3	21.0	31	1.7
Nebraska	—	—	16.4	5.4	24.1	45.9	32	1.7
Nevada	—	9.9	4.2	.8	3.6	18.5	71	2.9
New Hampshire	1.5	—	6.5	3.6	19.0	30.6	54	2.9
New Jersey	—	—	45.9	36.9	235.4	318.2	57	2.3
New Mexico	5.2	37.6	9.3	4.7	5.9	62.7	77	4.5
New York	476.3	402.8	96.1	80.6	469.9	1,525.7	95	3.7
North Carolina	52.9	73.6	49.6	13.3	28.1	217.5	49	3.7
North Dakota	3.4	14.2	4.8	5.8	5.9	34.1	55	3.7
Ohio	53.3	234.6	91.0	34.5	176.1	589.5	64	2.8
Oklahoma	12.6	49.8	30.3	22.5	19.2	134.4	59	3.6
Oregon	92.2	92.2	17.9	7.5	35.5	153.1	88	4.5
Pennsylvania	90.8	189.9	97.0	39.9	259.0	677.5	61	2.9
Rhode Island	16.4	15.1	6.5	4.7	21.0	47.3	55	2.8
South Carolina	—	53.5	25.2	3.3	5.0	103.4	44	3.7
South Dakota	—	13.0	5.6	5.1	7.7	31.4	45	2.9
Tennessee	4.4	92.4	36.5	11.9	36.4	181.6	53	3.8
Texas	10.1	—	82.5	48.7	108.2	239.4	26	1.5
Utah	9.1	23.4	8.6	1.6	11.0	54.7	65	3.7
Vermont	—	4.7	4.7	3.1	9.6	26.5	72	4.2
Virginia	106.0	.5	41.0	11.9	48.7	208.1	54	3.3
Washington	—	198.0	29.2	20.2	38.8	286.2	105	4.9
West Virginia	—	79.3	15.9	9.2	10.3	114.7	59	3.7
Wisconsin	110.3	—	40.3	20.1	106.7	277.4	72	3.7
Wyoming	—	9.7	3.9	.7	3.1	17.4	55	2.7
U. S. Total[b]	$1,753.8	$4,028.7	$1,645.5	$846.5	$3,449.5	$11,724.2	$69	3.4%

[a] Source: Column 1, U. S. Bureau of the Census, *1957 Census of Governments*, Vol. 3, No. 5, *Governmental Finances*, p. 30. Column 2, *ibid.*, p. 29. Columns 3, 4, 5, estimated according to methods described in text of this appendix. Column 7, calculated from column 6 divided by population figures. Column 8, calculated from column 6 divided by figures of current income (for which see U. S. Office of Business Economics, *Survey of Current Business*, August 1959, p. 15.)
[b] Excludes Alaska, Hawaii, and other territories.

District of Columbia were totaled to secure a national aggregate figure. The national figure so estimated was $1,646 million in 1957.

Motor Vehicle and Operators' Licenses

Most revenue from this source comes from the registration fees, but a portion comes from operators' permit fees. Since the figures for the automobile registration fees (available in *Highway Statistics, 1957,* Table MV-2) include the fees paid by taxicabs, a step is taken to eliminate this amount. For example, Alabama had 905,700 automobiles registered in 1957, and received $2,762,000 for automobile registration fees. Therefore, the average registration fee per automobile was $3.[18] The number of taxicabs registered in 1957 was 2,118 (preliminary table, Bureau of Public Roads), and therefore the aggregate registration fees paid on privately used automobiles in Alabama becomes approximately $2,762,000 − $6,000 = $2,756,000. This $2,756,000 of private automobile registration fees is combined with the operators' permit fees of $1,192,000 (Table MV-2) to give $3.9 million motor vehicle and operators' license fees eligible as a personal deduction.[19]

After a similar calculation is made for each state, the state figures can be totaled to secure a national figure of $847 million for forty-eight states and the District of Columbia in 1957.

[18] $2,762,000 ÷ 905,700 (*Highway Statistics, 1957,* Table MV-1).
[19] No adjustment was made to eliminate fees paid for chauffeurs' permits from the total operators' permit fees.

Index

Admissions tax, 150

Advisory Commission on Intergovernmental Relations, report, 17n, 22n, 27, 29, 30, 31, 32, 33, 34, 78n, 159, 161, 163

Alcoholic beverages, taxes on, 151-52

Australia, use of unconditional grants, 131, 133-35, 154, 166

Bishop, George A., 112, 113

Brazer, Harvey E., 66, 67n, 68n, 99, 100, 105, 106n, 111n, 121n

Burns, Eveline M., 37n

California conformity issue in unemployment insurance, 52-54

Canada, use of unconditional grants, 131, 133, 135-41, 154, 166

Cardozo, Benjamin N., 42

Cayton, N., 54n

Cigarette tax, 97n, 99, 150-51

Colm, Gerhard, 9n

Commonwealth Grants Commission, 133-34

Conant, James Bryant, 1, 66, 95n

Conditional grants, 126-27, 129-31, 154-55, 165-66, 167

Corporation income tax, application of assistance devices to, 144-47

Credits. See Tax credits.

Customs taxes, 3

Daly, Mayor of Chicago, 17n

Death tax credit, 19-35; origin and development, 19-29, 79, 128, 158-59, 162; revenue-maintenance, state, 31-32, 78n, 159; revision, recommendations for, 29-35, 159, 161

Death taxes, state, 9, 19, 30, 33, 34

Deductibility of state and local taxes, 96-125; comparative advantages to individuals and states of deductibility and of Heller credit, 119-21; comparison of deductible taxes and taxes deducted, 110-16; cost to federal government, 117-18; credits as substitute for or supplement to, 90n, 121-25, 163-64; degree of federal control, 127; justification for, 97-106, 126, 163; regressivity of state and local tax deductions, 116, 117; taxes eligible for deduction, 106-10

Defense expenditures, 4, 7, 8, 9n, 10, 17

Delano, Frederic A., 20

de Vyver, Frank T., 49-50

Diefenbaker, John G., 138

Double taxation, international, 20n

Driscoll, Alfred E., 60

Ecker-Racz, L.L., 142, 147

Eckstein, Otto, 9n

Economic Security, Committee on, 36, 38, 39

Education: Credit proposal regarding, 67, 125n; expenditures for, 1, 8, 13-15, 18, 95n; federal grants, 130, 154

"Effort" relatives, 12-15

Eisenhower, Dwight D., 29

Employment Security, Bureau of (Department of Labor), 49-50, 55n, 56

Equalization features of tax credits, 67, 83-86, 132, 161, 164, 167

36

To his brother Leo

April 7

Leo, buddy, today is your birthday, isn't it? I send you a big bear hug, but I'm sending it by mail. If I tried to deliver it in person, you would probably ambush me with a judo chop.

(. . .) Today is a great day for us Brazilians. Not only is it your birthday. It's also the day we commemorate Tiradentes.[33] (. . .) He fought against those who wished to tyrannize Brazil, and he died on the gallows for his love of justice and freedom. Funny, isn't it? In every age the people who fight for freedom end up in prison, and some of them are condemned to death by the judges of their day. I wonder what would happen to Tiradentes today? It seems ironic that Tiradentes, an early martyr for our freedom, should have this penitentiary named after him. Wherever he is now, I'm sure he's none too happy about that. But the prison, to commemorate its namesake worthily, could open its gates—or at least permit visits outside!

Tomorrow we commemorate a great date: the "finding" of Brazil by the Portuguese. Some philologists (Aurelio Buarque de Holanda, for example) distinguish between "finding" and "discovering." I'm not exactly sure what the distinction is, but I have the feeling that neither word fits the underlying concept. "Finding" implies that Brazil already existed as a country before the Portuguese ended up here one fine day. But in reality all that existed before the Portuguese came was an immense expanse of land inhabited by Indians, and only a mistake in navigation landed Cabral[34] on our shores (although today some people claim that he left Portugal with the explicit intention of "discovering" Brazil). History's funny, isn't it?

Tell everyone at home that my lawyer comes to see me regularly. He had forwarded an appeal to the Supreme Military Tribunal requesting our release on bail, but at the last minute he changed his mind and withdrew the request. As I hear the story, he realized that there was no chance for success. The report about us was highly unfavorable and drew quite a disagreeable picture of us poor creatures. Anticipating defeat, he retreated. (. . .) Now we are waiting for the charge being drawn up by the public prosecutor on the basis of the police investigation. In all likelihood we'll be charged on the basis of Articles 18, 23, and 25 of the national security law. But it is worth noting that almost all political prisoners are accused of violating those same Articles.

The bishops are fully informed of our situation.

37

To his parents

April 8

(. . .) It was the first time I had been out on the street since I came here last December. The journey from the prison to DOPS is a quick one, and you don't get to see a whole lot. I tried to imagine that the streets had changed, but actually everything was as before: the people, the cars, the weather, the polluted air of São Paulo. The city goes on living its own life oblivious to us prisoners and to the dead. I suddenly realized that I never really have had any tie to this city, even though I worked in it for three years. It has always remained alien to me, as characterless as its cold, grey skies and totally devoid of any charm. I passed through it as if it were a terrible figment of the imagination that kept disappearing and reappearing from a world of shadows.

I realized clearly that my world is different now. Five months in prison and the prospect of remaining here for some years have put real distance between me and the outside world with its schedules and obligations, work days and vacations, sunny days and moonlit nights, noisy streets and flowering gardens. My present world is made up of bars, of high walls guarded by machine guns, of cells lit even by day with electric lights, of meetings with my lawyer, and of young faces marked by sorrow and yearning for freedom. It's a world all its own, in which the imagination has full scope and we feel the living inner pulse of history.

Does a prisoner get used to prison? No, no one gets used to being deprived of freedom, which is always stronger than our patience. I would say rather that a prisoner adapts to prison life, which does not totally lack a rhythm of its own and which does have a certain interest. Anybody who doesn't adapt lapses into laziness, desperation, and moral debility. My expectations include the fact of prison, and so far I have been able to face it with my head held high. The important thing is not to let it overwhelm me (. . .).

38

To Pedro

April 11

Dear Pedro, I too find it strange that the clergy are so worried about the problems of celibacy and professional life. Such concerns might well be primary in Europe, but it's clear that here we still haven't cut the umbilical cord and are living in the shadow of the Old World. We forget that our reality is totally different and imposes its own peculiar tasks and concerns on us. It is not right that in an underdeveloped country like ours, on a continent in political and social ferment, the clergy should meet to discuss personal problems. It seems to me that this is not the response people expect from us. Does it perhaps signify a lack of the gospel spirit and apostolic aspirations?

In one of my last letters to you, I focused on the problem of Christian "praxis." Let me try to sketch out a few ideas on the subject. Contemporary philosophy is trying to tell us that a human being is essentially defined as a practical being, that is, as someone who transforms reality by work and action. The history of humankind is a history of praxis. And when we talk about a human being, we talk about his works and deeds, which give him definition and fulfillment. History is entirely

55

the result of human action. People do not exist on the margins of history and praxis, and history does not exist as some suprahuman, autonomous force. Humankind and history are inseparable. Indeed, we come to know God's revelation only through history, only through what he communicates to us of himself. A German philosopher stressed that history does nothing, that it is the actions of human beings pursuing their objectives. Human beings transform reality and themselves, and the story of these transformations is the real history. Every human being wittingly or unwittingly engages in praxis. Sometimes we act instinctively, seeking personal objectives without thinking ahead to the social impact of the action. So we have the common laborer, for example, who works to live and never thinks about the oppressive nature of the productive process with which he collaborates. Others engage in praxis that is consistent with some consciously held objective, and their intentions are in a certain sense directed toward the objectives of their actions. In any case the determining factor in practical activity is the result—what objectively happens as the fruit of this activity. A work of art cannot be judged by the intentions of its maker; it must be judged on its objective merit. For it is the practical result that counts: Sanctity does not consist of good intentions. Charity is fundamentally action.

I think that Christianity is praxis, first and foremost. It would be valueless if it were just a doctrine or a religious theory. A discourse on God (theology) would produce little that was meaningful.

According to the Old Testament, God's revelation is the revelation of a plan. Its elements unfold through the historical praxis of the people of God. In and through the objective results of this praxis, the people become aware of the divine word. The divine word is equivalent to action; the awareness is identified with love. The authors of the sacred book were sufficiently inspired to be able to read the plan of history. God is present, and God is guiding us: These are the two data derived from the actions of God's people. The inspired author does not theorize the praxis; he notes it, points it out, and demonstrates the divine activity present in it.

The Gospels too are the fashioning of a praxis. Jesus is seen to be much more concerned with teaching criteria of life than truths of faith. Almost all his parables are designed to stimulate a new way of behaving and living. He is implacable against the Pharisees, who do not act as they teach. He himself bears witness through his actions. He summons people to be aware, to be committed and courageous, to have faith, hope, and much love. This being the case, we cannot talk about instinctive praxis in the case of the Christian. The gospel embodies the example and the *conscious awareness* that should direct our actions. It is a criterion of life. Our fidelity to this criterion is confirmed by our capacity for self-giving, for loving, and for acting; and this action takes place in history, in the ongoing eschatological process.

It seems a very serious matter to me that we Christians today have lost this evangelical praxis. We are not even aware of its importance. We have religious habits, customs, and practices. Our spirits are lulled by the truths of faith in which we believe. But we have no practical activity in which we objectify our faith in all that has been communicated by God. Why? Perhaps the roots of this quietism are to be found somewhere in the Middle Ages. Medieval Christendom, characterized by *ratio, auctoritas, ordo universalis,* by speculative theology dealing in celestial categories, lost its apostolic vitality. It sought to preserve the Christian faith and the society that professed it, putting all its energy into the fight against heresy. Christians went on the defensive. But historical progress is stronger than forces for mere preservation. All unprepared, the church was faced with schism, the moral decadence of the clergy, and growing inner contradictions.

So this historical period left us with two things. On the one hand it left us with defensive apologetics (if you will pardon the redundancy); on the other hand it transmitted to us a body of crystal-clear doctrine. Since then we have been circling around that body of doctrine, so absorbed in it that we have only recently opened our eyes and caught sight of earthly realities.

Even today we Christians still lack an operative praxis that might transform and sanctify history. We lack it first of all because we are not consciously aware of the historical process. Despite the example of the Old Testament, this awareness is still reserved to a small elite in the church. And second, we lack such a praxis because we are used to using doctrine as our sole point of reference. Our doctrine provides us with all our answers—except that it does not tell us how to live with concrete facts. Third, we do not have such a praxis because we consider the society in which we live to be Christian.

Action requires a point of departure and a point of arrival. But where do we want to go? What are the chief objectives of the church today in a world devastated by famine and war? What is the aim of pastoral activity here in Brazil? It cannot remain on the level of mere intentions, as purely subjective activity. The point of departure (the original intention) and the goal (the practical result) are never equivalent. The created work of art seen by the public is never the artist's original vision. It is the working out and development of his intention in action that determines its objective effect. Isn't Christian life today a bit like subjective intention?

For example, you meet with a group of Christians in your parish. They read the Bible, study a little theology, learn to think about it. These Christians are consciously aware of and responsible toward their religious obligations. But don't you sense that something is missing? Specifically, some way of objectifying everything that they are pondering and assimilating, some praxis with spelled out methods and objectives that enables them to be as one with what they do?

We often say that the Christian is supposed to transform the world. But where do we prepare for this activity? In what Christian community can people learn to prepare the leaven that makes the bread rise? If we grant that Christian life does not admit a gap between intention and result, between subjective and objective, then we must grant that intentions are proved on the level of practical action. This action must not be spontaneous, naive, subjective, "spiritual." It must be consciously aware, critical, objective, and "material." In other words it must be capable of altering the present for the sake of an eschatological future that is already partly realized in the individual, physical future of each one of us.

As you can see, my dear friend, there is a whirlwind of ideas in my head. But they all are at the level of intuitions. I cannot systematize them in a critical way. I lack the theoretical framework since I was unable to acquire it during the years that I have dedicated to action. My activity was often very disorganized, but it was also rich in experiences and discoveries. Perhaps in the years of prison that lie ahead I will be able to study more. At least I hope so!

We remain united in prayer. Our joy is the awareness of the "new" that is coming into being in this prison. A hug of friendship and gratitude to all of you.

39

To a community of nuns

April 11

(. . .) We got the notes you sent us, and we're reading them. I think this attempt to make theology understandable to the laity is great. In the monastery I constantly fought against the currents of intellectual perfectionism (the European malady). It seemed to me that we should divulge our knowledge, especially since the laity are interested in theology but are fed such pap.

Some of our lay cellmates are reading the notes, and they like them a lot. I hear you're carrying on your fine work of liturgical renewal. I saw that clearly when I went to Mass at your place last July. It seems to me that you've managed to form a solid parish community for worship and study. I hope your apostolic vitality continues to grow stronger all the time.

40

April 26

Dearest Mom and Dad, *Estado de São Paulo* printed the news of the pope's visit to Sardinia on the front page of yesterday's edition. He walked through the streets of Santo Elia, the poorest section of Cagliari, and stopped to talk to the residents. He went into the house of a very poor family and spoke with Signora Graziella Murcia, who was sick in bed. Overwhelmed with emotion, the only words she managed to say were: "Your Holiness, find my husband a job." The newspaper does not say whether the pope answered her in the affirmative. It simply says that he exhorted the woman to have faith in God and then blessed her. Then he gave a commemorative medal of the visit to her husband and a box of candy to her little girl.

This simple meeting seems highly significant to me. The newspaper says: "The Pope left the comfort of the Vatican and went to one of the poorest regions of Italy. For the first time the splendor of his trip was marred by the protests of anarchists, who regard this visit as an affront to the wretched poverty of the Sardinians." Willing to share "the joys and the hopes, the griefs and the anxieties of the men of this age, especially those who are poor or in any way afflicted" (*Gaudium et Spes*, no. 1), Paul VI was embarrassed when confronted with the clear, direct, and concrete request of this woman: a job for her husband. Notice that she did not ask the pope for a cure, for alms, or for prayers for her family. She asked for the minimum that a person needs to fulfill himself and to acquire life's barest necessities. She asked for a job.

The pope made a request of his own in Sardinia. He asked the rich not to close their hearts to the needs of their neighbors and to try to lighten the suffering of the starving. He reiterated in a way the persistent appeal of John XXIII—that the developed nations give more aid to the poor ones, and give it disinterestedly. (The total aid of the United States to underdeveloped nations does not amount to 1 percent of the national budget.)

What is the difference between Signora Murcia's request and Pope Paul's? As I see it, the woman asking a job for her husband embodies the appeal of poor people and nations who are tired of receiving alms and blessings from the church, who want the church to contribute to their betterment without paternalism. What they are asking of the pope is not the same thing that the pope is asking of the rich. Signora Murcia did not ask for a favor or for pity. A job is the minimum that a human being needs for food, clothing, shelter, and human dignity. It is a human being's right and duty. But that brings us to a question: Is it the task of the church to give work to the unemployed? It seems to me that it is not the church's specific mission to maintain an international employment agency. Its task is to act so that there may be work for all, to fight for a social structure that can make use of all the available manpower. In short, its task is to fashion a world that is in line with the kingdom of God.

This is what the poor expect now from the church. They want its active participation in solving their serious problems. Not that they expect it to operate as a political party or a government agency or a class organization. They want it, in its own way, to serve humanity and establish God's justice among people: "My brothers, what use is it for a man to say he has faith when he does nothing to show it? Can that faith save him? Suppose a brother or a sister is in rags with not enough food for the day, and one of you says, 'Good luck to you, keep yourselves warm, and have plenty to eat,' but does nothing to supply their bodily needs, what is the good of that?" (James 2:14–16). What did Jesus do when he was surrounded by a hungry crowd on the lake shore?

The pope, on his part, asks the rich to have compassion on the poor. Now his appeal, it seems to me, shows a lack of perspective typical of many Christians. He does not encourage the poor to fight for their rights—which would be much more consistent with the view that man is the active subject of history. Nor does he even perceive the overall dimensions of the problem: that this situation does not depend on the good or bad will of the rich but is the fruit of a complex social structure, that it is based on a solidly established system with its own laws that determine the rules of the game between oppressors and oppressed.

Let us suppose that a rich Sardinian decides to alleviate the sufferings of the poor in one area. He decides to replace their wretched hovels with fine new houses. How will he pay for them? With the profits he has obtained from the work of laborers whom he has paid far less than their work is worth. In reality the wages are a way of fixing, unjustly, the price of labor-power. Labor-power produces goods that are sold in the marketplace at a price much higher than the sum paid to the workers for producing them. Now with this money the rich Sardinian will build new houses. But this will entail an enormous loss for him because the new houses will not generate new sources of profit. This unprofitable expenditure could lead him into bankruptcy, thereby causing his laborers to be laid off. So the solution of one problem will only have generated another problem. The rich man is rich only because he operates within the framework of the existing production system. And this framework is determined by the capitalist structure that now prevails.

The tragedy of the poor will be solved only by altering this structure and these relationships of production.

The church maintains a huge system of charitable works. All of them have been forced to play the capitalist game—not for profit but for sheer survival. Insofar as they reject the rules of this game, they will go bankrupt. And insofar as they (or the rich man in Sardinia) alleviate the sufferings of some poor people, they will be collaborating in the rise of poverty. It is a vicious circle that can only be broken at its roots, by altering the whole framework of society's present system of production. When will we realize this? When will we come to see that this analysis is not tendentious or seditious but rather a true picture of the real situation?

You are quite right. We pray for those who are taking risks in outer space, forgetting those who are here on earth. But God help the astronauts if NASA relied solely on prayer! Faith must be fleshed out in works, says Saint James. What works do we propose?

Let us remain united in unbounded love for this church that is searching for its proper path.

41

Dear Mom and Dad, I just finished reading your last letter. I think your idea of contacting the bishops is excellent. But on the other hand I must recognize the fact that the cardinals are not yet capable of taking a public stand in our favor. The support of the church is undoubtedly great; but confronted with the kind of thing that happened to Tito, it is imperative to *say* something. That's why I think it's important for you to go to Brasilia. All the bishops of Brazil will be there, and the laity can take part in their meetings. The efforts of our "church in prison" are bent in one direction: We want the bishops to take a stand against the tortures and injustices practiced by the military government and in defense of the human person, and we want them to make a public statement to that effect at the end of the conference. If you go there, you will be able to help us by talking to bishops, priests, religious, and other lay people. Think about it. I don't know what approach you have used in your contacts, but we must coordinate our positions. For our part, we have tried to get the following points across in all our conversations and contacts with them:

1. We consider ourselves engaged in the struggle for justice.

2. We have never belonged to any subversive group.

3. Everything we have done proceeds from the requirements of the gospel.

It seems that they are not going to transfer us to Taubate. Everything is still very much up in the air. I'm just fine. A big hug to all.

42

May 4

Dear Teresa, today is an exceptionally fine and sunny day. I felt the sun on my own skin for the first time since I've been here.

There is a young man in our cell who must take the sun every day, on the doctor's orders. He cannot get down the stairs because his legs were injured at the time of his arrest. I carried him down into the courtyard and we stayed there together, enjoying the most beautiful sunshine in the world. I sweated as if I were in a Turkish bath. Too bad it doesn't happen more often. Funny—exactly six months ago at São Leopoldo it was a beautiful day just like today. I had gone swimming in the lake at the seminary, and right after my shower, as I was getting dressed, I was informed that the police were looking for me. I immediately undertook my famous flight, which made the front pages of the newspapers but didn't last very long.

But who can foresee the ways of the Lord?

I don't know to what extent your impatience is justified (. . .). Don't worry, I have no objections to your religious choice, whatever it may be. The important thing is to search always for the truth as honestly as you can, without illusions. I find you sincere in the matter of religion. If Catholicism is not convincing enough for you, then faith in God, love, and generous dedication to others can be found in other religions. The essential point is not to lock yourself into an egotistical, individualistic lifestyle. We are happy only when we manage to come out of ourselves and dedicate ourselves to others, even if the price of that happiness should be our precious liberty, which is life. For authentic life, Teresa, is the life that awaits us on the other side of death. All our hope should be placed there.

I pray for you. Much thanks for your letter and your friendship. A kiss of joy and peace.

43

To Silvia, his sister's friend

(. . .) Your letter is wonderful. You were really inspired when you wrote it. It's true that friendship unites people into a single family. It is born of common interests, personal affinities, and encounters. It is sacrifices that have put us into communion with each other. Behind bars friendship is an extraordinary force, even toward people on the outside. Today I know that I have made some solid friendships, that I am surrounded by people whom I love and who love me. The only thing that bothers me is that I can't talk with these people, but I also know that my imprisonment speaks to them more clearly than any words I could say.

The flowers! Thanks from all of us for the seven marvelous roses. They opened up into countless petals, then died yesterday. But they lived long enough to bring us a ray of light. It doesn't matter that they didn't last long. The important thing is that they had the courage not to stay closed up in their buds, that they were wise enough to come out of themselves and rise toward the sun in delicate red petals. They left the mark of your presence here.

44

To a community of nuns

May 10

Dear Friends, (. . .) I view the renewal of the church with a lot of optimism. But it will take great sacrifices, and afterward it will no longer be such an easy thing to be a Christian, for it will entail risk. It will require concrete actions and taking stands. It will no longer be the vague, quietist, religious sentimentality of people who remain fiercely attached to this world while they wait for the next (. . .).

45

May 10

Greetings to you all! The most beautiful gift I've gotten recently was Mom's visit, bringing Dad's written statement about my imprisonment. It is remarkable in both form and content. I have no changes to make, no criticism to offer. Among other things, it's well written. Mom and Dad have managed to express beautifully everything that has been happening to me in this dynamic period of church renewal. There is a direct relationship between that renewal and my imprisonment.

For centuries the church has justified the social order in which it has lived. The values of that social order (the family, private property, tradition, individual liberty, democratic government, etc.), were considered Christian. Social order and Christianity became so closely identified that we came to speak of "Western Christian civilization." In reality this was an ideological interpretation of Christianity propounded by those in power. And the social order, which created its own peculiar abuses, found the justification for its existence in this interpretation.

So Eisenhower (who was Protestant) sends troops into Vietnam "to defend the Catholic minority."

Cambodia is invaded and its population decimated "in defense of the free world."

In South Africa Christians appeal to the Bible to prove the divine origin of apartheid.

And here at home Archbishop Sigaud[35] can say, without risking the accusation of heresy, that the class divisions into rich and poor derive from the will of God, who did not desire equality among people.

Now, in this postconciliar period, our problem is to return to the sources and to see clearly that Christianity is not identical with any social order; that it challenges and questions all social orders; that the state does not represent any divine right, that

66

laws are made by people and these people are wholly concerned with protecting their own privileges.

So we will inevitably see a clash between Christianity and the social order, between the church and the state, between Christians animated by love and those who are attached to their laws (. . .).

46

To his parents

May 11

Dearest Mom and Dad, thanks for the letters. If I don't write more often, it's because there is not too much to talk about in prison. It's like living on a desert island, except that an island is surrounded by water and we're surrounded by bars. And it's deserted here. When I arrived at Tiradentes prison in December, there were about a hundred prisoners here. Now there are almost three hundred, and more on the way. There is an attempted bank robbery in São Paulo almost every day, and after the young robbers are arrested they end up here. Whether ordinary criminals or political offenders, they all come under the state security laws.

We prisoners come from every social class and walk of life. The most important prisoner is certainly Caio Prado Junior, sixty years of age, a publisher, printer, bookseller (the "Brasiliense" book stores), and author of several books. He was sentenced to four and a half years because of an interview he gave in '67. Here he's just a prisoner like the rest. He gets up early to get the bread and milk provided by the prison. He cooks his own meals and does his own laundry. There are no rich or poor in here. Everyone is treated alike, and everyone has the same rights. Whatever one prisoner gets from the outside is divided among all. The only real differences are of intellectual ability, but we try to minimize them. We give Portuguese and English lessons to anyone who is interested.

Any prisoner might become a really good card player. I've learned to play bridge. (. . .) It's the most common mental hygiene in prison, particularly in DOPS, where you're rarely allowed reading material and, even if you were, the nervous tension caused by the interrogations kills the desire to read.

Contrary to what you people outside might expect, time passes incredibly fast for us. I'm astounded whenever I count up the time. I've already been in prison for half a year! We owe this to the rhythm we've managed to impose on our lives here. I try not to sleep more than eight hours a day. (By the way, I'm the one who gets to sleep first in our cell; the period of absolute silence begins at 1:00 A.M. and ends at 9:00 A.M.) I go to bed around 10:00 P.M. and get up between 6:00 and 6:30 A.M. I pray, read the Psalms, do yoga, and drink coffee. Then I devote the whole morning to studying French, taking time out to read the *Estado de São Paulo*. Our big meal is at 12:30 P.M., and silence is compulsory until 3:00 P.M. I spend the afternoon studying theology. We don't get a snack in the afternoon. At 5:00 P.M. the others do gymnastics together, but I don't participate. After supper, around 7:30 P.M., I play cards or read a novel. At this time, almost all the radios are tuned to the classical music program on Eldorado station. Every now and then we dance the samba a bit to the accompaniment of two guitars. Yesterday, as a matter of fact, thanks to the rich repertoire of two of our companions, we recreated the history of popular music in Brazil from the beginning right up to the start of the *bossa nova*.

I think our life here is more or less like life on a submarine—except there are no white rabbits and no date set for surfacing. (I've stopped writing to say goodbye to Caio Prado, who has been transferred to barracks. I take back what I said about all prisoners being treated alike. But I don't see the advantage of being in prison by yourself, no matter where it is!)

I'm glad to hear from Mom that you're settled into your new house, but I'm sorry to hear that the name of the neighborhood was changed. The old name was much more tropical-sounding and filled with folklore.[36] (. . .)

68

If your baby boy isn't afraid of cockroaches, you can be sure that he will become a great animal breeder like his father, who spent his childhood taking care of his little zoo, while I devoted myself to rock music and became an habitué of the Minas Tennis Club.[37] But my playboy career was interrupted suddenly when I began to frequent the "six o'clock tea" at São Jose (. . .).[38]

A kiss for you all. I am writing you from cell seven on the eve of C.'s birthday, which is two days before we celebrate the liberation of the slaves. Waiting for my own liberation, I greet you all.

47

To Sister Monica, a Brazilian nun

May 12

Dearest Sister Monica, your candy has sweetened the bitter taste of prison. All this solidarity on the part of our fellow Christians reminds us of Saint Cyprian's account of his fellow Christians' efforts to alleviate the sufferings and bolster the hopes of those who were to undergo martyrdom and set an example for others.

Today we had a fraternal visit from the president of CELAM, Archbishop Avelar Brandão of Teresina. He came to demonstrate what we had already seen by the visits of the apostolic nuncio, Cardinal Scherer, and others: namely, the church stands by those who suffer—be it in poverty, abandonment, or prison. Human justice is not identical with the justice of God. We who are "a scandal to the Jews and an example of folly to the Gentiles" know that God has chosen the foolish to confound the wise of this world. So Paul tells us, and he spent a great deal of his time in prison.

We fear nothing; we regret nothing. Prison is our Mount Carmel. Our prayer becomes all the more real and alive as we come to realize that the Christian's proper place is with the poor and the oppressed, with those who experience injustice or suffer for their love of justice. That is the message of Vatican II and of the gospel. The person who is imprisoned, be it behind bars or in sin, needs our love, not our judgment. Faith is not given to us so that we may condemn, but rather so that we may save. Transgression of law can only be understood in the light of charity. As Jesus said, the Sabbath was made for man, not man for the Sabbath. That is what he tried to get across to the Pharisees, who in their religious myopia could only see the legalistic side of things.

We don't know how long we'll have to stay in prison. So far there is no formal charge against us. But this period has been rich in evangelical revitalization. No one can take away our peaceful conscience or our inner joy. Indeed, how can our present tribulations compare with the promise that was given us, the future that awaits us? "How deep I find thy thoughts, O God, how inexhaustible their themes!" (Ps. 139:17).

Accepting this mystery, we contemplate God's wonders. Following the Lord, even into prison, we find true freedom.

Keep us in your prayers. The "church in prison" is united with its brothers and sisters outside.

48

To Pedro

May 16

Dear Pedro, the only news from prison comes from our own experiences and thoughts. Today I've been thinking a great deal about these six months that I've been in prison to date. You on the outside, who have never experienced it (I would not wish it on you for the world!), cannot imagine what it is really like, however much I might write to you about it. Although I have been here for six months, I think it's too soon to make a definitive judgment. That will have to wait until I have been free again for two or three years. Only then will I be able to say something about the meaning of prison life and its impact on us.

Based on my brief experience so far, I must say that prison is an absurd institution. It is as ridiculous as burying a man alive. It does not punish, and it does not correct. Its sole objective is to remove from society those who have threatened the security of its "masters." Countless human beings have spent long years in prison and, on leaving, returned to the same life they had led before. Their imprisonment did not increase or diminish the security of those outside one bit. Nor did it serve as an example. The example was provided by the ideals for which these prisoners fought and for which others would take the same risks.

It is abominable that society feels obliged to confine the best of its youth, those capable of transcending self-interest and egotism, behind bars. A waiting room is a good image of what prison is like. You wait there, among total strangers, for your turn to come. You wait for hours, and after reading all the magazines and chewing over all your thoughts you suddenly realize that the waiting time is indeterminate and that it is impossible to leave the room. So your only recourse is to start up a conversation with the other people there. At the same time every detail in the waiting room takes on importance. After several days, you know the pattern in the tablecloth and the upholstery, and you could describe every detail of the room with your eyes closed. The people and things in the room become as intimately familiar as the parts of your own body. To make the interminable wait less awful, you make up a game: Everyone changes seats—and you rearrange the furniture—but you have no chance at all to make any decision that will change the basic situation. The door can only be opened from the outside; no one inside has a key.

In the past six months I have passed through three different prisons and experienced eight different cells. I came to know each one of them as well as I now know cell seven. Although there are fifty of us in here, I have no trouble at all in finding

71

something I need. I know exactly where everything can be found, just as I know for a fact that my fellow prisoners are capable of loving. Prison can humanize a person or turn him into a brute. It teaches us to love, to smile at suffering, to get over moments of depression, to nurture patiently the strength of our will and our ideals. On the other hand, prison can drive a person crazy (it has happened to two people here), crush his moral strength, or fill him with hatred and destructive impulses.

Living together is a great help. It lightens the burden for all. There are also moments of tension, when the atmosphere becomes charged and everyone is suddenly transformed with fearful expectation.

As for myself, I feel that something has grown inside me, something firmly rooted. It is as if I have emerged from fog and can now see things clearly. I can see what I want and why I want it. I can see my capabilities and what I am up to facing. I feel I have reached some point of no return, from which it would be suicide or treason to go back. I must go on without a backward glance. I no longer have anything to lose because everything I now possess is within me. All that is left to me is the road ahead. Even if it does not take me very far, every step will make a difference (. . .).

49

To his parents

May 20

Dearest Mom and Dad, last week the newspapers indicated that the charge against us would be published any day now—if we can rely on the statements of the public prosecutor. So far there is nothing, but I expect to see a new campaign of vilification against us in the press. They will say absurd things about us. It is war, after all.

I am anxious to know the outcome of the bishops' conference in Brasilia. They were supposed to issue a document on church-state relations. But I am not very optimistic even though eleven bishops of Goias[39] have published a denunciation of the harrassment of political prisoners (see Sunday's *Estado de São Paulo*). I think there will be behind-the-scenes negotiations between the bishops and the government at Brasilia. Our church is not yet sufficiently free. The final report issued by the conference will reveal whether or not our bishops stooped to compromise with the regime.

Something odd has been going on here in prison. It is public knowledge, and I believe I can tell you about it openly. Some half dozen political prisoners have given their support to the present government platform, which they believe to be nationalist and opposed to all imperialism—North American, Soviet, Cuban. One of this group went to Brasilia and spoke with Colonel Manso Neto. Now they go from cell to cell, expounding their point of view. They assert that the government will move toward democracy, the first step being the release of those political prisoners who were not involved in armed resistance. This first step is related to the government's concern to erase the terrible image it has acquired for itself abroad. My impression is that these young people are in fact smoothing the way for their own release. They say that one of them had already been condemned to twenty-eight years. But to me it doesn't seem a very honorable way to win back your freedom (. . .). The Christian should say straight yes or no, no halfway measures. We must be utterly consistent. But mercenaries crop up everywhere.

I have no other news. It's very hot, and the routine is the same as always.

Have you read the gospel? We can only give Caesar what concerns him: money. God gets everything else, including our lives. A kiss and a hug to be shared by all.

50

To his brothers and sisters

May 21

(. . .) The text of the charge against me has finally been made public in *Diario Popular*. It's long, but it doesn't say very much. There is no serious charge against me. But I realize that my activities in the south will be regarded as crimes so long as people are not convinced that helping the persecuted is a right and duty of the church. The last part of the charge says this: ". . . falls under the sanctions of Articles 14, 23, and 25 of Decretal Law 898 of September 29, 1969, Article 53 of the Military Penal Code, and Article 154 of the Federal Constitution of October 17, 1970 [which abolished political rights for ten years]." Dad can explain to you what all those numbers signify. All the Dominicans were indicted on the basis of those same articles. Now we are waiting for the preliminary hearings. They've charged 138 people in this case, but only fifty-six have been arrested.

(. . .) I don't think dad should accept job offers from the government unless they are purely administrative. I don't believe he has a vocation to be a politician. Past experience suggests where his true vocation lies (. . .). A big hug to you, and the assurance that you are in my prayers.

51

To his parents

May 31

(. . .) Mom's hopes for the bishops' meeting were not realized. The Spirit is stirring, but it is not strong. I was realistic about it from the start. I know our bishops well, and I know how far they are capable of going. They put together a declaration that was the product of countless emendations, and it ended up as a patchwork of cliches. In short it epitomizes what they them-

74

selves are: naive, lacking a vision of history, lacking theological training, and insensitive to the great problems of the country. They wrote to save themselves. They shouted, "Long live the king!" and handed us over to the secular arm (. . .). Ah, how history keeps repeating the same droll story! Not once does the word "poor" or any synonym for it crop up in their report. It doesn't much matter what they might or might not have said with regard to us. Our fate is sealed, and Caesar has marked us out for the arena. But it was important that they speak of those who have neither bread nor circuses, who are screaming with hunger in the Northeast, who build everything yet possess nothing. About these people, there is not a word, not a single word: ". . . indeed the state of the nation is well and continually improving, thanks to the government." Let us wash our hands of the matter. And they are received smilingly by the king, who hands out chocolates.

The newspapers inflated the Eucharistic Congress into a great event. The church and the government were buddy-buddy. But in the eyes of a Christian it was an exhibition of paganism "because he who says he loves God and does not love his fellow man is a liar." Many will be saved thanks to the sacrament of ignorance. X. described the document as "muddle-headed and obscene." During World War II housewives in the small towns of Germany complained of the soot pouring from the chimneys of the Nazi "factories." No one saw anything; the only evidence was the soot. When the Nazis were defeated, the world learned that these "factories" were camps where the Jews were exterminated. The "deputy"[40] had remained silent. The air we breathe today is polluted, but who takes note of it?

But Vatican II tells us that the church is not the bishops; it is the people of God united in Jesus Christ. When has the church ever made a mistake by allying itself with the future? My confidence in the Spirit is enormous. It is not for nothing that he has allowed us to end up in prison, not for any merit of our own but for our openness to the gospel.

I hope all goes well at home.

P.S. I recommend that you read Mounier's *Personalisme* and that you study his writings and personal experiences in the French Resistance.

52

June 1

Thanks to all of you for your letter and for the texts that you sent. I am very interested in learning how to read the Bible. I very much like the comments on Saint Paul. You stress a point that exegetes have not paid enough attention to so far: the social conduct of Jesus and his apostles. The attention of exegetes is always concentrated on the texts themselves or on discovering how the primitive community understood the message, without regard to the context. In other words they don't consider the social behavior of Jesus and his apostles as a source of revelation (even though nothing was explicitly said when Jesus stood before Herod). To be sure, Jesus spoke in terms peculiar to his age and nation, and it is therefore useless to look for an explicit program of social reform in the gospel. But with the help of modern scientific disciplines we can ascertain what Jesus' vision of the world was, in what way his preaching did denounce a slave society, and in what forms Greek philosophy influenced the primitive Christian message so that it acquired an ideological overlay (natural right, etc.) that it had not originally possessed. You only have to look at the doctrine of divine right of kings to see that Christianity assimilated extraneous ideological elements.

I am convinced that we are living through a propitious time for profound Christian renewal. It is one of those periods that in an earlier day gave rise to new religious orders. Today it is no longer a question of establishing new institutions. It is rather the moment to bear witness to a new spirit whose substance is summed up in the terms *metanoia* and *kenosis*. To me, the document approved by the bishops at the meeting in Brasilia summarizes the whole agony of the old church. Everything in that document lacks consistency and foundation. Nowhere in it do we find reference to "the poor" or any synonymous term. From beginning to end, the text deals with issues that are of no interest to the people: seminaries, vocations, the ecclesial tasks of the laity. At the end this mosaic of shock absorbers tries to gloss over the pressures to which the church is being subjected and to confirm the policy of "peaceful coexistence" with the regime. It is all very sad. Not to mention that bandaid, the Eucharistic Conference, which is the supreme expression of a country where faith has been reduced to performance of the sacraments.

We are fine here (. . .). We still have not received permission to celebrate or receive the sacraments. We have written to the bishop about this, but we have not yet received an answer.

Thanks to you all for the friendship you've shown us. Let us remain united in grace.

53

To his brothers and sisters

June 7

(. . .) The television set came back to our cell for the World Cup games. This evening Channel 13 announced that in Argentina the "dictator" Onganía[41] had been deposed. It's funny: Until yesterday he was called "president." Now that he has been deposed, he is called a dictator and will go down in history as such. Clearly no dictator ever considered himself as such, not even Hitler or Mussolini. While in power they are presidents or generals or prime ministers. We don't call things by their right names until they've been rendered harmless. Only when the mighty have fallen do they get the name they really deserve.

The same news report stated that the military junta that deposed the "dictator" would designate a new "president" for the country within ten days. One comes down, another goes up; the labels change but the poison in the bottle remains the same, as if calling the new dictator "president" would lighten the despotism and make him more popular. The people of Argentina will continue to be oppressed. They will not have the right to vote nor will they have any say in the destiny of their nation.

With Onganía out of power, I am sure the church will pay homage to the new ruler. It may even go so far as to say that he arrived in the nick of time "to free the country from tyranny." What phonies and liars people in power are!

Well, that's a problem for the people of Argentina. We're here in Brazil, well guarded in this penitentiary where even the dust beneath our feet is familiar to us by now (. . .).

Right now it's fashionable to play the artisan here. We are trying to help those families that are in dire straits because the breadwinner is imprisoned here with us. Some of us are making fine purses out of colored plastic cord, and others are making rugs. It's good work, and our group is becoming more and more creative. I'm going to try to cut down on studying a bit and get involved in the handicrafts. You never learn enough, and here in prison I've learned a great deal. Besides my personal development that only time will reveal, I've learned to cook pretty well and to use my bed as a mini-apartment. I now know how to wash a floor, do a little darning, study and pray in the midst of noise, read lying down without falling asleep, be courageous, and love people.

Cardinal Scherer and Bishop Fontana from the south stopped by here on their way back from Brasilia. They brought us news of the episcopal meeting. It's my impression that things may have gone a little better behind the scenes than appears in the official statement.

The bishops sent a letter expressing their solidarity with us in our sufferings. Yesterday Cardinal Rossi, however, gave an interview to *Estado de São Paulo* in which he said that our attitude, objectively speaking, had nothing to do with Christianity. As if Christianity consisted in going to Confession and Holy Communion, which Jesus never did. In fact he said: "Not everyone who cries 'Lord!' will enter the kingdom of heaven" (. . .).

I hope everything is well with you people. Here we're simply prisoners—no formal charges, no news.

My feeling is that "they" are more interested in giving us a taste of prison than in condemning us (I prefer not to say "judging" us). A hug to all.

54

Thanks for the letter and the things you sent me. We all were vaccinated against smallpox; as usual my vaccination didn't take. (. . .)

Tito went to court yesterday in connection with the UNE case.[42] He learned that all the Dominicans will be charged under Articles 22, 23, and 25 of the National Security Law. We expected as much, since almost all the prisoners here are charged under the same articles. We're waiting for a visit from our lawyer for further explanations, but he's sick right now. Article 25 seems to entail a minimum sentence of five years and a maximim sentence of fifteen years.

I don't want to frighten you with this next piece of news—in fact, I'm the one who should be frightened, but I can't help viewing it as a joke in really bad taste. This week a young man was sentenced to three years in prison for having taken part in a meeting at a friend's house where Marxism was discussed. Three years in prison for a meeting! He'd been in prison for nine months, and he felt so sure of acquittal that on the day of sentencing he packed his bag to go home. This incident will give you some idea of the uncertainty that afflicts both lawyers and clients in our cases. The law says that a charge must be published within two weeks of the conclusion of the formal inquiry. Four months have already passed!

In the future when people talk about these things, they'll ask one question: Where was the church? Why did the church say nothing? It's not that I want the church to defend me but it ought to defend human rights, to aid the advancement of the poor, to combat injustice [censored].

The same question must be asked with regard to Germany, where six million Jews were murdered without anyone "noticing." It's what *The Deputy* is all about. It must also be asked about Vietnam because so far the church has not been able to say which side is right in that war.

This is the politics of silence, the sin of omission. Many will have to pay for the words that were not spoken and the deeds that were not done. It's all right to debate theoretical principles, but to be frightened by the hard facts is inexcusable.

It's rainy and quite cold. Lucky for those who don't have to leave their houses on a day like today! (. . .).

55

To Pedro

June 28

Dear Pedro, I don't think prison conditions will allow me to pursue my studies in theology as I had hoped. You need a guide, a library, and a little peace and quiet. Here our reading is often interrupted, and we have very little space in which you can be alone and create a little "distance" for yourself. So we must adapt to circumstances, make the best use we can of the few books we have, and discuss the more important theological themes among ourselves. Individual reflection and group discussion here bring out aspects of Christian experience that are usually not explored adequately. The fact is that we're living through a period of thoroughgoing renewal on every level of human activity. We might use the expression "new church" to convey the reality of this attempt to recapture the pristine aspects of Christian living, the aspects that came into the world with the preaching and witness of Christ and his apostles. I prefer not to use any adjective at all when I refer to the church. It has remained one and the same through two thousand years, undergoing constant renewal as it strives for greater self-identity. I believe that the renewal we are experiencing today will be the most profound and complete since the Council of Trent. For in a certain sense it is a "radical" renewal, full of innovations that are revelations to some people and heresies to others.

The renewal officially recognized by the church in the sixteenth century had its beginnings in the twelfth and thirteenth centuries. It took three hundred years for official doctrine to absorb the ideas and experiences that on first encounter aroused indignation and scandal. For example consider the impact of the theological reform of Saint Thomas Aquinas, which was based on the pagan philosophy of Aristotle. Church renewal always follows the same sequence: The Holy Spirit sets various charisms in motion, overthrowing concepts and institutions held definitive until then. Afterward these charisms are understood and assimilated into Christian faith and the teaching of the church. It is useless to try to find a direct and immediate connection between revelation and comprehension. Even the apostles, who were inspired, were unable to comprehend some aspects of the revelation transmitted to them by Jesus Christ.

Today we decry the Inquisition, which once was hailed as a way of bringing the faithful to salvation. Almost no one was able to understand the mystical life of Saint John of the Cross. His own confreres kept him in prison on a diet of bread and water. It's the same old story: What the past judged as evil is in the future acclaimed as good and vice versa. The history of the church is filled with examples of this. Wasn't Joan of Arc condemned to the stake by a commission of theologians?

In any period of church renewal one of the greatest difficulties is to distinguish faith from culture. Some elements of faith are absolute, definitive, and indisputable, such as the dignity of the human person. Other beliefs, which pass for elements of faith, are only constructs specific to a particular culture and period, like the identification of democracy with Christianity. It's obvious that this distinction occurs on various levels, and that faith always acquires a specific cultural expression as the faith-of-human-beings-living-in-history. The praxis of the faith is always clothed in a particular idiom that is the expression of a given culture. The danger lies in our ready tendency to generalize our own cultural values as if they were elements of Christian revelation. Progress, material well-being, prestige, and power are major values in our culture. From childhood we are taught that "to succeed in life" means to acquire a respectable social position, preferably one with a good income attached. Our culture is so imbued with this standard that we treat wage-earners and common laborers as "different" from ourselves. When advertisers wish to sell a product, they suggest that owning it is synonymous with power and prestige. Even the church is influenced by this scale of values, which has nothing to do with Christianity. The parish priest in some small town in the interior tries to stress the power and grandeur of the church by building a cathedral. Bishops live in mansions, and curates want their own Volkswagens, though such lifestyles conflict with the evangelical dictate of poverty, which should be the church's witness even more than its inner spirit. I don't mean to suggest that progress and material well-being are antievangelical in themselves. But when they belong to a small minority at the expense of the majority of the people, they are antievangelical.

What exactly is a true element of faith? Renouncing one's self-interest for the sake of one's neighbor is. Consider God's own example in Jesus Christ. He was born in a stable; he was a common laborer; he formed a community of uneducated men; he had no place to lay his head; he died on a cross between two thieves. Today, in a world where the vast majority of people are poor, I am convinced that the church should live entirely like them and identify itself wholly with their interests and aspirations. Our stately edifices and luxurious mansions are senseless, as are our classical culture and our bourgeois trappings. None of these things is an authentic sign. None of them will bring human beings to conversion to Jesus Christ. None of them breaks down the barriers of social class that we help to build up and are afraid to destroy, as if social differences between human beings are evangelical while social equality is not.

Facing this reality in this spirit, I don't find prison a burden. Prison is full of the poor, and now events have led us to identify with them. This is the home of those who have nothing, not even their freedom. Christ himself passed through this place and with him many others who would not accept injustice. It doesn't matter that now we are not understood, that we have to stay here for who knows how long. The important thing is that none of this will go for naught; in time it will contribute to the renewal of the church and the world (. . .).

82

56

Dear Pedro, all my thanks for your letters. I seem to gain
courage from confidence and solidarity. Such gestures are
very important to us now, for we are surprised by the silence
and fear pervading the world outside this prison. Everyone
seems to be waiting for it to "pass," as though it were a bad
dream, not reality. Meanwhile people tend their cattle, count
their money, and keep out of trouble.

We live in a world ruled by prudence, abstract principles,
and idealistic notions. It's as if reality didn't exist or were
neatly circumscribed by the satisfied consciences of the lazy.
It's ridiculous to argue about the color of the walls after the
house has caught fire.

Today, up to my neck in the tragic reality of prison, which is
the quintessence of a whole current historical process, I realize
to what extent the church is off target for lack of information
and a proper perception of the facts. What does the church
really know about transportation policy, foreign investments
in our country, the distribution of electric power? Practically
nothing, because churchmen are formed in a culture that is
artificial for our age. They cannot deal with a technological
project or an economic reality without first setting up a strict
scale of values that distorts the facts. For many years we saw
people only as contrite penitents kneeling in our confessionals
to recite their litany of sins. We exalt the individual at the
expense of the group. We can't believe the data of the social
sciences because we don't take part in the production process.
We don't work for wages. We're accustomed to reasoning
from theories rather than facts.

Long live formal logic! The indispensable transformation of
the church is too thorough to be accomplished quickly. But
when it is done, the change will be radical. It will not just
modify our ecclesiastical structures; it will mostly alter our
mental categories, which have been infected by a whole cultural atmosphere that proclaims certain values as if they were a

re-creation of Christian doctrine. That's why we stand about debating ends and means while history moves on without asking our permission or even our opinion. As if means could be predetermined without reference to praxis! As if a priori principles could be applied without reference to the objective conditions that determine the ways in which principles can be put into practice.

It's painful to see the church keep repeating the same principles without ever applying them. It talks about justice, freedom, and people's participation in the decision-making process, about the countless rights that are noted, recalled, and exalted in all the writings and teachings of the church. Meanwhile the government of Ecuador turns sharply to the right and no one says anything, although this would be the occasion for the church to practice what it preaches. The United States invades Cambodia and bombs the civilian population and no one says anything, although this would be the occasion for the church to practice what it preaches. Last year two hundred billion dollars were spent on armaments and no one says anything, although this would be the occasion for the church to practice what it preaches.

In short we keep silent in the face of facts. Or else we give the government a vote of confidence, forgetting that no nation or government is going to renounce its privileges in favor of a justice that it doesn't even perceive. Holy Innocence!

I am sure that *metanoia* will touch many people and that the ways of the world will change. We must give it time to happen. . . .

57

To his brothers and sisters

July 7

(. . .) The newspapers have published the charge against the Dominicans. It begins with a summary statement of various papal teachings, well chosen to prove how heretical we are.

It's interesting to note that according to the indictment we are more heretical than subversive. The public prosecutor spelled out the chief aim of the Dominican order (to fight the Albigensian heresy) and then pointed out how far we have strayed from that purely religious work. The one thing he forgot to mention, or perhaps didn't even realize, is that the Albigensians denied the human nature of Christ whereas the Dominicans taught that Christ was a human being in history. This precludes a Christianity devoid of incarnation and alien to the problems of this earth.

The text of the indictment notes that the accused Dominicans were living in an apartment in the underworld section of São Paulo. It fails to point out that near their apartment stood the Church of the Consolation and the Ministry of Justice. The indictment also notes with a trace of sadness that we didn't save the lost sheep that abound in that neighborhood. But this observation seems even more applicable to the local parish priest, who is specifically responsible for the souls in those particular bodies.

The charge will be formally registered next week. V. and C. were let out on bail. That's good because they had begun to feel the burden of prison life and were often depressed. Usually this happens to people who do not manage to figure out the real reason for their imprisonment. I'm the only one left of those who were arrested in the south. It's only fair, in my opinion, because I feel sole responsibility for everything that happened there.

The publication of the charge suggests that the preliminary hearing will take place soon, but it doesn't tell us anything about the sentencing. There are people here who were charged and found guilty a year ago and still haven't been sentenced. So I think this affair will drag on for a long time (. . .). An affectionate hug to all.

58

To a group of young Christians[43]

July 18

Dear Friends, (. . .) I owe you a letter but my hands have been busy with long hours of manual labor. To help out the families of poor political prisoners we've been making leather and plastic purses, ornamented rosaries, and embroidered wool rugs. Our cell has been turned into a crafts shop where everyone gets in on the work. The rate of production is reasonable, or at least good enough to keep some families from being evicted. We have the advantage of being able to work when we please, so we can work long hours. There are people who think that in prison irresponsibility is the rule because, closed in as we are, we cannot feel responsibility, but only anxieties that render us impotent. But that's not true. Wherever you find yourself, even on a desert island, you can create your own rhythm of work and impose on yourself set tasks.

I've been in prison since last November, and I can truly say that I haven't noticed the time pass. I'm so organized that I go to bed every evening contemplating the things I'm going to do the next day: finish reading a book, write a letter, or make a plastic purse. The great danger in prison is idleness, laziness, and lack of interest in the little things that make up your life here. The prisoner who starts counting off the days is lost (. . .). In that sense I may be lucky not to have been sentenced yet. I have an unspecified amount of time to spend in prison, and that doesn't upset me. At least I feel certain that I won't die in prison!

In your letter you speak of the work of Martin Luther King, Jr. I admire him too because he was able to make choices and give of himself, to die for love of others. But I confess that I'm not convinced of the validity, or rather, of the efficacy of his methods. Look at Gandhi: admirable, meritorious, but useless from the viewpoint of history. India has changed little. The power once exercised by the British is now wielded by the Americans.

A better world won't be fashioned by isolated initiatives, good intentions, and charismatic individuals. A better society is a joint endeavor for all those who want it and wait for it. It's hard to learn to swim without getting into the water.

I think, for example, of the social encyclicals. They're full of suggestions for improving human life in accordance with Christian inspiration. But they're ineffectual suggestions because you can't take medicine without its affecting your whole body. And it sometimes happens that certain chronic infections can be cured only by surgery—even against the will of the frightened patient.

The newspapers have already published the charge against us. Oddly enough, the text tends to emphasize the "theological" motifs of the charge by citing old church documents and isolated papal statements. I seem to be in Joan of Arc's situation, although I don't recognize the theologian who opposes me. It's interesting to see how history twists and turns and always returns to the same old ironies. Yet people never learn.

There are 138 of us listed in the indictment, of whom only fifty-six are in prison. The rest are on the run. Can you imagine how long it will take to question, charge, and try all these people? And on the day of the Last Judgment we will go over it all again. But Saint Paul says that patience breeds hope, and hope is even greater than patience. This gives us courage (. . .).

We are very grateful for your kindness. I think this is only the beginning of a friendship that will continue to grow. I join you in prayer and praise to the Lord.

59

To his brothers and sisters

July 28

I got the letter you sent this week. It's become less cold here the past few days, but I still haven't worked up the courage to do my gymnastic exercises. I'd rather wait till summer. In the meantime I'm doing a lot of studying and reading, even some novels by Machado de Assis[44] that I chanced to find.

Our lawyer hasn't put in an appearance lately. Now he's on vacation with his family. There's no additional word on the trial either. The court is overloaded with work.

The routine of prison life goes on: handicrafts, reading, conversation, cooking. Every once in a while we play cards out of sheer boredom. Cards were useful at DOPS, where there was nothing to do while waiting for the interrogators but fiddle with an old, frayed deck of cards. Now we have improvised a ping-pong table of sorts—improvisation being characteristic of prison life—and it works fine. We play with great gusto.

It's strange to see how human beings adapt to their circumstances. I remember the miners of Morro Velho[45] who were so used to the mine that the sun bothered them when they came out into the daylight. Suffice it to say that every Wednesday, when visiting hours are over, most of us go right to bed when we get back to the cell. We feel as tired as if we had just taken a long hike. I think a lot of things will bother us when we get out of here. I've heard of one such case of a person who got out of prison, went to eat in a restaurant, and couldn't stand "that racket." The fact is that here you get used to a strange silence, broken only by the same familiar noises, and you forget the typical hubbub of life on the outside. All your senses adapt, some improving and some deteriorating. Your sense of hearing grows very sharp—you can make out faint noises far away. Your vision deteriorates a bit, due to the lack of sunlight and the constant use of electric light for reading.

As far as my birthday goes, I can't think of a thing I need. I want for nothing. I have too many clothes as it is. It's pretty hard to choose a gift for a prison inmate! I think the best thing, if anyone is coming, would be to bring food. Anything will do. If you want to come on Saturday, call the lawyer's office so he can get the permit. A big hug.

60

August 7

Dearest Mom and Dad, it's too bad you didn't come. We had prepared a reception worthy of you (. . .) but the permit didn't arrive. In any case, Teresa's visit helped to allay the homesickness. It's good to see people from the "outside world" in here. In that sense my cell is a privileged place, because if we climb up on the bunk next to the barred window we can see the comings and goings on the street and not forget what cars look like. Really, this isn't my style, because I am not the nostalgic type who moons about the past. I prefer to tackle the present, even if it's terrible, and look toward the future. So this cell—160 square meters with bunks everywhere—and the forty-one people living in it now constitute my intense little world.

I know that many people outside think that we inmates idle away most of our time, feeling no sense of responsibility and doing nothing useful. It's not true. Something like that may occur during the first few days in prison, caused by the initial shock and the constraint of a new and strange way of life.

Here in prison, waiting (for what?), you learn many things. In particular you learn to respect other people. You begin to feel that the fellowship that can exist between human beings can work miracles. That's the source of your hope and your patience. Right now I'm in the "clergy corner"—three beds where we meet in the evenings to pray, read the Bible, talk, and tell jokes. Since we don't have any beer, we're eating the candy that Teresa brought and a few biscuits snitched from the pantry, along with a cup of tea. We talk about A.'s shirt, which is so old and threadbare that it looks like a spider's web. But he's terribly attached to it! He has other shirts, but he prefers that one. But the joke can't go on much longer because the shirt is on the verge of disintegration and A.'s sentence will be up on September 28. My release date will be around the turn of the century, when prisons will have become museum pieces. I wonder what people living in the future will think when they hear that human beings once imprisoned their fellows? (. . .)

61

August 10

Dearest Mom and Dad, I must confess that I too was impressed by the impact of the soccer world championship. Our cell is on the fourth floor, and through the bars I watched people running happily through the streets. It seemed as if a new ingredient had rendered joy more explosive: The winning of the Cup, which has by now acquired a mythic value of its own, has become the object of the contest. This Cup has become a goddess, desired and worshiped by players and fans alike. From all over the country, fans come as if on pagan pilgrimage to the Cup.

In this outpouring I see the emptiness in which our nation and its people live. We have to go back to the decadence of pagan Rome to find similar excitement over a circus spectacle. Any nation whose glory is the physical prowess and athletic ability of twenty-two human beings is in a bad way. It would be all right if the game constituted relaxation after productive labor, but that is not the case. Soccer lures crowds to the stadium, stimulates discussion everywhere, and turns the players into idols and national heroes. It's a clear indication of the mood and temperature of the country.

This phenomenon of pagan religious idolatry is more common among us than we might like to think. We gravitate toward abstract values, even in the realm of interpersonal relationships. It is a phenomenon called "reification." Things, mere objects, acquire in our minds a value unrelated to their utility. Ownership of an automobile signifies social superiority, for example. By the same token human relationships are reduced to the level of things: An individual's importance is proportional to his money and material goods. We confuse the human person with his function; the function stands for

90

and is the person. This is the cause of so much inner repression and neurosis and imbalance. This is the reason for all the safety valves we create to ease the profound loneliness and tension in which we live. I think we have reached the saturation point. Half-way cures and preventive measures no longer work for a malady that has become chronic. Clearly the culture we have absorbed has provided us with values only fit for blackmailers. We used to believe that the principles of the gospel could continue to exist perfectly well in this disordered mosaic. We thought we could straighten out the mosaic simply by shifting the pieces around a bit. Now we know that such an approach won't work; it would be like trying to use fireflies for lamps. The fact is that the mosaic doesn't work anymore. Time has shattered it, and its underlying framework has fallen apart. We must create a new mosaic with new pieces because the gospel tells us that we cannot put new wine into old wineskins. (. . .)

62

To his brother Luiz Fernando

August 11

(. . .) Last Saturday we had an unexpected visit from the apostolic nuncio. He was accompanied by Monsignor Expedito, secretary to Cardinal Rossi. They brought us Brazilian cigarettes and a package of medallions with pictures of Pope Paul VI and Our Lady of Perpetual Help. They said they had ordered American cigarettes, but they hadn't come in time.

We distributed the gifts among our fellow prisoners and then had a good two-hour conversation. The nuncio said he'd asked the minister of justice to expedite our case, and it seems that they just might do that. The nuncio also requested that we be set free on bail, but that was turned down. The minister of justice promised that our case would go as smoothly as possible. The nuncio also said that you people had come to see him and that he had appreciated your visit. We talked about the problems of the church in Brazil, exchanging ideas on clerical renewal and the apostolic task of Christians. He told some interesting stories about his experiences as apostolic nuncio in other countries. Now he is about to leave for Canada, where he will perform the marriage of a boy whom he baptized. Then he will go to Rome, hoping to discuss our case with the pope. He promised to come to see us again when he returned to Brazil. (. . .)

Cardinal Pellegrino passed through Brazil and wanted to see us, but he didn't receive authorization in time. (. . .)

Our lawyer has not shown up since his vacation ended. When he comes, I'll ask him about the visiting permit for the twenty-fifth. Let me know who's planning to come, because each visitor must be named in the permit. (. . .)

63

To his brother Tony

August 20

Tony, your letter made me very happy. You write very well, and your penmanship is excellent.

Do you know the story of the king who called a meeting to find out who could describe the wonders of the universe using the least number of letters? Many wise men entered the contest. One wrote a book on all of nature: sea, rocks, air, fire, land, plants, animals, and people. Another described the seven wonders of the world, like the Great Wall of China, the pyramids, and the Temple of Diana. And so it went, each wise man trying to describe the things that impressed him most in the world. The king ended up with a mountain of paper containing descriptions of countless things. As he was plowing his way through all this, he suddenly noticed one small sheet of paper on which was written: A B C D E F G H I J K L M N O P Q R S T U V W X Y Z. He realized that all the wonders of the world could be described with these twenty-six letters. He summoned the wise man who had submitted that sheet and gave him the prize: his daughter's hand in marriage. The wise man married the princess and lived happily ever after. A bear-hug for you.

64

To Cristiana

August 27

I've never met you, Cristiana, and yet we're already friends. Thanks for your letter. Teresa told me about you in her last letter. You say that the important thing is to *feel* what is happening. Well, I have really *felt* everything that's happened to me. Despite the bars prison is a good thermometer for taking the human temperature. In the near future human beings will find it absurd that people used to confine other people in cages, and set armed guards to watch these cages of unarmed prisoners, simply because they differed in ideology.

From all this I conclude that freedom is not always physical. Outside prison are many "free" people who are really prisoners of themselves. And many people remain wondrously free even in prison. It all depends on your attitude toward life. One of these days I shall find myself in the defendant's box in court, accused of conspiring against society and wanting to change the existing order. There in court I shall recall many things: Brazil's magnificent landscape—and its slums; girls parading in beauty contests like cattle at auction; movies that teach us that the world turns on sex and violence; garden-city villas and low-cost IAPI houses; Chacrinha's[46] TV program that mocks humanity; newspapers with obituary notices set in large type to be read by a peaceable population. I shall call to mind that kings are no longer recognized by popular acclaim but by their coats of arms. I shall call to mind that this is the society we live in, and perhaps it is I who have made a mistake by taking all this too seriously. And I shall come back to prison, condemned, because this society fears me.

The important thing, Cristiana, is that there's meaning in

93

everything that's happened to me. Life doesn't end at the prison gate. It surmounts prison walls and pulses inside me. You can't imprison the spirit any more than you can imprison a human being in whose spirit is faith and a relationship with Jesus Christ.

Thanks for your greetings and your friendship. I embrace you.

65

To a religious community

(. . .) I was delighted to get your letter and I thank you for your good wishes. Soon it will be the first anniversary of the day of my arrest. (And still neither trial nor sentence by the Military Tribunal.)

I no longer expect these things to happen quickly. I'm prepared to wait a long time without losing my joy or good humor. I feel that my spirit is tougher than the bars that surround it. I am not living for the day of my release, for that would be a great waste of energy. My life now has a rhythm made up almost exclusively of intellectual activity. I'm trying to put this time of seclusion to good use. I do not trust the justice of men as much as I trust that time will make everything clear. It would be presumptuous to ask that the ways of God be comprehensible to everyone at the same time! For many people God's ways remain a question mark. In my mind and heart I feel certain that I've chosen the right road. I was always aware that it would be hard and dangerous.

Thanks for your concern and your solidarity with us.

66

To his parents

August 30

Dearest Mom and Dad, I was delighted with the letter you sent. It shows that you understand and are on my side in everything that concerns me. I admire and appreciate your intention to raise the little ones in the spirit of justice and social equality. They should know everything that's being said about me, including what's written in the press. They should have an overall view of reality and be able to judge it for themselves. I believe that people of firm convictions will always be able to face life's conflicts and struggles. Such people will be able to live by their own choices, not merely to survive by the whims of fortune.

During the long interrogations to which I was subjected, I tried to sort out my convictions, which are based on my faith, against the background of a world in which all is not well. I wasn't concerned about how others would judge them. I had kept in mind only the words of Christ, himself a prisoner condemned: "Blessed are you when people persecute you and say all manner of falsehood about you for my sake. The time is coming when those who kill you will feel that they are blessed by God." It would be naive of me to think that I could make a Christian choice without travelling the road to the cross. Today I'm convinced that this road, instead of destroying you, renders you more worthy and noble. What really destroys a person, even in the midst of seeming security, is lack of a clear path.

My imprisonment has some odd aspects. From the very beginning I tried to keep calm and in shape. I'm just not cut out to play the tragic role of prisoner at the bar of justice. When I was transferred from Porto Alegre to São Paulo, I came on an FAB plane, handcuffed and guarded by six soldiers with machine guns. These precautions seemed a bit exaggerated. The thing that worried me was that we might hit an air pocket, the plane would start to shake, the soldiers would lose control over their triggers, and I would end up looking like a sieve. Deciding that the shortest point between two human beings was speech, I started to talk to the guards. I asked them how the guns worked. To explain, they had to point the gun barrels away from me. Then I asked them about their work, and pretty soon they were sharing their afternoon snack with me. When the officer in charge noticed the change in atmosphere between us, he told them they could put down their guns and take off their helmets. The handcuffs were left on, so I had to make sure I moved both arms in the same direction. Otherwise I felt a terrible pull on my wrists.

I still haven't managed to figure out the reason for all those security measures at three thousand meters above the ground. But such happenings have taught me that there is always a considerable distance between a human being and the work he does—a distance we often fail to notice or to admit. At bottom in all of us, soldiers or not, are certain existential concerns and a way of being that are unrelated to the activities we perform. We are always looking for understanding, human communication, and love (except for the hopeless cases among us). So I have always tried to discover the human being in the soldier or policeman interrogating me, even while clearly recognizing the ideological differences between us.

In Porto Alegre I was interrogated by a colonel in the First Army Corps. In no time at all he was telling me about his family and children, and we were exchanging ideas on child-rearing. At that point, I tried to convince him that the level of TV programming left much to be desired in a supposedly highly cultured society. Programs that exploit the public's sado-masochistic tendencies do so, not for their own sakes, but to attract the largest possible audience for their commercials. How can a society be well balanced if the communications media dispense nothing but violence and sex? We are still far from the desired ideal.

The truth is that people still imprison other people. Future generations will find this as incredible as we find slavery or racial discrimination today. It will be up to your children to fashion an ideal world. It will have been worth it to face all this if they and their generation come to realize that everything must evolve, that nothing can be forever. We are being sacrificed by those who persist in trying to stop the passage of time.

Thanks for your good wishes. A trusting hug to you all.

67

To a religious community

August 31

Dear Friends, thanks for the birthday wishes you sent me. As Heidegger would put it, I have progressed a bit further in life and also a bit further toward death. Each day that we live, we die a little. Faith enables us to penetrate this mystery and see its true dimensions. Vilaça,[47] one of those bohemian Christians found only in Europe, writes that there are three things that we lack courage to look in the face: sun, death, and self. As for me, though I haven't the deliberate courage of a fireman, I've managed to face myself and death. I have not yet looked at the sun (which isn't looking at me right now, either).

I saw myself for the first time during the novitiate, back in 1966. It was a tough nut to crack, but also one of the most intense and fruitful periods of my life. It was not easy to give up my busy, itinerant life in Catholic Action and resign myself to the anonymity of the novitiate. It seemed as if the circus grounds had emptied and suddenly there were no longer any spectators to watch the show. I had to let go of the illusions and face the realities of my choice of the religious life. I had to look at my future stripped of make-up and costumes. I saw then that it was not exactly what I had imagined, that the religious life was not a great adventure or an esthetic pleasure but first and foremost a life of witness, a thoroughgoing commitment to the faith. That was precisely what I lacked: real faith, a personal encounter with Christ, a certain inner conviction that this was my road. Doubts. Suffocating obscurity.

For many months I saw nothing, believed nothing. I seemed to be at a crossroads without signposts or directions. I had lived so many years as a layman, had discovered and talked and written about the role of the laity. Vatican II had exalted the role of the laity in the world and the church. And amid all this emphasis on the temporal, on the world, on the laity and its mission in the church, I had chosen the religious life. Why? Wasn't I taking a step backwards?

The obscurity of my situation kept me from thinking. I was simply there in my white habit, listening to the lectures of the novice master and tending the monastery garden. But it was all strange to me, like a bad dream in which events seem disjointed. I was looking for Christ and faith, and Christ withdrew from me, hiding himself, absurdly, in the eucharistic mystery. The liturgy seemed to me to be well made esthetically, but devoid of content. There was a steel wall between us that prevented communication.

Out of pride, a pride that I still have, I refused to look back, to accept defeat. This same pride also kept me from progressing, however falteringly. My confessor at the time was Father Martino. I confessed my doubts and my resistance to him. His answer was simple—banal, even—but it had its effect: "When you are lost in a forest at night, you shouldn't go forward or back. It's better to stop where you are and wait for daylight."

And so I did. I stopped and waited, not knowing exactly for what. The first ray of light came to me from an anthology of comments by the church Fathers on the Holy Spirit. Then I immersed myself in the mystics, John of the Cross and Teresa of Avila. Saint Teresa has had considerable influence on my life as a Christian. She was proud like me, and she is the person I most admire in the life of the church. No one has spoken to me so powerfully and pointedly as she has. When I was arrested at Porto Alegre, the first book I asked for was one of hers.

In the final phase of my novitiate my vision became not only clear but transparent. I savored the faith—all of it, the sweet and the bitter. Even today I am still looking for the intimacy that God granted me then, in the calm following the storm.

In the novitiate I looked myself straight in the eye for the first time. It was associated with my choice of the religious life. I was not interested in its superficial features, which are often mistaken for its essence. I was looking for a total encounter with Christ, looking to place myself totally at the service of the gospel. The Dominican order was simply the means by which I intended to reach my goal. I have always tried not to confuse one thing with another, not to identify ends with means.

Vatican II and my experience in Catholic Action had helped me a great deal. I wasn't used to blind obedience without dialogue or respecting rubrics as sacraments. I had never been overawed by classical culture. I was not devoted to reading the commentators on Thomas Aquinas or the old treatises. My preference has always been for people like Congar, Rahner, Chenu, Ratzinger, Schillebeeckx, Teilhard de Chardin, and De Lubac. But even so I have never felt a calling to be an intellectual, to do research and scholarly study. I have always read under the pressure of some immediate need, and this has left gaps in my intellectual training. My studies and my whole life have been oriented toward action. I am a person in search of effectiveness, a sort of theological technocrat. I am always interested in knowing how to apply something, how to communicate something, how to achieve concrete results, how to determine praxis. And at the same time I lug about with me an intense longing for the contemplative life.

This first period of encounter with myself lasted until I got to prison. Here a second period of encounter has begun, with new data, stages, and prospects. Real-life experience has always had great value in my eyes. Everything I have learned so far has come to me from experience, and only through experience can I assimilate it. It has become a game for me, sometimes a dangerous game, from which I derive my joys and in which I face great obstacles. Of these I am not afraid, because they are part of the game. They're not purely accidental interruptions disturbing the ordered sequence of proper moves; they are part of the game itself. Since I know the key to the game, I play optimistically, believing in victory and converting obstacles into strategic retreats that pave the way for further moves forward.

Today it seems I have a peculiar need to talk about myself (. . .).

68

To a religious community

September 7

(. . .) I have my doubts about this highly touted process of renewal. What exists, in fact, is an awareness of the need for renewal, a realization that we cannot go on as before and must seek out new forms, perspectives, and stimuli. But there is a gap between awareness and action, and so far we have not bridged it. As is normal in this first stage, our actions are still imprecise, tentative, and experimental. In reality there is no renewal yet; there are inquiries, attempts, initiatives. You cannot make qualitative alterations (leaving behind age-old forms) without feeling remorse or nostalgia, without feeling somewhat envious of our predecessors, whose world was untroubled by our problems and questions.

Insofar as the religious life is concerned, I think we must ask a basic question that deserves a precise answer: Why renew it at all? Something that is doing well does not need to be modified or altered. I think there is only one answer to the question: We must renew it because we have lost apostolic effectiveness. Our life and witness and preaching, our way of expressing faith and showing love, no longer say anything to the people of our time. Or perhaps it would be more correct to say that they speak only to a certain social class, to which our preaching is not a threat, an alarm, or a call to conversion. Our witness, in the final analysis, is of interest to this class because it serves to defend and safeguard its present status.

We have come to realize that we must step outside our cloisters, that we must let down the drawbridge between our monasteries and the world, that we must identify ourselves with the people of our time, particularly the poor. We have become aware that we have lost our apostolic effectiveness and have become religious professionals. We have acquired a certain social status, a source of income, and a means of survival, all of which have nothing to do with Christ's summons. We realize that there is an abyss between our vocation and intention on the one hand and our actions on the other. Our preaching is without effect, our witness meaningless to the present generation, and our methods inadequate for preaching the word of God. We realize that our methods must be totally revamped if God's word is to touch people. We must redefine our objectives in today's world.

So we have set off toward renewal, only to find ourselves riding madly in all directions at once. Some of us have taken off our traditional habits or abandoned our cloisters. Others have patched up the defects in their training with the aid of psychoanalysis, university education, or some of the countless courses in renewal now available in such profusion. Others have become secularized professionals, rejecting every form of clericalism. Some have abandoned the religious life, become laicized, married. There has been some kind of change in all areas: liturgy, pastoral work, theology, and so on. Today every parish priest has his own liturgy, his own kind of preaching, his own catechetical orientation; every confessor uses his own approach with his penitents. The same questions receive many different answers, some more careful than others.

All this is quite natural at the start of a period of renewal, particularly when it goes hand in hand with a clerical emancipation proclamation. And yet I cannot help asking myself: Are we really on the right road? Will we really achieve apostolic effectiveness? Will our witness engage future generations and restore the confidence of the poor in us?

My impression is that it will not if renewal is restricted to form. If renewal simply means community life outside the cloister, the abandonment of clerical garb, jobs within the system that obviate our dependence on alms, then we will have altered appearances but renewed nothing. A parish priest may take to appearing in shirtsleeves, telling jokes and unburdening his soul to his parishioners, and still, all this notwithstanding, cling to the same vision of the world and the same purposes that he held before.

What counts, in other words, is not appearance but content. What really must be profoundly changed is not our dress or our lodging but our outlook and attitude, as people of faith, toward the world and history. It is not that our lifestyle has caused us to lose apostolic effectiveness but rather that our actions and our lives no longer convey the power of Christ's gospel message. All the renewal, theological and otherwise, will profit us nothing if it does not move us to act. Here lies the key to all the renewal that must take place. Moving into action implies *metanoia:* that is, breaking with the past, undergoing conversion, and adhering to a new vision. Awareness and courage are indispensable. Many have the awareness. They talk incessantly about justice, poverty, human liberation. What they lack is courage to create the conditions that would make renewal possible. They do not have the courage to recognize and admit that a true church of the gospel cannot exist within present-day social structures, that such a church must come into conflict with these structures. They do not have the courage to acknowledge the harsh reality that we live in a materialistic society whose conditions do not permit people to find fulfillment in God.

This last point is particularly noteworthy. The materialism surrounding us does not originate in ideology but in practice. In our consumer society, people are reified. Things have as much value as people, if not more. The essential goals of the culture that is our matrix are embodied in profit, power, and prestige. There is an explicit denial of God, although religion is accepted to the extent that it forms part of a system for neutralizing frustrations generated by the fact that, for most of us, work is self-sacrifice rather than self-fulfillment. This materialism, which shrewdly manipulates religion, is far more harmful than the ideological materialism that denies God, because it tends to create a situation in which Christians actively or passively acquiesce in glaring social evil.

The conversion or renewal of religious life will be logical and evangelical to the extent that it transforms the causes of our passivity. Apostolic effectiveness will be achieved only when our view of life and our attitude toward this world have changed. It will be achieved only when our identification with the poor is transformed from utopian ideal into social reality. For only then will we be able to respond adequately to Christ's summons.

Pray for us. Pray for all who are prisoners, inside and outside prison walls.

69

To the Dominican community in São Paulo

September 7

(. . .) Thanks for your good wishes and for the New Testament published by the monks of Taizé. It's the best translation I've ever seen. Who is distributing it? We would like a few more copies, because there are other people here besides our group who would like to read it.

I finished *O nariz do morto* by Vilaça. It's hard to classify it in a few words. The book represents an important step taken by the author: He has broken with religious atavisms and has opened himself wholly to the world. When I met him in Rio, he seemed a timid, introspective type who could not say a word about himself. Now he stands revealed; he can even talk about his failings, his uncertainty, and his doubts. But there are too many quotations in the book, as if he wanted to show off his erudition. His analyses are restricted to situations in which he has been personally involved; they deal with effects but don't ever delve into causes. Perhaps that's typical of autobiographical writing. But the book is well written, in a pleasing and poetic style. The part that struck me most forcibly was his autopsy of the religious life, particularly his account of past experiences with the Benedictines. Life with the Dominicans is less cruel. But it makes you ask: What's the sense of such a harsh and methodical rhythm of life, apparently lacking any perspective, if it is not to be found in prayer and contemplation? I find the contemplative life to be valid today, but it must be based on new models. It seems to me that the passivity of which he speaks in his book is quite pervasive in the religious life today, even more so than it was in the past. Chance stimuli come along to rouse people from it (. . .).

70

September 7

(. . .) You're right in your observation that my comments on church history place little emphasis on the mystery of the Resurrection. My true concern has been with the mystery of the Cross, which is for me the axis of Christian life on earth, according to the eschatological promise. The hellenic conception of God (Parmenides' "eternal present" of being, Plato's "supreme idea," Aristotle's "unmoved mover") is probably too far removed from the God of "the promise." Contemporary historical awareness has lost sight of the historical Christ, when in fact it is only his historical dimension that enables me to know something about God. In other words what I must know about God is precisely that which he makes manifest in Jesus Christ. And Jesus doesn't define the attributes of God. God is our Father, with whom we have a relationship of obedience and love. Everything I can learn about the import of this obedience and love is shown to me by Jesus Christ. The God I know about is the God living on earth, and this clearly contradicts all these divine attributes that sent medieval people into ecstasies. Jesus is a poor, limited, powerless, suffering human being, who submitted to death on a cross. The legitimacy and grandeur of this *kenosis* is proved to me by Christ's resurrection, by his victory over death. But only through this *kenosis* can I find and come to know God.

On page 5 of my essay you'll find an explanation of what I'm trying to say. The Protestant reformers said that the kingdom of God is to be found *sub cruce et sub contrario*. By this they meant that the kingdom of God is here, hidden under its opposite: Its freedom lies concealed under loss of freedom, its happiness under suffering, its righteousness under injustice, its omnipotence under frailty, and its glory under marred appearances. In the cross God is denied, yet he affirms himself in and through this very denial. So the banquet is prepared for the blind, the halt, the poor, and the sick—for the dregs of humankind. We will find God insofar as we are capable of choosing the humiliating pathway of Christ, impelled by the Resurrection, which is the apogee of this mystery, the affirmation in the denial, the hope into which our faith is translated. The Resurrection is the indispensable experience on this pathway that entails death but leads to life. In this sense, the only self-affirmation lies in self-abnegating; the only exaltation lies in humility; the only riches lie in discarding all one has; and only those who suffer can experience divine happiness.

I intended to make all this clear in my essay even though I did not explicitly point to the Resurrection as apogee. The contradiction of the Cross seems to me to be fundamental in the Christian mystery. It encompasses the whole praxis of Christianity: its renunciation, its questioning, its identification with everything that says no to the superficial values of modern culture. It is the contradiction between *pneuma* ("spirit") and *sarx* ("flesh") in Saint Paul's writings. It is the restoration of Christ as the one and only access to the mystery of God. The real obstacle to our rediscovery of the Cross is our lack of faith in the Resurrection. Christianity has been turned into the ideological basis of modern culture. Insofar as Christianity has been identified with the values of this culture, it has lost its openness to the future, its note of eschatological expectation, its dynamic hope in the divine promise that is being fulfilled in history. The world has imprisoned us in a closed circle: Our achievements have been deified, and we have lost the meaning of the Exodus and fallen prey to the worst possible kind of utopianism—the utopianism of the status quo. And all this has been blessed by the silent, static God of Greek metaphysics whom we have transformed into a mere object of our awareness, so that we can talk about him but cannot listen to him, live by him, obey him, or love him.

Today the church finds itself too far gone in ease and comfort to be roused by the mystery of the Cross. It lives in a world too reasonable to expect the Resurrection, too sensible to live in hope of something to come. We have the feeling that the inauguration of the kingdom is at hand for us, though not yet apparent. So we clean the house and set the table before the invitation is actually sent out. In the end we may find ourselves in for a terrible surprise: We will find that the seats have already been reserved for those who are travelling hopefully through the darkness of this world. (. . .)

71

To his parents

September 14

(. . .) Here the unbroken calm of prison life goes on as usual. The only news is that A. has been freed. I read in the newspaper that the Dominican prior of Montreal, Father Demarais, will come to Brazil to observe our trial as representative of our father general. (. . .) He's the author of a best seller called *Optimism Pills*. I hope he brings some for us too.

Although we're neither pessimists nor optimists, prison is a degrading place for a human being. Not for Christians, who know that one way or another we must pass through such a trial. But as an institution, prison is abominable. It is such a contradiction of the outside world that it ends by teaching you many things, about freedom in particular.

Above all, prison makes you examine your life, thoughts, scale of values, and many things that outward freedom does not always teach. It is a darkness in which many things are glimpsed and you can judge your own worth.

Meanwhile we wait for them to decide our fate. There are many people all over the world in a similar situation, so there is no sense in feeling that we have a monopoly on suffering. Our suffering is a symptom of the age in which we live. Time will pass, and so will our suffering. It's a matter of patience and hope. Feeling certain that this period of gestation will bear fruit, I pray that you be inspired with the same faith that animated Abraham and Sarah in the matter of their son (see Genesis 12ff.).

72

October 11

(. . .) I've been making the rounds of São Paulo prisons. I've spent almost twenty days as an involuntary hermit in the prison attached to the cavalry division of the military police. The experience was both profitable and terrible. There wasn't much to do. Or rather there was absolutely nothing to do. I managed to devote myself more intensely to prayer. The days were long, as they always are when you await the unknown. I woke to the braying of bugles, paced the narrow cell with short steps, and said my morning prayers. I had some black coffee with bread and butter, then went back to pacing. Then I sat down on my bunk and propped my feet on the opposite wall. To divert myself I would sing whatever snatches of songs I knew, make up others, conjure up past incidents and mentally retouch them. Old times would spring to mind with the immediacy and clarity of a photograph. At night there was a different sort of diversion, but it was hardly pleasant: I would observe the comings and goings of the cockroaches, who seemed well fed for a place where food is scarce. I kept trying to get them off the bunk, because there was only room for me on it.

After a week there, I got my own copy of the New Testament. I gave myself up to reading it avidly, trying to memorize the passages most relevant to my position. I read the four Gospels, learned Saint Paul's itineraries, and was deeply impressed by the realism and topicality of the Apocalypse. I came to realize that I was at my proper post. The monotony was then broken by a visit from an official, the most humane and sensitive one that I have met in my tour of prisons. It was a moment of contact, catharsis, and relief.

Life has afforded me the opportunity to undergo all these experiences. I do what I can to profit from them, to extract understanding from them, and to grow in my vocation as a Christian. In my heart of hearts I feel great joy, not because I am a prisoner but because I can see how free I still am (. . .).

73

November 3

Dear Friends, I have learned that you were satisfied with my depositions in court. I believe that I made myself clear, and that I aptly expounded my position as a Christian and as a religious. I came back to prison greatly relieved, as one would be when a long-dreaded exam is finally over. But the greatest joy of all was the release of R. and A. I learned that you had a fine celebration in the monastery.

Now our cell is emptier. There are five Dominicans here, along with a Blessed Sacrament father who was sentenced to fourteen months for a sermon he preached in a small town in the interior of São Paulo state.

Right now we are completely isolated from the other prisoners. Our cells, visiting schedules, and recreation periods are completely separate. Little by little we are adjusting the cell to our needs as best we can. The main thing is that we now have the minimum we need to get some studying done. From the prison authorities we managed to get some crude bookcases and a table. Now all we need is more lighting, because right now we really cannot see well at night (. . .).

Today we were visited by a Dominican bishop, Tomas Balduino of Goias. The new archbishop of São Paulo, Evaristo Arns, came to see us the day after his appointment. We had listened to his inaugural address on the radio, and we liked his firm and direct style very much. I have increasing confidence in the action of the Holy Spirit within the church. He blows where he wills and when we least expect him, but always at the right moment. (. . .)

On November 9 I will have spent a whole year in prison, perhaps the richest and most surprising year of my life, or at least the one I have lived most intensely (. . .).

74

To another religious community

November 9

(. . .) I received your letters expressing your approval of our court depositions. The preliminary questioning really went well. We were not afraid to speak the truth or to point out that the Christian spirit, compelled by love, far surpasses anything that the human mind has invented to preserve private interests that are not always identical with the common good.

If I have made a mistake in explaining my conduct, it is the same error as the one in the parable of the good Samaritan. He did not ask the man lying in the road if he was good or bad, if he had been beaten while doing good or attempting a crime. Jesus says only that there was a wounded man lying in the road in need of help. The Samaritan helped him without asking questions about his past, his intentions, or his motives. He picked him up, brought him to an inn, and footed the bill for his recovery and care.

The point of the parable is summed up nicely in an old proverb: *"Faze o bem, sem olher a quem"* "Good you should do, no matter for who." (. . .)

75

To his parents

November 15

Dearest Mom and Dad, after a year in prison we have received the body of Our Lord in Communion for the first time in our cell. Last Thursday the chaplain of the military police celebrated Mass here and left us some consecrated wafers. He's a good guy who gave us a lot of support when we were in isolation in the barracks. Now every evening after our traditional card game we recite the Psalms and receive Communion.

Wednesday we saw Father Domingos[48] again, to our great joy. He brought us greetings and best wishes from the whole Dominican family in Europe, and a letter from our father general assuring us that we are still his sons and containing a beautiful photograph of a thirteenth-century stone carving of Saint Dominic. On the photograph are the famous words of Dominic's great friend and disciple, Jordan of Saxony: "Dominic revealed himself to all, by word and deed, as a man of the gospel." We each got a copy inscribed with our name and the blessing of father general.

It seems that there's a lot of sympathy for us in Rome. Father Domingos had expressed a wish to see the pope, but he wasn't optimistic about its being granted. Within twenty-four hours, he received a letter notifying him that he had been granted an audience for the following day. It is rare for the pope to grant an audience so quickly. When Father Domingos entered his presence, Paul VI made as if to rise and embrace him, but protocol did not permit that. He said that he was following our case closely and had advised the nuncio to help us in any way we needed. He said that he stood by us in our sufferings and sent us his blessing. At the end of the audience he gave Father Domingos a little gift for us as a token of his affection: a beautiful little box with a cross made of olive wood that grew in Jerusalem. Ordinarily Paul VI gives a gift of rosary beads to visitors (Charles De Gaulle was buried with his hands crossed beneath his). This extraordinary gift to us reveals his affection. You may recall that some time ago we sent the pope a little wooden cross with our names carved into it that we had made here in prison. Well, it seems that he did receive our gift.

Father Domingos also visited three Dominican contemplative monasteries in France. All three were deeply interested in our case and sent us various little mementos, and they pray for us. One cloister, the one in Blagnac, is rather out of the ordinary: It accepts sick and infirm people so that they too can dedicate themselves to the religious life. There is a young nun there who entered after a terrible automobile accident. She has already gone through several operations that she was not expected to survive. After hearing Father Domingos preach, she submitted a petition to her mother superior. Her note was simple, personal, and private, but the mother superior gave it to Father Domingos, and it ended up in our hands. I was deeply moved when I read it: "Dear Mother Superior, if you wish, you may tell Father Domingos that I am offering up my sufferings to the Lord for our brothers in prison. God knows how much I suffer! In particular, I am offering up my next operation, in which I will try to be more courageous, more faithful, and more religious with the aim of helping our brothers." It was signed "Sister Marike." We wrote to her.

The more we are forced to live in isolation, the more we feel part of a huge family that knows no boundaries of language, culture, or nationality (. . .).

76

To Sister Marike, a French nun

November 15

Dear Sister, the words you wrote so pointedly have reached us through your mother superior. They have pierced to the depths of this prison where we have spent the last year for the sake of Christ's gospel. Your words are here before us, and they make us weep. Suffering is the point of encounter for Christians because it is a proclamation of the Resurrection. Now that we are aware of your sufferings, we know that the Lord has already transformed them into grace for us. Your letter makes us feel a renewal of our conversion in intimacy with our crucified Lord. He has prepared a banquet, and by his grace we prisoners have been invited. There at the table we have met you, in the place of honor, joyous and radiant. You have asked to be "more courageous, more faithful, and more religious"; that you are. Today we too make the same request as we think of you, for we are united by faith, hope, and love. We know that neither lack of freedom in the world nor lack of bodily health can prevent us from growing in the freedom of the Spirit or the life of God. Everything is grace. The road to

111

the Resurrection passes through prison corridors and hospital operating rooms. In great friendship,

Carlos Alberto (Betto) Christo, O.P.
Yves Lesbaupin, O.P.
Fernando de Brito, O.P.
Helio Soares do Amaral, S.S.S.
Giorgio Callegari, O.P.
Tito de Alencar de Lima, O.P.

77

To a religious community[49]

November 15
Feast of St. Albert the Great

Dear Dominican Sisters, Father Domingos has brought us a little bit of your life. We are grateful for your news and your cards. We are glad to know that people in a little corner of Europe are praying for us and sharing our sufferings.

We too live in a cloister where Christ is present, barred and guarded by armed soldiers. Our life here is simple, filled with the unforeseen and with hope. We are five Dominicans and a Blessed Sacrament father. Roberto was released on October 28. We sleep in our cell, as well as study, pray, and cook here. All of us have learned to cook. It is not only a necessity but also a pastime. We give our imaginations rein by inventing dishes that can be found only on our menu.

Every evening we recite the Psalms together, and our chanting rings through the corridor of the prison. We are prohibited from celebrating Mass, but we can now receive Communion because the chaplain has left us some consecrated wafers. We are allowed outside our cells three hours a week, and we can have visitors every two weeks. Our cell is rectangular, small, and crude with a high, barred window at the back. Through the bars we can see the sky and experience a sense of the infinite and of the certainty that our spirits know no bounds.

We thank you very much for your prayers. For you we offer

up our sufferings in Christ, who was also imprisoned and condemned. We know that all this is part of God's design and can be found at the very origins of the church. Unfortunately, we are not always capable of echoing the "fiat" that Mary taught us, but a profound joy pervades our lives. We praise the Lord who has deemed us worthy to be in prison, for here there are many who have been invited to his banquet.

We are bound to your convent and to each of you by the strong bonds of sanctifying grace. In great friendship,

Carlos Alberto (Betto) Christo, O.P.
Yves Lesbaupin, O.P.
Helio Soares do Amaral, S.S.S.
Giorgio M. Callegari, O.P.
Fernando de Brito, O.P.
Tito de Alencar de Lima, O.P.

78

To another religious community

November 19

(. . .) We cannot complain of the church, which has given us its support. We know that many religious communities in Europe are praying for us. Even at Lourdes pilgrims have prayed for us. This makes us more keenly aware of the communion of saints, more a part of the invisible but real church. One small part of this church is here behind bars, but it also extends wherever human beings are suffering and thus taking part in the redemption of the world. It includes those who have fallen by the wayside, who are poor. The kingdom is growing in their hearts, though they may not know it, or may perceive it only dimly. It summons us to a deeper sense of responsibility.

On the outside, in another sector, we built a church of flowering gardens, erudite sermons, and a guaranteed number of baptisms. But here we find people who are living the mystery of the crucified Christ in a continuing augury of the Resurrection. Their suffering bodies are the temple, their spilt blood is the baptism, their existential communion with Christ is the Eucharist. The church on the "outside" cannot know this human reality theoretically. Only by real life practice can its manifold riches be known. But it is not easy to cross the boundary line between theory and practice. The church in prison sends you a big hug.

79

To Pedro

November 29

Dear Friend, in your last letter you mentioned how difficult it is to establish a dialogue with the poor because their language is nearly incomprehensible to the cleric. The difficulty is of our own making. We have dissociated ourselves from the normal concerns of most people's lives under the pretext of thus becoming available for preaching the gospel. Many of us come from working-class families, and more than one cardinal has come from peasant stock. Our early entry into the seminary tears us away from our native environments and our families and offers us a way of life that represents a step up on the social scale. Our classical education alters our way of thinking and our vocabulary. The long training period in the cloister removes us from the real problems that affect the lives of everyone except the clergy and the rich. Is it possible at this point to build a bridge between our world and the world outside our ecclesiastical institutions? Is it possible to alter our point of view and our way of life?

When Pius XI stated that the church had lost the working class, he meant that the church had become so bourgeois that it had lost a feeling for the poor. As a result, the worker-priest experiment came into being. I think the problem will be solved not by priests becoming workers but only when we get workers as priests, when workers can join our ranks without betraying their origins. To reach that point, however, we will have to break down many barriers, put an end to many taboos,

114

and move from doctrinal speculation to Christian experience. What good is preaching without witness?

What worries me is that this renewal will not come about by our choice and personal initiative but will be forced on us by circumstances. The fact is that these circumstances are already becoming apparent, exerting pressure on us, and forcing us to adopt new patterns of behavior.

As you know, we are not allowed to receive the sacraments here. Yet never in my life have I experienced the sacraments so vitally as I have here. I think our circumstances have forced us to interiorize the spirit of the gospel as never before. (All you need is the specter of death before your eyes!) The totality of prison becomes a great channel of divine life. And how visible a sign it is!

Only the term *kenosis* can convey all that we are undergoing, for we have come to the point where all values exist solely within us. We accept our existence as a stripping away of all externals, for we have no idea when we will get out of here or what our life will be like. The only certain thing is that this episode in our lives places us in the context of Christ.

Now I can understand what my parish priest in Rio meant by saying: "The poor, by the very fact of being poor, attain to a union with Christ as intimate and real as that of the mystic." He also used to say that the real presence of Christ could be found in the sacraments and in the poor. That is true, I think. It is easier for people to meet Christ and recognize him when their living conditions resemble his.

The hard thing is to get to this theological "reduction" that puts us on Christ's level. We are imprinted with the Hellenic conception of God and have lost sight of the reality of him who is the very negation of that conception: Jesus Christ. Our religious reference point is more the idea of God than the life of the poor and persecuted Jesus. So we have lost the Semitic, biblical, historical, and eschatological dimension of Christian life.

Thanks for the texts you sent. Our fellow prisoners' interest in Christianity is striking. The material you sent is a great help. (. . .)

80

To his brother Luiz Fernando

November 29

(. . .) Joy, Joy, Joy! You need a lot of courage to be happy in the midst of so much suffering. You need strength. What can we do but believe in ourselves as the Lord taught us to do? We must see the human adventure through to the end without hesitating or complaining.

I try to find this joy within myself and draw it out so as to give a little of it to those who inhabit the other cold and gloomy cells in pavillion 2. It's a dreadful building, old as the tragedy of the human condition. On the ground floor are those who have been invited to the Lord's banquet, one or two hundred people who live by the law of the jungle. At night they cry their bitterness to the wind, beating out the rhythm on tin cans. They sing their desperation and their impotence in the face of the world and of life. They endure in silence an existence unknown to the rest of the world. They are the alienated ones, the people who stand on street corners and make passersby afraid.

On the upper floor are a hundred or so prisoners who have been arrested and charged under the government's security laws. They are laid out in the cells like so many packages in a huge refrigerator. We, half a dozen Christians, are kept in the rear, isolated from the other prisoners. We cannot talk to the other prisoners, but now the prison chaplain is permitted to bring us the body of our risen Lord, who alone can know whether we are worthy of it or not. I know the effort it costs me not to hate. . . . This is no mere difference of opinion. We live in history, and the future will show who was right. The future will judge imprisonment to be as abominable as torture and the Inquisition.

I know just how much despair waits in ambush behind these walls. Like unshed tears, it corrodes the heart, even the hearts of the young. Not all of us have the wisdom or strength to resist the situation in which we find ourselves. Not everyone manages to see in the dark. To those who put you in prison, you are just another face. To you who are put in prison, this is your whole life.

Facing our cell there is a cell full of common prisoners —bank robbers. One of them is twenty-four years old and has been sentenced to the same number of years in prison. Does that strike you as a reasonable period for rehabilitating a person? Does he need that much time to make a new decision about life? Can he do it under these conditions, locked in a cage and left to his own devices?

We must be happy and love with all our strength to keep hatred and despair from taking possession of us. We must stay calm, or the vast corridor that runs the length of the prison will end by devouring us. We must remain patient, or the rattling of keys that are not ours will make us deaf. We must have trust and confidence.

Human existence is radically transcendent. Only this transcendence, felt even by those who do not believe, keeps you from commiting suicide.

Pray for us.

81

To Pedro

December 4

Dear Friend, we read your letter together yesterday evening, after reciting the Psalms and before receiving Holy Communion. What you say coincides with what we are thinking here in the darkness of this world. I would like to write you my opinions on some of the most hotly debated issues in the church today.

First of all, I agree with Bishop Fragoso's[50] remarks on the institutional church: "In *this* church we will reach renewal and salvation. Because *this* church is us." There is no heavenly church, no papal church, no church hovering above humankind like an intangible, venerable image. If the church has gone wrong, it is we who have gone wrong. If the church reflects the authentic image of Jesus Christ, then it is we who are letting ourselves be led by the Spirit. Quitting the church is as impossible as quitting ourselves. If the institution is ponderous, backward, and rusted, it is we who have made it so. And we can also make it light, flexible, and forward looking.

The church is the great responsibility that Christ entrusted to us. It is not identical with him, but it is identical with us. It was founded by Christ, but it is also the work of human beings. We can repudiate it and prostitute it, or we can purify and sanctify it. We can even dismember it. But the church is us; it is ours; and it is truly the church only if it is consistent with the gospel. We do not have a separate church for each aspect of life: the church of leisure, the church of social work, and so forth. We have only one church, the church of faith in God's word. Those who wish to renew the church "from outside" may be able to renew themselves, but never the church. If church renewal "from inside" is difficult, that is because we have neither the courage to speak nor the humility to listen because the seminary taught us that the bishop has a monopoly on truth; but the bishop cannot always distinguish between his personal truth and the truth of the gospel. The two truths do not always coincide.

When I was arrested in Porto Alegre, I heard that someone in the episcopate regarded me with misgivings. But I had prayerfully scrutinized all my attitudes, declining to commit a sin of omission. I did not become disheartened. Today the pastor of Porto Alegre came to break bread with us in our cell. But what if things had turned out differently? What if I had been refused orders and "furloughed" from my religious family? I asked myself these questions. I thought about the silence imposed on men like Congar, De Lubac, and Teilhard de Chardin, and how they kept faith nonetheless. Their faith assured them of hope. If the Lord has brought me to prison, where I never would have chosen to go, he can bring me elsewhere. There are many ways to serve him and many roads to redemption—even outside the institution of the church.

You write: "A growing number are leaving." That is true,

particularly among the clergy. There are many who are tired of being priests, who feel empty within, who are attracted by the delights and possibilities of lay life. In part this is the fault of the structures that we have fashioned, adorned, and canonized, and that we now wish to tear down. It is not the fault of those who pull out. They are leaving to be more authentically themselves, to live more realistically, to look for what they cannot find within the church. Their departure is a challenge to those of us who remain.

I do not mean to say that they are dissatisfied with the enduring institution of the church as such. I think that their dissatisfaction has to do with the structures of the institution which have only transitory worth. Such things as seminaries, religious constitutions, discipline, canon law, the curia, the college of cardinals, and parishes are part of this structure and have no eternal value. The church came into existence without them, and it can live without them. Crisis occurs when we absolutize these structural elements and then, when they are challenged, react as though a vital part of the church is being torn away—as though the very essence of the church is being mutilated. But Christ founded his church with twelve poor, uneducated men. We will ruin it if we do not remember its origins. Most of the priests who leave are abandoning the structures, not the church as an institution. Many of them would still like to exercise their priestly ministry—within the framework of *new structures*. But they don't have the patience to wait out the long gestation period necessary to change a church by now embedded in seventeen centuries of tradition.

Unfortunately their contributions to society from outside the church often fall short of expectation. Frequently they are so deeply involved with their own personal problems that they can see nothing beyond their new domestic lives. The most serious danger for those who leave the priesthood is the eventual loss of faith. It is serious for us who do not provide convincing witness. It is scandalous that people lose their faith within our seminaries. It means that our Christian life is sluggish, individualistic, moralistic, and short of courage and risk and daring. It means that our seminaries turn out priests,

119

preachers, philosophers, and theologians—but how many of them are Christians? How many of them would be able to risk their lives for the faith?

I know several priests who left to get married. Here we have the whole problem of celibacy. In my opinion we must pay much greater attention to the problem of training people for celibacy. We consider celibacy a charism whose value lies in making possible our total service to the kingdom of God and in bearing witness to its eschatological fulfillment. But we must not forget that this charism has to develop, that our awareness of this fulfillment must mature over time. As things now stand, the assumption is that every priest must have a vocation to celibacy. So it is most important that we train people in such a way that our celibates do not become neurotic, maladjusted people whose feelings of unease towards the sensual world produce conflict and disillusionment. At present, however, it is assumed in our seminaries that every candidate for the priesthood is a potential celibate. To protect this charism, obstacles are put in the way of any and all contact with the sensual world, in particular with women. It is worse when the seminarian has not had any adolescence, when he has been a seminarian since the age of eleven, plucked too young from the bosom of his family and from natural friendships and tossed into the artificial and inhuman setting of some minor seminary. At the age of thirty, such a person is still acting like a teenager.

Another serious matter is the illusion that we try to impose on the candidate: that love of God will be a substitute for human love. That is a lie. Celibacy is a real renunciation. The void remains, and nothing mystical fills it up. Saint Teresa of Avila speaks of this void. She says that it is there that we learn how much we are capable of loving and how much we are capable of giving up for the sake of love. In this void we learn to what extent we are human and masculine, capable of loving a woman and making her happy. One who doubts his sexuality will suffer greatly, because asexuality is an abnormality. A priest can find self-fulfillment in celibacy only if he is fully conscious of his masculinity.

The great value of this charism consists in liberating us for service and above all in bearing witness to the greatness of the faith. I don't think an asexual priest can bear valid witness to his celibacy. By the way, every prison inmate is a celibate by force of circumstances. Many inmates have said to me: "I would never have thought it possible, but now I understand through personal experience how you priests can live without women."

A man's emotional maturity does not depend on matrimony, but the fact remains that many clerics are emotionally immature. The explanation lies in their defective, rationalistic training that is too dissociated from real life. This is why we have so many intelligent and educated priests whose naiveté and insecurity are painful to see. And this is also why I feel that no one should enter a seminary before the age of twenty. It will be a great day when we celibate priests can live side by side with married priests. (. . .)

82

(. . .) We must interpret in the present God's will for the future, using our awareness of the community in history and our memory of the past. You indicate to me how the Bible is relevant today and the extent to which it provides us with an empirico-theological means of analyzing the present and the future in the light of faith. Your observations demythologize the Bible so that it is no longer a book of magic accessible only to experts. Quite the contrary, the Bible is God's loving colloquy with human beings in history. As you see it, any workingman can understand the word of God and seek in it a guide to conduct.

I have the feeling that all our theology is too erudite. We speak a language inaccessible to the man in the street, who remains satisfied with superstitions, syncretism, and magic. How can we make him understand the meaning of religion stripped of dreamy sentimentalism? How can we make him develop an attitude toward life that is consciously based on Jesus Christ? The spirituality we convey is individualistic, disembodied, and neutral. It is a spirituality of submission and resignation that turns people into slaves or bourgeoisie. It is not a socially conscious spirituality—not an incarnate, bold, committed, risk-taking spirituality of courage and redeeming faith.

Hence the attitude of the Christian in the Western world is frequently passive, fatalistic, submissive to anything that smacks of tradition, law and order, prestige, and stability. Faith does not evoke a critical attitude. Religion is a kind of anesthetic to dull the sufferings of life, a consolation in misfortune, in short, an opiate. Christians settle down in a church in which they are assured of salvation and promised a reward hereafter. Their religious concern is to lead honest and well-regulated lives according to the false, opportunistic precepts of bourgeois society and culture. Good Christians are the good citizens, the ones who dispute nothing, challenge nothing, question nothing, protest nothing, claim nothing, subvert nothing. Sin for them is a purely individual phenomenon. God is a white God, a colonizing, land-owning, governing God—the God of the European who hoists the banner of liberty, equality, and fraternity and then uses it to shaft the peoples of Asia, Africa, and Latin America.

It will take more than an act of contrition to wipe away our sins from history. Our debt is still great. The crimes continue, and we preach peace and lack courage to denounce the assassins or to side with the victims. For us everything becomes "a delicate matter" requiring "prudence." Isn't prudence the church's greatest sin, the cause of all its sins of omission? This is one of the questions for whose answer we must look into the Bible. (. . .)

83

(. . .) Nothing is so attractive to a human being as freedom. Even animals and plants grow toward the light. Even a condemned man, whose freedom depends on serving out his prison sentence, will still count off the days bringing him closer to freedom. A boy who had served three years in prison told me that the worst time of all was the last year. It was then that he suffered most, for it passed so slowly. Every passing day was like the end of a great battle that would have to be fought over and over again until the war was finally over. A prisoner sentenced for an indefinite period suffers less because he can always hope that his imprisonment will be brief, although he may suffer more if he cannot be patient in the face of uncertainty.

In any case freedom exerts an irresistible magnetism on everyone. To be free, to be able to walk about at will, to be alone (which is impossible in a crowded prison), to plan for the future: All that is a dream right now. Since I don't even know when the future will arrive, I can only wait and regard my present situation as normal. I must create a certain rhythm of life here in prison, trying to improve myself despite the limitations. I must not give way to laziness, depression, or illusion.

Illusions weigh heavy in prison! Often you meet a prisoner doomed to a long stretch who nevertheless insists that, for quite inexplicable reasons, he knows he is getting out at the end of the month or the year. Imagination takes over; you begin to perform all sorts of mental acrobatics and end up crediting your wishful thinking more than your actual legal situation. From one newspaper article a prisoner will draw a thousand deductions and from them convince himself that he is about to be freed. It happens often here, and it is an awful thing to see.

Every now and then such a person regains his senses and realizes that his imagination has run riot. Then he gives way to confusion and depression, to a sense of failure, and to rebelliousness. But the madness is cyclical, and soon he falls prey to his imaginings again. They tranquilize him and temporarily lessen his pain, although his wound remains.

When you run into such an individual, it is useless to point out to him that he is mistaken. You must resign yourself to listen to him, pretend to agree with his reasoning, and share his harmless euphoria. Trying to contradict him would be like kicking in a child's sandcastle at the beach. (. . .)

84

To his parents

December 11

(. . .) I have so much to say, but my powers of expression are as limited as the space in this cell. It's hard to think in a situation in which the unforeseen can happen at any moment. You exist in a state of absolute uncertainty. Everything is waiting, tension, surprise. There is no end in sight, nothing we can count on. Destiny becomes for us either a palpable presence or a matter of total indifference.

This is the third kidnapping of a diplomat[51] that has reverberated through this prison since I've been here. It's curious that you never really get used to an event like this. It always has a tremendous impact on your unconscious. Even a prisoner who is sure that his name will not be selected finds it hard to disregard the possibility of being unexpectedly free. He shares the sense of expectancy that grips everyone. At every bit of news, every step of the negotiations, he feels as if his life is riding on a throw of the dice. There is little basis for predicting what will happen. You only know, for example, that those who will be freed will probably be prisoners charged with offenses carrying long sentences. But there are many surprises.

I don't see why the groups who carry out these kidnappings should have any interest in me. The only organization to which I belong is the church. The case of Mother Maurina[52] can be explained, I think, by the fact that she is a nun, the only woman arrested on such grounds in the West. Freeing her was designed to have political repercussions. Too many priests and religious have been arrested in too many places for us to be newsworthy.

What gets to us is not so much the possibility of personal liberation as the psychosis, the uncontrollable sense of expectation created among the prisoners at these times. In short it is the imminence of freedom for a whole group of people who must otherwise remain in prison for a long time. (. . .)

85

To Pedro

December 18

(. . .) Everything that society banishes from its midst ends up here. It's like a giant sewer into which refuse drains on its way to the ocean that is freedom. Living in a sewer is an indescribable experience. Here all sorts of castoffs meet, both the bad and the good. Each cell is one tank in the great dam that is prison. We live here together with the moles and cockroaches that breed under the city. We smell of our lack of freedom, almost unbearably. Above us the rest of the city goes on as usual, chewing, digesting, and excreting what it produces. Through these sad and narrow tunnels of cement and iron run people's dreams, ideals, blood, hopes, and unalterable faith that the water of the ocean is not far away. One day we will get there, and then the desert will bloom and the oases will dry up.

Here underground great things are happening. There are seeds germinating, a stream of water wearing away the rock, life asserting itself. Here lie the roots that will flower in the spring. It is underground that we find gold and silver and the roots of ancient oak trees. It is here that everything is born, blossoms, and grows toward the sunlight. From the earth comes power, nourishment, richness, and security; but since the sun is above, everything reaches ineluctably toward the light. Ascent is the natural motion of everything that exists.

Life in the darkness of this world teaches us to see things differently. It makes us morose as cockroaches, terrible as plague-bearing rats. It obliterates many of our former values, and makes us friends of the dark—which conceals what should be laid bare. We learn to feel our way, to see in the dark, to tell things by their smells. We know how to walk through potholes and puddles. Our only light against the darkness is the light of the Holy Spirit. We hear voices and can't tell where they come from, but they don't sound incoherent. Someone says, "This way!" Another cries out, "That way!" Holding each other's hands, we look for the way out of the darkness. Sometimes we are dashed against the walls and lose contact with each other. Sometimes the silence is broken by outbursts of mocking laughter or convulsive weeping. We fall, and love stops the bleeding of our wounds. Only hatred causes them to hemorrhage, although salvation may require a complete transfusion.

After a while, we become familiar with the mysteries of the darkness. We lose our fear, our need for security and consolation, our attachment to what the darkness has rendered invisible. We also lose our absolute certainties, our dogmatic truths, our interest in defending perfection, order, and purity. We come to believe in sin, anguish, need, uncertainty, and risk. We cling to the refuse that thickens on the walls, finding acceptance and repose in it. It is useless to be holy, pacifist, meek, resigned, and good, and we no longer are any of these things. We are pariahs, criminals, dissenters—banished, oppressed, and alienated: the wretched of the earth. If we are granted a little more life, it is because we are sure of this now.

But it is in all this that we find salvation. We identify with one who was born in a stable and died on the cross. We bear in our own flesh the stigmata of sorrow and suffering. Our faces are drenched with tears, but our hearts go on beating. Their beating rouses us. It keeps our blood moving and quickens our lives. Ill treated and in rags, we hear the voice of him who bids us to the banquet where the chalice of his blood will slake our present thirst. The more we try to control our feelings of expectation, the keener they become.

This is our path. It leads to liberation. It winds, but it never turns back. To turn back is to betray, to be afraid. We have passed the point of no return. We cannot look back. We can only go on. (. . .)

86

To his family

December 25

Dear Ones, it's Christmas night in prison. It brings back our childhood, midnight mass and gift-giving, the feast of meat and wine. I feel like writing a poem, but I know I'm not a poet. Tonight I feel very close to you. I feel freedom and tremendous joy that has been forged out of suffering, like the water that comes flowing from the rocks.

Today a contagious joy infects our prison. Clearly all of us here feel tremendous longing for those we love who are "outside." But it is also clear that even here, by living together so long and so intimately, we prisoners have become a family. In each of us who hunger and thirst for justice, peace, and liberty, he who embodies these ideals is being reborn: the infant Jesus.

The best gift of all was the release of Giorgio. He went off like a kid on the first morning of summer vacation. Radiant with happiness, he was reborn into the world. Now there are four of us in cell 17, and we may be reduced to three. Tito is among those whose release is demanded in exchange for the Swiss ambassador.[53]

Christmas night in prison. The guards came to wish us a Merry Christmas, and we wished them the same. Shortly before midnight we celebrated our liturgy. We chanted the Gloria, meditated on the Nativity according to St. Luke, sang the Magnificat, and recited the Psalms. Our Christmas dinner consisted of meat sandwiches on rolls, eggs, and tomatoes. For dessert we had a box of chocolates, which were gotten past the authorities with some difficulty because they have a little bit of liquor in them.

Now the whole prison is singing, as if our song alone, happy and free, must sound throughout the world. The women are singing over in their section, and we applaud. Bars and walls cannot imprison voices; they burst forth from hearts filled with friendship and love and united by a shared hope. On the floor below the nonpolitical prisoners are singing too. They beat out the *batuque*—the rhythm of the slums—on cans and boxes. Everyone here knows that it's Christmas, that someone is being reborn. And with our song we testify that we too have been reborn to fight for a world without tears, hatred, or oppression.

It's quite something to see these young faces pressed against the bars and singing their love. Unforgettable. It's not a sight for our judges, or the public prosecutor, or the police who arrested us. They would find the beauty of this night intolerable. Torturers fear a smile, even a weak one.

The acoustics of the prison corridor are very good. The whole place seems to be vibrating, as if everything that's meant by living free were blowing on the gentle wind of this summer night.[54] We can feel it because we are prisoners for the sake of other people's freedom.

In front of our cell stands a huge black man with a powerful voice, directing the singing. He is the top singer in this prison. He spends his days shouting from his cell: "Do you mean to say that besides being a prisoner I must put up with promiscuity? Let me out of here; I know your kind very well." He was arrested this year and probably won't get out for twenty years. Now he is telling us to get to *la* because our *re* is falling flat. (. . .)

This is another world. Many things cannot be told now. But I will remember it all forever. We will never be free of this experience, especially because it has taught us so much.

I hope that you are as happy as we are. Especially tonight, the bonds of faith bring us together. May our Father grant you all the best for the new year.

87

To his brothers and sisters

December 26

(. . .) Last Wednesday the Military Tribunal reviewed the petition for freedom on bail and house arrest that had been presented by our defense attorney, Mario Simas. The answer was no. The decisive factor in the eyes of the public prosecutor was the recent terrible fire at the Volkswagen plant in São Paulo. It must have been the work of terrorists, and it cost thirty lives and left many injured. I cannot figure out the relationship between that fire and our petition. It must be astrological, especially since the true cause of the blaze has not yet been ascertained.

All the same I must confess that the outcome is all right with me. I don't like the idea of house arrest, even in a monastery or episcopal residence. It's a matter of principle. I don't think I should contribute to turning a church into a prison or making a bishop into a jailer. The church's mission is to proclaim freedom, not to help suppress it. The church is a gift from God. Out of love of freedom and respect for this gift, I prefer to remain in the hands of those *who force me* to be a prisoner. I prefer to stay here. The church cannot and must not ever become a branch of the Brazilian prison system. There can be no fence-sitting in matters of principle. The easiest way is not always the right way. Hence I feel a certain relief at the decision of those who are my de jure and de facto jailers not to grant me house arrest.

88

To a religious community[55]

December 27

(. . .) I am deeply attached to the monastic life. I have always defended it, because I know that in the monastery one leads a committed life, a committed, contemplative life. And this contemplation is not unmindful of the Resurrection as the consummation of God's incarnation in history. We reach heaven via the streets of earth and God through encounters with other people. This witness to this faith, received in the monastery, has kept me from lapsing at various times into disdain for the contemplative life. I have always kept it in mind, and I have always felt a secret attraction for that way of life.

Insofar as the active life is concerned, the Lord has helped me to surmount obstacles that seemed insurmountable. My paths have always been turbulent and dangerous. Today I accept all that as part of my vocation. The Lord has called me through the voices of unbelievers. He has brought me to the very center of life in the world—to prison. He has cast me into the darkness of this world and this life. There, where I once thought only malice, indifference, and sin existed, I have found grace, fidelity, love, and hope. Christ's missioners may well be inclined not to stick their necks out; they may well prefer to keep close to the safety of parish and cloister, of catechism class and the dinner tables of the bourgeoisie, where the priest is an honored guest. But Christ stuck his neck out. He wasn't afraid to be tempted, vilified, and cursed, or to be friend to prostitutes and sinners. It didn't bother him to be called drunkard, glutton, law-breaker, and flouter of tradition. Christ went where we haven't the courage to go. While we look for him in the temple, he is in a stable. While we look for him among priests, he is among sinners. While we look for him among the free, he is a prisoner. While we look for him in glory, he is bleeding on the cross. It is we who have created distinctions, dividing the world into good people and bad. We think that God is bound by our ideas and preconceptions and formulations; but time and time again he sits on our doorsteps and asks for a slice of bread. . . .

I too was brought up in a milieu much given to expressing disdain for the poor, the blacks—whomever we considered the scum of the earth. Now I find myself among such people. Thrown into a narrow, stinking cell where the air reeks of sweat, I find myself surrounded by criminals—gangsters, murderers, thieves, child-molesters—people I would be afraid to run into on the street at night. And in my petit-bourgeois arrogance I think: "I must bring Christ to these people. I must improve them." But what do I discover? I discover that it is they who are revealing the true image of Christ to me. They stand alongside the crucified Christ and join him in accomplishing our redemption. I am ashamed of myself. I no longer know what to say. I only know that I must lay myself open to receive God's gift, to understand, like these people whom I call "the guests at Christ's banquet."

Of one thing I am certain: They are saved. Their thefts and murders are not their fault but ours. Why? Because we have not been wise enough to respect the rights of our neighbor. Because we have been selfish, greedy, and rich. Because we have drawn our blinds to shut out the sight of their slums. Because we have consented to the division between rich and poor. Because we have looked on these people with suspicion, disgust, and fear. They are poor, lowly, rejected, and condemned—like Christ. They are the living image of the Lord. (. . .)

89

To Sister Stella, a Brazilian contemplative nun

December 27

(. . .) I'm sure you weren't expecting a letter from me. But I suddenly felt the urge to write you, God knows why. It's daybreak, the time when I pray, meditate, and write. A prisoner's time is not rigidly scheduled. Today for example we ate our midday meal at three in the afternoon (mashed potatoes). Sometimes we have supper at four in the morning. Here we are at least free to ignore the clock, a freedom almost impossible on the outside.

I have many reasons for wanting to dialogue with you. It was eleven years ago that I first tramped up the stone path leading to your convent. It was carnival time, and I was making a retreat with a Catholic Action group in your chaplain's quarters. I visted the convent faithfully from 1959 to 1962. There I came to know Father M., who seemed to me poles apart from us, incapable of looking without suspicion upon the Catholic Action movement. That was the time when we were discovering the social dimension of the Christian message. A person with fond memories of the movement for liturgical renewal[56] had a hard time feeling kindly toward all the social agitation that, following Vatican II, became the preoccupation and mission of the whole church. Then I made friends with Father A., a plain man forged in the harsh and humble school of missionary work among the Indians. I wonder where he is today.

In those days I became friendly with a boy who used to serve Mass every day at the convent. I would jump out of bed every morning at the sound of his motorbike turning the corner of our street. We would climb the hill for Mass in the poor and somber chapel of the convent. Its walls were faced only with brick, and from the other side of the broad wooden grating we could hear the sweet and moving chanting of the nuns. Then we would have coffee in the little parlor. What a beautiful time it was! (. . .)

Now I'll talk a little about myself. There are four of us Dominicans in this cell, which is no bigger than the parlor of your convent. We get out only twice a week, for an hour-and-a-half of sun. The date of our release is not yet set, so we are still waiting. Roberto and Giorgio have already been released, along with the former Dominican, Maurizio. Fernando, Ivo, Tito, and I are still here. Tito is included in the list of prisoners to be exchanged for the Swiss ambassador, but the government is still putting off a final decision. We have suffered a great deal during these fourteen months in prison, but we are well and in good spirits because we know that this is the road we must follow. We have had much support from our brothers in the faith, including Archbishop Paulo Evaristo[57] and the apostolic nuncio. We realize that we are prisoners here so that others may be free, and our hope makes us content.

Pray for us, and rest assured that we are offering our meager suffering to the Lord in the hope that he may grant grace and blessings to your community. An affectionate hug to you all.

90

To Sister Ruth, a Brazilian nun[58]

December 31

Dear Cousin, it was a great joy for me to receive your letter and best wishes on this last day of the year. I am replying immediately primarily because I want to get back in touch with you. I value our friendship.

In your letter you told me that you're trying to integrate your life with the world's, that you have come to realize that "structures depersonalize us." This is a marvelous insight, particularly coming as it does from a city like Rome. We too have been thinking about the same things, and we have reached a conclusion that will not be pleasing to many people: This structure is not undergoing renewal, it is doomed to die. New wine cannot be put into old wineskins, a new patch cannot be sewn on threadbare material. The experiments in renewal that we have seen so far are for the most part artificial. Many people think that renewal means working outside the cloister and earning your own living. This is a necessity of the times. In our desacralized world, the cleric has lost his social function because no one derives vital benefits from cultic worship. At the same time the bourgeoisie no longer supports the church because the church is gradually coming to oppose bourgeois values. So we are obliged to go out and work, but often in jobs that have no apostolic thrust to them. We become enmeshed in the gears of the capitalist system. We "experience life."

But Jesus did not create fishermen-apostles. He took fishermen and made them apostles. We should have the sense to imitate him, to make working priests. For even though we hold jobs, we still live in luxurious houses such as only the rich can afford. So do we really deserve to be called disciples of the poor fishermen of Galilee?

Yes, structures are depersonalizing us, because they have gradually become more important than the gospel. Within these structures we are thought of and treated like helpless children. Naiveté has corroded our critical spirit. We have

133

become masks of blind obedience to the details of our discipline. In our cloisters we are molded into mummies, and creative initiative is condemned as lack of discipline. Alongside our well-appointed houses we have built schools to educate the bourgeoisie, setting our seal of approval on their right to possess *things* in a world where most people possess nothing but hunger and misery. We have lost the apostles' daring. We have given our blessing to European colonialism in Asia, Africa, and Latin America. Time and time again in mission lands we have tried to proclaim the gospel in French and English, and we have drunk deep at the well of social and racial prejudice. To conceal the fact that the skin of the black is repugnant to us, we have said that he is "not very intelligent," that he practices "evil customs," that he is a "savage." We doubt the honesty of the mulatto; we consider Orientals "primitive." But God is not bound by our classifications, as I have discovered here in prison.

I came here filled with lofty intentions. I was going to bring the gospel to these "creatures"—thieves, murderers, brutes you'd be afraid to meet in broad daylight. *But God was here long before I arrived.* Believe me, it is they who have revealed Christ to me. Before we arrived, he was here with them, accomplishing the redemption of the world. They are crucified alongside Jesus. Whose fault is it? Our fault: because we have closed our eyes to human misery, closed our windows against the sight of the slums, avoided the red-light districts, and adopted the bourgeois lifestyle available only to the privileged few.

Living with these people here, I have learned how despicable are our prudence through which we avoid these people, our customs through which we shirk the radicalism of the gospel, our ever-so-sensible counsels through which we convert no one, our lethargy disguised as patience in the face of oppression and social inequality and institutionalized violence.

We have faith in these new stirrings of the Holy Spirit within the church. Perhaps the Spirit has cast us into the world's darkness so that we may learn to view history differently. This suffering is profoundly redemptive.

This is the last evening of the year. As we did at Christmas, the prisoners in each cell along the corridor have formed samba lines. Our sorrows are forgotten and our hopes rekindled. We pray, and we offer up part of this cup of suffering for your sake and your community's. Is Sister Matilde there with you? If she is, give her a big hug for me. Pray for the church in Brazil, for it is living through a difficult time. An affectionate and nostalgic hug for you.

91

To his cousin Maria

December 31

(. . .) There are three Dominicans left in prison with me: Fernando, Ivo, and Tito. Tito is included in the list of prisoners demanded in exchange for the Swiss ambassador, but the negotiations have bogged down. Roberto was freed on October 28 after he had attempted to commit suicide by slitting both wrists. It was the psychological effect of prison life that led him to it. It was not an act of weakness but the protest of a man who had been in prison for almost a year without any charge whatever having been lodged against him. Maurizio, who has left the order (he decided to leave even before his arrest), was freed in November. Our Christmas gift was the release of Giorgio, an Italian, on December 24. There had been no charge against him either. So the four of us are left, waiting for a trial whose date has not yet been set. We are accused of a "crime," namely, that we hid people wanted as subversives by the police and helped them to flee the country. This is an offense according to Brazilian law, but not according to church tradition. Church precedent for aiding fugitives dates from the time when Mary, Joseph, and the child Jesus fled into Egypt to escape Herod's persecution—as I told the Joint Military Council.

There are more than three hundred political prisoners here, both men and women. For seven months there were forty of us in a cell that had room for twenty. For four months I slept on the floor. In September the inmates organized protest demonstrations against the terrible prison conditions and the excessive slowness of the judicial proceedings. Because Giorgio went on a hunger strike, retaliatory measures were directed against us priests. We were taken from prison and sent separately to different barracks. I spent twenty days in solitary confinement in a cell belonging to the cavalry barracks. It measured one meter by three, with hardly room for a bunk. It had no water or sanitary facilities, and I was only allowed to use the washroom once a day—at 8:00 A.M. I faced total solitude there, surrounded by soldiers but unable to exchange a single word with anyone. My only reading material was my New Testament. I was later transferred to headquarters where conditions were slightly better. There at least I could wash up, because there was a water faucet in the cell.

At the end of October we were brought back to Tiradentes prison. We were kept completely separate from the other prisoners, confined in cell 17. It measures two and one-half by six meters. The walls are damp and gray, and there are a lot of holes in the ceiling. So there is a constant dripping of water when it rains. At the back of the cell is a water pipe with·a faucet. There we wash up and get water to drink and to cook with. We cook our own food that is sent to us from the monastery because the prison food is unbearable. We get out of the cell for an hour and a half in the sun only twice a week, and we have visiting hours once every two weeks.

We spend our time in prison reading, doing calisthenics, and studying theology. We are not idle. Every evening we get together for prayer. We recite the Psalms, chant hymns, and receive the body of our Lord. We have not received permission to celebrate Mass, but the chaplain of the military police comes with consecrated hosts every so often.

For me all this represents a revival of the life lived by the church during the first three centuries of its existence. It would be incredible if the church were not present somehow in prisons under a regime that oppresses the human person. Here we are in fellowship with "the wretched of the earth." We are in communion with those who have been invited to the Lord's banquet. All this is grace, as is any suffering endured in a Christian spirit.

I can assure you that prison has effected radical transformation—a profound conversion—in us. Behind these bars many things lose the value they once had, and new discoveries turn us into new people. It is good for the church to go through prison. There it rediscovers the way that Christ had pointed out, the way of poverty and persecution. (. . .)

1971

92

Dearest Mom and Dad, my first letter of the year is to you. I was hoping to send it by T., but I don't think it will be ready in time. She came to see me. Her decision to come to São Paulo seems sound to me. There comes a time when it's important to take off on your own.

We had our New Year's Eve party here in prison. It was pretty much the Christmas party all over again. We sang everything we knew, in a concert that lasted from eleven at night to three in the morning. Very lively and very off-key. I listened more than I sang. I don't have the gift of song, which belongs to the birds and which God has kindly granted to some people. But my three companions sang till they were hoarse. They are the most singular trio that I have ever encountered. Tito knows the lyrics of all the songs, even the old *boleros* that were popular at the same time as the maxi-skirt. Ivo knows the tunes, and Fernando shouts them out. From every cell a small chorus sang together, making the whole prison resonate. And hands thrusting through the bars beat time on the heavy iron doors.

One year has ended, another begun. For some of us it means one year less in prison, for others one year more of waiting.

We, for instance, don't know how much longer we will have to stay here. Now rumor has it that we'll be out soon, and we hope the rumor turns out to be true. But rumor does neither us nor you any good. It's better to assume that we'll get out when the discharge papers arrive. These flights of fancy may nurture hope, but the prison bars remain impassable as ever, with us on the inside. I prefer not to cherish any illusions because nothing is more dangerous for a prisoner than impatience. Imprisonment is not like illness, in which the doctor's contagious optimism is a real psychological aid to the patient's recovering. This is different, as I noticed with Giorgio. In the last six months of his internment somebody came by at least once a week to assure him that he would be released the following week. Result: As the weeks passed and his irritability mounted, he gradually lost all power of concentration. So it is better to wait for freedom to come to you than to try to grab it. I suspect that the family's impatience is greater than mine.

(. . .) And I see people here who will not go free for ten or twenty years. There was a kid here, just recently transferred to a penitentiary, twenty-nine years old and sentenced to sixty-seven years in prison. He has already served ten. I have thought about it for a long time, and I ask myself how in the name of justice it can take sixty-seven years in prison to rehabilitate a nineteen-year-old! Compared to people like him, I have no right to feel sorry for myself, particularly since I always knew what I was getting into and why. Some people are convicted for actions for which they are not wholly responsible. In a sudden burst of anger they commit an act that has irreparable consequences. There are prisoners who will have to pay for such a lapse with many years of their lives. For example, I think I would not be able [censored]. A longing bearhug to you all.

93

January 12

Dear Friends, it is not too late to thank you for your best wishes. The past few days I've been very busy with my Christmas mail because I always answer everyone who writes to me. Besides the mail from our families we get letters offering to pray for us from many Catholic convents. It does us good. Personally I have blind faith in the value of prayer although I don't care to turn it into a list of petitions. In God's plan nothing happens by chance. So I know that I will get out of here at the right moment, no sooner and no later, though everybody (including me) hopes that the right moment won't be too long in coming.

In prison it is important to wait patiently for the moment of liberation. You have to know how to derive benefit from every aspect of this experience. The fact is we are learning a great deal about people and about life. Particularly now, because we are in a cell-block of common prisoners, despite the fact that by law we are entitled to a special prison of our own. Here we see the other side of the coin. Being in this prison puts us in contact with all those who are detested and condemned by our society, and there is no doubt that it alters our personalities. Our web of illusions is torn apart by every breeze that blows. It becomes plain to see that we do not live in the best of all possible worlds.

Though I have been in prison for fourteen months, I can't say that I've gotten used to it. Even birds don't get used to it, much less people. But intelligence enables us to adapt to even the most deplorable circumstances; at least it keeps us from being overwhelmed by them. In a time of suffering we must preserve our dignity and recognize the fact that this trial is not in vain. It is only one moment in our chapter of history, which keeps moving ahead. I have every confidence in the future.

Now there are three of us Dominicans here. We are in a small cell with gray and white walls and a triple-barred window. At this time of year the heat is almost unbearable, but we still manage to read, do some handicrafts, exercise a bit. It is not exactly a debilitating routine. In a prison filled with inmates something new is always happening, particularly right now when there is a lot of coming and going.

I hope you all are well and I send you a big hug filled with fond memories.

94

To his brothers and sisters

January 14

Dear Ones, everything is OK here. Tito was released Monday morning. For many days he was under extreme tension. He was taken away several times for identification purposes, and he was photographed in the nude. Then he videotaped a statement of his reasons for leaving the country. He stated that his only interest was in saving the ambassador's life. I think he'll have lots of opportunities for study abroad. Probably he'll go to Europe.

So now there are three of us in the cell. We have more room and a situation more conducive to work and study. (. . .)

95

To Pedro

January 20

Dear Pedro, you are quite right in saying that we can't read the Bible without reference to our own condition (being careful not to define our "condition" solely and narrowly as the circumstances of our own life). Through my condition I come to recognize myself in God's word. It's a shame that the church's preaching has not always respected these human conditions,

144

which are simultaneously subjective and objective. Herein lies the mistake of those who concentrate exclusively on the *letter* of the Scripture, a way of thinking that comes of concentrating on the letter of the law. We need only recall the missionary enterprise in colonial Brazil, when the Indians were forced to undergo baptism. Today the pope's frequent appeals for peace are unrelated to objective conditions. People want peace, undoubtedly, but insofar as it is the fruit of justice.

In the notes you sent me I read the following: "The Bible does not purport to transmit a specific cultural and historical view of the world, *because the word of God is adaptable to all.* It seeks to bring all human beings in the course of their lives into contact with Jesus Christ under conditions that make possible a true conversion, both individual and collective. It's this latter aspect of conversion that calls for the transformation of the world in which we live" (p. 7).

There is no denying what you say about the results of conversion (which means fulfillment of the promise through the manifestation of God's kingdom). But I doubt that the word of God is adaptable to *every* cultural and historical view of the world. I think that some views are the negation of God's word: for example, the mechanistic and the liberal views. The first reduces the autonomy of human activity and hence human freedom. The second is fundamentally individualistic and anarchic. Unfortunately the word of the church often adapts itself to this liberal vision, thus flagrantly contradicting the word of God. Many Christians have a subjective and alienated vision of the world that causes them to read the Bible myopically. They cannot break out of the shell that imprisons and corrupts their understanding. If our present is to be explained solely by the past, and its meaning for the future is shown us by the past, then clearly we must consider the Bible to be God's word to us here and now. In other words what God does has continuity in history. It is a permanent and lasting activity. We can perceive it at times, but we can never know all its principles and its instruments. We know that God's activity does not and has not ever reduced the force of human activity. Believe it or not, man tends naturally to act in conformity with God. On the other hand, God's activity intends the good of the world and its people. It does not have as its object single individuals, and it certainly does not propose the triumph of a heavenly kingdom and the dwindling into insignificance of this earthly one. It exists in the world and in time and identifies itself with every longing for justice, progress, freedom, peace, and love. It escapes the limitations of our condition and it does not necessarily well up among those of God's people who constitute the church. It is the activity of the just person for his people. The Bible is precisely the mirror in which this activity is reflected most clearly. So it is clear that God's activity is not present where a concern for the future is lacking, where the present is turned into an absolute and the past into the subject of an incurable nostalgia.

In your notes you say: "The same God who gave direction to our lives in the past continues to do so today. In our present God draws the course of the past toward the future."

This indicates the historical awareness inherent in the Bible and the need to have such awareness in order to understand God's word today. It seems to me that the catechesis based on "salvation history" has not produced such understanding. There are many ways of thinking about history. Many catechists are capable of thinking about it only episodically or allegorically. They know the history of the Hebrew nation as they know the history of the Persian Empire or the French Revolution. They cannot see the present historical moment as part and parcel of salvation history. They do not recognize today as history in process, hence they cannot establish continuity between past and present in salvation history. But if the God of Christians were not present in the currents of today's history, then he would not be the God of Jesus Christ.

So contact with the Bible should make us feel inextricably linked to the past and inescapably committed to the future. But the future will not be brought about by intentions alone, much less by the preservation or perfecting of an inhuman social order. Building the future means breaking with the present because a bad tree cannot bear good fruit. That is what the

Bible teaches us. The Hebrews separated by violence from the Egyptians. They realized that their future called for a new reality, and since they could not persuade the pharaoh, they had to break with him.

Now I ask myself: To what sort of future is the church committed? Can the peace so much desired by everyone come from the hands of those who provoke war? Can the future arise from the ruins of a social order that has reduced the person to the level of a tool of production? The difficulty experienced by the church in answering such questions indicates how much we lack historical awareness that would immerse us in fashioning the future, that is not limited to vague and abstract yearnings but committed concretely and specifically to the struggle for such a future.

Like the prophets, people who plunge headlong into denunciations of the present in order to inspire commitment to the future risk their necks. So, like our bishops, people prefer simply to decry the "abuses" of the present and to believe that the future will arise spontaneously out of a corrupt and agonizing present. The minority of activists who choose to break with the present must face up to the painful consequences of their choice. Living for the future, they can expect only cruel persecution in the present. It is the age-old dialectic of history.

Perhaps, to get on with the subject, we should define more carefully what we mean by history. From the Bible we can deduce a theological concept. But I get the impression that Christians are not yet capable of interest in this theological concept, much less in any other concept of a philosophical nature. They accept history only with subtitles—a chronicle of Past Events involving Great Men. There are people who think they know the history of the Roman Empire because they know a bit about emperors and their conquests. That is like trying to recount the history of Brazil through the biographies of its presidents. My first impression is that the church, or rather its teachings, has an idealistic concept of history, one in which events are considered to be independent of human activity, as if history were the motive force of human

147

beings instead of the other way around. This is virtually to "identify history with God." Church teaching also tends to the belief that history is always made by "others," and our task is solely to advise and inspire, to certify and judge. But those who commit themselves to action, who struggle and suffer and endure the pangs of childbirth, will be the "others."

The Bible presents the past as a normative standard. What was the attitude of the people of Israel toward history? They placed themselves in the vanguard of history, consciously fighting for their own liberation and their own future. They admitted their own mistakes and trusted in God's promise. But what is the attitude of contemporary Christians toward history?

Your list of suggestions (p. 32) on learning to read the Bible is very good. The fourth says: "The Bible calls upon us today to recognize that God is journeying with us." We must be imbued with this awareness. God is present in the history that is unfolding around us, that is reported in the newspapers and on TV. But how are we to recognize his presence? It is easy to say that God is present in history. But it is hard to assert God is present in the Vietnam war, in the Middle East, in the struggles of the Black Panthers in the United States and the Jews in the Soviet Union, in the guerrilla movements of Latin America. And yet that is precisely what the Bible teaches us. Cyrus did not have to be virtuous for Isaiah to see him as one sent by the Lord. The important thing was the historical function that Cyrus embodied for Israel at that moment. Hence I can say to you that I can recognize the presence of God in all the wars and revolutions going on today. But why is it that we today cannot glimpse the signs of this presence? The truth is that we are living in contradiction to our own principles. Either the word of God gives us our bearings amid concrete, tangible facts, or it makes no sense to us. We are imprisoned in vague theoretical principles that we don't know how or when to apply. In the West we defend with tooth and nail the individual's right to private property, but in the East we allow the United States to trample on the collective right of a people to be sovereign in its own land.

148

You write: "The Bible is a book born from people and meant to guide them along their way." It is God's plan for human history. A great responsibility rests on those who are cognizant of this plan by virtue of their faith. Great blame attaches to those who try to shirk their part in carrying out this plan. You are perfectly right when you say, "Today there is no absolute division between textual interpretation and life." But it will not be easy to establish the connection between the two. The long period during which the Bible was a closed book for Catholics is costing us dearly today. It is still not easy to find a Catholic who reads the New Testament, . . . and if you do find one, you don't know if he has managed to take off the blinders that keep him from seeing the light. . . .

I also want to touch upon your fine explanation (pp. 61ff.) of "how the Bible deals with God's activity outside his people." This activity is great, and as divine pedagogy it forces God's people to recognize their mistakes and get back on the right road. The Catholic church has begun to do this with Vatican II. I have no doubt that God is challenging us by inspiring an avowedly atheistic movement that seeks at least to eradicate material misery [censored].

I like your proposal to extend the concept of salvation history to our own history. But we must keep in mind the fact that many people are not capable of discerning in their own history the signs that point to the promised future. There is so much alienation around. We won't break out of stagnation until we break the hold of alienation on our awareness. And this is an extremely difficult thing to do.

Your notes have been extremely enlightening. I forbid you to stop sending me such food for thought. Remember me in your prayers. (. . .)

96

January 24

Dear Sister, I know that you have been operated on and are now, thank God, convalescing. I'm afraid that at times like these we don't always have the courage to treat suffering as something temporary and bearable. But it should not be difficult for us Christians because we know that the way to Resurrection is through the Cross. That does not mean we should simply resign ourselves. If pain is the result of evil, I don't see why God would want only resignation from us. Instead God asks us to have the courage to face suffering and surmount it. In any case pain does liberate us; this is the discovery we all must make through our own passion.

Today I am more than ever convinced that I cannot complain of my situation; but neither can I call it the will of God. First of all I realize that my suffering is insignificant compared with that of countless other people. I think of whole families living in poverty and hunger, of people born physically or mentally defective, of the common prisoners now in my cell who will tomorrow be taken to police headquarters. . . . Second I think that God would be denying his own goodness if he wished to see us suffer. God wishes us good, peace, joy, well-being, and mutual respect. If I am a prisoner here, it's not God's will but the will of people who judge me to be a political criminal, a danger to the security of the state.

If you are sick, it is a bodily disorder that science is trying to overcome. Nevertheless it is certain that God intervenes in every moment and in each event of our lives. It is not God's will that I find myself here, but his will is revealed to me in this place just as I am sure it is being revealed to you. He asks us to be strong, to be wise enough to carry our cross and not succumb, because his yoke is sweet and his burden light. He also asks us to transform our suffering into an act of solidarity with all those who suffer in the world. This is the communion of saints, which leads us to liberation, restores our strength, and fills us with courage.

So we need fear nothing. We don't let pain grind us down and triumph over us. Only for the Christian can suffering be a freely chosen option, as it was for Jesus Christ. He chose the way of the cross, not out of masochism but because every true redemption, like every new life, is born of pain.

People are talking about the canonization of a Polish priest who was pastor of a village during World War II. When the Nazis invaded Poland, they decreed that ten civilians would be summarily shot for every German soldier killed. A soldier was killed, whereupon the Nazis rounded up all the men of this village and took them to the town square. Among them, unbeknownst to the Germans, was the priest. Ten villagers were picked at random to be shot for the death of the soldier. The priest was not one of them, but a workingman standing near him, father of five small children, was. Immediately the priest stepped forward and asked to die in his place. Since the selection had been random, the exchange was permitted; the children's father was spared, and the priest was taken away. The Nazis quickly discovered that he was a priest. The other nine they shot; him they locked up alone without food or water. Days later, he died, overcome by the torture of total abandonment.

Can we say that this priest willed his suffering? No. He willed to save the life of a man who had five children to take care of. We should not will that our suffering be extinguished but that while it exists it should bear fruit in Christ's mystical body for the liberation and salvation of humanity. (. . .)

97

To a friend

January 31

Dearest Alice, prison does not afford much happiness, it is true, but it does lead us to many discoveries. I can say that 1970 was as important a year for me as 1965, the year of my novitiate. In 1965 I learned the nature of faith; now I know how to live it. I may not be able to carry what I've learned much further, but I'm sure that I can never again know the tranquil conscience of the Christian who goes to Mass on Sunday and is content with a minimum of spirituality.

In prison you realize that it's impossible to be free simply by chance and furthermore that we are prisoners of the many useless limitations we allow life to impose on us. At least here the complete physical limitation—living behind bars for an indefinite length of time—completely dissolves all the other limitations that we have acquired from a bourgeois education full of falsity. You cannot cheat here. It's a clean game, and the only thing that counts is the truth of each individual. Words, appearances, and illusions lose their significance. We are all reduced to our human essence. You see yourself in a mirror, stripped of disguises and fantasies. Two alternatives are open to you: You can take flight in laziness, fear, or madness; or you can break with the past and commit yourself to the future, though it cost you your life.

After a certain length of time (more psychological than chronological), the prisoner begins to glimpse the moment of liberation. It is like a hoped-for vision of resurrection. Freedom does not mean simply physical liberty. It also entails a new manner of living, a new set of values, the overcoming of old habits. For us Christians it means continuing in the poverty that we have come to know here. It means a new spirit of service, one that is much simpler, more radical, and coherent.

That's why this past year has been so important for me. I have come to half a dozen conclusions that I consider fundamental to my life. No one can remain the same after spending so much time in the darkness of this world. For lack of light we have learned to see ourselves in the dark. We have learned to see into things, to perceive the essential qualities by which they exist and are defined and expressed. We realize now that our task is a terrible one. If we have faith besides, then nothing can go on as before. All that remains for us is to figure out how to act from here.

In short I have no reason to complain. Despite everything, so profound an experience is worth the cost. I know that on my own I would never have encountered certain situations that prison forces upon me. Finding myself here, I accept these situations and try to make the most of them. (. . .)

98

To a religious friend

January 31

Dear Ernesto, (. . .) For two days we have not had a drop of water in this cell, which seems like a pressure-cooker. The roof of this cell block is not tiled, so the ceiling gets scorching hot during the day. And there is no ventilation. Don't try to imagine what it's like; it's indescribable. It feels as if there will be a riot at any moment. In the overcrowded cells the smell is unbearable. When it rains, we try to collect a little water through the holes in the roof. But the heat is intolerable. Prisoners shout for water day and night, but our cries echo uselessly down the dismal prison corridors. At these times we see how easily a human being can cease to be rational and become a brute. Every so often we get a pitcher of dirty water from God knows where; we boil it before drinking. With every sip we take, our bourgeois habits—already pretty well corroded by these fourteen months in prison—crumble a bit more. Even our scale of values has been altered by our circumstances here. Many things lose their importance to us, and new criteria appear. In other words we undergo a change in social class. Our whole worldview is profoundly changed —from theory to practice. Whoever doesn't adapt gives way to despair.

Throughout this period my chief concern has been the church of God in Brazil. Only now do I see clearly my vocation within it. We have a great task to carry out. We must stop pointing to the past with the Gospels in our hands. We must live and learn how to live. I am trying to analyze, as scientifically as possible and without confining myself wholly to the realm of ideas, the impediments to and possibilities of living a

Christian life. It would take too long to discuss it now, but I can assure you that this preoccupation makes time fly for me in prison. How do we overcome the dualism between faith and life? Between divine revelation and history? Between faith and politics? I make every attempt to put this period of seclusion to good use. It is cruel, but it is not in vain. Many things will be born in this darkness.

Your being in court when I gave my deposition made me so happy. Christ was right: We shouldn't be concerned about what to say; the important thing is to bear witness.

Thanks for your prayers. I pray for you too.

99

To Pedro

February 2

Dear Pedro, your postcard made us very happy. It had a particularly good effect on the psychological atmosphere here. Locked up all day in this pressure-cooker and melting in this terrible summer heat, it was a real relief to look at the snow-covered mountains of Albiez-le-Vieux and to know that you had thought of us there. Here we would be satisfied with a sliver of ice to melt in the warm water that flows from our tap after boiling its way through the city pipes. The ceiling of our cell is red hot.

I was once up at an altitude of 5300 meters. There was no snow, only ice. I didn't have oxygen, or even adequate clothing. Being inexperienced, I started drinking whisky. My heart began to beat so hard I thought it was going to jump out of my mouth. I came down the Andean slopes in a jolting old pullman car and was immediately taken to an oxygen tank.

Today I'm having the opposite experience. Here we have oxygen but no ventilation. Our cell has two iron bars and a plate of sheet metal with minuscule holes in it. The door is a slab of dark iron with the usual barred opening in the middle. The oxygen is inside us; it is the force that enables us to rise above this oppressive situation and face it courageously. Many people who come up to visit us wonder whether they could stand prison. The fact is that there are cases of deep depression and even of madness.

At dawn this prison is the image of hell. Banging and shouting and songs of desperation reverberate through the cell block, exploding from hearts steeped in bitterness. These outbursts are typical of the common prisoners with whom we are thrown together. Political prisoners have more endurance, particularly more solidarity. None of us is alone. The important thing is to succeed in conquering our old habits. By now we are no longer upset at living together in a cell where the sanitary facilities are in the middle of the room near our beds and where there is only one faucet. You lose your physical freedom but you gain the freedom of awareness. You learn to accept the radicalization of your life.

At the age of twenty-six I suddenly realize that all my adolescent dreams have gone up in smoke. I feel very young and very realistic about the future! Faith is too serious a thing not to effect profound transformations in us. But you cannot foresee this. Equally unforeseeable is everything that brings us fulfillment (love, for example) and everything that leads us to the truth of ourselves—such things as poverty, prison, pain, struggle, and hope in a future that will flower in our hands though today we clutch only a thorny stalk. All the principles that once resounded in my head and made me the prototype of the Western Christian have now broken to smithereens. (. . .)

I can never manage to leave out my prison experience when I write. It is an exceptional period, and I cannot let it go by without making the most of it. Your family is in our prayers. An affectionate hug for you.

100

February 7

Dear Little Cousins (please don't call me uncle, or else I'll feel old. . . . Just between ourselves, we are brothers, but keep it quiet, otherwise your mom might also feel old. . .).

Today I'm going to tell you a story, not a bedtime story, but a waking-up story. . . .

Once upon a time there was a man who could never resign himself to the fact that he was not like a bird. He felt imprisoned because he couldn't warble and fly and be free like a bird. No matter how hard he tried, he could never manage to get off the ground. He felt nailed to the ground because he couldn't fly like the birds, who live in the vast expanses of space and time. He would open his mouth to speak, and out would come only grunts that no one understood. He would never be able to sing like the birds, with that beautiful sweetness.

One day this man decided that the best thing to do was to reverse the nature of his unsatisfied desire. And he had the *power* to do it. Since he couldn't be like the birds, he would try to become their master.

The man built a trap, put a worm inside, and set the trap on the branch of a tree. A lively bird, flying around the tree, noticed the worm and swooped down to take this food for his children. The man was close by watching. No sooner did the bird's foot touch the edge of the trap than it sprang shut and the bird was caught. The bird beat his wings furiously to escape the snare, but to no avail. His leg remained caught. The man observed his desperation without pity; indeed he took delight in the bird's anguish. The bird would fly no more, its children would die of hunger, and its song would grow sad as the winter nights. The man approached the trap and grabbed the bird. He was going to strangle it to death, but then he realized that the bird's suffering would end too quickly if he did that. It would be better to shut the bird in a cage where he could hear him cry for his lost liberty.

156

The bird was imprisoned in a cage. No more flights over fields and gardens, no more scent of leaves and flowers in bloom. The man took delight in seeing the bird a prisoner like himself. There was only one hitch: The bird could still sing, and he could not.

As time went on, the man added many more traps and invented new snares to catch birds. He replaced the old cage with a huge birdhouse in which he kept all his prisoners. *It gave him pleasure to look upon his imprisoned birds because they testified to his power.* Somehow it made him feel more free even though he could never be a bird.

Birds, however, reproduce faster than people. Although the man could imprison some birds, the rest remained beautiful and free as the man could never be. Faced with whole flocks singing anthems of freedom in the sky, the man was forced to admit his powerlessness. But he persevered in his wickedness and continued capturing birds when he could.

When his time came, the man died. From his grave a tree grew, spreading its leafy branches high in the air. One glorious summer afternoon a huge flock of birds descended and began to build their nests.

My dear little cousins, I love you very much, and I think of you often and I miss you. Some day we will all be together again. Then we will be able to sing and to fly like the birds. . . .

A great big hug.

101

To his parents

February 18

(. . .) This morning we had a visit from the apostolic nuncio. He came with Bishop Benedito Ulhoa, the chaplain of the Pontifical Catholic University, and Father Angelo Giannola, the episcopal vicar for the southern district of São Paulo. Our newest fellow prisoner, Father Giulio Vicini, comes from there. As usual, the nuncio brought us a touch of happiness and some cigarettes. He said he had been to see you at home and that he will come to dinner again as soon as I've been freed. He was impressed with Mom's tranquillity, and said that "any other mother would be in tears." He didn't say anything about the annual meeting of the National Episcopal Conference except that you two were there. We are waiting to hear about it from you. (. . .)

Right now I'm reading about the results of the bishops' meeting in Belo Horizonte.[59] I gather from the newspapers that for the first time a bishop has gone on record as demanding an inquiry and has been backed up by the rest of the episcopate. Times have changed. It appears that the era of the silent church—the church that couldn't take a stand when we were arrested—is over. Now I understand Jesus' words to the authorities who wanted him to silence the acclaim of the crowds: "If they were to keep silent, the very stones would cry out."

It's best to have faith in the Holy Spirit. The election of the new board of directors seems to me a good thing. The cardinals' primacy is at an end. The board has ceased to be a rubber-stamp for authority and has begun to exercise its executive function. I think that the seventies will be a time of decision for the Brazilian church. I get the impression that we are beginning to reap the first fruits of the seeds sown by Catholic Action in the sixties. But these fruits are still tender, delicate, and weak, borne on a tree that sways in every breeze.

The letter to Bishop Valdir was also a success. I can well imagine the joy it must have given him. (. . .) I am thinking of him, now a frail old bishop in the Northeast who has walked on water without any public support from those around him. He has been slandered and silenced, judged by some and condemned by others. No one has spoken out and said that he is on the side of the gospel. I think the church of the future will venerate him as a saint and a prophet. (. . .)

On the other hand, I was frankly not pleased with the letter they sent Father Domingos. It should have been more incisive. It opens: "The central commission has received your letter requesting a statement from the episcopate concerning the brothers who are prisoners in São Paulo.'' Does that mean that if Father Domingos had not written the letter, no one would have spoken out? The whole first paragraph is useless. The letter goes on to say that ''the imprisonment and trial has dragged on for fifteen months.'' But it is stated impersonally, as if they were afraid to mention the prisoners by name. The letter is good where it notes that our plight is the same as that of many prisoners, but it does not publish (on purpose?) the bishops' opinion of our case. The pope has already shown his sympathy and sent us his blessing. The papal secretary of state has said that there is no evidence against us. Our order has given us its full support. Yet the bishops are unable to say whether we are innocent or guilty. They are waiting for the verdict of the Justice Department of the military regime. There is a kind of implied support in the fact that while they say nothing in our favor, they say nothing against us either. *In dubio pro reo.* [60] Isolated voices don't count. (. . .)

102

To Sister Ruth

February 27

Dear Cousin, your letter comes to us like a friendly and encouraging presence. It's the kind of support that comforts us most. It makes us feel that we are not alone, that we no longer live in a silent church. The church's silence, unfortunately, was what first impressed us after our arrest. After so much talk about the Christian presence in today's world, some priests were astonished and dumbfounded by our praxis. It reminded me of Jesus' conversation with his disciples when he revealed that everything foretold earlier he would have to live in his own body: ''From that time Jesus began to make it clear to his disciples that he had to go to Jerusalem, and there to suffer much from the elders, chief priests, and doctors of the law; to be put to death and to be raised again on the third day.

159

At this Peter took him by the arm and began to rebuke him: 'Heaven forbid!' he said. 'No, Lord, this shall never happen to you' " (Matt. 15:21–23).

Peter had no trouble assenting to ideas and programs, but he could not accept such things happening *in reality*. He was afraid to face reality. He thought that the gospel pertained *to others*, to the church, but not to his particular community of disciples and apostles. Peter wanted a Christ for himself, a nicely protected Christ, safely removed from life's contradictions and conflicts, from cruel suffering, and from the cross. He didn't want a Christ who would follow his commitment to its final consequences. Prudent Peter thought he knew and could interpret God's thoughts. What was Jesus thinking of! How could he die on a cross like a common criminal! Such fates were for *other people*, not for Christ and his disciples.

Today, echoing Peter's logic, we may ask: What are you thinking of! A church of the oppressed, the ragged, the starving, the alienated, the persecuted and imprisoned? An outlaw church?! Jesus, however, did not have the patience to explain to Peter why he was mistaken; nor did he keep silent in the hope that Peter would understand him later. Jesus got angry because Peter hadn't grasped the essence of the mystery of redemption. He must have thought: "Is all I've taught only a subject for sermons rather than a rule for living? What you want is a community of 'Establishment' Christians, well dressed and on friendly terms with the rich and powerful, supporters of the status quo. No risk, no daring, no radical break with the way things are." So angry was Jesus that he saw his friend as the very incarnation of the Enemy: "Away with you, Satan; you are a stumbling block to me. You think as men think, not as God thinks" (Matt. 16:23). The fact is that human beings do want a church triumphant rather than suffering, a church upheld by the laws rather than one in hiding in the catacombs, a church capable of pardoning sin rather than one capable of extirpating evil at its root.

This is the experience of God of which you speak in your letter. It's the experience of walking the same road that he walked, of learning through faith about things that are beyond

160

poor human reasoning. Prison enables us to live this experience of God intensely. There are five of us in this cell now—Fernando, Ivo, and I are Dominicans; Father Giulio Vicini[61] and Laercio Barros, a seminarian from the diocese of Lins, are with us. Laercio is serving a one-year term, which will end in 1972, for using a book by Michel Quoist (*The Diary of Anna Maria*). Father Vicini will be interrogated by a military court next Monday. We Dominicans were interrogated last October, almost a year after our arrest, and as yet the date of our sentencing has not been fixed. We are serving the sentence ahead of time.

Recently we have been visited regularly by the new archbishop of São Paulo.[62] Last week the apostolic nuncio, Bishop Mozzoni, came to see us, bringing us as usual gladness and cigarettes. We are expecting a visit from our superior general[63] in April.

We thank your community for their prayers that our suffering may bear fruit within the church and that our spirits may be stronger than the bars that confine us. With you we wait for the Lord's Easter.

103

To his family

March 3

Dearest Parents and Brothers and Sisters, last Sunday Father Ettore Torrini, who has spent twenty-one years in Acre,[64] came to celebrate Mass in our cell. (. . .) The mass was simple—as life in prison and the things that pertain to God are simple. There is more intensity in the Masses here than I have ever found in Masses celebrated on the outside. Christ is more intimately, almost tangibly, present. They remind me of the catacombs. Father Torrini wept because something here reminded him of certain experiences of his in the East that evidently made a profound impression on his life. How much more beautiful Mass is when the chalice is a cup, the altar a wooden bench, the church a small cell, and the worshippers are prisoners. Over the centuries we have made things too complicated. We have transformed the familiar, unstudied rite into pomp and ceremony, the dialogue into protocol. Now we have reached the critical point. We don't cast off ceremony because we don't want to offend other people's sensibilities, and we wait for these sensibilities to change so that we can cast off ceremony.

People have sent us a huge stack of Italian, French, and German magazines (in the German ones I can only look at the pictures). In the *Paris Match* of October 1969 were several letters written at various times by John XXIII to his family. They are taken from an anthology of his letters that is about to be published. Here is an excerpt from one of the letters:

> I cannot in conscience, as a Christian and a priest, vote for the Fascists. Everyone is free to judge the matter from his own point of view. In the end we will find out who was right. Do what you think is best. In my own opinion, however, you would do better to vote for the popular slate if you have the freedom to vote as you choose. If that freedom does not exist, then it might be better to stay at home and let things take their course. Otherwise you could be in for trouble. I am sure of one thing: Italy's salvation cannot come from Mussolini, even though he may be an able man. The goals he envisions might be good ones, but the means he employs are wrong and contrary to the gospel. . . . Affectionately, your Don Angelo.

He wrote that in April 1924. What historical insight that man had! (. . .)

104

To a Dominican fellow student

March 6

Dear Robert, locked up in this cell, listening to the rain beating down on the grating, I keep reading your letter over and over again. It gives me comfort, peace, and courage. I feel now that suffering is worthwhile, that every sorrow is a harbinger of redemption. Although I would not exactly have chosen this, I know that God has chosen precisely this for me.

As you put it in your letter, "I am simply carried along by Him." Sometimes I resist, but the power of attraction that he exerts on me is stronger still. I think he asks a great deal of me, more than I have strength or ability to give. Who am I, Lord? In my inmost heart, I swear, I envy the humble lay brother in a Trappist monastery, who gives glory to God in the silence of his anonymous life, milking cows and making cheese. But then reason prevails. Once I have put my hand to the plow, I have no right to turn back (Luke 9:62). I know that salvation lies there where the cross looms, roughhewn and terrible. If death should overtake me now, I could die knowing that, despite all my mistakes, I have tried to live the teaching of Jesus.

You ask me to write something relevant to your calling that would be "less of reason and theology and more of inner experience." I'll tell you what I feel—which doesn't mean that I live accordingly. I have still more breaking with the past to do before I'll be able to say that it is now Christ who lives in me (Gal. 2:20).

What really does exist in me is an irresistible attraction to God. Whether they know it or not, people speak of this attraction using many names, such as justice, peace, progress, or freedom, and they live it out on the political, economic, religious, or social plane. For me this divine summons is made explicit in Jesus Christ, and it is handed down and brought to life in the community of faith that is the church. This is the origin of what I feel: a profound and all-encompassing love for the church of Jesus Christ. It is the church that has made him known to me. It is the church in which his word lives, errors and omissions notwithstanding. Indeed it is these defects that make it ever clearer to me that the church is a human community and not a divine one, a historical community and not a heavenly one. The church is us poor sinners continually seeking to become one with him. If what I am doing is meaningless for the church, then I have not achieved what I was really looking for. I have given my life to the church. Today in all

163

humility I realize this is true. Not a week has gone by since I was a child that I have not been occupied with meetings or readings or some activity for the spread of the gospel and the growth of the church. So I love this fulcrum of my life, this mainspring of my existence. It pains me when the church is unfaithful to Jesus' word. It pains me that we are not like the poor fishermen of Galilee. It pains me when I find myself un-Christian. And I become very jealous when anyone tries to take over the church and use it like a prostitute.

The church's mission is gratuitous service to human beings. We cannot delude ourselves that we are serving the church if we do not serve people, particularly the neediest. When I took my vows, I realized that they set the seal on my commitment to serve others. A promise to give myself to the service of others would therefore have made more sense than the vows I took.

Thanks to the secular upbringing and training that you and I have had, we have never found it possible to separate the church and the world. There is no such dualism in our thinking or our lives and this makes certain things a lot easier. It saves us from thinking of service to the church and service to the world as mutually exclusive commitments. The church is a movement in the world. Its mission arises there and is carried out there. This perspective reveals most clearly the existential aspects of contemporary vows within the traditional institutions of religious life in the church.

Let me say a little first about how I think we should live these vows and then about how I look on them as a whole in relation to the meaning of contemporary religious life. When we talk about the vows of obedience, chastity, and poverty, we could be talking about vows of fidelity, gratuitous generosity, and justice. What's important is that the three really are one and that they represent a choice. Unfortunately, in this matter we are still subject to ecclesiastical jurisdiction. But since this is the *form* through which we make official our commitment to the religious life, we see that these vows can indeed be made meaningful.

I think that obedience is owed to God, who speaks to us through the Bible, the church, the world, and history. God speaks through the signs of the times. If my superior or my community are at variance with the will of God as I perceive it in real life, then I owe them no obedience. I owe obedience to the poor whom Jesus served. I owe obedience to the pathways of hope in the life of my time, to concrete and effective love for others. I do not owe obedience to anything that renders me less free, less human, less committed, less aware. I do not owe obedience to laws that shackle human beings and stifle the spread of the gospel; to traditions that drain Christian life of its pristine force; to anything that makes me look more obedient and less Christian, more prudent and less evangelical. Obedience cannot mean cowardice, conformism, egotism, overprotectedness, and fear of risk. Obedience should lead me to the cross, not to the throne (see Matt. 16:21–23).

When Jesus revealed to Peter that the road he must take was the road to the cross, Peter objected. He wanted a community without problems. He wanted Jesus to walk in his footsteps rather than the other way around. Peter wanted to preserve the appearances of respectability, to prevent Jesus from dying like an outlaw and tarnishing the community's image. In *The Brothers Karamazov* the Grand Inquisitor will say the same thing to the outlaw in whom he recognizes Christ. Jesus did not restrain his anger at Peter's way of thinking; he saw in his friend the image of his enemy. And what about us? How many times have we, in the name of obedience, sinned by omission? How many times have we failed to see that God's ways seem foolish to people? How many times are we more heedful of the letter of the law than the appeals of the living?

As far as the vow of chastity is concerned, you know what I think. It is to free us for service to others, but it is also a great renunciation. It is a charism if God permits us to live so without its withering our emotions. From one moment to the next I can expect to feel the need for a female companion. Life itself, the greatest gift we have received, is the fruit of human love. It is wonderful that I feel the attraction of this love and that faith enables me to live it in a new dimension. I am deliberately and firmly set on making this renunciation, but the resultant void not even God can fill, for that would amount to altering human nature itself. Love remains, and it is beautiful to experience the capacity to love outside the confines of the flesh. Those who limit themselves to these confines have not yet reached the starting point of love. There is no fulfillment in love unless that love is generous and expansive. A couple who think they love each other but don't love other human beings have not yet discovered love. A man's love for other people is mediated through his love for his wife, and vice versa. This love is most completely expressed in the physical union of the two, which is the sign of their communion with other human beings. God's gift of faith permits a mystical expression of this same union. This is no abstraction. The love I feel for people becomes more real insofar as I freely place myself at their service.

On a more personal plane it is obvious that I love some people, to whom I am bound by ties of friendship and fellowship, more than others. Christ himself had preferences, and this is a mystery that only the gratuitous nature of love can explain. If these ties were to be established with a woman, then I would naturally discover all her beauty and be enchanted by her charms. But I know the boundary between gift and possession. If I don't include having a family among my plans for the future, then I have no reason to encourage a state of affairs requiring exclusive possession, particularly since I see no relation between love and any kind of sentimental escapade. It is people damaged by egotism who get involved in sentimental adventures which are always an attempt to be loved.

So celibacy has meaning if faith enables us to express mutual reciprocal human love through the exclusive mediation of God, if celibacy itself permits us to recognize how great and real human love is, above and beyond mere physical union. After all, physical union itself is never a point of departure, as the pervasive bourgeois culture makes people think. It is rather a final goal of full mystical and physical communion. This communion is a harbinger of our mystical union with God that is made possible by contemplative action. But mystical union with God is not a privilege reserved for the celibate. Purity, daring, and detachment are not inaccessible to a married person. Indeed Jesus chose married men to be his apostles, and I have known many married men capable of a selflessness that few religious can equal. . . .

So I cannot evaluate celibacy in terms of advantages or disadvantages. Marriage does not diminish people, and celibacy does not exalt them. *Celibacy is a gift. One accepts a gift from God not as a privilege but as a responsibility undertaken for the sake of a mission.* I accept this gift in complete consciousness of my masculinity. It is important not to confuse celibacy with sexlessness. No one loses his sex because he is celibate, and it disturbs me that many religious should give that very impression.

I don't want to pursue this discussion any further, however, because I would end up going beyond the realm of personal experience and reality. I thank God for the gift he has granted me, and I hope my ability to love will continually increase.

As for poverty, I am embarrassed to talk about it. First of all, because I am not poor. I was educated in middle-class comfort, and I have lived my life under the spell of its alienating attractions. I have not struggled to survive; I have not been dehumanized by the production system. At the same time, however, I have never had income or human relationships that were supported by this form of alienation. I have never labored to perpetuate the dominion of the bourgeoisie. On the contrary: I have always been preoccupied by the plight of the poor and the oppressed.

My first personal experience of poverty was this imprisonment. But it seems to me that the poor are born so and that it is almost impossible for us to cross class lines in the sense of escaping from our class consciousness. I realize that I live in a church that is rich and seems rich in the eyes of people. Even here in prison, whenever anyone needs anything, from an onion for soup to a hospital bed for a relative, they come looking for us priests. Priests, after all, have money, connections, prestige, power. We do what we can, but it is irritating to realize that this is the image of the church evoked by our presence. I wish we were the neediest of all, living witnesses to a poor church.

In my eyes poverty means putting yourself entirely at the service of the poor. If that seems very bourgeois, so be it! The important thing is that all my plans be directed to the effective liberation of the poor by effectual means. That is the poverty that I can and must live. I must be accountable to the disadvantaged and oppressed, not to the rich and powerful. It is the former who are the living image of Jesus Christ. The God I have come to know in the Bible is the God who liberates the poor and exalts them, who topples monarchs from their thrones and sends the rich away empty-handed.

This choice provokes the wrath of the rich. They are persecuting me because they will not allow anyone to destroy the evil they have set up. It is only natural that there should be conflict. (. . .) Prison has taught me to know freedom, has freed me from needing superfluous things, has freed me from the values that are part of the alienating machinery of the present social order. Goodbye to the myths of the bourgeoisie! Prison has reduced us to the plight of the poor by depriving us of our freedom, making us suffer, humiliating and traducing us, and leaving us completely at the mercy of others. This experience has taught me a lot. If the lessons I have learned survive the coming of freedom and its charms, then I will have succeeded in living the poverty I have chosen. I absolutely do not wish to return to the social class from which I came.

Now let's consider all this in the context of the religious life. Here we must do just a bit of theorizing, but I will simply tell you what I mean by the religious life. To begin with, the religious life antedates Christianity. The Essenes lived in monastic communities before the birth of Christ. Monasticism arose in the church about the fourth century, a time when the church was already allied with the Empire and Christianity was beginning to show signs of decadence. Persecution and martyrdom were things of the past. The group of Christians that would not accept concessions to the temporal power and wished to remain faithful to the inspiration of the church's first three centuries chose to live apart in the desert. There they were joined by fugitives from earlier persecutions. The communities they formed were intended to be the church's "final" witness. "Eschatology" is the word that defines the true meaning of the religious life, which arose as a *challenge* to the world.

As time went on the religious life became established and institutionalized and acquired formal rules; the poor monks of former times were replaced by rich abbots and lords of the manor. The cloisters no longer challenged the world, feeling that they had planted the kingdom of God on earth. The religious life proliferated and became so strong as to absorb the church itself, taking control of the hierarchy and the papacy. The cloister began to feel a desire to dominate the world. Attempts at renewal always consisted in establishing new forms of the same institution: Religious orders multiplied.

There was one clear call to radical change, but it proposed an idea whose time had not yet come and therefore went unanswered. Francis of Assisi came too soon: He will be understood by those who come after us. Francis did not wish to found a new order, much less an institution of the accustomed kind. He wanted to initiate a *movement* within the church of return to the gospel and to the poverty that should characterize it. But his successors betrayed him and destroyed his witness. Large and lofty monasteries replaced his bare shelters.

The religious life has continued to subsist on the margins of history. The last century saw a new flowering of religious foundations devoted to the philanthropies in which the church was beginning to engage: orders devoted to teaching, to hospital work, to the communications media.

What now? Without wishing to be a prophet, I predict the extinction of the institutional form of religious life. Our ranks will gradually empty; the membership of orders and congregations will progressively diminish. In their place I envision St. Francis's prophecy: movements within the church inspired to carry on a specific course of evangelical action without requiring their participants to live under the same roof or rule. These movements will comprise lay people, priests, nuns, and bishops. They will not have formal rules. This is how I envision the return to the gospel—not separate communities but movements originating within the church. (. . .) I am preparing myself for this new stage. It is already being born. (. . .)

105

To his parents

First a big hug for dad. Another year of life, another grandchild. (. . .) I'm sure the grandchild was the best present of all. Every time I see a child born, I realize more and more how good life is. The struggle for existence is hard but beautiful. I feel as if I were careening along in a sailboat, subject to every puff of wind on the sea of history. Sometimes I fall overboard, but it doesn't matter. I can swim. (. . .)

In between a book on theology and one on philosophy, I've read two interesting novels. The first was *One Day in the Life of Ivan Denisovich* by Solzhenitsyn. It is well worth reading. It's a brief and disturbing account of a situation much like mine. The subject of the other novel, by Ilya Ehrenburg, could not be more different: *Factory of Dreams* deals with the world of Hollywood movies, and what makes it interesting is the author's approach to his subject. He shows that the United States has been able to manufacture and export not only refrigerators, automobiles, soft drinks, and chewing gum but also illusions that have conditioned the lives and mentalities of countless moviegoers. (. . .)

A big hug to you all, especially to Dad, who is a real friend.

106

March 29

Adriana, your grandpa has just left.[66] I was so moved and cheered by his visit that I could hardly talk. He seemed in great shape, with a spiritual and physical youthfulness that would be the envy of many people. I told him to give my love to your mama, Claudia, and to your aunts Vera and Maria Eugenia, just as if I were the brother they never had. How I envy your grandma Glaucia, who still swims in the pool! I've had enough of the Turkish baths we get here! . . . The snapshots your grandpa brought are great. You look like a typical newborn baby, all of whom look the same to me though to its parents each one is undeniably unique. Your mama's smile is a masterpiece of love.

In the darkness of the world I am thinking of you. I think that you have just been born for freedom and that you will spend your whole life seeking it. At some point you will discover that the key to freedom is love, and love has its stages. In the first stage we free ourselves by searching for someone to love, that is, we find *our* freedom in loving. Then we come to love so that others may be free. Finally we are willing not to be free so that others might be. You cannot understand this now, but life will teach you things that go beyond my words.

I pray for you. If what my body is suffering (though my spirit is joyful) can have any merit, then I ask the Lord to let this merit benefit you. God loves you so much that he wants you to take part in life, which is the best gift he can give. In the course of your life you too will wrestle with an angel. You will know times of doubt and times of certainty, times of discouragement and of courage, days of rain and days of sunshine. But you will prevail over the angel if you have faith in yourself, in others, and in God.

Adriana, I want you to be beautiful as a flower, pure and without vanity, genuine as the sun that does not ask permission to shine through prison bars. I want you to be strong as

171

the rock from which flows the water that cleanses and quickens all that lives on earth. I want you to be patient as the butterfly, which turns beautiful inside its cocoon and does not fear the blowing of the wind as it flies. I want you to be brave as the sand on the beach, which does not fear the waves advancing to cover it. I wish you the faith of those who fight to win, the hope of those who bear the present in order to build the future, the love of those who do not fear to die because they know that love ends not in death but in rebirth.

All this I wish for you. I entrust you to the safety of your parents' arms. Today they carry you, tomorrow they may lean on you for support. That's the way life goes. Sometimes the road is tortuous and hard to follow, but that doesn't matter. The important thing is to keep alive inside us the meaning of the journey. If we can do this, we shine with an inner light that may blind others but can also awaken them.

To conclude my first letter to you, Adriana, I ask one thing of you: *Never forget the poor.* A big hug to papa Roberto and a kiss of peace and happiness to your mama and yourself. Peace and joy!

107

To Pedro

March 22

Dear Pedro, homesickness was beginning to get the better of me when your letter arrived. (. . .)

The prison world has led me to discover what lies back of and beneath reality. I've learned that beneath the rose petals are thorns, that beneath the broad avenues run refuse-laden sewers, that a tree that bears bitter fruit must be cut off at the roots. Neither medicine nor grafting will help it. The gospel tells us that we must cut it down and burn it. But how many people go on hoping for a harvest from a barren fig tree! When I think about your freedom to come and go, to attend theological meetings, to read and write, I must confess I envy you.

But I try at once to resist the feeling because I know that my place is not yours and that my contribution to God's plan is different from yours. (. . .)

Sometimes I'm afraid I won't be able to see this thing through because I feel theologically undernourished. What keeps me going is an immense, exaggerated confidence in divine providence; I cling to providence like one waiting for a miracle. But I know the nature and the risk of my own work, and I don't expect God to do it for me. I only ask him to help me do it well and to let my unending self-offering be meaningful and bear fruit.

During these sixteen months of imprisonment I have not yet lost my nerve. At no point have I felt that the past was useless or the future lost. On the contrary, I'm optimistic about both. For me this time in prison is a passage to liberation, a period of waiting for Easter. It counts as a second novitiate, in which I'm reaching a more profound understanding of the mystery embodied in Jesus of Nazareth. Now I know how false are any concepts of God that do not refer to the young man of Galilee. In him I find myself and define myself. But I do realize how ill prepared people are—even Christians—to hear and understand Jesus' summons. Not because his summons is complicated but precisely because it is too simple. It's difficult to come out of the labyrinth into which our traditional conditioning has led us. We aren't yet strong enough to face the temptations Jesus underwent in the desert. We adore temporal power, we look for security, and we fail to grasp how corrupting it is to bow down to the wielders of wealth and power. If we had Jesus' certainty that a legion of angels would come to our aid, we would not hesitate to cast ourselves from the hilltop. But we haven't this certainty, so we prefer to be a legal church rather than an evangelical, endangered church. Clearly the Holy Spirit is working to get the church moving. But I think we tempt him too much, always hoping for *him* to act. By the time he has acted too many sacrifices have already been consumed. He speaks to us primarily through events. It is events —sometimes tragic ones—that guide the church, though it would be better if the church guided events. It often seems to me that the church has an enormous capacity to pardon and absolve historical situations, but a glaring inability to initiate, advance, or prevent them. It's said that history is a good teacher. That may be, but human beings are poor students! God's intent moves toward fulfillment with or without the church and whether Christians like it or not. It's the history of salvation that is moving. As Teilhard de Chardin said, everything moves toward convergence despite detours and momentary reverses. Let us have faith; Easter is coming.

108

To his parents

April 6

(. . .) We're approaching Christianity's most important holy day: Easter. Saint Paul said that if Christ had not risen, our faith would be in vain. But he has risen, proving that death is not the end of life. The liberation proclaimed of old by the prophets came to pass in Jesus Christ, and the import of this fact is enormous. If Jesus had not been resurrected, then we could go on with life indifferently. We could eat and drink and dance, indifferent to all else, till death ended us and our revels together. But we believe that the young carpenter of Nazareth still lives in his Father's bosom and that we live and move by the power of his Spirit, and that changes everything. No one can ask me to live as if the resurrection had not been a critical event. The fulcrum of our earthly lives shifted in that moment when Christ conquered death. Since then anyone wanting to know why and for whom I live should try to understand the meaning of Christ's cross and resurrection rather than indulging in amazement at my seeming folly.

All this is easy to say but hard to carry out. If we believe —and establish our life on the belief—that resurrection, not death, is the end of earthly life, then it follows that nothing on earth is absolute. It is foolish to accumulate riches, to wrap oneself in prestige, to pile up guarantees, to attain a mediocre tranquillity. Probably these needs are so deeply rooted in our upbringing and our culture that we cannot easily relinquish them. But in Christ they are rendered absurd. He knows that the way to life leads through the cross. He saw in his death neither disgrace nor sorrow nor the frustration of all his purposes, but glorification: "The hour has come for the Son of Man to be glorified. In very truth I tell you, a grain of wheat remains a solitary grain unless it falls into the ground and dies; but if it dies, it bears a rich harvest. The man who loves himself is lost, but he who hates himself in this world will be kept safe for eternal life. If anyone serves me, he must follow me" (John 12:23–26).

Can a mother understand that her son was glorified precisely because his body was nailed on a cross between two thieves and would have been buried in a common grave but for the good will of Joseph of Arimathea? What could Mary have thought when she saw her son hunted, persecuted, imprisoned, beaten, and crucified? What mysterious glory was concealed in all that ignominy? Jesus was afraid. I know something of the fear that must have been his: "Now my soul is in turmoil, and what am I to say? Father, save me from this hour. No, it was for this that I came to this hour. Father, glorify thy name" (John 12:27–28). And his Father, as if wishing to infuse new strength into his Son, breaks the silence: "I have glorified it, and I will glorify it again" (John 12:28).

In the cross God revealed his inmost secret: his solidarity with the oppressed. The most incredible conversation in human history is the exchange between one of the thieves and Christ. Hanging on the cross, the thief acknowledges Jesus' innocence and asks: "Remember me when you come to your throne." He does not ask for a place in the kingdom or even to be saved; he simply asks to be remembered by someone. Jesus replies: "Today you shall be with me in Paradise." The first saint of the church is a thief condemned to death alongside Jesus.

Jesus' glorification is complete in his Resurrection. Now we know that we will preserve our lives if we are willing to lose them. We know that death no longer terrifies us. We also know that Jesus' innocence is suspect in the eyes of the world. What use is it for one convicted man to call another innocent? Yet by these dubious proceedings God brings liberation to humankind.

The prefiguration of Christ's Easter is the Exodus, the liberation of the Jews from bondage in Egypt. The God who reveals himself and leads his people through the wilderness is the same God who liberates this people and causes them to go on through human history. Through faith we are sure of Resurrection. In Easter we celebrate having been redeemed and saved in advance. We are the freest of human beings. All the barriers have been burst asunder.

But I wonder: Are we living like people who carry within themselves this certainty, who do not fear the painful aspect of this liberation brought by Christ, who are free enough to free others? We were challenged by Marxism a century ago, but it seems we have not yet succeeded in becoming a living image of the Resurrection. We are not yet wholly witnesses to Easter, artisans of liberation. We cling to life and reject death because we find it hard to believe that death too has its limits. We are still afraid of the cross, and we see no glory in Christ's sacrifice. He bore it for us, but we cannot bear it for him and for others. We still prefer the common sense of the world to the folly of the cross. We still strive to store up treasures on earth, though we know that in time to come they will not be worth one hair of our heads. The judgment of Caesar means more to us than the insight of the crucified thief.

But the most curious and tragic fact—our real challenge—is not that Christians lack the strength to inhabit a climate of Resurrection but that many non-Christians do inhabit such a climate, even though they do not believe that there is anything beyond the moment of giving up their lives. Surely these people are acting under the influence of grace. Their number grows every day, as if they were living the word of God even without believing in it.

Here we are trying to prepare for Easter by meditating on the relationship between Cross and Resurrection. Prison gives special meaning to our liturgical life. It puts us in direct touch with the passion of Christ because it makes us participants in his agony. But it also leads us to believe even more strongly in the reality of Easter. (. . .)

Archbishop Evaristo[67] has returned from Europe and is supposed to visit us one of these days. He may celebrate Easter Mass here in Tiradentes Prison. Father Torrini[68] is going from cell to cell, preparing the prisoners. Giulio[69] will be here for another two months even though his lawyer appealed his sentence. Maybe you've read in the newspapers that we've asked to be freed on bail.[70] But it wouldn't be soon even if they granted it. Laercio[71] appealed last September, and he will be finishing his sentence this coming May. The Superior Military Tribunal moves slowly because it has too many cases to handle.

I'm pleased that Dad is reading Mounier. There was a time when his books influenced me greatly. I read everything of his that I could lay my hands on, and from him I learned the meaning of Christian commitment. Happy Easter and a big hug to you all.

109

To his sister Cecilia

May 12

Dearest Cecilia, I would so love to spend your birthday with you and your little family. (. . .)

When we are imprisoned and unable to embrace those we most love, the roots of love grow painful in our hearts. There are bars separating us, and hands like ours made and set in place these bars that keep our hands from touching.

My love for you is as great as the distance that separates us. Something in your simplicity and silence has always moved me deeply. You are one of those rare people who are always familiar with poverty and therefore have great inner riches. Many things in you correspond to my image of Mary. Perhaps it's because you don't have to make any effort to love God. He loves you, and your life shows it.

My relationship with God is very different from yours. I live in constant struggle with him. I get angry and argue with him; I am never satisfied. You, on the other hand, are at peace with him. Like Mary, you have been wise enough to say, "Be it done unto me according to thy will," and to leave the rest to him. When I was still very young, God tore me from my family, laid a heavy yoke across my shoulders, and sent me to live among strangers in a strange land. Of you he demanded nothing exceptional. He laid no yoke on you, nor did he tear you from your family. I resisted him, but he won and compelled me to a vocation I never thought I had. You, however, seem never to have resisted him, and he has always been your neighbor, your confidant, and your friend.

It's been different with me. There have been times when he has shaken me to the depths. There have been times when he has been silent and I couldn't find him anywhere. There have been times when his silence so enraged me that I threatened to abandon him. But he's used to my temper and has never taken my threats seriously. You he has let go your own ordinary, uneventful way, undistinguished except by the love that is reborn in you each day.

But look what he has done to me: He has led me from place to place; he has let me make good friends and then taken me from them; he has led me in strange paths, made me front-page news, and brought me in the end to this prison.

Sometimes I ask: How long, O Lord? And I think he is not yet done with demanding of me much more than I can possibly give.

There are days when I have remained standing only because he willed it. If it had depended on my own strength I would have fallen a thousand times. In my heart of hearts I ask God to let me be like you: peaceful and possessed of a faith as transparent as a mountain stream. But it's no use! He wills me to live amid storms and tempests, so I must cling to the thread of faith that he grants me.

Cecilia, the real tragedy is that God trusts too much in us. He

178

wants us to be his presence among people. Sometimes I imagine what it must be like to be pope—head of the church of Jesus Christ on earth! Who are we? What are we capable of?

You have been wise enough to entrust yourself to him and let him act in you. Not me. I always want to anticipate him. I don't have your calm. I'm always in a hurry, always wanting to do something. And after I've rushed into something, God comes and tells me that it's not exactly what he had in mind. Then I must start over from the beginning, changing the plans and putting in more work. Does he think I have your infinite patience?

I imagine your prayer as being wholly silent. You tell God you love him, and God replies that he loves you even more. I don't pray. I debate. When I pray, I propose a set of problems, ask for solutions, propose tentative solutions of my own, analyze, argue. . . . There are days when I feel he doesn't even want to listen to me, but I keep talking. I ask for something, he gives me something else; I imply something, he infers something else. Perhaps it will go on like that till we meet face to face. . . . Then we'll come at last to an understanding.

I was thinking about sending you a gift, but you've already received the best possible gift—your son. By the time I get to meet him, he probably won't be a baby any more. I remember something that happened when you were teaching slum kids. On Teacher's Day the students brought you gifts, and the poorest of them, the child of a candy peddler, gave you a tiny jar of guava jam that his father had given him. It was the most beautiful gift of all. I'm in the same spot now as that little boy was then. I can't buy you anything, so I'm sending you something I made with my own hands—a necklace of glass beads, like the one I gave Teresa. Mom told me that you all liked hers.

A big hug to your husband, whom I like. A kiss for the baby. And to you all my love.

179

110

May 12

Dear Pedro, Ivo's solemn profession of vows was an immensely important event for us. The setting couldn't have been more meaningful: Some wooden planks that usually serve as our writing desk and kitchen table on that day became the altar.

After a year and a half of "retreat," he was more than prepared. I should like to be ordained a priest here because here I have become the one who sacrifices and is sacrificed. Will I be granted that grace? The fact is that I have already been granted it. As Ignatius of Antioch said, we can consecrate bread and we can turn ourselves into living bread. Priesthood as charisma, in the profoundest sense of the word, is far more than a set of churchly functions. Here this is the common priesthood. Priesthood as a function within the ecclesial community exists only to the extent that it is at once the expression and result of a life of giving, of service, and of witness. A person who simply "conducts services" has not yet discovered the true dimensions of the priesthood. Body and blood are something much more real than "services," don't you think? What is the use of daily re-enacting Christ's sacrifice if we don't undertake it in our own lives? Dear friend, it's not very disturbing to deal with soul and spirit and mind; it's only when one deals with body and blood that the fear and trembling begin. We are capable of living for the gospel, but are we capable of dying for the gospel?

I see that you have great plans for study. Here, lacking books, we extract our lessons from our daily lives. I envy you because I've always wanted to study methodically, but reality shattered that dream. So I can only write letters, but even that is something. I've made up a thousand study plans, but they all come to nothing. I've managed to study a little theology, philosophy, and economics (not thoroughly—I just read the books I can get). It's the least one needs to know in order to decipher the complex reality in which we live.

I see you have managed to free yourself of the label "scholar." "Exegesis as a discipline of interpretation" is precisely what we need. What good does it do to read the Bible if we can't apply it to concrete contemporary events? (. . .)

It's almost unbelievable how many churchmen live in a vacuum, isolated in their own utopia. They don't know where Laos is, who the prime minister of Israel is, how much a liter of milk costs, what the average salary is in their part of the country, or what social and health services are available. They don't look for causes, they never ask why, they take poverty and wealth for granted, they find war scarcely objectionable, and they are convinced that good will, patience, and prudence will remedy all ills. How are we to preach the gospel to people who look upon us as aliens, who don't understand our language, to whom we represent another class and a different world?

You sent me a poem, so I will send you a story. There was a family of small farmers, poor and religious. One son went into the seminary. At night the mother in her naiveté dreamed that her son would come home a bishop, clad all in red, admired and honored by all the rich landowners who lived in town. From the seminary the boy wrote to his sister, the only one in the family who could read and write. In the evening she read his letters aloud by candlelight. He always wrote about the same things: the athletics at the seminary, roast-chicken dinners on Sunday, classes in Latin and Greek and history. He told them that he had the whole day to study, that he could see movies on the weekend, and that the liturgical feasts were beautifully celebrated at the seminary. In the evenings his parents would thank the Lord for the good fortune that had befallen their son. He had been freed from the bondage of the hoe, he had shelter from the rain, and even in times of drought he could be sure of a good meal. One day the son returned home for his vacation. His parents killed the fattest hog and the tenderest cow and barbecued them. They even managed to find a nice mattress for him. But when the whole family got up

181

at dawn to go to the fields, he stayed home in bed. While his brothers were hoeing the stony ground, he was bent over his books. In those books, thought his family, was all the knowledge in the world. His brothers didn't have the courage to address a word to him because they were ashamed of their ignorance. His mother noticed that her son had difficulty in drinking the well water and that his feet were so smooth he could no longer walk barefoot over the earth that gave them sustenance. When he spoke, everyone listened with awed respect. No one replied or offered ideas. They knew that his life was "over there," on the other side of the mountain, in the big city where the seminary was located. When vacation was over, the boy left his home and went back to his studies. He left behind in his parents' poor cottage neither longing nor sadness—only the certainty that this son who had left them to enter God's house would never come home again. (. . .)

111

To a student friend

May 13

Dear Paulo, I am delighted to be in touch with you again. I like talking to you because you're the kind who is always thinking about things and looking for solutions, like me. Here, of course, there is too much time for thinking and rethinking everything. In prison you acquire a more comprehensive view of historical events. Out of the game and sitting on the bench, you can better observe the plays of those still on the field. The very fact of being shut in—we get out of the cell only five hours a week—prompts questions and discoveries we would never have dreamed of before. It's a centripetal process, yet it never degenerates into mere subjectivism. This is no place for contemplating your navel. A prisoner is always in the company of others, and that forces him to reveal himself for what he really is. The demand for objectivity is constant, and this results in stripping away all bourgeois falseness of feeling.

It's a situation that can humanize a person or dehumanize him. Just try to lock up a few rats together in a box: They will destroy and devour each other. When people are locked up together, there is always the same danger, but it never happens among political prisoners. Just the opposite occurs, in fact: People become humanized to an amazing degree. Once the individual has no recourse to flight, isolation, or fantasy, he is constrained to confront himself in the process of confronting others. He is constrained to think, to assess his own limits and those of others. Living together day after day gives rise to profound fellowship, to the ability to live together all day every day, to the discovery of self and other in the context of mutual relationship. In this barred world externals don't count; all that matters is what you are. What are social position, family tradition, or cultural level worth if the thing that saves you is your openness to others? The one who suffers here is the person who is incapable of being simple, relaxed, openhearted, and friendly.

The metamorphosis in some prisoners is astounding. They arrive here with class delusions intact, but gradually they lose interest in pretense and reveal themselves in a surprising way. They cease pretending and posturing and adapt to the prison lifestyle, which in other circumstances might lead to total brutalization. Only our endurance, our inner strength, enables us to live with dignity in prison.

Sometimes I think that this is the ideal we have not managed to attain in our religious communities, namely, an integration that demands the total and unreserved personalization of each individual. In our religious communities we get just the opposite. In the name of an integration that is purely juridical, the individual gives up his own personality. Such deception is possible only so long as we cling to "our own" lives, "our own" friendships, "our own" interests, "our own" rooms. When we can no longer turn back, when everything necessarily belongs to "the other," then very few things are "ours," and this really is community life. You learn to be responsible for yourself and for others. I've lived in a cell with forty people of the most widely differing backgrounds, upbringing, and educations. We formed ourselves into groups, each with an assigned task—cooking, cleaning, recreation, study. The system worked fine; we had no need of anyone to give orders. That was because any one person's failure to do his share would inevitably hurt the whole community. When one can withdraw (or shirk) without the community's noticing it, then there is no longer a community, just a group of individuals who share nothing but the fact that they live under the same roof. (. . .)

I ask your prayers for all those living their passion here. In one way or another they all hope in the resurrection. I know that the freely given love of our heavenly Father is not to be measured by our yardsticks. A big, affectionate hug to you.

112

To Pedro

May 16

Dear Pedro, I have just now finished reading *Octogesima Adveniens*.[72] I notice myself becoming increasingly demanding by comparison to the teachings of the church. The root of my severity and my impatience is a profound and passionate love for the church. I want to see the church free and untainted and poor—at one with its founder. If I note errors in this latest document, I don't blame them on the pope but rather on the limitations inherent in his function under contemporary circumstances.

Certainly, you can see advances in this document—in certain respects surprising advances. For example, the document criticizes democracy and accepts a socialism that safeguards the values guaranteeing integral human development, especially liberty, responsibility, and openness to the spiritual (no. 31). But I cannot accept certain flaws that keep showing up in documents of this sort and turn them into two-edged swords.

One clear advance is the fact that no one is arguing about

words any more. Remember the publication of *Mater et Magistra?* Everyone wanted to know exactly how the Latin should be translated. Now the terms are clear-cut and unambiguous—though their *practical import* for the pope may still be unclear. Just a short few years ago the word "socialism" sounded like blasphemy to Christian ears. How times change!

Octogesima Adveniens presents a well-thought-out list of world problems, though with certain inexplicable limitations. It is written by a European for Europeans. Once again you get the impression that the universality of the church is confined to western Europe and the rest of the world is heathen territory still to be converted. Not a word about war or the arms race, and only a glancing reference, in comparative terms, to the dizzying escalation of military expenditures.

Obviously it isn't possible to broach every problem in one document. But the principal ones certainly should be tackled. This document talks about the problems as if they were simply "abuses" of a social order that in itself is quite natural and Christian. . . . I suspect Pope Paul prefers a country where contemplative monasteries and pornography fairs stand side by side (I can hear him say, "At least they have freedom there!") to one where such contrasts are less glaring and human dignity is more respected but Western religions are regarded with a certain coolness.

On the other hand, this document does suggest that a new social order is justified because no existing model is "completely satisfactory." The author's analytic methodology seems defective. He can list the surface manifestations of problems, but he never gets down to their historical causes. How are we to overcome these problems? Must we simply wait for those in power to undergo some sort of conversion? This is the most dangerous element of utopianism in the church's teaching. It doesn't seem to me that Jesus directed his apostles to the religious and political leaders of their day. Instead he himself turned to the poor and tried to initiate a dialogue with them. One positive feature of *Octogesima Adveniens* is its recognition that there can be no one, universally valid solution and that some decisions properly rest with the local churches. This decentralization will benefit the church because experience has shown that imported official solutions only exacerbate problems.

The pope states that "it is the role of each Christian community to analyze objectively the situation in its own country and elucidate it in the light of the Gospel" (no. 4). This increases the responsibility of the rest of us; we may no longer wait for Rome to speak before we act. It is not the pope who will tell the churches of Haiti, Senegal, or the Philippines what to do, but the Christians who live in these countries. The same faith can lead different people to different undertakings (see *Gaudium et Spes,* no. 43). But none of these undertakings may contradict Jesus' meaning in proclaiming the good news to the poor.

The condemnation of liberalism in *Octogesima Adveniens* also represents a step forward: "Philosophical liberalism is at its very root a false affirmation of individual autonomy in action and motive as well as in the exercise of freedom" (no. 35). We have lived so long under this ideology that it has even contaminated church doctrine. Incredible that it has taken us until now to realize how antievangelical it is. We are still not aware of all the mischief wreaked by liberalism. Section no. 18 clearly reveals the author's belief that, serious problems notwithstanding, the existing system incorporates "a general movement of solidarity, through an effective policy of investment and of organization of trade and commerce, as well as of education." He still believes that the members of international organizations are capable of suiting their actions to their words.

This is the most difficult point to accept. International organizations such as NATO and the International Monetary Fund unilaterally serve the interests of the stronger nations that control them. They do not accept pluralism at all. Small nations that refuse to play the game by the rules of the game are shoved to the sidelines. An orange tree cannot bear apples. If we want apples, we must create conditions in which apples can be produced.

In short this document does not tackle the etiology of the

problems. Along with ingenious analysis it offers unfounded assertions like the following statement that "certain ideologies produce nothing but a change in masters who, while their power lasts, envelop themselves in privilege, restrict the freedom of others, and establish new forms of injustice." There are places where this has actually happened, but the document does not name them; nor does it say what conditions obtained in these places before the changes occurred. For the most part these changes are to the people's advantage, but one cannot compare the newly established orders with corrupt and decadent liberal societies. (. . .)

It is worth noting that the author addresses himself to Christians in general, never to Catholics in particular. But how does he think of the church? In his own words: "In some places they [Christians] are reduced to silence and regarded with suspicion [totalitarian societies]; in others they constitute a weak, scarcely noticeable minority. In yet others the church's position is recognized—or even officially established." I get the feeling that the author judges the last-named situation to be the most fitting. Naturally we should hope for complete freedom to preach and practice Christianity. But the most convenient situation is not always the most evangelical. We are in grave danger of making convenience our criterion. In many countries the church's position is recognized but at the price of its silence. The price is too high. The church must walk the road of poverty and persecution—so *Lumen Gentium* tells us, but we don't seem too convinced. We regard poverty as a heavy yoke and persecution as a disgrace that limits our freedom. That which is truly grace we regard as misfortune or disaster. We have fallen into opportunism and have lost the meaning of the gospel. We are not ready for poverty and persecution. Do we really trust in the Holy Spirit, in the Lord's promise to be with us always? What does it matter if our position is not recognized, if we become—again—a "tiny remnant"? God has need of us so that human beings may come to know him, but he does not need us to save them. The gratuitousness of his love transcends all our efforts.

Section 48 is the one that alarmed me the most. The author

implicitly confesses what was previously admitted by Pius XII, namely, that we have lost the working class. In other words the pope is aware that the church is enmeshed in the bourgeoisie. By saying that the church "has sent priests on an apostolic mission to the working class," the pope raises the question: *Where was the Church* when it sent these priests? Where else but among the rich? But matters should have been exactly opposite. We should have sent worker-priests to the bourgeoisie. We should be rooted in the world of the poor. Then we would not be required to pass through the eye of the needle to attain salvation.

There are, finally, two passages I should like to cite in order to convey two of my fundamental principles. The first is in section 36: "In serving his fellow-men the Christian must —without allowing himself to be compromised by any system—endeavor to reveal through his choices the specifically Christian contribution to the transformation of society." I would change it to read: "In serving his fellow-men the Christian must—while questioning all systems—. . . . "

The second passage occurs in section 48: "It is not enough to recall precepts, to state intentions, to note crying injustices, and to intone prophetic denunciations. It is all empty talk unless accompanied—on the part of every Christian—by intense awareness of personal responsibility and by effective action." As was said at the Medellín Conference,[73] the present still has time for words, but it is swiftly becoming a time for action.

There are other comments I would like to make but can't in the present context. Underlying this critical examination is a great love for the church. I do not want it to be, like a prostitute, the tool of anyone who can pay. I want it to be the image of Jesus Christ.

All of us in here send a big hug to all of you out there. Let us remain united in the Holy Spirit, who has made the cross a signpost on the road toward the future.

113

To Luciano

May 17

Dear Luciano, if you only knew how much Mom admires you and likes you. . . . When I read her description of you, I felt as though I'd known you for a long time.

Your letter is a little embarrassing. It makes me sound as though I'm not made of flesh and bone at all (in reality I think I'm more flesh than bone). If my witness—as God has permitted me to bear witness—has such impact on people, it's because the church is in bad shape. We should be the rule, not the exception. We are simply living according to the gospel and taking all the consequences. When Jesus warned his disciples that they would face many hardships, he didn't consider it a tragedy. The tragedy is elsewhere, in an established, officially recognized church that calls to mind a feudal aristocracy more than a manger in Bethlehem. The tragedy lies in the realization that God's word no longer rouses and converts but is restricted to alleviating the sufferings of the poor and justifying the egotism of the rich. (. . .)

I have never wanted to be a prisoner, just as Jesus never wanted the cup that was given him to drink. But since I find myself here, I want to put the occasion to good use. Human wickedness does not limit God's plan. In this place I've had a chance to see the other side of the coin, to deepen my aims, and to renew my conversion. I know my weaknesses, my limits and defects, but now I know that suffering does not destroy me, human and vulnerable though I am, that prison doesn't snuff out freedom, that darkness does not shut out my light, and that death will bring me to resurrection. Now I know what the parable of the sower and the seeds means.

I've learned a lot here, primarily that we discover our true selves only when we are confronted by our own limits. The animal pursued by a hunter measures its own strength. Look at the story of Job. Although he didn't know God's plan, he didn't despair. He trusted, and his hope was rewarded.

Why is the church so upset when its possessions are threatened? Why do we fear poverty and persecution? Why are we so afraid that the church's image might suffer? If the church doesn't communicate Jesus Christ, then it ought to be not just disfigured but destroyed. Unfortunately such changes are more often forced upon us by circumstances than freely embraced by us for the sake of the gospel. But the changes will come. Very soon we will forget our own personal problems and commit ourselves to something very different.

Luciano, I hope to be able to continue this newly begun dialogue with you. I know that in my house they like you very much. Take my place at table. Some day we will be together to celebrate our deepening friendship.

114

To his sister Cecilia

May 19

(. . .) Here they are suspicious even of our breathing. The food that is sent to us every week is inspected minutely and maliciously. (. . .) Countless little humiliations are repeated every day. You'll get an idea of what it's like if you think back to when we were little kids and the grownups were always saying, "Stop that! What have you got in your hand? Beat it!"

That's the kind of thing that goes on here, and it's not easy to take when you're over twenty-one (some of us are over forty). The poor slobs who guard us have gotten a raw deal in life. They are treated like dirt by their superiors, and they take out their rage on us.

If one has not had a certain upbringing and therefore lacks a certain point of view, as is the case with most of the nonpolitical prisoners, all that bad treatment leads to silent revolt. That is the source of the brawls that break out almost daily among the nonpolitical prisoners. It is their only way of shaking off the humiliations put upon them. The political prisoners, on the other hand, never lose their heads and can demand and get more dignified treatment, though it's not easy when you're dealing with a guard who comes to work half-drunk and worried to death about his unpaid bills.

The life we live and the tragedies we witness can only be understood by someone who has been here. At night terrible shrieks break the heavy silence of people who by now are accustomed to feeling powerless and showing no reaction to anything. A prisoner howls and howls, or cries like a baby, and when you ask the guard what's going on he says that someone has gone crazy or that there was a fight in the cell. It's also possible that the prisoner in question has been tortured. But there are frequent cases of madness here, and last month there was another suicide. A prisoner tied his pants to the window-bars, looped them around his neck, and then jumped as hard as he could (because the cell windows are not that high). Like the other suicides that have happened here, the whole affair remains shrouded in mystery. No one knows where his cell-mates were or where the guards were. No one saw anything. No one says anything.

In the beginning such things bothered me terribly. In time I learned that someone living in the jungle cannot afford to be afraid of snakes.

If in one way I have become thick-skinned, like the grave-digger who earns his living from the dead, in another I have learned to direct all these experiences into a profound and continued conversion, by which my faith and my ideals become greater and purer. I see our little problems of the outside world for the molehills they really are. Some of our bourgeois concerns are completely silly and out of place. Human reality is very serious, and we privileged souls must not permit ourselves to live apart from other people's sufferings. We must reach their suffering and eradicate it.

I hope to be a guest in your new home. May it be as simple and hospitable as you are.

115

To Sister Ruth

May 25

Dear Cousin, when I read your letters I realize that you and I think alike about the Christian life and that we two experience with particular intensity the mystery of the cross and of joy. I am becoming more and more convinced that it is really a privilege to live in this postconciliar period of church history, in which we are required to play a responsible part in the process of renewal. But the renewal will come from below, from prophets, not from experts in canon law, from those open to the future rather than those attached to the past. Our excessive attachment to juridical values—a hallmark of the Western mind—has too often caused us to forget that the human person is a being in continual evolution, capable of transforming and being transformed, full of questions that are infinite in scope and that only faith can answer. We often take refuge in the status quo, believing that the present is definitive and unchangeable. But in reality, if we don't prepare ourselves to face the cyclone that is devastating our age and driving it toward an unknown future, we are in danger of running aground on the myths and utopias of the present.

The same phenomenon occurred in the fifteenth and sixteenth centuries, when human creativity overcame many barriers that till then had seemed insurmountable. Navigation and international trade broke down the barriers between peoples and enlarged geographical confines. Technology and science increased man's dominion over himself and nature. Philosophical subjectivism turned the universal order upside down and made man the center and the measure of all things. All barriers crumbled—economic, social, artistic, political, and religious—and the world grew wider. Man felt somehow insecure and lost in its immensity. Many people thought it was the end of everything, when in fact it was the beginning of a new era.

Today we are living through a similar situation. The moon,

once a symbol of romance or madness, is now a real place on which human beings have walked.

How will we go about reconciling our old values with the new world of space, the progress of automation, artificial insemination, the dizzying rate of scientific advances, and the capacity to probe the deepest mysteries of the universe? Everything familiar seems to be crumbling around us while these new realities seem to be infinite in dimension and absolute in their power. The cyclone raging around us for the last few decades has shaken not only the outside world but also the foundations of our inner world. Moral and religious barriers have toppled, and the younger generation has launched itself on a frantic search, looking everywhere and not finding much. Atheism is a collective phenomenon; sex is a commercially furnished diversion and very profitable; earning-power becomes the supreme criterion of professional achievement. At the same time contradictions multiply: We talk a great deal about peace and live amid wars; poverty and wealth live side by side.

Clearly these convulsions will end sooner or later, even if we don't know when or how. A Christian cannot be pessimistic about the future. These are the pangs of childbirth that bring a new world, a new promised land that is our journey's end. It is the goal we seek, but like Moses we will probably never set foot in it.

What, then, should be the attitude of the church toward a materialistic, unbelieving, and exploitative world in possession of scientific knowledge that challenges our religious faith? Should we go into the desert and wait there apart till the storm subsides? Should we abandon our faith and plunge into the whirlpool of a world in turmoil? Surely these are not the only two alternatives open to us. We can no longer barricade ourselves inside the church, praying and doing penance on behalf of the "outside world." Our vision must be based not on despair but on faith.

How does God see the world? This may seem like a rhetorical question, but for me it is a radical and basic problem. The Bible tells me that the Lord is not only involved in human

193

history but also reveals himself through this history. I open the newspaper to read the plans of God. Every human action, wherever it may take place, is an act of salvation or perdition. The criterion of judgment is easy enough, and it is provided by the gospel: We are saved when we are willing to lose ourselves for others, but we are truly lost when we are concerned solely with our own salvation. So I think God sees the world very clearly. He does not experience crises as we do because he knows that his kingdom is eschatological. We have crises because we forget this fact and concentrate all our hope on the present or live nostalgically in the past. If human beings seem to us to be moving farther away from God because they are abandoning the church, it is because we confuse the church with God. I think that human beings are seeking God more anxiously than ever before. If they withdraw from the church, the fault is ours because we bear witness to a god of nationhood and private property who no longer chooses to suffer on the cross, to a god who is not the God of Jesus Christ. If a world in turmoil frightens us, what kind of leaven do we propose to be?

It should be crystal clear to us Christians that our task is not to judge the world. Our mission is to save it. Or rather, *human beings will be saved by the gratuitous gift of God's love, which is the essence of our proclamation.* This being the case, how can we think that human beings are far removed from God? The very fact of being a human being in the world is a blessing from God. Hence I think that human beings are imbued with the values of the gospel, eager for love, and full of hope, even though they do not recognize the revelation of Jesus Christ as the expression of the foundations of their existence.

There is sin, it is true. But it is also true that grace is stronger than sin. God looks upon the world with love and confidence and therefore so must we.

Sometimes events trouble us. Discouragement overtakes us, and the feeling that anything we might do would be absolutely useless. Who is mistaken, we or the world? I always prefer to think that it is we who are mistaken. We have been well trained to teach catechism to children according to the

Tridentine formulas, according to medieval theology and neo-platonic philosophy. We are locked into an illusionary spirituality and becalmed amid aristocratic institutions. If we cannot renew ourselves, we will never understand the nature and scope of the changes that the world is going through. The gospel says that we are to be the leaven of the world, not its image, but we succumb to the temptation to be image and not leaven. The shape that the world may take in a particular age is not important for us. Our concern is to be truly its leaven, utilizing everything we have learned from our faith. Mystical experience should help us to recognize the presence of God, not only in our own lives but in the lives of all people and in the evolution of the universe. (. . .)

Today we had the pleasure of saying goodbye to Father Giulio Vicini, who was released after serving four months of his sentence.[74] Now there are three of us in this cell.

A hug to you and your sisters. Much friendship.

116

To Sister Alberta, a Brazilian nun

June 17

Dear Sister Alberta, your postcard was a welcome surprise because I have always esteemed your faith and your vocation. I know that you can understand what we are feeling and living through here precisely because of that faith and vocation. (. . .)

The judge has personally assured us that we will come to trial in July. It does not seem likely to us, however, even though the progress of our case has picked up in the last few months. On the first of June we learned that our request to be freed on bail under house arrest had been denied. From that fact we gather that we will be sentenced to at least two years. It's ridiculous, but there is nothing to be done. Now we are hoping that the Supreme Military Tribunal will okay our appeal. It's a matter of waiting. No suffering, no privation is eternal.

There are now three of us in this cell. We are neither resigned to our fate nor despairing. We try to understand it in the light of faith, to explore the possible import of such an event in the life of a Christian. In this respect we can say that ours is a privileged situation, one that furthers our efforts toward a lasting conversion to Jesus Christ. This does not mean that coercion acts upon us as a tranquillizer; rather, it enables us to see more clearly that our situation and our actions can have a positive impact on the life of the church. If it did not, rebellion—or despair—would be inevitable.

But when we realize that the fact of our presence here is a sign of the church's vitality, then all we need do is give ourselves up wholly to the Lord's intentions. This is not vanity. On the contrary, we are aware of a great responsibility—the responsibility and humility of the sown seed, the fidelity of the useless servant. Neither conscience nor the church nor God accuses us. So why should we fear "the wisdom of the world" when we know that our redemption rests in "the folly of the cross?"

My companions and I thank you for your words of friendship and support. We entrust ourselves to your prayers and promise to pray for you. Peace to you all.

117

To Liana, a friend

June 20

When I read your letters, Liana, I feel as if they had been written by an angel. They breathe pure-heartedness. You scarcely seem to be flesh and blood at all. The only hitch is that you call me "holier" (?) than yourself. That's a real joke! If you only knew how much I have to grow! Besides, the traditional image of the saint does not appeal to me at all. . . . I prefer to have my feet on the ground, to be human among humans, to participate in life. I know that you do the same because you work and keep up friendships outside the limited circle of your own church. If you want to be leaven in the dough, there is no point in staying inside the package.

I don't know very much about the structure or history of your church. You will have to explain it to me. As far as my own church is concerned, it will have to make an about face before it can become leaven in the dough. The story of the Catholic church is very similar to that of the monk who forsook his land and goods to go into the desert and live a life of strict poverty. Since he was cold and a little ill he accepted heavy clothing from a friend who came to visit. As time went on, he was surrounded by an ever-increasing multitude who came to venerate him and to express their gratitude and leave gifts in exchange for favors received through his intercession. The monk replaced his bowl with a plate, ate with a spoon instead of his fingers, put boots on his bare feet, and left the cave and the hard ground for a dry dwelling and soft bed.

To the people who began to voice a suspicion that he was no longer poor, the monk replied, "Just gifts! Simply gifts!" His possessions (to which he claimed he was "unattached") mounted, and he had cultivated land and plenty of food to eat. Eventually he produced more than he needed and began to sell the surplus. Concerned over the growing number of his disciples, he had a large monastery built to house them. This monastery was in all respects like the fief of a feudal lord. It produced the best wine in the area, as well as a great many other things that the monks sold. Everyone praised the monastery's prosperity, kings acknowledged its economic importance, and the monk who had founded it became a veritable prince. He was given, among other things, a title of nobility.

But the monks continued to take vows of poverty and to tell the poor, "You are the Lord's favorites." They praised the poverty of the Servant of Yahweh and were convinced that, despite the wealth of monastery and fief all around them, none of it was actually "theirs." Since it didn't belong to the poor either, the monks insisted that "it all belonged to the church and to God." It was God and the church who made sure that the monks had bread and wine everyday, while outside the monastery the poor went hungry and consoled themselves by thinking of the poverty of Christ, whose minister and representatives on earth the monks felt themselves to be.

What am I to do? How can I preach what I do not live? How can I teach what I do not do? I am a liar because I do not bear witness to what I proclaim. I am full of false pride because I wish to be taken for what I am not. It is the old schism between faith and witness, theory and practice, ideals and life.

Today the church is aware of this problem. Vatican II represented an effort to pinpoint and overcome the causes of this schism but we still have a long way to go. In theory many things have already been accomplished: We have rediscovered the Bible, we have formulated a new definition of the church as the people of God, we have perceived that God is present in human history, we have reformed the liturgy and entrusted tasks to the laity, we have come to esteem poverty as an essential precondition for apostolic work, we have acknowledged the autonomy of the temporal world and the service to humanity that the Church must undertake. And there are attempts to move from theory to practice.

But to practice what we profess we must break with the past. Once and for all the church must renounce its privileged position in society. It may not be a church *for* the poor; it must be a church *of* the poor. If the rich wish to enter this church they must pass through the eye of the needle.

Whenever you can, tell me about the problems of your church. Probably they are different from ours. But we do have much in common: faith in the same God and a desire to save the same world. As far as I know, your church retains the characteristics of its country of origin. This is true of us too. We have tried to force the Catholic church into a Roman mold, even in countries that have no connection with Western civilization. Today we see the error in that, and we are trying to remedy it.

I think that our common religious concerns can serve as a basis for dialogue. We should exchange ideas on our experiences. Thus we can help each other to be more authentic.

Here life goes on as usual: iron bars and not much sunshine. But we feel the serenity of knowing that all this has meaning even if it is slow to bear fruit. It seems absolutely certain that we will not get out of here before the end of the year.

We pray for your apostolate, offering up our sufferings that you may be successful and grow in faith, hope, and love. Fernando, Ivo, and I send you a big hug and all our love.

118

To Marlene, a friend

June 20

Marlene, your letter, which I've read twice from beginning to end, is very human and as beautiful as the sunflowers you have planted on your farm. It is like you. To be in touch with the earth is a good thing. Here I miss it very much. It's been quite a while since I've seen fields, or anything green—my landscape is all cement and iron. It's an oppressive panorama. I miss the open air and the vistas in which you can lose yourself. . . . I was born in the mountains and spent my first years on the seacoast. My earliest memory of myself is that of a small boy playing with a little pail on the Copacabana beach. That was when I was three or four, and it's my only memory of that time—the rest is gone. This has stayed with me because I love the sea above anything else in nature. It frightens me and consoles me at the same time because it hides a mysterious richness.

There is another spectacle I never tire of contemplating: human beings. What could be more beautiful or more terrible? People can cultivate roses, write poetry, compose music—and they can also make weapons of war, oppress each other, and condemn each other to death. We have a long way to go to recapture the unity described in the first chapter of Genesis. Right now we are a mass of contradictions, undoubtedly because we are self-deceived.

199

One of the most important moments of my life came when I realized that my existence had a social dimension. Only then did I begin to grasp its personal dimension. Until that moment I had believed in the law of the jungle, in which competition, not cooperation, was the key. I left off competing in order to cooperate. I ceased wanting so that I would be able to choose. It suddenly came to me that every choice entails a renunciation. You cannot flutter through life from one possibility to the next without ever committing yourself to any. Choosing one path at a crossroads necessarily excludes the others. At times you are overtaken by the temptation to turn back or take dubious shortcuts that at first glance seem easier but always turn out more tortuous. You must keep going, patiently and determinedly, trusting your own legs and nurturing your hope in the destination that awaits you.

The things we have been taught don't emphasize the social dimension of human existence. . . . I learned to read and write from the Uncle Paperone books. I piously believed that one day I would be as rich as he. I spent my childhood with Captain Marvel and Zorro. My heroes were strong men, and they won with force. I could sleep in peace because they would protect me. . . . The enemies of my heroes—the outlaws, thugs, and trouble-makers—looked a little bit like Mexicans. All these books taught me that crime doesn't pay, but also that it was no crime to make money. They also taught me that the ideal man, the prototype of virility, was super-fed, super-equipped, and super-envied. I learned that I must become one of them at all costs, and I dreamed of my future as I chewed gum and drank Coke. I had a passionate admiration for Uncle Sam.

My sensibilities were further developed by the movies. They continued the education that my comic books began, reinforcing the same values vividly and crudely. They taught me that love is a pretty face and a nice figure, and that I would have to plunge headfirst into incredible adventures in order to be a real man. From the movie screen I learned a whole host of things that no one would have the courage to teach anyone in real life. The fulfilled man was rich, clean-shaven, stylishly dressed, successful with women, and surrounded by flunkies who jumped to satisfy his every whim. When I left the movie house, I was convinced that my own life would duplicate in every respect what I saw on the screen, provided that I could make money. This was the primer of Uncle Sam, who was to me the incarnation of progress, civilization, and freedom.

My adolescent idols were the technicolor images of movie stars. David Niven in his Rolls Royce, driven by a black chauffeur from Harlem. Elizabeth Taylor as the queen of Egypt, worshipped by thousands of Oriental slaves. Gary Cooper leveling his unerring rifle at the head of some Mexican bandit. John Wayne carrying victory over death around the world. They were the invincible whites, superhuman and superb, every man capable of winning a blonde goddess for his love.

In every feature of body and mind I sought to resemble Marlon Brando, James Dean, Frank Sinatra, and Glenn Ford. I wished to be nothing like the bandits whom they killed, the enemies they conquered, the servants who catered to them on the screen. I tried to identify with my heroes and their glory, their wealth, and their power over women. But most of my illusions died with the death of Marilyn Monroe, and a good thing too.

In the city I learned the law of the jungle and the use of intelligence to accumulate riches. I too could learn to be insensitive to other people's sufferings.

Women were brought up to believe in even worse illusions than ours. You were trained to be man's living tools. You were taught to be beautiful. You were taught to walk, smile, sit, bat your eyes, speak, eat, diet, and dress so as to arouse men's desire. You were taught that men are the ones who study, make decisions, build things, make mistakes, give orders, and fulfill themselves. Man is the warrior, woman the warrior's rest. You were to satisfy his whims; to be beautiful, docile, and patient. You must belong to him alone, even if he amused himself with other women. All you had to be was beautiful. It didn't matter if your head had nothing to recommend it but hair. You were the body; he was the mind. He thought; you did. His body was not supposed to matter to you, only his

201

money, his social prestige, his intelligence. That is what you were to look for in him, even though he saw neither your mind nor your spirit, only your body.

The worst poison in our society is not sold at the drug store. It is sex. It is an effect, not a cause. It is the fruit of our inability to love, a symptom of contemporary man's asexuality. We are preoccupied with sex because we are impotent. All the supermen of our childhood were asexual beings. All the movie stars of our adolescence were romantic fakes: They could kiss beautifully, but love was only supposed to happen *after* "The End" flashed on the screen.

In this school we were taught the artifices and the vicissitudes of love, but we never learned to love. A line was drawn between mind and body. As mind, the male has lost his virility, his ability to perceive his body; his sexual aggressiveness stems from the repugnance he feels for his own body. As body, the female has lost her personality, her inner self; her sexual passivity is that of a mere receptacle.

The Don Juans of our day are not supermen, as James Bond might suggest. They are impotent, never-satisfied creatures who must always be trying someone new. And the super-seductress in reality is super-frigid. The body cannot satisfy the mind, and the mind is unaware that it must satisfy the body's spirit.

If you walk in the rain, you are bound to get wet. If we have deceived ourselves about love, then our lives will be ones of amorous deceit and deceptive loves. Only when we discover the social dimension will we free ourselves from this modern Babylon!

(. . .) Only then will we recover the unity of body and mind, of flesh and spirit. Competition will be succeeded by cooperation. Personal success will come to mean success in and for society. Heroism will be the prerogative of the whole people, achieved in the fulfillment of common aspirations. Power will mean service, love, self-giving.

(. . .) Why all these years of psychotherapy? Why all these incurable guilt complexes? They are the price of the illusions in which we have grown up, of the daydreams to which we were addicted. We are maladjusted to life.

At this point it seems to me that the only cure for the evil is to uproot it. But first we must find the roots.

Next time tell me about your daughter. Much friendship to you and your family.

1972

119

March 27

(. . .) Today I wrote to Father De Couesnongle asking him to forward an appeal to the monasteries that are keeping in touch with our cases. I would like them to help the prisoners' families living in their vicinities. Such a gesture would signify support for us. Only an inmate can appreciate the suffering of a father who knows that his children want food and clothing and are totally dependent on charity. During the past two years we've tried in every way and through various people to organize a permanent relief organization for the families of political prisoners. But our efforts have not succeeded. More than one bishop who has visited us and even the apostolic nuncio promised to set aside a special fund for this purpose and to get help from Caritas International. But nothing concrete has been accomplished, and what aid there is, is intermittent and insufficient.

We have tried to collect a little money for these people by doing all sorts of handicrafts. We have made plastic bags, belts, and leather cigarette cases for the families of poor prisoners to sell. But the market is small, and the prices must be lower than what the stores charge. At least we may have helped a little bit.

Families of political prisoners face far more serious difficulties than families of ordinary offenders. They are the object of general mistrust. The systematic propaganda of the military dictatorship labels us "terrorists" and has managed to panic many people. They are not so much afraid of us as of the police repression that envelops our circle of friends and relations. The wife of a political prisoner loses her job because her boss doesn't want "trouble with the police." His children have trouble finding a school that will accept them, the house is under constant surveillance, and friends gradually fade away. If the family gets any help, the police assume that it comes from some political party or from "the organization" and that it is part of the take from a bank robbery. In some ways the fear and insecurity that the family suffers are worse than what the imprisoned husband must bear.

(. . .) And this is only a small part of the prevailing atmosphere in Brazil today. (. . .) On the surface everything seems just fine. Economic progress is spectacular, and the government supposedly enjoys popular support. This is the image of Great Brazil that they try to project both at home and abroad in order to attract foreign credit and investment. But the reality is very different and has never been as bad as it is today. The lie is well told, however, even as it was in Nazi Germany. The people will end by believing it, just as the Germans believed that Hitler was the savior of Europe.

(. . .) The facts about the situation in Brazil are told in the official publications of the dictatorship, even though official propaganda tries to twist these facts into a favorable interpretation. Just don't believe anyone who comes to Europe to tell you that here everything is fine. German families calmly contemplated the smoke rising from Nazi Germany's "factory" chimneys. When the war was over, they learned that the chimneys belonged to crematoria where human beings were burned to ashes.

A small segment of the church has reacted to the present state of affairs in Brazil. Pedro Casaldaliga, the bishop of São Felix di Araguaia, is our voice crying in the wilderness, our "wilderness" being the *sertão* of Mato Grosso. He courageously defends the small farmers of that region against the huge agribusiness companies that are trying to take away their land at gunpoint. The superintendent of police ordered Lulu, the small farmers' leader, to appear at headquarters for interrogation, and soldiers went to arrest him and escorted him in handcuffs through the streets. The bishop, too, was summoned. But he replied publicly that he was no different from Lulu and that he would wait for the soldiers to arrest him and escort him through the streets in handcuffs. Don't you think that Christ would have done the same?

Repression against the church continues. Last week Father Comblin was expelled from the country. There was no word of it in the press.

Pray for those who wait hopefully to see this sorrowful passion transformed into a glorious resurrection. I want to thank you and your companions for all you have done for us. Hug them all for me, your friend and cousin.

120

To a brother in Rome[75]

Presidente Wenceslau Prison
June 12

(. . .) I am writing to you on the morning of the fourth day of a total fast. It's a magnificent, sunny day that seems to reflect our own feelings.

(. . .) We are reviving an age-old tradition that of late has fallen into oblivion. Fasting fortifies the spirit. It is as if we are living Christ's words: "The flesh is weak but the spirit gives life." The atmosphere is one of spiritual retreat. We pray continually and nourish ourselves on God's word. It is a kind of Exodus. We are crossing a desert with only manna for food, accompanied by the certainty that we will attain the liberation of the Brazilian people. This certainty is grounded in our faith in Christ the Redeemer, and in our loving communion with the people. We choose to be present among the people and to walk with them through this parched and seemingly endless desert, bearing in our hearts the certainty of liberation. We are not downhearted and we never have been. We are happy because the Lord is with us and the church of God is here in our two-by-five-meter cell. . . .

June 30

(. . .) To prevent any misunderstandings, I will try to give you a detailed and faithful account of recent events.

At the beginning of May we learned that fifteen political prisoners would be taken from Tiradentes Prison and isolated from their companions. They would be the first group. The aim of the military was to gradually weed out the "incorrigibles" from those who could be "rehabilitated," naturally according to the military's definition of these terms. We were in immediate danger of maltreatment and even murder, presumably incurred while "attempting escape" or "attempting revolt" or "during brawls with other prisoners." There have been nasty precedents for this happening in other places. An enormous number of political prisoners have "disappeared" while "resisting the police." In reality they died as a result of terrible torture or were murdered in cold blood after unspeakable suffering. The method is much used today by the political police all over Brazil.

In the face of this imminent great danger, our lawyers lodged all sorts of protests. They were summoned, questioned, and exhaustively investigated by the political police. Petitions were sent to newspapers, journals, and prominent people. All in vain. Only one defense was left to us: to stay together in the prison for political prisoners. We had to adopt a common position that corresponded to the gravity of our situation.

On May 12 eighteen of us were taken out of Tiradentes Prison and transferred to the state penitentiary, where we were to be treated like ordinary offenders. (. . .) Once we got there, we were put in cells with the most dangerous criminals. We then began our fast, declaring that we would not touch food until we were returned to our companions. Those who had remained at Tiradentes Prison joined in a sympathy fast. Our archbishop, who fully grasped the situation, agreed to serve as our negotiator with the authorities. He did everything he could to meet with the participants in this gesture of denunciation and protest, but humiliating obstacles were put in his way. Meanwhile our friends in Tiradentes who were fasting in sympathy were transferred to the São Paulo House of Detention.

On the sixth day of our fast, a member of the São Paulo judiciary came to us, stating that he had carte blanche to resolve the situation. He promised us that if we stopped our fast, within a week all political prisoners would be reunited in one cell bloc in the House of Detention, and that women prisoners would be taken to a nearby prison so that their relatives could visit them again. On the basis of this formal commitment from the authorities we broke our fast, and two days later we too were transferred to the House of Detention. But as time went on, we realized that we had been shamefully deceived. Only those who had gone on a hunger strike out of sympathy with us would remain in the House of Detention. We and other "dangerous" prisoners would be kept in isolation. Our situation had not changed; indeed it had become even more perilous. We repeatedly asked to see the official who had made the promise to us, but without success. But we did get to explain our plight to Archbishop Arns of São Paulo, and he did succeed in getting to see us.

On June 8, without notice, we were awakened at 4:00 A.M. to "take a trip." There were six of us: three Dominicans, a lawyer who had been arrested with Mother Maurina, a godson of Monsignor Alano du Noday, and a student. The judge made some veiled threats, but we were not told where they intended to take us. The guards were from DOPS, the political police unit that has tortured and killed countless people. Among them are some members of the death squad in São Paulo. We were pushed into a windowless police van, and in airless darkness and suffocating heat we traveled all day without food or water. Fernando fainted, the student had a violent attack of dysentery, and the lawyer, who had been tortured, suffered

211

racking back pain. At 9:00 P.M. we arrived at our destination and found ourselves at Presidente Wenceslau Penitentiary on the border between Mato Grosso and São Paulo, 660 kilometers from where we had started.

Faced with this new official lawlessness, we again took up our fast. It was the only means of defense available to us. (. . .) We began on June 9, so we are now on the twenty-second day. (. . .)

Of our companions back in São Paulo we have heard relatively little. They are all in isolation. On June 9 two of them, Paulo de Tarso Vanuchi and Paulo de Tarso Wenceslau, were carted off to the headquarters of *Operação Bandeirantes* and brutally tortured for five days in an attempt to get them to stop their fast. Right now they are in São Paulo prison hospital, in what condition we do not know. (. . .) For a week we have been subjected to real psychological tortures by the doctor assigned to "take care" of us. . . . Bishop José Gonçalves of Presidente Prudente has been of great help and comfort to us. He has done everything possible—and some things impossible—to help us. Without him I do not know what might have become of us.

That's what has happened to us in the last month. We do not know how long this situation will go on. We only know that our fellowship with other political prisoners—present and future—is the Christian witness that we are called upon to bear. Nothing compels us to this course except the love of Jesus Christ, who chose to give his life for humanity's salvation. One figure is constantly in our minds' eyes: Blessed Maximilian Kolbe. If he could lay down his life for one laborer, then we feel that risking ours to save thousands—workers, farmers, students, intellectuals, religious, and priests—is truly meaningful in God's plan.

We were not surprised to have lost our appeal to the Supreme Tribunal. It was just another attempt. But that tribunal, like all the others in Brazil, is mostly composed of and dominated by military men who have inflicted an unlawful government on us and have turned torture and political assassination into our bitter daily bread.

We are determined to continue our fast as part of the Chris-

212

tian witness we must offer at this terrible moment in the history of our country and the Brazilian church. It must continue at least until we have news of our companions in São Paulo. In this connection the return of our archbishop to Brazil is most important, for he continues to be our negotiator.

I hope I have clarified everything. We count on your support.

July 28

(. . .) Our situation today is not what it was when I wrote my last letter to you. We were then in the infirmary, in the course of a total fast that lasted thirty-three days. (. . .) When we finally ended the fast, we went through days of tense waiting. Would we be kept here? Would we be returned to São Paulo? (. . .) Finally we learned our fate: We will be kept here like common prisoners. (. . .) On the twenty-fifth we were processed into the population of this prison. This means that we are now known by numbers: Betto 25044, Fernando 25045, Ivo 25046, Vanderley Caixa 25047, Maurice Politi 25048, Manoel Porfirio de Souza 25049. We wear the prison uniform, we are not allowed food parcels from home, and we must follow prison regulations. Since they were made for a population of four hundred inmates, they are hardly flexible enough to allow for individual needs.

We are also subject to the same punishments as the other prisoners. These range from a simple warning through loss of visiting rights to solitary confinement. We live in individual cells, two meters by three, one next to the other. In each cell is a toilet, cement blocks that serve as chair and table, and a faucet for washing our dishes and ourselves. In the afternoon we can be together in one room; there we study theology.

(. . .) The other prisoners' attitudes toward us are excellent. They all come to talk and listen to us. They show us great sympathy and seem immensely curious on the subject of faith. We feel useful. (. . .) We protest the regimen to which we have been subjected, but we find ourselves adapting to it bit by bit. It is the radicalism of the gospel that bids us to do so. Now we

213

must share our lives wholly with our brothers, the ordinary offenders, and carry on our struggle for the justice to which we are entitled. As always, we are counting on your prayers.

121

To his cousin Agnese

> Presidente Wenceslau Prison Infirmary
> July 15

I am rereading your letter of June 4, which came together with a most beautiful postcard. Receiving it amid these tribulations was like sighting a port of hope in a storm. You simply cannot imagine what these last three months have been like for us. In the granaries of the Lord the seed is winnowed for a long time. . . . Is it so that it will bear more fruit?

On May 12 Fernando, Ivo, and I—with fifteen fellow prisoners—were taken from Tiradentes, which housed the political prisoners of São Paulo, and transported to the state penitentiary, where the ordinary offenders are kept. For the first time since we had been deprived of our physical liberty, we were obliged to wear prison uniforms, to be clean-shaven, and to inhabit individual cells, and were forbidden to receive mail from friends or relatives. Even religious assistance was denied us, and Archbishop Arns of São Paulo was forbidden to visit us.

For these reasons, and also with a view to returning to Tiradentes where political prisoners are held, we began a total fast, taking only water. After a week we were again transferred, this time to the House of Detention in São Paulo, which houses five thousand ordinary prisoners. But we had been promised that all the political prisoners would be reunited there in a cell block of their own. We stopped our fast and got some improvement in our condition: We still had to wear uniforms, but we were allowed visitors.

About three weeks went by and the promised reunification of all political prisoners did not take place. On June 8, toward

214

evening, the colonel in charge of the House of Detention informed us that early the next day we three Dominicans and three other political prisoners would be transferred again, but he did not say where. We traveled 660 kilometers, handcuffed to each other in an enclosed truck without light or air, which the burning sun turned into an oven. Toward evening of that day we arrived, more dead than alive, in the town of Presidente Wenceslau, on the border between São Paulo and Mato Grosso. We are now interned in this regional prison, which presently holds about four hundred ordinary prisoners.

On June 9 the six of us who were transferred here and the other twenty-six political prisoners remaining in the House of Detention began to fast once again. We fasted until July 11—thirty-three days in all. Try to imagine what it was like to go all that time without food, stretched on a bed, being fed intravenously. The catabolism induced by undernourishment consumed our fat and our muscles, causing infections in some of us and various manifestations of hyperacidity in others. Our nervous systems were abraded by isolation and by the effort of resisting those who tried to get us to eat. I kept thinking about the martyrdom of Eleazar, in chapter 6 of the second book of Maccabees.

Finally, on July 10, our fellow prisoners in São Paulo broke their fast and asked us to do the same while waiting for a response from the authorities. We heard about it on July 11, but it was not until yesterday (July 14) that we were able to take solid food. That's how weak we had become.

In all this, however, I feel that God's grace is lending strength to our weakness, that our inner selves are maturing and developing. I am content to think that this sacrifice may, in a more evangelical church that "does justice," turn into a boon.

I thank you for your words of encouragement, and for the love of all of you who pray for us and think about us. You are ever present in my prayers. A big hug and much friendship to you all. May Our Lady of Liberation bless us.

122

To the Dominican Provincial Chapter

September 6

Since circumstances prevent us from attending the upcoming Provincial Chapter in Belo Horizonte, we are sending you this letter in response to your request. It is a modest summary of what our lives as Dominicans have been during these three years in prison.

For us prison has become a privileged locale of Christian living. Although we did not choose prison, it has all the same forced upon us a transformation that would have been very difficult to accomplish on the outside. Suffering, viewed in the context of the cross, cannot but be purifying and liberating.

The very fact of being arrested tore us away from the essentially bourgeois world in which we had been living. Accidental and superfluous things ceased to be regarded as fundamental and indispensable. In our fellow inmates our apostolic vocation found a very specific focus, freeing us from the vacillation of continual searching for a genuine field of missionary endeavor. . . .

Prison has defined a mission territory for us, and in a way it has forced us to take it seriously. . . . Prison has imposed on us the great responsibility of being the only church presence within various prisons. . . . We have come to realize that it is impossible to know people unless you live with them. Our living with other prisoners has afforded some of them a chance to rediscover the church, to see the advent of a church without privileges. Yet we know we are still very far from being as poor as they. We have many friends and brothers in the faith who are interested in what is happening to us, whereas most prisoners spend five, ten, even fifteen years in prison without one visitor!

Among our fellow inmates, we try continually to stress the Christian and ecclesial character of our life. We have been doing this since our first days in prison. . . . Even though most of the prisoners are not Christian, yet in a way they expect and implicitly demand that we live as men of faith here in prison. They marvel at our attitudes, which might seem very traditional, and they lose confidence when they see something in us that contradicts their image of a Christian.

We practice common prayer and meditation on the gospel. Our prison companions would not understand living among Christians who did not pray. We commemorate, simply but meaningfully, all the important feasts of the liturgical year. And in their fashion our fellow inmates have always participated.

We have often asked ourselves what it means to be Dominicans in prison. In practice, very little. Perhaps a certain type of Christian education marked by respect for theological reflection. What's important here is not the label attached to our way of being Christians but just our way of being Christians. Thus it doesn't matter whether one is a secular priest or a Jesuit or a Franciscan. Here reality imposes on everyone the same pattern of life and the same tasks and forces us to form a single community. Only rich people can distinguish between one congregation and religious order and another. To the poor we all are priests and Christians, and what matters is how we act.

Although we are outside the framework of monastic life, we have never before lived such a deeply communitarian and regular life. Here there is no room for theory divorced from practice. We are among prisoners and guards twenty-four hours a day, and this imposes upon us consistency and integrity. We cannot be one person in public and another in private. We must put up with everything: For us there is no "getting away from it all" to the company of close friends, or to a movie, or on a vacation. We cannot even choose our friends. Prison brings together very different people—there is no way of avoiding each other. Prison discipline imposes on us a life of strict observance.

In actual fact the little Christian community we form amid our fellow prisoners represents a communion with them. Despite the limitations imposed on us by prison, we try to provide a basis for our thinking and to continue our study of philosophy and theology. To answer our fellow prisoners' challenge—which is also the challenge now facing the church—we must pay attention to philosophy, economics, and sociology. These disciplines have afforded us a more scientific picture not only of human relations but of just how it is that *people make history*. The fact that we are, of necessity and by the very nature of our discussions, self-taught has allowed us to discover which theological problems rank highest among the concerns of God's people. This is one of the most interesting aspects of our life in prison.

Sharing the same life as the other prisoners has given us a better understanding of what it means to be leaven in the dough. Personal problems of a psychological and subjective nature disappear when we devote ourselves to other people's problems. Here we are continually called upon for something; we are laden with present tasks.

We have never allowed discord among us. So far this unity has certainly been one of the most important aspects of our witness. Many fellow inmates express their regret at not being able to achieve a similar unity among themselves. We also refuse to accept privileges without, however, ceasing to fight for our rights. In every situation we make a deliberate effort to think and act with the full realization that we are the presence of the church in prison. . . .

We are convinced that in the wake of Vatican II God's Spirit has initiated a new *metanoia*, a process of conversion, in God's people and in human history. We believe that this time the renewal of the church will not be effected by isolated individuals like Dominic and Francis but will grow out of the evangelical life of the Christian community as it learns to follow the Lord along the path of poverty and persecution (see Luke 8). Our experience among these people has provided us with some building blocks toward a people's pastorship.

There are many difficulties, some of them insurmountable. The prison officials will not let us do apostolic work or even administer the sacraments. But is it not more important that we Christians ourselves become the Lord's sacrament among the people?

Such has been the nature of our presence in prison so far.

There is no merit in what we are doing because there is nothing else we can do. Either you try to live what you preach or you become a prisoner of your own charade. Affectionate greetings to you all.

123

To his cousin

I got your letter of November 1 last Friday. I'm surprised that you haven't received mine, the one in which I commented on your meetings in Sotto il Monte regarding Christian praxis and prayer. In that letter I also spoke of the meaning that we are trying to give to our presence here among the ordinary prisoners and I pointed out the vast difference between a church that does good works for the poor and a church that is in communion with the poor. I said that unfortunately we are used to *going to* the poor with armloads of gifts, but it would be better if our arms were empty so that we could embrace the poor and shake their hands. I reminded you that now is the time for the church to *align itself with* the disinherited and the oppressed, as Peter and John did with the cripple outside the temple: "I have no silver or gold; but what I have I give you: in the name of Jesus Christ of Nazareth, walk" (Acts 3:5–6). I also asked you to send me the book by that young monk who spoke to you on the subject of prayer. That was the gist of my letter that was apparently lost.

Here in Brazil it's often said that Vatican II has made no difference at all in Europe, but from your letter I gather that this is not generally true and that there are people and groups intensely engaged in the process of return to the gospel. I am convinced that authentic renewal will come, with us or without us. The Holy Spirit does not ask permission to act. Those who have ears to hear will hear, those who have eyes to see will see.

Early every morning, before the cart with the carafes of

coffee comes around, I meditate on the gospels. Today, reading Matthew 27:33–50, I was struck by the atmosphere of failure surrounding Jesus' agony. It is easy to follow him through the triumphal entry into Jerusalem, but there is a real temptation to abandon him when the persecution begins. Jesus could have confounded his persecutors by coming down from the cross and proving he was the Son of God, but he did not give in to triumphalism and would not use any means not in accord with the will of his Father. At times I feel that the church has never learned to tolerate disdain and derision, that it preens itself in the mirror of worldly wisdom. We are afraid to experience the dynamics of failure. We are afraid that the cross will turn out to be a real cross that lacerates our body and spirit. We prefer to remain safe and secure inside the city walls.

In contrast to Jesus, we want to prove to the powerful of this world that we are the children of God. We do not wish to be confused with those whom the world rejects. . . .

I think the subject of your meeting in Sotto il Monte was well chosen. Praxis is a very serious problem for Christians today. We live in a world whose political and juridical principles —which we accept—do not correspond to its existing social relationships. Religion is in the same boat to the extent that we fail to live the faith we profess.

Our social relationships are profoundly characterized by individualism. It isn't easy to preach love in a situation where competition and getting the better of others seem to be the only road to professional success. Hence it is of fundamental importance for us to create fellowship with those who possess nothing except the power to make all people free and equal. This is the fertile soil in which we must plant the seed of God's word, the seed that fructifies the world.

Our lawyer has requested that we be released on bail, and the Military Council will make its decision next month. We are prepared to spend another year in prison. It would be a real surprise to get out any sooner. What others regard as privation is gain for us. (. . .)

1973

124

To his cousin Agnese

January 2

This is in reply to the letter you wrote me exactly a month ago on the First Sunday of Advent. So far I haven't been able to find out whether you got my other letters. I have answered all of yours, but I have no idea whether you got mine because you make no reference to them. Besides I don't have your new address, so I can't write to you directly.

You say that in Italy a lot of people are asking: "What do you believe in now?" You also talk about the need for finding new sources of spirituality. It is precisely this need, I think, that makes it possible to answer such a question.

The problem is a consequence of theology's growing maturity expressed in its ability to criticize its own premises. Nowadays there is nothing that cannot be questioned. Just as in the latter half of the nineteenth century, post-Hegelian philosophy criticized the methodology and the objectives of everything that had come before, so today theology is impelled to a similarly radical self-revision. Among Catholics this process began with Vatican II and constitutes a real Copernican revolution. Just consider the problems raised by Bultmann, for example. . . .

Scientific progress is the root of all philosophical progress. One cannot write a history of philosophy without taking into account the data arising from man's perception of nature. Plato was the genius beneficiary of Greek mathematics, as Descartes was of Galileo's physics, Kant of Newton's discoveries, and Marx of the English economists.

Theology is not an isolated science. It cannot help but reflect innovations in science and philosophy. But theology has had a falling-out with the secular sciences. Science has definitely become the mainspring of all human progress. Philosophy has ceased to contemplate the world and has decided to change it. But what about theology? Will it manage to be more than a polite way of saying something about revealed truths?

"What do you believe in now?" People find the question

hard to answer and the reason for the difficulty, I think, is the centuries-long divorce between theology and spirituality in the Western church. You say, quite rightly, that we must discover new sources of spirituality. I think we can only accomplish this through a new mode of theologizing in which theology and spirituality will be inextricably linked. The foundation of theology nowadays is threefold: divine revelation, tradition, and signs of the times. Theological interpretation of the signs of the times is not something new; the Old Testament prophets did it long ago. It is new only for us who have reinstituted it after long disuse, albeit we still lack the tools to practice it. We must clean our glasses well to see what's happening in the world. Otherwise we will be in danger of mistaking the burning bush, the breeze on Mount Horeb, and the star over Bethlehem for purely natural phenomena.

Every historical period has its own structures. To understand the period we must know how these structures were formed, for the word of God is supposed to reverberate through them. Hence a contemporary theologian simply must know how to judge the impact of economics as a determining element in the lives of peoples and in international relations. It is not enough to say *what* we must do to be faithful to the Lord. One must also spell out *how* we are to do it, what our praxis should be, how we must act within the context of our fidelity to him. Chapter 21 of Luke's gospel presents a masterful lesson by Jesus on reading and interpreting the signs of the times. He tells us the sign: Jerusalem besieged by an invading army. He tells us the outcome: Its destruction is at hand. Then he tells people how to act according to their circumstances: Those in Judea are to flee to the mountains; those in Jerusalem are to get away. Those in the countryside are not to enter the city. Then he reveals the meaning of the event: These are days of chastisement in which all that had been written will be fulfilled.

The church finds it hard to interpret present-day events prophetically. It seems perplexed by events like the war in Vietnam, the struggle in the Middle East, the various wars of liberation, the emancipation of women, student and worker movements, dictatorships. . . . In general the hierarchy limits itself to voicing vague desires for peace without giving any concrete indications of how committed Christians should act in these real situations. Hence it's hard for the church to show the profound significance of Christian praxis for the course of salvation.

I believe that two ideological factors influence the positions that the hierarchy takes. First of all, prophecy has given way to diplomatic expediency. Pronouncements are phrased so as to offend no one, therefore they touch no one. They provoke no questioning, no changes of heart. The second factor is the false notion that the world can evolve without birth pangs. This fallacy is reflected in the pessimistic attitude toward all social conflicts, as if they represented a backward step. But Jesus tells us exactly the opposite: "When you hear of wars and insurrections, do not fall into a panic. These things are bound to happen first; but the end does not follow immediately. . . . When all this begins to happen, *stand upright and hold your heads high, because your liberation is near*" (Luke 21:9–28).

I can see the possibility of a synthesis between theology and spirituality only in an evangelical praxis. We ask each other, What do you believe in now? because the object of our faith is a body of doctrines subjected to rigorous criticism. That sort of faith should not exist among us. The true object of a Christian's faith is a person, Jesus Christ; and the relationship established by faith is one of love. Whoever experiences a crisis of faith because the assumptions of theology are being revised confesses thereby that he lacks spirituality. By spirituality I mean a way of possessing Christ in one's own life, not merely as someone believed in but above all as someone loved. Theology must be rooted in love.

When we observe Jesus' relations with his apostles, we are amazed to find that he was never concerned to transmit to them a body of doctrine. He did not copy the Greek Academy or even the Hebrew synagogue. He did not train his disciples in the manner of Plato and Aristotle. We do not find in the gospel an academic Jesus, concerned to demonstrate to his disciples the principles in which they are to believe. In Christianity the object of faith is a person, which implies a relationship of love.

225

Jesus is one who loves and who is loved. He lives with his friends and teaches them what the simplest happenings of life mean in the light of the "good news." He is not in a hurry, and their vacillation does not upset him. Peter vacillates. So does Thomas. And Matthew tells us that some were unsure even after they had seen him risen from the dead (Matt. 28:17). But they all loved him.

So the question should be phrased differently: "What do you love? A person may believe everything that the church tells him to believe, and still love worldly wisdom, the trappings of luxury, money, and power. When a person tells you what he loves, he reveals who he really is: "For where your treasure is, there will your heart be also" (Matt. 6:21). Belief without love is possible only when theology and spirituality are completely separated. We have much to learn from the Eastern church about how to overcome this defect. The Eastern church has no such dualism. Its theology is not *rational science* but *wisdom,* and it grows out of and is nurtured by a profoundly spiritual life.

Latin rationalism has so subdivided the duties of Christians that we have ended by losing the unity and dynamism of the gospel. Some are to contemplate; others to act. Some are to be concerned for the poor, others not. Some are to follow the beatitudes, others may even observe the evangelical counsels.

This is a serious distortion. I don't think that Jesus established different categories of Christians. The so-called evangelical counsels are for all: priests and laypeople, married people and celibates. So are prayer and contemplation.

The only allowable differences are in charisms and functions. All the other differences derive from our imperfections and our infidelity.

Well, I'll sign off. At home everything is fine. Mom and Dad have celebrated their thirty-first wedding anniversary, and Leonardo has gone to the United States. Please let me know whether you've gotten this letter. Keep writing to me. Fernando, Ivo, and I send you and your friends all our best wishes for a happy 1973.

A Prisoner's Prayer

Lord,
when you look down on those who have imprisoned us and given
us over to torture,
when you weigh the actions of our jailers and the heavy
sentences imposed on us,
when you pass judgment on the lives of those who have
humiliated us
and on the consciences of those who have cast us aside,
forget, Lord, the evil they may have done.
Remember instead that through this sacrifice
we have been brought closer to your crucified son:
Through torture we have received the imprint of his wounds;
through these bars, the freedom of his spirit;
through our sentences, the hope of his kingdom
and the joy of being his sons through humiliation.
Remember, Lord,
that this suffering has borne fruit in us,
like the winnowed seed sprouting.
It is the fruit of justice and peace,
of light and love.

Epilogue

Betto was released from prison in October 1973, and today lives in a shanty in a desperately poor section of Vitória, capital of the state of Espírito Santo. Together with other young people, he is participating in the life of the poor to concretize his commitment to the oppressed. According to him it is not a matter of trying to serve them but above all to be one of them. Betto believes only in a church that is born of the people.

One year after his release from prison he said: "We have finished the first year in freedom and we have not found freedom; it still does not exist. I try always to be prepared, knowing the next time will be the last." (Betto is referring to a new imprisonment.)

With regard to his status in the Dominican order, Betto has written to his general superior asking that he be officially considered a lay brother: "I do not want to be ordained a priest because it would be the first step in rising to power within the church. I am more convinced every day that any type of power tends to corrupt. Furthermore, the priority is no longer sacramental but rather evangelical and I can continue to evangelize without being ordained a priest."

Notes

Foreword

1. All abbreviations are explained on page xiii.

2. Later, in 1969, when the military dictatorship had gained firm control, Bishop Padim felt compelled to point out and denounce the Nazi matrix of the doctrine of "development" as propagated by the War College of the Brazilian generals.

3. Insofar as prison witness is concerned, Christian resistance to fascism was elaborated doctrinally by Emmanuel Mounier and Dietrich Bonhoeffer. Mounier, a Catholic philosopher, was prosecuted and imprisoned by the Vichy government in 1942. Bonhoeffer, a Protestant theologian and minister, was hanged in 1944 by the Nazis in the Flossenburg concentration camp. This thinking found its most forceful embodiment in the German Evangelical community known as the "Confessing Church," whose leader and inspiration was the Berlin minister, Martin Niemöller. It was Niemöller who raised the cry of resistance against Nazism. During Hitler's rule, eighteen of these "Confessing" ministers were shot and several hundred were imprisoned. Niemöller himself was imprisoned for eight years.

1969

4. "If the world hates you, it hated me first, as you know well. If you belonged to the world, the world would love its own; but because you do not belong to the world, because I have chosen you out of the world, for that reason the world hates you. Remember what I said: 'A servant is not greater than his master.' As they persecuted me, they will persecute you; they will follow your teaching as little as they have followed mine. It is on my account that they will treat you thus, because they do not know the One who sent me. . . . I have told you all this to guard you against the breakdown of your faith. They will ban you from the synagogue; indeed, the time is coming when anyone who kills you will suppose that he is performing a religious duty. They will do these things because they do not know either the Father or me. I have told you all this so that when the time comes for it to happen, you may remember my warning."

5. Tiradentes is an old prison in downtown São Paulo, built in the colonial

231

era. Abandoned for decades because of its unhygienic conditions, it has recently been returned to use, primarily for political prisoners.

6. A secondary school run by the Barnabite Fathers in Belo Horizonte, where Betto studied.

7. Teresa is Betto's sister. She moved to São Paulo to be near him in prison.

1970

8. All subsequent letters are written from Tiradentes Prison in São Paulo unless otherwise noted.

9. "Acts" are official pronouncements and decrees. Here Betto is referring specifically to presidential proclamations which suspend constitutional guarantees and promulgate extraordinary measures.

10. Café Filho was president of Brazil during the transition period between the violent death of Getulio Vargas and the electoral victory of Juscelino Kubitschek (1956–1961).

11. Pinto is an outstanding lawyer, still living, who has served as attorney for the defense in many political trials under various dictatorships.

12. The son of Luiz Fernando, Betto's older brother to whom this letter is addressed.

13. Dom Pedro I (1798–1834) was the son of the Portuguese ruler, Dom João VI, who fled to Brazil as Napoleon's army approached his country. Pedro grew up in Brazil. On September 7, 1822, on the banks of the Ipiranga River in São Paulo, he proclaimed Brazil's independence from Portugal. His proclamation is known as the *Grito do Ipiranga.*

14. A division of the political security police in São Paulo.

15. Betto is referring to another Dominican, Tito de Alencar. He was one of the seventy political prisoners released in exchange for the Swiss ambassador in December 1970.

16. In this torture the victim is trussed to a bar and swung back and forth. Electrodes and other torture devices may be used on him.

17. *Caritas Internationalis* is the Holy See's equivalent of the Red Cross.

18. The New State was the fascist regime inaugurated by Getulio Vargas in 1937.

19. Felinto Muller was the infamous chief of the political security police under Getulio Vargas.

20. Taubate is a small city in the state of São Paulo.

21. Betto's youngest brother.

22. Betto shared a cell with "nonpolitical prisoners," that is, ordinary offenders.

23. "Leo" is Betto's second youngest brother, Leonardo.

24. A national daily of conservative bent, now the official voice of the regime.

25. Kidnapped by antigovernment guerrillas, the Japanese consul was released in exchange for five political prisoners.

26. Mother Maurina Borges was the mother superior of an orphanage in Ribeirão Preto. She was arrested for giving refuge to members of a resistance group. When it became known that she had been tortured, the bishop of

232

Ribeirão Preto excommunicated the local chief of police. She is presently in exile in Mexico.

27. Demetrius was the silversmith of Ephesus who incited a riot against St. Paul because he feared Paul's preaching would put an end to his livelihood (see Acts 19).

28. Pedro is a member of a religious order and a biblical exegete.

29. The "Dominican Affair" was the name given by the secret police to their campaign against the Dominican order.

30. Antonio Carlos, the youngest child in the family.

31. Seminary in the city of São Leopoldo, in the state of Rio Grande do Sul, where Betto was studying at the time of his arrest.

32. Giorgio Callegari, an Italian Dominican. Betto refers to him as Giorgio or Father Giorgio.

33. Tiradentes (1748–92), a Brazilian patriot whose real name was José Joaquim da Silva Xavier. He led a revolutionary movement against Portuguese rule and was eventually executed in Rio de Janeiro.

34. Pedro Alvares Cabral (ca. 1467–ca. 1520), a Portuguese navigator, discovered the coast of Brazil in 1500.

35. Gerardo de Proença Sigaud, Archbishop of Diamantina, and two or three other bishops constitute a faction of the Brazilian episcopacy that is aggressively opposed to church renewal. Founder of the TFP movement (Tradition, Family, Property), he is a friend and advisor of the military government.

36. From this point on Betto is speaking to his sister Cecilia and her husband, though the letter is addressed only to his parents.

37. A club in Belo Horizonte much frequented by playboys.

38. From 1960 to 1964, students active in the Belo Horizonte JEC used to meet for Mass every day at 6:00 P.M. in a downtown church. This daily mass became so well-known a meeting-place and so significant for the development of a theology of history that is was prohibited and its participants persecuted after the coup of March 31, 1964. Among the students this Mass was known as the "six o'clock tea."

39. State in the central Brazilian plateau, where the present capital (Brasilia) is located.

40. A reference to Rolf Hochhuth's play of the same name about Pius XII.

41. Onganía was president of Argentina from 1966 to 1970.

42. The case dealt with the clandestine activities of the UNE, which had been officially disbanded in 1964. Nearly all of its members were ambushed by the police and arrested in October 1968 during their clandestine national convention at a farm near São Paulo.

43. The letter is addressed to one of the many Christian youth groups in São Paulo.

44. Author of classic Brazilian novels in the realistic tradition.

45. A gold mine in Belo Horizonte.

46. Brazilian TV personality.

47. G.A. Vilaça, *O nariz do morto* (Rio de Janeiro: JCN Editora, 1970).

48. Father Domingos Maia Leite is at present the provincial superior of the Dominican order in Brazil.

49. The convent where Sister Marike lives.

50. The bishop of Crateus, a small diocese in northeast Brazil. He is well known for his stand against the large landed estates and in favor of rural unions. On several occasions he has defied the military in order to protect the

rights of the peasants. He divided the property of his diocese into small holdings and gave them to anyone willing to cultivate them.

51. Betto is referring to the kidnapping of the Swiss ambassador, who was later released in exchange for seventy political prisoners.

52. See letter 22 and note 26.

53. Tito de Alencar, released in exchange for the Swiss consul.

54. The reader must remember that when it is winter in the northern hemisphere it is summer in the southern hemisphere.

55. A Brazilian convent of contemplative nuns.

56. The movement of liturgical renewal was introduced into Brazil in about 1940 by Benedictines in a monastery in Rio de Janeiro. It was associated with the movement of Catholic Action at that time.

57. The new archbishop of São Paulo, appointed after Archbishop Rossi was transferred to Rome.

58. Sister Ruth is Betto's cousin and contemporary.

1971

59. In a plenary session (held in Belo Horizonte, February 1971) the Brazilian episcopate sent letters of support and solidarity to the archbishop of São Paulo (Evaristo Arns), the bishop of Volta Redonda (Valdir Calheiros), and the provincial of the Dominican order (Domingos Maia Leite).

60. "The defendant receives the benefit of the doubt."

61. A priest from Milan serving in the Pontifical Foreign Missions.

62. Archbishop Evaristo Arns, O.F.M.

63. The newsletter of the São Paulo Catholic Information Center reported this visit in its May issue. The superior general of the Dominican order (Father Aniceto Fernández) was allowed to visit the Dominican prisoners, and he concelebrated Mass in their cell. Asked for his impressions, he expressed his wonderment at their high spirits. He said the prisoners were not "downhearted, aggressive, or dispirited but rather strong and serene in their priestly and religious vocation, . . . imbued with a strong sense of the Christian import of their presence in prison."

64. Italian missionary in the Congregation of the Servants of Mary. Acre is a "territory" belonging to the Brazilian Federal Republic, located in the far north of the country near the borders of Peru and Bolivia. It differs from the regular Brazilian states in being still partly unexplored borderland and not fully integrated into the juridical, economic, and political structure of the country.

65. The baby is the daughter of Claudia, Betto's cousin.

66. Dr. Gilberto Gomes Libanio, brother of Betto's mother.

67. Archbishop of São Paulo. See letter 102.

68. The missionary mentioned in letter 103.

69. Father Giulio Vicini. See letter 102.

70. The request was rejected in June 1971. See letter 116.

71. Seminarian mentioned in letter 102.

72. Apostolic letter of Paul VI, issued in May 1971 to commemorate the eightieth anniversary of *Rerum Novarum*. An English translation appears in *The Pope Speaks* magazine, Washington, D.C. 16:137–68, and in *The Gospel of Peace*

and Justice: Catholic Social Teaching since Pope John, presented by Joseph Gremillion (Maryknoll, New York: Orbis Books, 1976).

73. General Assembly of the Latin American Bishops held in Medellín, Colombia, in 1968. The full proceedings are available in English translation from the Latin American Division of the United States Catholic Conference in Washington.

74. After serving his sentence and being released from prison, Father Vicini was acquitted on appeal in August 1971.

1972

75. These are excerpts from three different letters, grouped together because they deal with the same subject and are addressed to the same person. These and all subsequent letters were written in Presidente Wenceslau Prison.

Index of Major Themes

Numbers refer to letters in this volume, not to pages.

law, Christians and, 14

liberation, *see* freedom

love, meaning of, 104, 106, 112, 124

Marxism, listening to the message of, 26, 108

materialism, the concrete praxis of a consumer society, 68, 115, 118

metanoia, 23, 52, 56, 68, 114, 122

Nazism, comparison of Brazil's situation with, 16, 18, 51, 53, 54, 96, 119

nonbelievers
    author's concern for, 18
    holiness of, 9

noosphere, 25

novitiate, as critical experience, 67, 97

obedience, meaning of, 104

political prisoners
    as different from ordinary offenders, 99, 111, 114
    sufferings in families of, 34, 58, 119
    switching to support regime, 49
    treatment of, 13, 16, 19, 22, 120

poverty
    absence in church of, 55, 112, 117
    as means of union with Christ, 79, 97, 123
    meaning of vow of, 104

praxis
    as key to human life and history, 38, 56, 99, 123, 124
    renewal of Christian, 28, 38, 68, 70, 117, 122

priesthood
    and celibacy, *see* celibacy
    charisms of service and self-sacrifice in, 110
    flaws in priestly training and religious life, 38, 69, 79, 81, 90, 110
    as riding in all different directions, 68
    those leaving, 81

prison
    as theological experience, 13, 23, 25, 47, 71, 85, 107, 111, 113, 122
    degrading conditions of, 10, 13, 31, 48, 71, 72, 80, 85, 91, 98, 99, 114, 121
    experience of, summarized, 7, 122
    liturgical celebration in, 86, 103, 110, 122
    routine, activities, and opportunities in, 3, 6, 7, 8, 9, 11, 13, 14, 17, 18, 20, 21, 22, 25, 33, 35, 37, 46, 48, 53, 58, 59, 60, 71, 72, 73, 77, 80, 83, 85, 86, 91, 92, 93, 98, 99, 111, 114, 120, 121
    suspicions in, 13, 114
    tortures in, 13, 16, 19, 114, 120

rage, feelings of, in prison, 16, 17, 114

240

241